Created and Directed by Hans Höfer

INSIGHT GUIDES
Hong Kong

Updated by Saul Lockhart
Photography by Bill Wassman,
Alain Evrard and others

Editorial Director: Geoffrey Eu

HOUGHTON MIFFLIN COMPANY

APA PUBLICATIONS

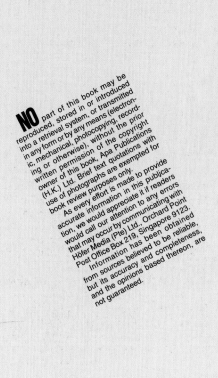
Hong Kong

Eighth Edition (Reprint)
© **1994 APA PUBLICATIONS (HK) LTD**
All Rights Reserved
Printed in Singapore by Höfer Press Pte Ltd

Distributed in the United States by:	Distributed in Canada by:	Distributed in the UK & Ireland by:	Worldwide distribution enquiries:
Houghton Mifflin Company	**Thomas Allen & Son**	**GeoCenter International UK Ltd**	**Höfer Communications Pte Ltd**
222 Berkeley Street	390 Steelcase Road East	The Viables Center, Harrow Way	38 Joo Koon Road
Boston, Massachusetts 02116-3764	Markham, Ontario L3R 1G2	Basingstoke, Hampshire RG22 4BJ	Singapore 2262
ISBN: 0-395-66204-4	ISBN: 0-395-66204-4	ISBN: 9-62421-008-X	ISBN: 9-62421-008-X

ABOUT THIS BOOK

With change the watchword, *Insight Guide: Hong Kong* offers an anthology of old and new images of the incredible island colony. The national bird of Hong Kong is still the construction crane, but there is so much more to the tiny state with its pockets of rich Chinese culture, sophisticated shops and sheer beauty offered by the classic mixture of rock and water.

The streets of Hong Kong are filled with political activists now along with the bustling businessmen, frenetic visiting shoppers, and smartly-dressed secretaries and boutique assistants. The Union Jack will soon be coming down and the flag of Chinese communism raised. But will Hong Kong change? The pages that follow attempt to provide an answer.

Words and Pictures

With *Insight Guide: Hong Kong*, the visitor is prepared for the hustle and bustle that has always marked the colony and to understand the portending changes. This is the goal of all Apa Publications books: to provide serious travellers with the material to make every tour a complete experience. The *Insight Guides* feature outstanding writing, great photographs and clear, straight-forward journalism. This formula was devised by Apa founder **Hans Höfer** when he produced his first book, *Insight Guide: Bali* in 1970. The ensuing library of new travel literature produced by Apa reflects Höfer's Bauhaus training in Germany in book design, printing and photography. *Hong Kong* was the ninth in a list of titles that now approaches 200.

This new edition of *Hong Kong* has undergone a major face-life, featuring updated text and extensive new photography, reflecting the many changes that have occurred in the colony since the first edition appeared in 1980.

The original *Hong Kong* book was the product of the combined talents of former Apa executives **Leonard Lueras** and **Ian Lloyd**, and **Saul Lockhart**, a Hong Kong-based writer and editor.

Lueras, who also produced the best-selling *Insight Guide: Hawaii*, arrived in Hong Kong in 1970 as a roving correspondent for *The Honolulu Advertiser*, Hawaii's major morning daily. Lueras has written and edited many books on Asia-Pacific subjects, and has contributed articles and photographs to numerous publications in the United States and Asia. He is now based in Bali.

After contributing to several more *Insight Guides* titles, Lloyd ventured out on his own and has made a name for himself as one of Southeast Asia's leading photographers.

Lockhart wrote the book's introductory essay, the Macau travel section, most of the lively feature essays, and nearly all of the Travel Tips section. He is also responsible for the extensive text updates in this edition. After a stint as a freelance correspondent in Vietnam, he moved to Hong Kong in 1967 to establish a permanent home.

Harry Rolnick takes us on a non-format tour of Hong Kong Island. Rolnick, a native New Yorker, worked as a free-lance writer. He has published a restaurant guide to China, a history of Macau books of humour and written articles for numerous international publications in Hong Kong.

Roger Boschman, a Kowloon resident, wrote about the wonders of Kowloon and the

Lockhart

Lueras

Huang

Maitland

New Territories. Boschman, who was born in Carrot River, Saskatchewan, Canada, moved to Hong Kong in 1974 and has since free-lanced for several regional and international publications.

Another free-lancer, **Derek Maitland**, contributed articles on Hong Kong urbanity. Maitland, a British-born Australian novelist, moved to Hong Kong in 1976.

Alan Chalkey, who analyzes Hong Kong's penchant for making money is an economic journalist who has spent 30 years in the Asian region. A native Briton, Chalkey works on many newspapers and magazines in Hong Kong.

Frena Bloomfield considers the scheming and dreaming that permeate all life in Hong Kong, then takes us on a strange collection of ferry boats to the colony's lovely outlying islands. Bloomfield was born and educated in London, qualified as a librarian but escaped into journalism. As a free-lance writer, she has contributed to *The Guardian*, *New Society*, *The Far Eastern Economic Review*, *Asia Magazine*, *Asiaweek* and the *British Broadcasting Corporation* (BBC).

Other writers who have contributed are **Veronica Huang**, formerly a reporter for *The Asian Wall Street Journal*, and Hong Kong food and festivals expert **Lesley Nelson** and **Linda Wong**.

Thanks are also due to **Jane Ram**, whose early editorial advice was most helpful, **Spencer Reiss**, a magazine writer-editor; **David Watts**, **Paul Maidment** and **Nedra Chung**; as well as to **Stephen Siu** who wrote and edited the Travel Tip's guide to "Survival Cantonese."

Calling the Shots

Two long-time Apa hands contributed most of the spectacular new photographic material for this book. **Bill Wassman** and **Alain Evrard** spent many days combing the colony for the perfect pictures. As anyone who's been there knows, the amount of construction that goes on in Hong Kong makes any skyline shot virtually redundant the moment it's taken. Still, they succeeded admirably in capturing the mood of the place. They also had lots of help. Photographers from Hong Kong-based Globe Press – **Earl Kowall**, **Keith MacGregor**, **Richard Dobson** and **Gerhard Jörén** – provided a refreshing new perspective to a well-photographed theme. Other lensmen whose work appears in this book include **Max Lawrence**, **Ian Lloyd**, **Dallas** and **John Heaton**, **Jean Kugler**, **GP Reichelt**, **Adina Tovy**, **Jean-Léo Dugaste**, **Liau Chung Ren**, **Rick Strange** and **Manfred Gottschalk**.

Institutions and others who contributed to this book in one or many ways were Hong Kong's Urban Council, the Hong Kong Art Museum, the Hong Kong Tourist Association (HKTA), the Macau Tourist Information Bureau, the Hongkong and Shanghai Bank, Cathay Pacific, Jonathan Cape Limited (London), the London Public Record Office, Hong Kong Publishing Company, *Discovery* magazine, *Pacific* magazine (Emphasis Inc.), *The South China Morning Post*, and The Academy of Motion Pictures Arts and Sciences (Los Angeles).

—Apa Publications

Rolnick

Bloomfield

Chalkey

Evrard

Wassman

CONTENTS

History & Features

Maps

TRAVEL TIPS

**For detailed Information
See Page 273**

PASSAGE TO DESTINY

When George Orwell bestowed such ominous significance on the year 1984, so many years ago, the tiny colonial outpost of Hong Kong had no idea it would be its own year of destiny. Nineteen-eighty-four was the year Hong Kong's future was decided – in the form of an agreement between Great Britain and the People's Republic of China, initialled on September 26 in Beijing and signed on December 19 in the same city.

At midnight, June 30, 1997 – the moment the 99-year lease on the New Territories (90 percent of the colony) expires – the British Crown Colony, including the two areas (Hong Kong Island and the Kowloon Peninsula) "ceded in perpetuity" in 1841 and 1856, will be returned to China.

During the often-acrimonious negotiations over almost two years, Britain, which clearly came out second best, managed to extract a 50-year guarantee from China (beginning in 1997) which, on paper, ensures Hong Kong's basic freedoms. Hong Kong will become a Special Administrative Region of China on July 1, 1997. That arrangement is conveniently accommodated by the official Beijing stance of "one government – two systems." In refugee-minded Hong Kong, where almost half the 5.8-million population has fled from turbulent upheavals in China, trusting the Middle Kingdom for the 50 years after 1997, and the time remaining before then, is more than a moot point of academic interest.

"Borrowed time, borrowed place" is the perfect description, coined by novelist Han Su-yin, of Hong Kong. Historically, the colony's citizens have tried to ignore the perpetual uncertainty of their future – their "borrowed time" – and have preferred to make their pile quickly in the fervent hope that destiny will unfold without severe or permanent disruptions. Hong Kong is reassuming the very real Chinese self that always lay just below the modern urbane facade; it believes its destiny is in the hands of fate, influenced perhaps by hefty doses of good *joss* (luck).

Preceding pages: glass, steel and concrete – Central's impressive skyline; harbour crossing; ancestral hall at Kam Tin; maiden from the Middle Kingdom. **Left,** Cheung Chau resident.

The Hong Kong Chinese always reckoned this British Crown Colony to be a "three-legged stool," with one leg in Beijing (Peking), another in London and the third in Hong Kong. That idea was immediately coshed by the Chinese in the opening rounds of their protracted negotiations with Britain over the territory's future after July 1, 1997, the day the 99-year lease on the New Territories (90 percent of the colony) expires.

Trade Superintendent Captain Charles Elliot, RN, annexed Hong Kong Island on his own volition, and by force of arms, to obtain trade concessions, to recover compensation for thousands of chests of British opium confiscated earlier at Canton, and to redeem a bent British pride. Six days later, Commodore Sir J.J. Gordon Bremer led a British naval force onto Possession Point for the ritual planting of Her Majesty's flag. It was all grand impe-

WENCHOW TRADER

But that metaphor still suggests Hong Kong's historically unique balancing act. If one leg is chopped off just a wee bit, the stool is askew. If the legs are of even more unequal length, the stool tilts crazily and doesn't fulfill its original (and stabilizing) function. And if a leg is accidentally broken, or deliberately lopped off, it will topple.

From the moment of its controversial 19th-century birth, Hong Kong has been at centre-ring, delicately resting its fate on that improbable set of legs.

This fragile tripod arrangement officially began on January 20, 1841, when Britain's sole remaining plenipotentiary in China –

rial theatre, but this annexation was instantly unpopular with higher-ups in London and Beijing – so much so that both Elliot and his Chinese counterpart Kishen, were reprimanded by their superiors and given huge boots in their lower-ranking bums.

Hong Kong's founding fathers: Kishen, the Chinese negotiator (who was Viceroy of the metropolitan province of Chihli), was roundly taken to task by his superiors for capitulating and giving away a bit of the Middle Kingdom to red-bearded British barbarians. He bowed, withdrew into his robes, quietly lost face, and was banished to Tibet.

Elliot, who, like Kishen, meant well, suffered similar ignominy. The opium traders – for whom Elliot blockaded Canton and occupied three forts in order to secure "one of the islands …conveniently situated for commerce intercourse" – attacked Elliot after the fact because in their opinion his Convention of Chuen Pi was too conciliatory: indeed, the "foreign mud" merchants *still* had to pay customs charges to the Chinese, even though trading from desolate Hong Kong was less convenient than trading at Whampoa (their traditional entrepôt at Canton).

London was livid. Lord Palmerston, Queen Victoria's Foreign Secretary, dismissed Hong of this Victorian White Elephant. The dishonoured captain was chastised for negotiating a dud settlement and for not using "the full employment of that force which was sent to you expressly for the purpose of enabling you to use compulsion, if persuasion should fail" to gain a more formidable concession from the Chinese. This upbraiding effectively ended Elliot's professional career. His next posting was as Britain's Consul General to Texas.

Thorn in the Lion's paw: Today, nearly a century and a half later, Elliot's name is still not honoured in massively successful Hong

Kong as a "barren island with hardly a house upon it." It would never become a trading centre, he harrumphed. Victoria herself clucked about the deal: "*All* we wanted might have been got if it had not been for the unaccountably strange conduct of Chas. Elliot… He tried to obtain the lowest terms from the Chinese."

Poor Elliot was recalled to Whitehall, probably by fast return clipper, and another chap, Sir Henry Pottinger, was given the dubious honour of being the first governor (1843–44)

Far left, Chinese junk. **Above**, Victoria, Hong Kong, 1860, artist unknown.

Kong – not even by a street, sandbar or park bench. The names of his successors, however (whether middle or senior-ranking civil servants), adorn highways, buildings and waterways throughout the colony.

Perhaps Elliot is still a non-person because Hong Kong has not yet fully proven its worth to Britain. It certainly cannot be called a "barren island" any more, but maybe it needs to do more penance. Or perhaps, in the insular view of Whitehall, Hong Kong is not really worth all the hassles it has caused the British Lion.

Is it really worth Britain's time and energy to cope with and be responsible for Hong

Kong's 5.8 million Chinese? Mother England periodically attacks the Hong Kong immigration "problem" with controversial and restrictive Nationality Bills. She growls even louder when Hong Kong's British civil servants lead movements against their own countrymen to argue the colony's case against trade restrictions imposed by the United Kingdom and the European Economic Community.

Even though more than half the population have British Dependent Territory British National Overseas Passports, there will be a safe haven in Britain come July 1, 1997 (when the Chinese take over) for only a few Chinese civil servants and community leaders.

There must have been many times during

for the privilege of having a token contingent of British troops stationed here to show the flag. Indeed, economically depressed Britain is so short of troops and funds that Hong Kong has been paying 75 percent of the colony's defence costs and from 1988 till the changeover in 1997, 65 percent, just to keep a few battalions of British and Gurkha troops, a few Royal Navy Ships and a squadron of vintage Royal Air Force and Army helicopters on hand to "defend" this 413-sq.-mile (1,070-sq.-km) territory, its 22 miles (35 km) of contiguous land border with China and thousands of miles of coast line spread over 235 islands. The cost of these defence agreements is nearly HK$2 billion.

the Sino-British negotiations from 1982 to 1984 when British civil servants wished Hong Kong would just slink away and leave London alone. Do those same people today rue the day Elliot occupied this "barren" place?

Hong Kong is still the world's 11th largest trading entity (excluding OPEC and COMECON) and the second largest port in the world; it is, in short, an economic force to be reckoned with.

High-rise Hong Kong has proven its "viability," but despite its successes – evidenced by recent economic recoveries under political uncertainty – the colony still has to negotiate financially with Mother England just

Ironically, these defence agreements don't mean much because China, if it wished, could take the colony back without a shot – with only that proverbial phone call to Her Majesty. So, the local troops are really here only for "internal security," usually to assist the police and to "protect" the colony from periodic invasions by illegal immigrants.

Managing in a "borrowed place": The Hong Kong government now has near complete internal self-government and even has the power to conclude certain negotiations with sovereign powers. The colony, for example, regularly negotiates its own economic treaties with other countries and belongs to international financial institutions such as the Asian Development Bank. When it could not "belong" to something directly, it joined a British delegation. The 1984 Joint Agreement gave Hong Kong the right to hold membership certain types of international organisations like the ADB or the GATT. It also allows the territory to negotiate certain types of agreements like those dealing with aviation rights or trade.

But for all its apparent strength, Hong Kong constantly would balance its very existence by catering to colonial masters in London and impulsive Communist Party mandarins in Beijing. Hong Kong has no real power. Hong Kong can only make money for

to improve Hong Kong's infrastructure and housing. The hope is that such plans can continue uninterrupted past the change of government in 1997.

Unfortunately this bodes for an uncertain future. As Chinese author Han Su-yin has described this dilemma, the colony, though "squeezed between giant antagonists crunching huge bones of contention …has achieved within its own narrow territories a co-existence which is baffling, infuriating, incomprehensible and works splendidly – on borrowed time in a borrowed place."

With more than nine-tenths of the colony leased from China, the vibrant economic entity that is Hong Kong today would not exist

every party concerned and exhibit a marvellous capacity to be flexible and bend with every problem that blows its way.

Historically, problems have been tackled in a rather ad hoc manner – like plugging holes when the leak comes instead of planning for such events. Many of these stop-gap measures surprisingly survive the test of time. The system has gradually changed to where far reaching, sweeping plans are now generated – mostly massive building projects

In the past century Hong Kong's suburbs have risen from the sea. Old Causeway Bay, 1846, left, and the New Causeway Bay, above.

without the New Territories. The "borrowed time in a borrowed place" is to be returned at midnight June 30, 1997, and the "loan" will presumably be marked "paid-in-full."

Ironically, that controversial Convention of Chuen Pi, negotiated by Kishen and Elliot was never signed, but that minor legal detail did not stop the occupation and settlement of Hong Kong Island.

The first governor, Pottinger, felt Hong Kong should be retained, but during subsequent fighting in 1841 and 1842, Hong Kong was just regarded as another pawn in ongoing negotiations with the Chinese – until subsequent instructions issued by Palmerston on June 5, 1841, arrived and reversed his earlier decision.

In spite of the fact that the "home country" had been a bit lax in declaring sovereignty over its newest acquisition, Pottinger felt so strongly about Hong Kong's potential future that he encouraged permanent building and awarded land grants. These practices he ordered stopped when he went north to take part in renewed hostilities against the stubborn Chinese. A long round of fighting ended at Nanking – on August 29, 1842, with the signing of a Treaty of Nanking – when the Chinese capitulated to the "Outer Barbarians" just as Pottinger's forces were preparing to attack that city. At the time, Pottinger,

British traders wanted a place of their own to build godowns and process and sell profitable "foreign mud," as opium was nicknamed by the Chinese. Hong Kong was also a well-sheltered (from typhoons) harbour near enough to China to facilitate trade, but far enough from the Middle Kingdom to allow the British private concessions with a minimum of interference.

By fortuitous accident, Hong Kong Island became both a swashbuckling embarrassment and lucrative money machine for England. Hong Kong was taken for trade and continues to exist *only* for that commercial reason. Everything else in life was, and still is, secondary to this business of earning profits.

like Elliot, was being politically chastised for spending too much public money on "useless" Hong Kong development projects. With the Treaty of Nanking, however, those arguments ended and Britain gladly accepted the Island of Hong Kong in perpetuity, so that it could have "a Port whereat they may careen and refit their Ships, when required, and keep Stores for that purpose…"

Previous to this time, Macau and Whampoa were the major China trade ports. But with the eventual silting of Macau's harbour – located adjacent to the Pearl River Estuary – and the weakening of Portuguese power in Asia (and the growing strength of England),

Biting the Dragon: As Dr. Norman Miners of the Political Science Department of the University of Hong Kong expresses it, the Treaty of Nanking was the first of three "indefensible bites" the British Lion took out of the Chinese Dragon's rear.

During the six months Pottinger was away from the colony, much progress had been made in settling this barren island. Though there was confusion over land sales, astute British traders recognised that if Hong Kong did indeed become a prosperous colony, the key to success here would be land. And of course the local Chinese were always – as they are today – one speculative step ahead of the "barbarians"; they readily sold land whether they had title to it or not. Good *joss* (luck) apparently was with the traders, because on June 26, 1843, Hong Kong was officially declared a British Crown Colony.

The second of England's three bites occurred as a result of the Arrow War (also called the Second Opium War) when a Hong Kong-registered *lorcha* (a junk-rigged schooner with a foreign hull) named the *Arrow* was boarded off Canton in October 1856 by Chinese sailors. The *Arrow*'s crew was detained, and this impropriety properly irritated the British.

Hong Kong's Consul General, Harry Parkes, retaliated in force, hoping to use

met, but the key question of access to Canton was not. The Viceroy said he could not guarantee the safety of foreigners if they were allowed in the city.

Shortly thereafter, guerilla warfare broke out and foreign-held factories in Canton were attacked. Until that time, Hong Kong had been only a minor commercial dependence of Canton. The *hong* (the original trading houses, some of which still do business in Hong Kong today) at this time transferred their headquarters to the security of the new British colony at Hong Kong and that trading situation was reversed. Hong Kong took its first step forward towards becoming a full-fledged Asia entrepôt.

this *casus belli* to force the Chinese into allowing foreigners back into Canton. (Entrance into Canton was guaranteed by the 1842 Treaty of Nanking, but had never been asserted.) The local British fleet sailed up the Pearl River, breached Canton's city walls and forced their way to the Chinese Viceroy. Immediate British demands inspired by the *Arrow* incident were quickly

Left to right: Jui-Lin, the Viceroy of Kwangtung and Kwangsi province in 1870; the prim Victorian look of *gweilo* ladies; the mandarin lady in her courtly best for this 1870s portrait; and Sir Richard Macdonnell, Governor (1866–72).

Tsimshatsui in perpetuity: Increasingly, local acts of terrorism continued to occur in Hong Kong, Canton and along the vital Pearl River. British forces, this time joined by French allies, fought back, and in December 1857 captured Canton yet again. By the summer of 1858, allied forces had moved to the far north, where they eventually forced another Chinese capitulation and negotiated stronger concessions known as the Treaties of Tientsin. Under the terms of these agreements, foreigners now gained the rights to station diplomats in Beijing and travel at will throughout China. On March 26, 1860, under a subsequent Convention of Peking

(Beijing), Kowloon Point (Tsimshatsui) was leased in perpetuity from the Chinese.

In October that same year, another battle took place in the north and the emperor's Summer Palace in Beijing was sacked by the allies. Lord Elgin, the British plenipotentiary who negotiated for the British this time, secured on October 24–25, 1860, the cession of an additional 3.75 sq. miles (6 sq. km) of new territory consisting of Kowloon Point (on which the British had built a harbour defence fort in 1842) and Stonecutters Island (in the harbour) with the signing of two Conventions of Beijing.

With that second British "bite," Hong Kong now consisted of nearly 36 sq. miles of

long history of "bursting at the seams."

Hong Kong's inscrutable landlord: England's third and last "nibble" of the Middle Kingdom occurred in 1898 – and it is this final morsel which now keeps Hong Kong nourished and economically alive. By the mid-1880s, the colony's powers were concerned about the territory's security. What pushed Britain to force China's hand once again was a coaling station grant to France on the South China Coast opposite Hainan Island. After expressing Her Majesty's displeasure regarding the grant, Britain duly informed Beijing that for defence purposes (nothing was said about "balance of power with France") the colony would require additional territory.

sovereign territory. The colony's harbour could now be defended on both sides and the colony's British residents had a convenient haven across the water where they could engage in nefarious – mostly sexual – intercourse with Kowloon's natives.

Hong Kong's 20th-century *laissez-faire* image and beliefs were shaped in those early days. However, Hong Kong's perennial population problems also began during those days. During that century's long Taiping rebellions in China, the colony's population increased from about 90,000 in 1859 – of which only a few thousand were Europeans – to 150,000 by 1865. Hong Kong began its

Eventually a demarcation line was drawn from Deep Bay to Mirs Bay and Britain forced China to lease it additional New Territories for 99 years from July 1, 1898.

Britain recognises that piece of paper promptly every year by paying HK$5,000 in rent. The People's Republic of China refuses to recognize Imperial treaties signed under the duress of gunboat diplomacy, but despite this non-recognition, China inexplicably accepts the annual rental fee. Britain feels that the New Territories lease is a valid contract being legally fulfilled. The Chinese say there is no contract, or the contract is null and void, but they inscrutably accept and thank the

British for their annual donation.

In that third bite, the Crown Colony gained 350 sq. miles (565 sq. km) spread over the mainland and 234 outlying islands. They also inherited a late 20th-century headache – an uncertain Hong Kong future.

Though the constant question in Hong Kong's collective psyche – what will happen in 1997? – was always deeply buried, in spite of bitter riots in the 1950s and 1960s, it bubbled to the surface with a vengence in mid-1982 with the lead up to Prime Minister Margaret Thatcher's visit to Beijing in late September/early October that year.

That question, though officially answered with the signing of the Sino-British Agree-

ern businessmen and tourists have since flocked to China. Mao's death in 1976, and the subsequent arrest of the "gang of four," cleared the way for the more practical leadership of Deng Xiaoping. In 1978, Hong Kong received its first "official" visitor from north of the border since 1949. Significantly, the caller was Li Chiang, China's Minister of Trade. The following year, Hong Kong's Governor, Sir Murray MacLehose, was invited to Beijing where he met with Deng, who advised Hong Kong investors "to put their hearts at ease." The assurance effected an ecstasy in Hong Kong and other international boardrooms. It was as if Deng had personally signed a 1997 New Territories

ment in December 1984, has of course spawned two additional questions: What will happen when Hong Kong reverts to China as a Special Administrative Region in July 1997 and what is going to happen in the "lame-duck" time in between?

It was in the 1970s that the peaceful economic and diplomatic upswings began racing head-long into "modernization."

Meanwhile, the Chinese Dragon turned its back on a former ally, the Russian Bear, and overtly embraced the capitalistic West. West-

lease waiver in blood.

MacLehose belatedly reported publicly during the ofttimes acrimonious negotiations in 1983 and 1984 that Deng also stated China would take back Hong Kong. He said the comment passed back to Whitehall and No. 10 Downing Street – something the British government has never acknowledged.

The end of the 1970s and beginning of the 1980s also ushered in even closer co-operation between Hong Kong and Chinese authorities. British and Gurkha troops on this side of the border worked closely with units of the People's Liberation Army (PLA) to stop the flow of hundreds of thousands of

Left, traditional yet modern. **Above left**, cool in Kowloon. **Above right**, *gweilo* on call.

refugees. The PLA gladly accepted the tens of thousands of these illegal immigrants caught by Hong Kong forces.

A Communist country club: On the economic front, a Special Economic Zone established on the Chinese side of the border at Shenzhen had embraced thousands of local co-ventures, with Hong Kong usually providing the expertise, money, quality control, marketing and transportation infrastructure paired with China's abundant land and labour.

China-controlled companies have actively, and for the most part openly, participated in Hong Kong's subsequent property boom by investing billions of Hong Kong dollars in local enterprises. The new capitalistic Communists get along just fine with Hong Kong's very astute property barons; both exult in the regular increase of the value of their joint property shares.

also to training a leadership and an administration to take over the decision-making and running of the colony from July 1, 1997 – the date the lease on the New Territories expires and the entire British Crown Colony of Hong Kong reverts to China in the form of a Special Administrative Region. The agreement was signed in Beijing on December 19, 1984, by Britain's Prime Minister Margaret Thatcher and China's Premier Zhao Ziyang.

Increased elective representation in the District Boards and the Urban and Regional Councils have proved successful. More electoral changes came with the advent of a partially-elected (albeit indirectly via functional constituencies) Legislative Council.

munists get along just fine with Hong Kong's very astute property barons; both exult in the regular increase of the value of their joint property shares.

China, however, does not completely ignore the political workings of the colony in favour of quick money-making. The Chinese took a long and serious look at the Hong Kong government's plan to create district advisory boards throughout the colony in 1981. But the plan eventually went through.

With the advent of the Sino-British Draft Agreement and a white paper on representative government, the colonial government committed itself not only to elections but

Of the few political options available to Hong Kong, full independence – a common goal of most colonies – was not a viable option. Previously, even tiny steps towards more representative and democratic government here were taken only with due consideration of Beijing's authoritarian views.

But during the two-year negotiating period, as Hong Kong rocked with anxiety, it was the Chinese, specifically Premier Zhao Ziyang, who announced the colony's 50-year (from 1997) guarantee, forcing the British to scramble for plans to give the local citizens more say in government in order to prepare them for a time during which they will, for the most part, be self-governing. So it is indeed ironic that the Chinese are now directly responsible for the British instigating political reforms when successive British and Hong Kong governments used the same Chinese government as an excuse not to reform.

Ironically, Hong Kong's continuing prosperity, which is partially nourished by China's modernization is at the same time the colony's greatest weakness and strength. It is common sense here to say that China only tolerates Hong Kong's and Macau's existence because they act as convenient foreign exchange windows to the outer world. Investments from Hong Kong and Macau rep-

ogy which China taps regularly. With the combination of its Western style economy, free and open marketplace and Chinese culture, Hong Kong serves as a "commercial laboratory" for China's own venture into modernization, which includes modern management. It is a place where China can buy or borrow nearly all the know-how the capitalist world has to offer. Many Chinese trade organizations have set up representative offices in Hong Kong, including those from the Special Economic Zones, open cities, provinces and municipalities. As an international business and financial centre, Hong Kong provides a venue where Chinese enterprises can seek out business opportunities, engage

resented a staggering 80 percent of that foreign investment.

Hong Kong also serves as a transhipment centre for China export goods because China's own such transport infrastructure is lacking. Besides, Hong Kong is, literally, China's window on the world. Its excellent trading, communications, and transportation facilities help China gain greater access to international markets. It has a large reservoir of management skills and modern technol-

Far left, at the dragon boat races in Aberdeen typhoon shelter. **Left**, that Golden Smile. **Above**, cellular phones are a common sight in Central.

in joint ventures with foreigners and find an access to the international financial market.

Hong Kong could become China's centre for international trade and investment, if promises concerning the Special Administrative Region (to be set up when sovereignty is handed back on June 30, 1997) and, most important, the lead-up time to 1997, are kept.

However, as China's economic prosperity grows, so grows the Chinese infrastructure, a development process which means that one day China may catch up or even surpass Hong Kong – a potential reality which would more and more dilute Hong Kong's role as the country's only good entrepôt.

Mutual ventures across the Sino-British border, for example, are bringing prosperity to many Hong Kong companies and people because they allow businessmen to keep land (Hong Kong's most expensive commodity) and labour costs under control (thus enabling local manufacturers to undercut competitors in Singapore, Taiwan, Japan and Korea).

But most of these venture agreements are for 5 or 10 years and when the contracts expire, the factories and technology revert to China. China will eventually use this new expertise and hardware to compete directly with Hong Kong, and given present economic inflationary trends, Hong Kong may not be able to compete with the mainland for business when the contracts end.

Seductive neon: The still booming economy also exposes another Hong Kong weakness: people. The very bright neon lights of this glamourous colony are reflected in the sky for many miles. More tempting are Hong Kong television stations, which during every broadcast minute emphasize on mainland TV screens the differences between living standards and lifestyles here and in China.

During Sir Murray's meeting with Deng in 1979, the Governor discussed the subject of illegal immigration. Sir Murray wanted Deng's help in stemming this human floodtide. Deng promised to do what he could and he eventually sent another battalion of PLA troops to police the border. He also made a very astute appraisal of the refugee situation. The Vice Premier, noting that the real cause of this problem was the obvious discrepancy in Hong Kong and Chinese living standards, suggested that the only way to combat the refugee situation was to "equalize" these two disparate living standards.

At first interpretation, China-watchers and men-on-the-street here thought this was a reference to Deng's modernization program. But following Deng's comment, there was a great surge of even more illegal immigrants across the border, causing fears that Deng was again flooding Hong Kong in order to lower the colony's standard of living, a move that would "equalize" standards of living in another way. Eventually this most recent flood of refugees was dammed, and once again Hong Kong gasped and wondered aloud what the next subtle swish of the Dragon's tail would *really* mean.

End-of-the-lease days: No one can really predict what will happen in Hong Kong's near or far future, but the government has not backed off its commitments due to the 1997 lease expiration or the increased population which is expected to reach almost 7 million by 1996.

By the end of the millennium, HK$100 billion would have been spent on construction by the pre- and post-1997 Hong Kong government, in addition to the HK$127 billion earmarked for the Port and Airport Development Strategy.

The dreaded question of "What will happen to Hong Kong in 1997 when the lease on the New Territories runs out?" had always

been around, but only discussed by government officials discreetly, never in public or for quotation – until the negotiations began in 1982.

British Prime Minister Margaret Thatcher's visit to the Middle Kingdom and Hong Kong in September 1982 brought the dreaded question from a closet off stage to a centre stage. The initialling of the Sino-British Agreement in September 1984 (and its subsequent signing in May 1985) answered many questions – and created many new ones – about Hong Kong's future.

If Hong Kong is to continue to survive as one of the world's top 15 trading entities, as a source of more than half of China's foreign exchange and as a living symbol of China's modernization and political aims, there will have to be more giving and understanding on China's side, or Hong Kong will deteriorate into a burden well before the "50-year guarantee" from 1997 expires in 2047.

Lord MacLehose was the first to recognise that some sort of special status situation would have to be worked out. Ironically, he also stated that the Chinese intended to take over sovereignty when the time was ripe.

Though Mrs Thatcher reiterated her moral responsibility for the colony's population, the Hong Kong Chinese were under no illusions. Britain's new nationality law – effec-

Kong. China refuses to recognise them because they are non-Chinese and Britain will not take them in because they were born outside the United Kingdom to non-Britons.

Hong Kong suffered badly from an acute case of the S&P (stability and prosperity) syndrome during the Sino-British negotiations. And it continues to have relapses frequently, depending on the political and economic climate. The most severe symptom is the wholesale emigration of professionals, entrepreneurs and the young to Canada, Australia and the United States. They were the key words in the Sino-British communique and have since echoed forth at every pronouncement from either side.

tive in 1983 – makes this plain. Hong Kong people's worthless Hong Kong British passport was diluted further when it changed to a British Dependent Territory passport.

The BNO (British Nationality Ordinance) passports, to be issued only to Chinese citizens of the new Hong Kong Special Administrative Region, are extremely unpopular because they cannot be passed on to subsequent generations.

Another sticky problem for Britain is the 15,000 or so non-Chinese residents of Hong

Left, Sunday artist brushes up on his technique.
Above, now, police do border patrols.

China's 13th National People's Congress ended in December 1982. It approved a new constitution which, under Article 31, allows for the creation of Special Administrative Regions, a political entity aimed directly at Hong Kong, Macau and Taiwan.

Perhaps more significant, the 6th Five Year Plan launched by the same Congress restructured China's economy quite drastically. An example: State companies will now pay taxes to the government and are allowed to keep profits. Does that not sound suspiciously like capitalistic Hong Kong?

Hong Kong has taken a severe drubbing in the international press since Prime Minister

Thatcher's visit. In addition, global recession which hit the colony in 1982 (exacerbated by the negotiations with China) affected the liquidity of the over-extended property companies and Deposit Taking Companies (the local version of Savings & Loan Associations).

The backlash of the drop in property prices affected Hong Kong government revenues because they represented more than 50 percent of the government's income. Hence, the first deficit in a decade because land sales have fallen dramatically.

Business is still being conducted. By the end of 1983, there were more than a dozen contracts with payment schedules beyond 1997. There are many more now, including mortgages.

It was also in 1983 that China signed her largest deal – a US$3.5 billion nuclear power station in Daya Bay (30 miles/148 km northeast of Hong Kong). The Hong Kong Government formed the Hong Kong Nuclear Investment Co. for a 25 percent joint venture stake with the Guangdong Power Co. to build, commission and operate the plant. Due to negotiating delays, the construction contracts were only signed with British and French firms in 1986.

China, for her part, is still investing directly in Hong Kong through property, construction and stock investments. China went into the commercial money market for the first time in 1985 to float a loan of HK$300 million.

In spite of the political uncertainties Hong Kong faced since Mrs Thatcher first stepped foot in China in 1982, economically the territory has managed to surge ahead, slowed down only by the recession and the Gulf War in early 1991.

This was no mean achievement considering that many of Hong Kong's best and brightest – the professionals, entrepreneurs and the just plain wealthy – expressed their faith in the Sino-British view of the future by emigrating primarily to Canada and Australia, but also to the United States and Britain. What started as a manageable 10,000 a year in the early 1980s (which was more than matched by the return flow) ballooned to 60,000–70,000 a year by 1991, with less than 10 percent returning after they got their new passports. The emigration put severe strains on all sectors of the community – politically, socially and economically.

While coping with its own political problems, Hong Kong is still centre stage in the world's perennial Vietnamese boat people problem. While other countries in Asia have scrapped their First Asylum Policy (meaning if your country is the first place they hit, you take care of them, either providing care until they are resettled or giving them a home), Hong Kong soldiers on.

With resettlement in the West at an all time low in early 1991 and involuntary repatriation blocked by the United States – which has thrown its guilt-laden veto around at all international conferences called to resolve the problem – Hong Kong is stuck with 55,000–60,000 Vietnamese locked away in depressing camps. Most have little hope of settlement but that does not deter the thousands arriving on Hong Kong's shores annually.

This policy, as felt by the proverbial man-on-the-street and expressed in Legislative Council, is viewed as one having been foisted on the colony by a distant colonial master. Well-meaning and charitable though it may be, Hong Kong people are not pleased with resources being spent on ever-increasing number of Vietnamese – there has never been any love lost between Vietnam and China throughout their long history.

As hard as that view may seem, it is softened when you realise that concurrent with the First Asylum Policy there exists a strictly enforced policy of returning all illegal immigrants (I.I.'s in the vernacular) from China. Once they are caught – and much manpower is expended by the government in searching them out – the I.I.'s are unceremoniously trucked to the border and dumped back across the border. Severe fines and imprisonment are in effect for anyone harbouring an I.I., even if that person is a relative like a spouse or brother.

To tighten the pressure-cooker lid even further, China has stated publicly that it wants all the boat people out of Hong Kong and the problem resolved by 1997 – and has insisted that Britain promised this.

So where does all this leave Hong Kong? For a moment, she sits here – economically viable, frustrated at times, but somehow coping with the problems caused by her long and improbable existence on a three-legged stool.

The Empire Strikes Out?

Sealed by the Plenipotentiaries on board
Her Britannic Majesty's Ship —
"Cornwallis" this twenty ninth day of August
1842, corresponding with the Chinese
date, twentyfourth day of the seventh month
in the twenty second year of Taoukwang.

Henry Pottinger
Her M.'s Plenipotentiary

大清欽差便宜行事大臣等

大英欽奉全權公使大臣各為

約者

君上定事蓋用關防印信各執一冊為據俾即日按照和約開載之條袒行妥辦無礙矣要至和

道光二十二年七月二十四日即英國記年之

一千八百四十二年八月二十九

由江寧省會行

大英君主汗華帥大臣關防

AD 61: A Roman envoy, perhaps the first western tourist in the Orient, follows the Silk Road east to somewhere that may have been China. His account of an enormous, civilized empire is dismissed as fantasy.

100: Wandering monks bring the teaching of Buddha across the Himalaya from India. In concert with China's native Taoism, this new "Way" spreads quickly during an era of disaster and discontent. By 589, with the rise of the first "alien" dynasty from Western Mongolia, Buddhism becomes China's official state religion.

758: Sea-going Arab traders burn and loot Canton, then, as now, South China's principal city. To the north and west, after two centuries of vogue, Nestorian Christianity vanishes from China, leaving behind a few stone tablets.

1100: Pressed by "Northern Barbarians" – known and feared along the Danube as the Mongol Horde – gentry farmers from central China flee south to fertile valleys in today's New Territories. Among them are the Tangs, Hong Kong's oldest family, whose descendants still live as a clan in Kam Tin.

1279: While Kublai Khan treats Marco Polo to a 20-year Far East tour, his horsemen rout the last Sung emperor – a 12-year-old boy – from a rough hide-out near present-day Kowloon Bay. Polo's account of "Cathay," published in Europe at the turn of the century, is widely dismissed as fantasy.

1405: Commanding 62 ships and 28,000 men, imperial court eunuch Cheng Ho sails through the Straits of Malacca to India and the Persian Gulf. Ho's later expeditions reach east Africa and even Mecca, but the Emperor remains unimpressed and in 1431 bans further forays into the barbarian West.

1498: Vasco da Gama, with four ships and less than 100 men, leads Portugal's "Age of Discovery" around Africa to Mozambique and India. Over the next 10 years, the Portuguese seize Goa and Malacca, building forts and replacing the Arabs in control of the lucrative East Indies spice trade.

1513: Connecting Malacca's "Chin" merchants with Marco Polo's fabled "Cathay," Portuguese officials send Jorge Alvares east in a junk to investigate. Though refused entry to Canton, he does some small trading at Namto (a coastal town north of Castle Peak) and returns with the news that a great Chinese empire indeed appears to exist.

1517: Uncertain where or what "Portugal" is, Peking officials spend two years pondering Alvares' successor, envoy Tomé Pires. Though finally brought before the Dragon Throne itself, Pires' request for a trade agreement is judged insufficiently humble, and he returns to Canton empty-handed. Greeted there by news of an unsuccessful Portuguese naval assault, ever-hopeful envoy Pires is jailed, and dies shortly after in captivity. Eschewing revenge – or diplomatic nicety – his countrymen finally find their profits smuggling silk, tea and porcelain from small ports up and down the coast.

1540: Encouraged by local merchants, Portuguese privateer-traders pull in for the winter at Liampo, a small island south of Shanghai. Never more than a rude group of waterside huts, creative mapmakers quickly make Liampo a city – "Europe's first settlement in China." En route there two years later, storm-blown adventurer Fernão Mendes Pinto by accident discovers Japan – and a friendly, lucrative new market.

1549: Chinese troops, ordered to suppress the burgeoning Japan trade, set upon and destroy Liampo. Undeterred, Portuguese survivors regroup 90 miles south of Canton on windswept Sanchuang, where three years later St Francis Xavier expires – having visited Japan but denied his dream of converting China. Undeterred still, smuggling operations move in 1553 to Lampakkau, a larger island nearer the mouth of the Pearl River. By 1556, the place boasts of 400 matshed huts and thriving Chinese supporters.

1557: "The mandarins of Canton, at the request of the local inhabitants, have given us this port of Macao," writes Japan-finder Mendes Pinto. The concession is a reward – albeit tacit and grudging – for driving off "dwarf-robber" pirates. But with the port comes a richer plum: permission – in fact, a monopoly – for regular trade in Canton. The Japanese and the Chinese make the Portuguese their middlemen in the lucrative trade between two countries, and Macau became a winter stopping point for an "Annual Royal Japan Voyage" originating in Goa. Moving quickly to shore up their gains, the Portuguese by 1665 have warehouses, churches and stone-walled villas on the hills that surround this old fishing village.

1600: Macao (commonly spelled Macau) hits its zenith, *A Fé o Império* (For Faith and Empire) not necessarily in that order. Macanese carracks rule the Far East waves, trading Chinese silk for Nagasaki silver, bringing Indies pepper, Indian cotton and European manufacturers to Canton, then sending back to Macau and Lisbon silk, porcelain, pearls, silver and tea. Two hun-

1601: Having been bested by the Portuguese, Spain, Holland and England form India companies and send their own ships east. The Macanese do not view competition kindly: the first Dutch arrivals are attacked, beaten and publicly hanged. Later skirmishes – culminating in 1607 with a naval battle off present-day Lantau Island – spur Macau to fortify and the Dutch to build an outpost on Taiwan. In 1627, the Dutch invade Macau, only to be repulsed by a lucky cannon shot fired by a Jesuit father.

1637: Captain John Weddell's four armed merchant ships shoot their way into the Pearl River Estuary. Though turned back short of

dred percent profits make a disappointing voyage, and the now solid town of 6,000 – complete with its Praia Grande – is said to rival Venice in the richness of its trade. For Faith, scarcely a street lacks some sort of church, and a Jesuit seminary tops the highest hill. Missionaries following St Francis Xavier convert 150,000 Japanese, while in Peking, Father Matteo Ricci wears mandarin robes and lives as a court philosopher.

Preceding pages: signatories page of the Treaty of Nanking, 1842. **Above,** Marco Polo spent 20 years on his grand tour of the Far East.

Canton, they demolish a fort, burn several villages and establish the English in Chinese eyes as the "most ferocious of all the Western Barbarians." Blamed for allowing these "red beards" through, the Portuguese forfeit their 80-year-old trading rights at Canton. Shogun Iemitsu closes Japan in 1639 – in the process crucifying Christian missionaries and exterminating tens of thousands of converts. The Dutch two years later take Malacca. Portugal's Far East commerical empire effectively vanishes.

1685: Emperor K'ang Hsi, a noted patron of Jesuit scholars, reopens trade in Canton on a limited basis. After *HMS Macclesfield*'s profitable visit in 1699, British ships begin arriving annually from East India Company "stations" on the Indian coast. Fifteen years later, already the world's largest commercial organization, the company asks for – and receives – permission to build a warehouse (a "factory") near Canton.

1687: The ancient Confucian Classics are published in Latin at Paris, sparking the Enlightenment's China craze. For writers from Leibnitz to Voltaire, against strife-torn, bigoted Europe the Celestial Empire seems a model of order and reason: just laws, a learned bureaucracy, and, above all, a benevolent

(and squeezes) Hong merchants, who govern (and squeeze) barbarian traders. Terms of business for foreigners are severe: they may reside in Canton from September to March only; may not bring arms, warships or women; must pay for everything in hard cash, normally silver; and, except for special occasions, must stay within the carefully marked confines of their waterfront factory district. Trade, despite all this, prospers, and even impoverished Macau has a minor renaissance, supplying the new merchant princes with sumptuous off-season retreats.

1773: While "Indian" revolutionaries dump East India Company tea into Boston

CHINESE MERCHANTS,&c.
1 in the Summer Dress.....2 in the Winter Dress.....3 a Merchant's Wife.

philosopher-king. Chinese porcelain and furnishings, mock-Chinese landscapes and architecture rise to the height of fashion, topped off in 1763 by a 10-storey pagoda built in London's Kew Gardens. The illusion lasts just about a century, then dims when Europe reads more current reports of Chinese corruption, vice and tyranny.

1757: By Imperial edict, a Canton merchant's guild – the "Co-Hong" – gains exclusive rights to China's foreign trade. The privilege is paid for with "squeeze," an old, notably Oriental system of royalties, kickbacks, bribes and fees: The Emperor appoints

Harbour, British traders at Canton unload 1,000 chests of Bengal opium containing 150 lbs (68 kg) each and together worth a million silver dollars. The two events are not unconnected: with its tea trade expanding worldwide, the Company hits on Indian opium to balance purchases of Chinese tea. A decade later, as trade in both directions booms, 13 foreign-devil factories line the Canton waterfront, the larger belonging to the East India Company. In 1784, Canton sees its first American ship, the *Empress of China*, and a novel cargo of Turkish opium carried all the way from Smyrna.

1793: Lord Macartney, fresh from successful negotiations with the Russian Czar, arrives at Peking's Court of Heaven seeking new ports to open for trade. In a flush of high British honour, his lordship evades the *kowtow* (crawling in on all fours, then performing "The Three Kneelings and Nine Prostrations" at the Emperor's feet) by insisting that a mandarin of comparable rank do the same before a portrait of King George III. During breakfast with the Lord of the World and Dispenser of Light, however, the clever envoy gets an undiplomatic goodbye: "We possess all things in abundance," says the Imperial Dragon, "and have no need of

the manufacturers of outside Barbarians."

1800: Despite the Emperor's boast, China's taste for "foreign mud" (opium) tops 2,000 chests a year. Alarmed at the drain of silver – and the growing horde of addict-subjects – Peking thunders an edict totally banning the drug trade. But Canton has other

Left, early British sketches of Chinese aristocrats inspired a China rage in Europe. **Above**, though "official" approval was, well, unofficial, Her Majesty's East India Company dealt sticky opium by the clipper-full all along the South China Coast. Drugs are now a no-no.

ideas, and with everyone's connivance, lured by profits and squeeze, the high days of open smuggling begin. To keep its own hands officially clean, the East India Company holds auctions in Calcutta, where private, usually British "country" traders load swift and heavily armed "opium clippers" for the voyage east. Though the dealing is done at Canton, the chest stay safely out of sight of Lintin, the "Solitary Nail," as the Chinese call it, that stands in the mouth of the Pearl River. Squeeze takes care of official complaints – in 1804, the *Hoppo* alone nets some £200,000 – and from Lintin oared "crab boats" run the drug on its final leg to quiet coves around the delta. By 1816, when Macartney's successor, Lord Amherst, is rebuffed from even entering Peking, yearly imports total 5,000 chest – ¾ million pounds.

1802: British warships invade Macau as France invades Portugal. Fearing a Portuguese accommodation with the invading French armies, Lord Wellesley, Britain's Governor-General in India, sends an expeditionary force. Word reaches the fleet of the Peace of Amiens before troops disembark and Macau is saved from an invasion. But a couple of years later, the Portuguese colony is not so lucky. Again, France is the enemy in Europe and after taking Goa, Britain sends a force to occupy Macau. This time the British troops occupy three forts. British traders in the Portuguese colony are delighted until they realize they have misjudged the Chinese reaction. Portugal relies on negotiation, instead of force of arms, for its strength in China. Now the East India Company faces the possibility of a Chinese army crossing into Macau to throw them out. Trade stops and the merchants persuade the British admiral to leave. Afterward the Chinese enter Macau to verify the situation. Trade continues again.

1833: The East India Company's monopoly hold on the opium trade with China is broken and Queen Victoria's Foreign Secretary, Lord Palmerston, appoints Lord Napier of the Royal Navy, Chief Superintendent of Trade. Palmerston instructs Napier to induce British subjects to obey Chinese laws, which of course would be the end of the lucrative but illegal opium trade. Unfortunately for his lordship, the Foreign Secretary also instructs him to proceed to Canton and deliver a letter to the ruling Viceroy. Napier has no right under Chinese law to enter Canton because only merchants are so privileged. Furthermore, under the very Chinese laws he is charged with upholding, he has no right to pass a "letter" to the Viceroy; only a "petition." His lordship refuses to pass his "petition" through an intermediary. Deadlocked, Napier returns to Macau whilst the Viceroy orders the cessation of all trade with the British barbarians. Napier sends two frigates up the Pearl River to force passage past the forts, but the ships are cut off and hopelessly stranded. He dies three weeks later.

1839: Opium is still *the* key to British commerce in the East and Palmerston writes

Navy, the fourth Superintendent of Trade in China, fell the thankless job of trying to protect the interests of British merchantmen and sort out the political mess in Canton. He is under instructions from Palmerston to not only solve the trade problem, but also to find a "conveniently situated" island to "afford natural facilities for defence and be easily provisioned." By a quirk of fate, Elliot becomes Her Majesty's sole plenipotentiary in China due to the illness of another more senior naval officer. When negotiations break down with Lin's representative, Kishen, Elliot's fleet attacks Canton and occupies the city's protecting forts. Three days later, on

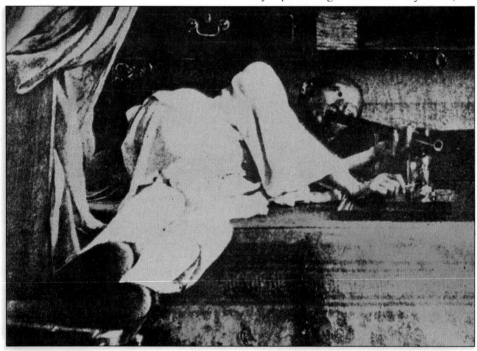

Napier that "it is not desirable you should encourage such adventures, but you must never lose sight of the fact you have no authority to interfere or prevent them." A strong anti-opium viceroy, Lin Tse-Hsu, is appointed by the Dragon Throne to clean up Canton. He orders all foreign merchants to obey the laws and confiscates their opium – some 20,291 chests in all. Additional British forces begin to arrive to force Lin's hand in opening Canton once again to the opium trade. Lin exerts his authority over foreigners by making an "official" visit to Macau.

1841: To Captain Charles Elliot, Royal

January 20, the Convention of Chuen Pi is to be signed. Its terms include the annexation of the island of Hong Kong, a point of land included at Elliot's request.

The fact that the treaty is never actually signed does not bother Commodore Sir J.J. Gordon Bremer, who leads a contingent of naval men ashore on January 26 at Possession Point to plant the Union Jack. Both Kishen and Elliot displease their superiors with this deal and are recalled. Hostilities break out again and this time Hong Kong's first governor, Sir Henry Pottinger, who replaced the discredited Elliot in August 1841, marches his troops as far as Nanking before the Chinese capitulate on August 29, 1842. The Treaty of Nanking cedes (amongst other things) Hong Kong Island "in perpetuity."

1845: Macau is freed of rule from Goa after nearly 300 years and joins with Timor and Solor as part of a single provincial region. Inspired by Hong Kong's forced British annexation, the Portuguese Territory rebels at paying rent. A British Protestant religious teacher refuses to remove his hat during a Corpus Christi procession and is arrested, only to be freed by a contingent of British Royal Marines who cause the death of a Portuguese soldier.

1849: The governor of Macau is assassinated by rebellious Cantonese who have learned that the Portuguese territory is not under British protection. The Portuguese blow up a Chinese border fort which had peppered the Portas do Cerco (border gate) with gunfire. Macau reasserts its independence from the Chinese with that assault.

1856: On March 26, the Chinese cede Kowloon Point (Tsimshatsui) and Stonecutter Island "in perpetuity" to the British colonials. By 1864 the Taiping Rebellion is crushed, and by 1878 the Dragon Throne has dispatched its first ambassadors to the world of outer Barbarians.

1860: An unprovoked attack on a British-registered *lorcha* (a junk-rigged schooner) by Chinese soldiers triggers the Second Opium War (or the "Arrow War," after the name of the *lorcha*). Attacks on the East India Company headquarters in Canton forces the British to regroup in Hong Kong. In retaliation, British takes Canton yet again in 1857, and Peking in 1858.

1862: A Sino-Portuguese treaty is signed, granting Macau a colonial status similar to Hong Kong's. A second treaty in 1887 confirms Macau's Portuguese status in perpetuity and defines the colony as the old town and two offshore islands, Taipa and Coloane.

1898: In an effort to strengthen its defences, Britain forces China to lease it another 350 sq. miles of territory, including 233 more islands, for 99 years, beginning July 1, 1898. (The lease expires three days before June 30, 1997.) The opium trade now has more breathing room and the Hong Kong

government naturally collects increased revenues on profits. By the turn of the century, the Home Office is pressing Hong Kong to decrease opium consumption. (Opium use was not completely banned in the colony until after World War II.)

1900: The Boxer Rebellion begins and Chinese prejudice against foreigners surfaces all over the country.

1905: Dr. Sun Yat-sen leads an anti-Manchu movement that aims to topple the Dowager Empress' Ching Dynasty. Japan triumphs in the Russo-Japanese War. In Hong Kong, meanwhile, workers lay 28 miles (45 km) of railway track for the new Kowloon-Canton Railway.

1911: Dr. Sun overthrows the Dragon Throne, and the Republic of China is born.

1912: The 85-mile (137-km) railway linking Hong Kong and Canton is completed.

1914: Despite an exodus of 60,000 Chinese fearing an attack on the colony after the outbreak of World War I, Hong Kong's population begins its evermore claustrophobic climb – from 530,000 in 1916, 630,000 in 1912, 725,000 in 1925, 800,000 in 1930, and 1 million in 1937 to 1.6 million by 1941.

1922: Hong Kong experiences its first seamen's strike, a walkout which cripples the colony. China, meanwhile, had already coped with its first general strike two years earlier when Manchurian Railways workers quit their jobs. Like the strikes in China, Hong Kong's are directed against foreigners and inequitable treaties.

1927: General Chiang Kai-shek's Kuomintang troops escalate their Nationalist campaign to rid the country of Communists. The Chinese Civil War divides the country.

1928: Mao Tse-tung establishes his first guerilla base. The Japanese occupy Manchuria in 1931 and the following year the Communists declare war on them.

1935: Mao gains control of the Communist Party and the following year Chiang Kai-shek is kidnapped during what becomes known as the Sian Incident.

1937: The Sino-Japanese War erupts, so the Kuomintang and Communist armies "unite" temporarily to fight a common foreign enemy.

1941: On December 8 (December 7 in Hawaii), the Japanese Imperial Fleet attacks Pearl Harbour and commits America to another World War. British, French, American

Left, the Imperial Dragon frowned on the use of opium, *the* Chinese drug of choice.

and Dutch colonies fall before advancing Japanese like bowling pins. Japan occupies this colony on Christmas Day. As Hong Kong's Europeans are herded into Stanley Fort, Japan recognizes Portugal's neutrality and tiny Macau becomes the only "neutral pocket" in China. Macau becomes a refuge for escapees who successfully run through Japan's military gauntlet.

1945: On August 6, an American atom bomb drops on Hiroshima. That same month, Sir Cecil Harcourt steams into "Fragrant Harbour" at the head of the British fleet to re-establish Her Majesty's presence in the war ravaged British Crown Colony of Hong Kong.

flying boat en route to Macau from the colony is taken. The pilot was shot by the lone hijacker and the plane crashed, killing all but one of the 27 passengers and crew.

1949: Routed Kuomintang forces flee to Taiwan. Communist Chinese troops stop at the British border and a heavy Red Bamboo Curtain seals off the Middle Kingdom. While China's civil war was being fought, Hong Kong's refugee population swelled, and the colony's residents now number nearly 2 million. This time, however, many of the new refugees are affluent Shanghai entrepreneurs and proprietors, some arriving in the colony with complete factories.

1946: The Bretton Woods Agreement is signed, thereby forbidding the importation of gold for private purposes. Britain signs, Portugal does not. Thus begins a Macau-to-Hong Kong gold-smuggling operation which lasts until 1974 when Hong Kong abolishes a law which requires special licenses to import gold. Tiny Macau becomes one of the world's greatest importers of gold (which then usually finds its shiny way to Hong Kong where it is then sold on the open market). China's civil war rages on.

1948: Hong Kong's first skyjacking took place on July 16 as a Macau Airways' catalina

1952: In March, riots break out in Kowloon when the government refuses the entry of a Canton mission to provide comfort to victims of a squatter fire. In Macau, waves of immigrants threaten to swamp the tiny territory. Macau signs an agreement with China pledging co-operation with the Communist regime.

1953: On Christmas Day, Hong Kong's Shek Kip Mei squatter area bursts into flames leaving 53,000 homeless. After the debris is cleared on Boxing Day, Hong Kong begins an emergency housing programme.

1954: Dien Bien Phu falls and the French lose Vietnam. A conference in Geneva is called to guarantee Indochina's neutrality and John Foster Dulles, the American Secretary of State, snubs Chinese Prime Minister Chou En-lai by refusing to shake hands.

1955: China, in a show of force, blocks Macau's plans for a 400th birthday celebration; in a genuflection to diplomacy China later frees American prisoners-of-war captured during the Korean War.

1956: Another wave of immigrants hits the colony, pushing the population above 2.5 million. Squatter huts spring up everywhere and rioting between Nationalists and Communists explodes in the streets. At ongoing Geneva peace talks, China proposes cultural exchanges with the United States. Hong Kong gets cable television in time to catch some of this year's political and military action.

1962: Yet another wave of immigrants – estimated to be between 60,000–100,000 – crosses the border, but this time they are shunted back and forth like ping pong balls as Chinese border troops herd them towards Hong Kong while colonial forces try desperately to keep them out. The deluge stops as quickly as it began – when Mao orders it to stop.

1964: Legal gambling begins at Macau, turning this somnolent territory into a "Las Vegas of the East." Hong Kong makes history by being the only city in the world in which Britain's famed mopheads – the Beatles – lose money.

1965: The war escalates in Vietnam with the first US air strikes against North Vietnam. Marines land at Danang and a "protracted" ground war is on. Hong Kong braces for an American invasion. R&R (Rest & Recreation) troops begin trickling into the colony on leave from the war, and during the next 10 years this trickle expands to more than 3,000 GIs a month. US Navy vessels become as familiar a sight in the harbour as do servicemen from all three of the United States' armed services in the bars and nightclubs of Wanchai and across the harbour in Tsimshatsui restaurants.

1966: Rioting flares up again, this time over a price rise in the first class Star Ferry fares. Peking, however, remains mute. Mao starts his great proletarian "cultural revolution" to regain control of the country. Young

intellectuals take over the ancient Middle Kingdom and traditionally revered elders are cast aside, sometimes with brute force.

The chaos in China spills over into Macau as Red Guards plaster the tiny Portuguese territory with posters. Portuguese troops fire on rampaging Red Guards, killing eight. Macau's governor, Brigadier Nobre de Carvalho, negotiates from a position of weakness because Portugal cannot come to its aid and Macau's tiny police force and garrison is helpless. In Hong Kong, Chief Superintendent John Tsang of Special Branch, one of the colony's highest ranking Chinese policemen, is unmasked as a Communist spy and disappears across the border, only to become the chief of security for Kwangtung Province. By this act he establishes himself as a character in all subsequent fiction written about the colony.

1967: Brigadier de Carvalho plays a last trump and suggests that the Portuguese leave Macau. Peking pulls back its Red Guards. China doesn't want either Portugal or Britain to pull out at this point in time due to economic considerations. On January 29, the Portuguese make a public apology for the Red Guard killings and pay China HK$2 million in compensation. The Hong Kong government is shocked at this Portuguese capitulation. Meanwhile the Britain Embassy in Peking is sacked and Red Guards take to Hong Kong's streets. The government fights back, but just about all aspects of the economy are paralyzed – except R&R nightlife business. Stories circulate that special "triads" are keeping Wanchai free of Communist cadres so that police can concentrate on protecting other districts. Peking responds vociferously when major Hong Kong riots break out and tension is mounting. By the end of the year, the "disturbances" are quelled and Hong Kong and Macau are still Western-run colonies.

Hong Kong's first vehicle tunnel, the Lion Rock Tunnel, opens as a symbol of the government's regard for the future.

The pound sterling is devalued and Hong Kong loses a third of its sterling reserves. Hong Kong devalues, revalues in the same week and then pegs its currency to the US dollar.

1969: The Hong Kong government stages its first Festival of Hong Kong to thank "residents" who have tolerated the past few

Left, Mao inspired a socially realistic school of art with visions of the Great Helmsman and his people.

years of the cultural revolution across the border with nervous patience, aware of the potential danger to the colony.

1970: Pope Paul VI visits Hong Kong, the first Roman pontiff to do so. A "Jumbo Jet" arrives for the first time at Kai Tak Airport.

1971: The United States cannot muster enough support for Taiwan in the United Nations General Assembly and the People's Republic of China is eventually recognized as the "real China" and takes Taiwan's place in that world body.

Sir Murray MacLehose becomes the first Hong Kong governor to be appointed from

ny's time-consuming, but pleasant, cross-harbour vehicular ferry cruises.

The cruise liner *Queen Elizabeth*, bought by shipping magnate C.Y. Tung to be converted into a Seawise Floating University, mysteriously catches fire and rolls over in Hong Kong's harbour.

1973: Britain floats the pound sterling because it cannot afford to artificially prop up that currency any longer. But Hong Kong is prepared this time and has long since diversified its cash reserves.

The first of the "spiralling" OPEC oil price rises hits Hong Kong; de-energising effects

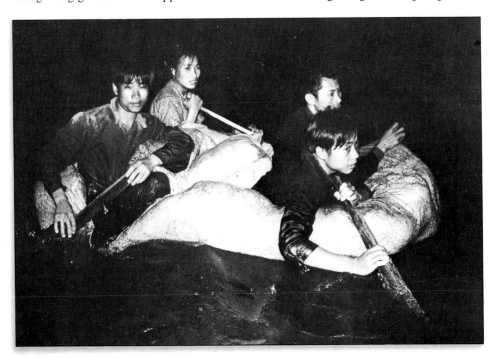

the British diplomatic corps. This is a signal to China that Britain is concerned about Hong Kong's future. Shortly after Mac-Lehose's arrival, a new Jumbo Floating Restaurant at Aberdeen catches fire.

1972: The entire world is caught off guard by the once unthinkable sight of US President Richard Nixon visiting China. He has audiences with the aging Mao Tse-tung and Chou En-lai, and treats the Middle Kingdom to a Western-style media circus as the world's press flocks into the Forbidden City and other Chinese places.

In Hong Kong the cross-harbour tunnel opens and motorists bid farewell to the colo-

are felt immediately by one and all.

The United States officially "recognizes" China, sets up a Peking liaison office, closes its Taipei embassy, and creates a China institute to handle consular matters.

Hong Kong's stock market collapses. The colony's first "new town," Tuen Mun, is opened in the New Territories and will eventually house 200,000.

During this shocking year, Hong Kong's rampant police corruption becomes common knowledge when senior police officer, Peter Godber, slips out of Hong Kong to escape arrest, taking with him more than HK$4.6 million, six times the amount he officially earned during his Hong Kong police career.

1974: In response to public outcry – and pointed nudging from an embarrassed governor and Whitehall – Hong Kong sets up an Independent Commission Against Corruption (the ICAC) with a wide mandate to stamp out corruption. The police force is the first government department on the commission's check list.

Following this year's revolution in Portugal, Macau's governor, Brigadier Nobre de Carvalho, is called back to Lisbon and ordered to resign from the Portuguese army. A young technocrat, Lt. Col. Garcia Leandro, ain, Thailand and the United States, in addition to Hong Kong police.

The infamous Peter Godber is extradited from England, stands trial and gets four years. He is convicted partly on the testimony of another copper, Taffy Hunt, who was given judicial immunity in exchange for fingering Godber. Hunt later bragged to reporters at his home in Spain that he made more than a million US dollars working for the Royal Hong Kong Police.

Her Majesty Queen Elizabeth II and H.R.H. the Duke of Edinburgh arrive for a royal visit; they are the first reigning British roy-

replaces him. Since China refuses to take back Macau, the colony's status was changed to a "Chinese territory under Portuguese Administration."

The Macau-Taipa bridge is completed.

1975: The police bust a Mr Big in the local heroin trade – Ng Sik-ho – and his assistant, Ng Chun-kwan, who were sentenced to 30 and 25 years in prison respectively. This narcotics crackdown on big drug syndicates involved law enforcement agents from Brit- alty ever to set foot in the colony.

1976: After a mass demonstration by off-duty policemen on Queensway in Central, the Governor orders an amnesty for all crimes of corruption committed before January 1, 1977. With hundreds of staff assigned, the ICAC drive against corruption becomes one of the world's most effective.

Both Chou En-lai and Mao Tse-tung die and China begins "a new era" under Deng Xiaoping and Hua Guofeng, the "new" Celestial Kingdom's Vice-Chairman and Chairman respectively. And in a conscience-cleaning move which shocks the world, Mao's widow, Chiang Ching (Jiang Qing)

Left, a group of illegal immigrants is spot-lighted by a patrol boat just off the shore. **Above**, a restaurant at Aberdeen erupts in flames in 1971.

and three other zealous revolutionaries – the infamous "gang of four" – are arrested.

1977: Rumours hit Macau that Portugal is trying to give the colony away, but the Chinese will not take it back. The Deputy Prime Minister of Portugal visits the 400-year-old colony in a show of faith.

London continually pressures the Hong Kong government for more social services, but the colony's conservatives resist. Fears grow that Whitehall, under a Labour government, will turn the ultra-capitalistic colony into a welfare state.

namese boat people to the colony for Christmas. In Kowloon, a Sung Dynasty Village opens, offering visitors an easy journey into ancient Chinese "living" culture.

1980: In October, Hong Kong ends its "touch base" immigration policy which previously allowed Chinese refugees to remain in the colony if they reached an urban area safely. Such illegal immigrants will no longer be home free here.

The colony's longest running sideshow –

1978: Peking and Lisbon exchange diplomatic niceties and Col. Garcia Leandro, Macau's governor, visits Macau's old landlord, China. As a sign of improved relations, China approves in principal a Hong Kong-Macau helicopter service.

Vietnamese refugees fleeing the south (after buying their way out with gold) start piling up in Southeast Asia. Eventually, 70,000 of these "boat people" settled in Hong Kong.

The gigantic High Island Reservoir opens and begins quenching Hong Kong water problems, while in China the Bamboo Curtain opens wide and for the first time in many years tourists are allowed to visit the People's Republic.

1979: Hong Kong's US$1 billion Mass Transit Railway (MTR) opens. The rusty freighter *Huey Fong* brings 3,000 more Viet-

an enquiry into the alleged suicide of Inspector John MacLennan (who according to official police reports shot himself in the chest five times) reveals sordid details about police undercover agents who stalk after homosexuals. Chinese who regard homosexuality as "white man's disease" are exposed to an unseemly side of life in a big city.

1981: The Housing Department admits that more than 1.2 million people in 250,000 households – 20 percent of the population – still live in "unsatisfactory conditions."

In Macau, a new administration led by governor Commander Vasco Almeida de Costa takes office.

1982: The highpoint of the year is the visit of the British Prime Minister, Mrs Margaret

<u>**Above**</u>, **Chou En-lai and giggling comrades on a 1977 People's Republic stamp commemorating the first anniversary of his death.**

Thatcher, to Peking and Hong Kong in September. During this visit, the first talks on Hong Kong's future (the 99-year lease on the New Territories, nine-tenths of the Colony, expires in 1997) began. The negotiations and subsequent jitters thus generated overshadow the departure of Sir Murray MacLehose from his office as the 25th governor for more than a decade. He was replaced by Sir Edward Youde, another Mandarin-speaking, old China-hand diplomat (instead of a colonial administrator).

Hong Kong's stock market takes a dive on Thatcher's visit which acts as a catalyst to bring down the soaring property market.

China's 13th National People's Congress meets and releases the 6th five-year plan which completely restructures the economy. The Chinese also announce they are putting in US$100 million in infrastructure construction into the Shenzhen Special Economic Zone on Hong Kong's border.

1983: The Sino-British negotiations on Hong Kong's future continue to hold headlines, affecting every facet of the colony's existence.

Property market continues to fall, pulling with it a number of deposit-taking and real-estate companies, the largest of which was the Carrian Group which owes HK$10 billion to the banks when the plug was pulled on the year-long rescue effort.

In July, the Chinese tip their plans for Hong Kong to a group of universiy students: Hong Kong will become a Special Administrative Region, will keep its own capitalistic system, judiciary and police, but the future head will be a Hong Kong Chinese.

The tone of the negotiations changes for the better around autumn after China leader Deng Xiaoping reportedly receives a letter from Mrs Thatcher in which she concedes Hong Kong's sovereignty to China.

1984: Hong Kong's most important day, September 26, equal in significance to the day the colony was founded in 1841, is added to the calendar. On that day the British Ambassador to China and the Chinese Vice Foreign Minister initial *A Draft Agreement on the Future of Hong Kong*, ending two years of often acrimonious negotiations between the two countries on Hong Kong's fate.

The government sets up an Assessment Office to gather opinions on the Draft Agreement, as promised by Mrs Thatcher. (Opinions collected are sent to London to assist Members of Parliament in thier debate on the matter.) "Catch 22" is that both the Chinese and British governments announced after the initialling that "no changes could be made." The real choice for Hong Kong's population is to accept China's takeover in 1997 with the agreement as writ (including safeguards therein) or to accept China's takeover in 1997 *period*.

Almost as important as the agreement itself are the government's plans for Hong Kong's administration in the years running up to 1997. Key points include elections to the Legislative Council, the District Boards and new Regional Councils. The government has stated its intent to train local decision-makers in the intervening years to 1997 to prepare the territory for its semi-autonomous, almost-self-governing role as a Special Administrative Region of the People's Republic of China.

Hong Kong-appointed Legislative and Executive Councillors, who have been left out of the Sino-British talks, gain strength and stature as they fly to London several times passing on Hong Kong's anxieties and arguing forcibly with various British Members of Parliament and politicians.

1985: Britain and China ratify the Sino-British Joint Declaration initialled the previous year and subsequently register it as an international treaty at the United Nations. Beijing (formerly known as Peking) proceeds to appoint a Basic Law Drafting Committee (BLDC) of 59 members, 23 from Hong Kong. Its job is to write the mini-constitution for the Special Administrative Region created by the Declaration. The BLDC in turn creates a Basic Law Consultative Committee of 180 members, all from Hong Kong, to tap local Hong Kong opinion about the new document which will rule Hong Kong for 50 years from July 1, 1997.

The tripartite (Britain, China and Hong Kong) Joint Liaison Group, also created by the Declaration to liaise and coordinate matters to the year 2000 and held two meetings in London and Beijing. Britain announced it will faze out its garrison by 1997 while the PRC stated that the contingents of the People Liberation Army will be stationed in Hong Kong after the hand over.

Hong Kong is also abuzz with its first elections to the Legislative Council, for the first time in its history. Twenty-four of the 56 members take their place through indirect elections from member of two groups; Functional Constituencies (representing the professional and various sectors of the economy) and an electoral College (made up of members from existing group like District Boards, and the Urban and Regional Councils).

Out of a total population of 5.5 million, only 70,000 will qualify for this franchise under a restricted system of which of the 47,000 registered, only 25,000 actually go to the polls. Nevertheless, this election fever is enough to touch off a debate about how

director of the New China News Agency, lashes out just five days before the second Joint Liaison Group meeting, insisting Britain is deviating from the Joint Declaration. Fear and anxiety pervade Hong Kong as a backlash, forcing Ji Pengfei, a member of China's State Council and Director of its Hong Kong and Macau Office, to downplay Xu's remarks during the scheduled visit in December. (He is the highest ranking Chinese official ever to visit the Colony.)

The territory takes a big step towards improving its arts education with the opening of the Academy for Performing Arts. The Tolo

future Councils should be chosen and whether Hong Kong Government will allow open elections for the 1988 elections, as promised in the 1984 White Paper.

British Minister of State, Timothy Renton, arrives in Hong Kong after his appointment to assure the Hong Kong people that London will not interfere with constitutional reforms here nor foist a parliamentary democracy on the territory, stating that Hong Kong must develop its own system.

Meanwhile, China looks with great askance at the territory's fledging attempts at the democracy and the ensuing debate about the future. Its top man in the territory, Xu Jiatun,

Highway project in the New Territories is completed.

1986: Politics continues to dominate the headlines, but takes a different glance, as the hottest political issue becomes nuclear power plan at the Daya Bay across the border in Guangdong Province, a mere 9 miles (15 km) from the territory.

In the light of the Chernobyl accident in April, the cry is to get out of this project which is backed by Iron Major Hong Kong Company, China Light & Power and the Chinese Government with the Hong Kong Government, which is also a shareholder. The Legislative Council sent fact-finding missions to the US, Japan and Europe to study nuclear power stations.

April saw the opening of the Unified Stock Exchange of Hong Kong, enabling disparate exchanges under one rule. The Hong Kong index is also created, while the Hong Kong Commodities Exchange introduced Hang Seng Index Future Contract.

The Joint Liaison Group created under the Sino-British Joint Declaration met in Hong Kong, London and Beijing. This is the territory's first step in severing its ties with Britain while simultaneously creating different ones with China.

This year also saw Hong Kong acting as its own contract party rather than as part of the British delegation.

Queen Elizabeth II and her husband Duke of Edinburgh visited Hong Kong for the second time in October after their trip to China. The territory's Governor, Sir Edward Youde, died unexpectedly in his sleep on December 5 in Beijing where he was engaged in a series of consultations over Hong Kong's future.

1987: Sir David Wilson, former political advisor to the Hong Kong government, is sworn in as governor and steps into the middle of the Green Paper debate on representative government, as focused in the 1988 Legislative Council elections. In the 1984 White Paper on Representative Government, the government promised to institute direct elections in the 1988 elections, aiming for an elected council by the handover in 1997. Opposition to this idea comes from within and without the territory as the Hong Kong's business elite and wealthy ally themselves into the Group of 81 which calls for a benevolent oligarchy (of the elite and rich) to rule after 1997. Against them are various grassroots organizations and a few liberal Legislative Council members, formed into the Group of 81, representing the middle and most liberal political viewpoints respectively.

The Group of 81's most powerful ally is of course China which becomes more and more upset as the debate gets increasingly acrimonious and widespread. Eventually, Lu Ping, the Deputy Director of the Hong Kong and Macau Affairs Office of the PRC's State Council lashes out, stating that the political

changes that do not follow the Basic Law will be overturned in 1997. China's top man, Deng Xiaoping, weighs in stating that universal suffrage might not be beneficial for Hong Kong. Britain and Hong Kong get the hint and Lord Glenarthur, the official in charge of the Hong Kong desk at the Foreign and Commonwealth Office arrives. He rejects calls for a referendum.

The mutual distrust, the underlying anxiety within the Hong Kong population over what will happen in 1997, continues to bubble over. The first sign of this is the brain drain – the emigration of the territory's professionals to better political climes, exacerbated by changes in immigration laws in Canada, Australia and the US, the more popular destinations. The government denies there is a brain drain.

In a move earmarked as a legal tidying up exercise, the government tries to introduce non-jury trials in complex commercial cases. The timing is bad as the fear of the future overrides the more practical judicial aspects. The government introduces legislation to control publications creating a great outcry regarding the definition of "false news" the keystone of the new ordinance. The government is also embarrassed at disclosures that it has been censoring films for 34 years without the legal authority, in the full knowledge it was doing so.

The British National (Overseas) passport is issued by the Hong Kong government, a document meant to replace the British Dependent territories passport. Though the new BNO passport will be valid beyond July 1, 1997, it proves unpopular as the overriding anxiety about the new citzenship becomes apparent. The Carrian trial, for alleged criminal fraud and alleged conspiracy to defraud, ends as the government case is thrown out of court in one of the most controversial decisions in Hong Kong's history.

The economy booms, recording a 13.6 percent gain in GDP and the government announces once again that it will study the problem of a new airport.

A HK$2.7 billion programme is implemented to clear the infamous Walled City, the notorious non-walled section of Kowloon which has been the subject of many jurisdictional arguments between the colonial and Chinese governments for nearly a century.

On Black Monday, October 19, Hong

Left, Margaret Thatcher, Britain's former Prime Minister takes tea in a resettlement estate flat during her visit to the colony in 1982.

Kong's stock market, alone among the world's financial centres, closes for four days. The controversial closure, condemned world wide, rocks Hong Kong and nearly destroys the Futures Exchange. The government puts together a HK$4 billion rescue package to forestall collapse and distances itself from the exchange hierarchy which has been accused of running the place like a club.

In December, a Sino-Portuguese Agreement initialled in April is signed. The handover date for Macau, the first Western enclave on the China coast and the only one ceded, not taken by force of arms, is December 20, 1999. The agreement is similar to Hong Kong's but China, in an about face, recognizes

the community). A flood of 8,000 arrives in the first six months causing the government to crackdown and create a new category effective June 16. After that date, Vietnamese boat people must prove they are political refugees, not economic migrants, or face repatriation. The flow continues as another 9,000 arrive between June 16 and end of August. The government imprisons 4,200 newly arrived Vietnamese boat people in a 12-storey factory building, hastily made fit for human habitation, in a desperate attempt to house the new arrivals. (Total refugee expenses since 1979, when the first ones arrived, now top HK$1 billion.)

The factory building becomes the focus

the Macanese can hold dual nationality: Chinese and Portuguese. (This was not the case with the Sino-British Joint Declaration.)

And, as if more signs are needed about China's emergence into the modern world, a 2,100-mile (3,380-km) Hong Kong-Beijing motor rally is held; 50,000 troops are mobilized for the 3-day event to hold back crowds so that 36 rally cars and 124 support vehicles can drive through China unhindered!

1988: Hong Kong started the year with 9,500 Vietnamese refugees, divided into open (those whose population is free to leave and work in the community) and closed camps (those incarcerated, forbidden to mingle with

for worldwide criticism as the UNHCR washes its hands of the matter and refuses to help in the selection of political refugees. The government announces it will liberalize the conditions of refugees in closed camps who arrived before June 16.

The Vietnamese invite the Hong Kong government officials to Hanoi to discuss the problem and make it clear that money talks; if Hong Kong coughs up some aid then Hanoi will consider taking its people back providing they are willing. China enters the fray with the announcement by Lu Ping, Deputy Director of the Hong Kong and Macau Affairs Office of China's State Council, that the Vietnamese issue should be settled by the handover in 1997, stunning the colony.

A White Paper on representative government is published, postponing direct elections to the Legislative Council in 1988. With indirect elections via Functional Constituencies (representing professionals and various sectors of the economy) and an Electoral College (drawn from exisiting councils and boards), less than 100,000 people out of 5.5 million are eligible to vote in September, of which only 61,519 registered. Due to the number of uncontested seats, a mere 18,326 have a choice from which to cast a ballot.

A draft of the Basic Law, Hong Kong's future constitution when it becomes a Spe-

radio and television licensing, which now includes proposals for cable television. Radio Television Hong Kong, now a government department, takes steps to become a chartered station in the image of the BBC.

The government's press law, passed in 1987, gets its first test of the definition of "false news" as a local Chinese paper prints an interview with high ranking Li Hou, another Deputy Director of the Hong Kong and Macau Affairs office, who, according to the paper, stated that direct elections may not converge with Basic Law and would not be in the spirit of the Joint Declaration. The statement causes an uproar and is then corrected in the *China Daily*. The press calls on

cial Administrative Region of China in 1997, is published in April for a five month discussion period, evoking widespread criticism. In an unprecedented move, China sends some of its leading Basic Law Committee members to the colony to find out first hand the objections. For the first time in Hong Kong's history, the members meet the press and public on television. Hong Kong's brain drain continues unabated.

A Broadcasting Authority is created to run

Left, the infamous Walled City before being torn down. **Above**, making their sentiments quite clear about 1997.

the government to define false news in the light of this occurrence. Later, the government announces it will review the press law.

In Macau, Governor Carlos Melancia travels to China to review the handover and returns with Beijing's blessings for massive projects – the long-discussed deep water port and airport. A Basic Law Drafting Committee to write Macau's new constitution is appointed.

1989: The pro-democracy movement in China excites Hong Kong which sees the territory's future in it. The People Liberation Army's massacre of students on June 4 in Beijing's Tiananmen Square, and the subsequent crackdown, hits the Colony's collective heart. A million people take to the streets peacefully, culminating in a huge rally at the Happy Valley racetrack, in sight of the New China News Agency, the Chinese quasi-diplomatic mission. Hong Kong finally sees itself on the road to democracy, but China views the Colony as a place fomenting trouble and harbouring criminals, particularly student leaders who flee through Hong Kong.

The action at Tiananmen Square exacerbates Hong Kong brain drain which is now over 50,000 annually. Britain tries to internationalize its Hong Kong problem by bringing the subject up at the Group of Seven meeting in Paris in July and the Common-

direct elections in September 1991.

After various visits and consultations, Hong Kong and Beijing governments decide that members elected to the Legislative Council in 1995 will serve through 1997 to 1999 and that they will be part of the 400 people who will select Hong Kong's first post-1997 Chief Executive. The scheme is nicknamed the "thru train."

In response to complaints, particularly from the UN Human Rights Committee and the UK, the Governor, Sir David Wilson, announces in October the government's intention to draw up a Bill of Rights. China objects and threatens to ignore the law after the 1997 handover. The Chinese are also annoyed at a

wealth Heads of State meeting in October. It receives only tea and sympathy in return. Foreign Secretary Sir Geoffrey Howe's visit in July to calm Hong Kong after the events of June 4 is met with hostility. By year end, Britain offers a very limited nationality package encompassing no more than 50,000 heads of household, 225,000 people.

On the democracy front, the government walks a thin line between previous promises and China's displeasure at free elections for Legislative Council, the territory's law-making body. Shaken by budding political alertness, Hong Kong government agrees to speed up the process, offering to put 18 seats up for

Central District reclamation plan which moves the British military headquarters from its present waterfront site at HMS Tamar to Stonecutter's Island in the harbour. The Chinese claim they were not consulted, but it is widely assumed that the People's Liberation Army, which will station troops here in 1997, wants the valuable real estate for itself.

With confidence at an all time low, government announces a confidence boosting scheme in October – a HK$127 billion Port and Airport Development Strategy. It plans to have the first plane touching down at the new airport, located off Lantau Island's northern coast at tiny Chep Lap Kok Island, by early 1997. Most of the finance for the scheme will be private.

The move is a calculated risk as Hong Kong pushes its autonomy to the hilt. But China objects, saying it should be consulted because its future (post-1997) Special Administrative Region government will be saddled with debt.

Vietnamese refugees, arriving by boat faster than they can be resettled, still plague the Colony with more than 50,000 languishing in camps, the largest concentration of Vietnamese boat people in the world. The tab touches HK$1 billion for housing them as both the Police and Correctional Services Departments are stretched to the limit with

Eastern Harbour Crossing, opens.

The Prince and Princess of Wales visit Hong Kong in November to open the Hong Kong Convention and Exhibition Centre as well as to lay the cornerstone of the University of Science and Technology. In spite of evident ill feelings at Britain because of its inaction over the plight of Hong Kong's 3 million Hong Kong-British passport holders, the visit goes off without a hitch.

1990: The massive Port and Airport Development Strategy begins to hang heavily on Hong Kong. Instead of restoring confidence, it drains it as China vents its anger at not being consulted. The Hong Kong government finds itself in the unenviable posi-

extra duties. The first volunteer returnees fly back, 75 in March and 68 in May as a Geneva Conference on the problem is called to push for mandatory repatriation. The first group of mandatory repatriated refugees, numbering 51 men, women and children, are flown back in December in the dead of night. Following the adverse international publicity, Britain and Hong Kong call off mandatory repatriation.

The second cross harbour road tunnel, the

Left, the walla-walla offers an alternate mode of cross-harbour transport. **Above**, grim scene at a Viet refugee camp.

tion of being at loggerheads with its giant neighbour and future master.

The international finance to make the scheme a reality is not forthcoming. Pressure builds as the draft Bill of Rights is published to which China objects and vows to ignore when it takes over. In April, the Basic Law, Hong Kong's post-1997 constitution, is promulgated giving the China's National People's Congress final say over Hong Kong affairs.

In October, the government announces it will self-finance – to the tune of HK$7.8 billion – the Lantau fixed crossing (a series of bridges to the airport) because it cannot get international financing and contracts must be let if the airport is to proceed on schedule. China takes the announcement as a direct snub and a challenge.

Emigration, particularly to Canada and Australia, of Hong Kong's best and brightest tops 60,000. The UK calls on its allies to help. The US amends its immigration laws to increase Hong Kong's quota to 10,000 until 1994 and 20,000 thereafter. Another 12,000 Hong Kong visas, valid to the year 2000, are being offered to employees of American companies.

The aftermath of the June 4 massacre still affects Hong Kong as the former New China News Agency director, 74-year-old Xu Jiatun, a 52-year veteran of the Chinese

in favour of China's inclusion in the MFN.

With Berlin Wall's demise and the political changes in Eastern Europe, the government eases restrictions on visits from Eastern Europeans, previously banned. Macau begins reclamation for its own airport and the neighbouring Special Economic Zone of Shenzhen announces plans to enlarge its airport, already under construction.

The long-awaited helicopter service to Macau begins in November and Macau's new governor Carlos Montez Melancia takes office and quits office in the same year.

In December, Hong Kong gains its own shipping registry but is shocked that the Hong Kong and Shanghai Banking Corporation,

Communist Party living in retirement in the neighbouring Shenzhen Special Economic Zone, flees to the US with some of his family – after he is ordered to report to Beijing.

With the granting of a one-year Most Favoured Nation (MFN) status to China by President Bush, in spite of Congressional fury at China's human rights record – a continuing reflection of the negative aftermath of the 1989 Tiananmen Square massacre – Hong Kong breathes a sigh of relief. With its economy so intertwined with that of Southern China, any restrictions on China's exports would hit Hong Kong too. It was this fact which reportedly swayed the President

the territory's biggest bank and *de facto* central bank, moves its headquarters to Britain.

After the collapse of cable TV license talks, a 12-year satellite TV license is awarded to Hutch-Vision to beam Star TV throughout Asia.

1991: Hong Kong's acknowledgment of its 150th anniversary on January 26 is so officially low-key that only new stamps and newspaper supplements betray the occasion. The reason? The government feels it is a sensitive subject due to the continued conflict with China over the proposed HK$127 billion Port and Airport Development Strategy, particularly the HK$78 billion airport scheme due to receive its first planes in 1997. So it is left to the Post Office to celebrate their founding on August 25, 1941, with new stamps.

The anxiety level of the general population grows – reflected in an increase in emigration which tops 60,000 – as the argument now moves beyond consultation and airport finance to the basic question of Hong Kong's autonomy during the remaining years until the 1997 handover. Various visits to Beijing by both Hong Kong and British government representatives, including Foreign Secretary Douglas Hurd, throughout the year to sell the airport while retaining Hong Kong's full autonomy fail.

At the end of June, the British Prime Min-

related Questions" has been initialed, ending 20 months of acrimony.

The Understanding, like the 1984 Sino-British agreement, is concluded without Hong Kong's participation. The document gives China's support for the project in exchange for fiscal guarantees and membership on the board of the Airport Authority.

As a fillip for the Chinese, Major goes to Beijing – the first Western leader to do so since the Tiananmen massacre in 1989 – and signs the document on September 3 with Chinese Premier Li Peng. While in Beijing, Major is "blunt" on the West's dissatisfaction with China's human rights record and hands over a list of jailed dissidents from

ister John Major makes a last ditch effort to try and settle the argument by sending his Foreign Affairs Advisor Sir Percy Craddock, the former British ambassador to Beijing and one of the key negotiators of the 1984 agreement, to Beijing for secret negotiations. On July 4, it is announced that a "Memorandum of Understanding Concerning the Construction of the New Airport in Hong Kong and

Left, the Goddess and the Governor (Sir David Wilson): contrasting symbols of the pro-democracy movement and fading British influence. Above, getting their points across at a pro-democracy rally.

1989 (one of which, Hong Kong businessman Lo Hoi-sing, jailed for helping two dissidents, is freed and returns to Hong Kong to a tumultuous welcome shortly after the PM's return to London) forcing the Chinese Foreign Office to tell the gathered press that the PRC knows all about human rights because it was under foreign domination for a century. The irony of Major touting human rights in China and then signing a document that curtails human rights in Hong Kong is not lost on the colony.

A few days after the Memorandum announcement, the Colony's stock market indicator, the Hang Seng Index, closes at an all-time record high of 4,009.35, having reached 4,025 at one stage during the day. Economists gleefully predict the airport will add 0.5 percent to Hong Kong's GDP, but government officials disagree whether 2,000 or 20,000 extra workers will be needed for the massive airport scheme, one of the biggest civil engineering projects of its kind in the world. (When finished, it will have the world's longest bridge.)

The mid-year floods in China provides a non-political opportunity for Hong Kong's population to help the motherland. The territory raises HK$700 million for flood victims, HK$100 million alone in one Sunday rally featuring, ironically, many stars who

is the place where the refugees are cared for), as legislators emphasize the territory cannot bear the full brunt of this international problem by itself.

The collapse of the Bank of Credit and Commerce worldwide hits Hong Kong on Saturday, July 6. Some 40,000 depositors, many of them small businessmen, are hit hard.

With the British defense cutbacks in July, Hong Kong's Brigade of Gurkhas is cut from 8,000 to 2,500. The police announce they have no intention of making up their manpower shortage, caused by increased duties on the border and their vigil at the Vietnamese camps, with the Gurkhas.

The economy receives another boost with

performed at a rally for the pro-democracy movement in the same place in 1989. However, fear of corruption in China forces many of the donating agencies to monitor the funds themselves.

On June 8, Hong Kong's new Bill of Rights becomes law, much to China's chagrin, backing the "rights and freedoms" guaranteed in the 1984 Sino-British Agreement.

With mandatory repatriation of the Vietnamese boat people at a standstill and record numbers of boat people continually arriving – five arrivals for every departure – Hong Kong people push for an end to the First Asylum Policy (whereby the first port touched

the decision in August to allow China to retain Most Favoured Nation Status for another year, in spite of the US Congress annoyance at its human rights record. (The economies of Hong Kong and Southern China are now so intermixed that curtailment of China's MFN status would severely affect Hong Kong.) The extention of the Multi-Fibre Agreement at the eleventh hour in August also portends increased blows to economic growth.

Major makes a whirlwind 30-hour visit to Hong Kong (September 4–5) after the signing ceremony in Beijing. He announces he has "unblocked the rupture of confidence" on Hong Kong. China's blockage within the Joint Liaison Group to the establishment of a new Court of Final Appeal (which must be implemented before the 1997 handover) to replace Britain's Privy Council is lifted as a by-product of Major's visit. But it transpires that the decision on judges will not be left to the Hong Kong government and China will now have a very big say on appointments.

Stalking Major in China and Hong Kong is none other than former British Prime Minister Margaret Thatcher, who is travelling on behalf of the Thatcher Foundation. On September 12–14, Mrs Thatcher follows the British PM into Hong Kong. The first direct elections in the 150-year history of the Leg-

islative Council take place on September 15 when 18 directly elected seats from geographical constituencies are contested by universal suffrage for the new 60-member Council. In a separate election three days earlier on September 12, elections for the functional constituencies take place for the second time. Government prepares itself, for the first time in its history, for opposition, namely the United Democrats under barrister Martin Lee and a potential legislative defeat sometime during the session.

Left, a princess in Hong Kong. **Above**, Gurkha in symbolic silhouette.

On September 1, China through Hong Kong's New China News Agency announces Hong Kong voters should take candidates' "attitudes toward the Mainland" into account when casting their votes. The comment is widely interpreted as vote for the correct (i.e. pro-China) candidates and not those of the more liberal persuasion (i.e. the United Democrats).

Actually, the government's first legislative defeat comes when councillors in March voted against the government budget forcing the Financial Secretary to halve an unpopular cigarette tax, reducing it from 200 percent to 100 percent.

The government announces another world record – 273 vehicles per 0.6 mile (1 km), reportedly the densest concentration of traffic in the world. It also now sports the fourth and fifth tallest buildings in the world, Century Plaza (1,228 feet) and the Bank of China Tower (1,209 feet) respectively. And "grape treading" makes its first appearance in Hong Kong's history in a competition at a local wine bar. For the first time in many years, Hong Kong's airwaves expand – Metronews Radio begins broadcasting on three channels, including an all-news one; Star TV, the Colony's first satellite channel goes into action; and Business News Network, another satellite venture opens.

As a year-end treat for the people of Hong Kong, the British government announces in London on December 31 that the governor, Sir David Wilson, would be retiring when his term is up mid-year. Though Sir David has had his differences with the Foreign Office vis-a-vis Beijing's ever-growing list of demands, no one, not even the Chinese, expected him to be preemptively fired before the 1992 British elections. John Major and the Conservatives win a closely-fought election victory in April 1992. Later that month, Conservative Party chairman Christopher Patten is named as Hongkong's new governor.

Across Pearl River Estuary, Macau also gets another new governor, Vasco Joaquin Rocha Vieira, its second in as many years. Work proceeds on Macau's ambitious airport and port plans.

Across the border in the Special Economic Zone, the Shenzhen airport receives its first planes.

The arrival of Chris Patten in 1992 signals the onset of, politically, interesting times. He announces proposals for increased spending on welfare, health, housing and the environment. Every government department dealing with the public will introduce a performance pledge, aimed at improving services. A Governor's Business Council will be established to ensure Hong Kong's continued success and to advise on a 'comprehensive competition policy'. And he also proposed a reform of the political system.

China wants no such shift towards greater democracy. Patten has barely finished speaking when the New China News Agency fires the first salvo at him and his proposals.

On 13 October, the *Wen Wei Po*, a newspaper that serves as a mouthpiece for Beijing, accuses Patten of wasting time in dressing himself up as a 'God of Democracy', and of gambling with Hong Kong's future.

On his first official visit to Beijing, Patten is snubbed by Premier Li Peng. The highest official he meets, China's Foreign Minister Qian Qichen, tells him the Hong Kong Government is jeopardising cooperation between Britain and China.

In response to the Chinese criticism, the Hang Seng index drops 200 points on 26 October. Brokers warn that unless Patten makes a U-turn on his push for greater democracy, the stock market could suffer further falls.

In November, senior National People's Congress member Li Hou says Patten is 'openly lying to Hong Kong people and the world'. The overseas edition of the *People's Daily* says Patten is conspiring with Western allies against China – a strategy that is doomed to fail. Beijing declares that the validity of all contracts, leases and agreements signed or ratified by the British Hong Kong administration without that approval of China will not be not be honoured after 30 June 1997. The Hang Seng index falls 308 points.

Panic selling continues. The Hang Seng Index – which had stood at a record level of 6447.11 on November – is at 4978.21 at the close of business on 3 December.

The next day, the index jumps 290 points.

It dips again on 18 December, as Beijing accuses Jardines of being the black sheep of the business community, of prospering (in its early history) on selling opium and continuing to make money from Hong Kong and China unscrupulously, and of working closely behind the scenes on a political agenda to help Patten.

1993: Early 1993 sees a lull in the war of the words, as China celebrates the Lunar New Year.

Rumours that China might be willing to give ground at impending talks on political developments send the Hang Seng Index up 91 points on 15 February – the biggest rise in a day since 1987. China denies the rumours.

In early March, the index rises to a record level on hopes that talks will resume between Britain and China.

On 12 March, after deferring gazettes on four successive Fridays, Patten gazetted the electoral bill for the 1994/95 elections. He makes his announcement in the afternoon, and the Hang Seng Index loses 260 points in the final half hour of trade. At night, the Chinese Foreign Ministry says Patten has seriously damaged the foundation for discussion and cooperation between the two sides.

In the opening address to the Eight National People's Congress, Premier Li Peng accuses Britain of trying to instill unrest in Hong Kong before the 1997 takeover. Patten has 'perfidiously and unilaterally' crafted proposals to alter Hong Kong's political system and violated previous Sino-British agreements. Britain's Foreign Secretary, Douglas Hurd, says London remains 'ready for talks at any time.'

Within minutes of the stock market opening on Monday 15 March, the index loses almost 400 points. It rebounds a little, steadies, and waits for the next developments.

On 17 March, in a press conference that is broadcast live in China, Lu Ping, Director of the State Council's Hong Kong and Macau Affairs Office, says the Governor will be condemned in Hong Kong's history as a 'man of guilt'. But Lu is more conciliatory towards Hong Kong, saying Beijing will honour its commitment to 'Hong Kong people ruling Hong Kong, which will enjoy a high degree of autonomy.' Even before he starts speaking, money begin pouring into the stock market; the Hang Seng Index, which had dropped in the morning, rebounds to finish the day little changed.

In April 1993, Sino-British talks resume. The Hang Seng Index leaps, and once again reaches record levels.

Harbour high-rises.

LIFE IN HONG KONG

Dreaming high over Hong Kong, staring down across the kaleidoscopic sweep of the harbour, Wong Ming – our man in the street – gazes at far-off islands misting into the horizon. Up here, on Victoria Peak, he sees the whole range of Hong Kong's life-styles sprawling out below. Scattered sparsely across the jade green hillsides are the white mansions of the rich and super-rich: European-style country houses and a few traditional Chinese homes, the latter usually tiered with ceramic tiled roofs and curved eaves.

Below snuggles the lower executive belt, suburban Mid-Levels and its smart apartments. Farther down, the city anthills into tiny alleys and the ups-and-tumble-downs of ladder streets, each connecting one main road with the next and linking mid hill with sea level. Here rise the old tenements of Western, Wanchai and Kennedy Town. The flats here are overcrowded and iron-barred, but each has a neat balcony garden – a tiny growing reminder of the farms and small land holdings of neighbouring Kwantung (Guangdong) Province. Here, in a dense city, love of earth is reduced to the tender care of flower pots.

Even farther away, round the curve of a hill beyond Wong Ming's eyes, are the housing estates. In these dingy overcrowded hives humming with the *mahjong* clack of worker bees, labourers rest noisily on their one-day-off-a-week; windows are bedecked with a working man's flag – shirts, pants and children's socks.

Wong Ming turns to watch a Rolls Royce purring up The Peak. In the back seat a man in a dark suit sits pensively, alternately staring at the back of his chauffeur's head and reading afternoon papers. He's Chinese, of course, as are most of Hong Kong's super-rich. There are wealthy foreigners too – after all, this is not a *laissez faire* economy for nothing – but when it comes to being a straight-up out-front super-rich, only the Chinese really qualify.

Preceding pages: high and not-so-dry in a rooftop rowing facility. **Left,** modern couple in a modern world. **Right,** a traditional chauffeur surveys her lot.

Indeed, it is these people who make up the nearest equivalent that Hong Kong has to an aristocracy. Hong Kong is neither old enough, nor perhaps honourable enough, to boast a society marked by good breeding or proper lineage. Money, not genealogy, makes the man here. The great names of Hong Kong are those which dominate business: Hotung, the merchant prince; Tung, the shipping magnate; Lee and Li, the banking and real estate barons; and the rest of the mandarin.

Most foreigners trail far behind, both in

terms of their money and certainly in terms of their significance, in the real thread of life in Hong Kong; but there are those who catch up and even overtake. The Kadoories, Baghdad Jews who made their family fortunes in Shanghai during the time of the merchant adventurers and later moved to Hong Kong, are, as well as rich, a local byword for charitable ventures. Noel Croucher, alas now dead, was a traditionally stingy millionaire who doled out secret acts of kindness but regularly walked home to save bus fares. The Harilelas are leaders of an Indian community which is largely comprised of Sindhi merchants. Bona fide philanthropists abound, but so do the rich who become noticed through public acts of extravagance which exceed even Hong Kong's normally self-indulgent standards. Chantal Millar, a stunning South American beauty, will long be remembered as the socialite who paid a million Hong Kong dollars for a three day fund-raising social bash. She flew guests in from all over the world to party with her, than donated the proceeds to charity.

Silver shadows and gold phantoms: Even more conspicuous are the Kaibong Chaus, well known for their fancy dress costumes and his-and-hers Rolls Royces. Their 3-ton "works of art on wheels" are a pink Silver Shadow and a sparkling Gold Phantom. The couple, both Cambridge-educated lawyers

and scions of two of Hong Kong's leading families, live in a converted garage called Villa d'Oro. Talking of their famous Rolls-Royces, they gush: "We *love* glamorous *things.*" Kaibong Chau, who describes himself as really quite shy, explains that the cars were conceived to fit two of his wife's favourite moods – the pink for "when she feels like Jean Harlow," and the gold for "Cleopatra occasions." Matching clothes (including a pink mink) and interiors – not to mention a colour-coordinated chauffeur in pink or gold uniform – "adds to the mystique," explains Mr Chau. The paintwork was done in Hong Kong, because Rolls Royce officials

in England apparently could not quite bring themselves to understand what moody wife Brenda and shy Kaibong had in mind for their opulent beats.

Wong Ming watches the Rolls Royce with wonder, but does not for one moment think life is unfair to him, who has so little. Instead, as he stares at the car he thinks wistfully of the day when he will make it, when he too will join the privileged ranks of the super-rich. Indeed, his is a dream dreamed by every poor factory worker, street hawker and construction site labourer in Hong Kong. It's a vision which feeds many local fantasies because, for many hardworking others, the dream has become real. This real dream sequence starts with a cheap watch with Russian works, a little status symbol. Then a cheap digital watch. Then a Rolex. Then a gold Rolex and/or a gold Cartier lighter. Ultimately, one wears monogrammed shirts from Italy, silk ties from France, and collects fine jade and ancient ivory.

But, however fanciful a Chinese dreamer becomes, he never forgets his heritage. A rich businessman may modernize himself in a watch, suit, tie, and stiffs under a silk shirt, but the fine jade amulet is worn for more traditional reasons – to repel evil influences and bad luck.

In later dream stages, the same man will frequent auctions held now in Hong Kong by the West's great auction houses – Christie's, Sotheby's and Stanley Gibbon's. These dealers regularly come panting into acquisitive Hong Kong with their best Oriental treasures. (They know well that if a buyer in Hong Kong wants such an object, the price means nothing beside the desire to have the treasure and to take it from those others who want it too.) And if Wong Ming makes it by luck, good business sense, well-applied dishonesty, or hard work, he will readily buy and carry such goods off to a house with a garden, the other sure sign of wealth. In Hong Kong only the wealthy – and farmers – have gardens. Everyone else lives in a highrise apartment.

The queuing-up life: Wong Ming throws down his cigarette, sighs, and sets off for the Peak Tram with his small singing bird in a wicker cage. A breath of morning air for Wong Ming and his bird and then back to ordinary life again. Wong Ming is going home – to a bleak tiny flat in an old public housing estate, where he, his wife and their three young children live the life of Mr and Mrs Hong Kong Average.

The silent and rather impassive majority which play little part in decision-making in Hong Kong, for whom life is not Rolls-Royces, pursue a lot which is a monotonous mixture of hope and ennui. From the womb to the tomb they survive great pressure.

Such people are usually born in one of the government hospitals (home delivery and midwifery are now rare) where medical treatment costs only a nominal amount but where inevitable overcrowding makes conditions uncomfortable. If they want to be born in more pleasant surroundings, their

The kids are all at school, even the 4-year-olds, boiling water in Hong Kong's education pressure cooker, bringing their homework back and spending weary hours every night studying for tomorrow's tests. Lots of tests here, even for the 4-year-olds. But how else will winners be chosen? Exams determine who gets to attend the best kindergartens; then they qualify kindergarteners for the best primary and secondary schools; and, finally, they decide who gets to take university exams. After university one then begins a lifelong climb up a fiercely competitive employment ladder.

In spite of a lack of good secondary schools, and strict Confucian ethics which often render

parents must pay more to go to one of the colony's government-assisted hospitals or private ones. If they become ill later, but not seriously enough to enter a hospital, they have to queue up for first-come first-serve medical aid at one of the colony's government clinics. Treatment there costs only a nominal sum, but Wong Ming often chooses to pay for a more expensive private doctor. It's easier to do that than queue together with the sickly crowds that begin waiting at 6 a.m. for clinics to open at 9.

Left, gold coins are preserved in plexiglass at Villa d'Oro. **Above**, street shopping in Wanchai.

a passive student unimaginative and uninspired, education is still the best leaping-off point for those who want to succeed in life, and for their families as well. With only limited places available in Hong Kong at universities, many families scrape and save to send a son or daughter abroad, usually to the United States, Canada or Australia, where they can establish a family beachhead and eventually sponsor the rest of the family over and out of claustrophobic and uncertain Hong Kong. One of Hong Kong's biggest unseen exports is its young, sent away for education. Taxi drivers, factory workers, and all their family members will often club together to pay for one child's leap overseas.

Unreal estates: Wong Ming, like more than half the population of Hong Kong, lives in a public housing estate. It was only in the early 1950s that the Hong Kong government started thus to house its poor. The colony's first such estate, the now dilapidated Shek Kip Mei tenement, was built after a huge Christmas fire made 53,000 squatters homeless in 1953. Immigrants, who had fled from hunger and poverty in China, and had erected ragged huts wherever spare patches of land could be found, were burned out of their shelter in a few short hours. This tragedy inspired the start of an ambitious government programme to house workers who have

Illegal Chinese immigrants, many of them discontents from the communes of Kwangtung Province and the streets of Canton (Guangzhou), only contribute to this chaos. Upon finding life here much harder than they imagined – work tedious, language difficult and money less valuable than they thought – these disillusioned dreamers have turned to crime and drugs to improve and anaesthetise their dreary lot. Some have joined the legendary "Big Circle," an association of mainland criminals said to be behind Hong Kong's many bank robberies.

Ironically, Hong Kong, despite such squalor, has become the hottest property market in the world. Rents are higher than in

since become the backbone of Hong Kong's current prosperity.

More recent estates are fine examples of urban renewal, but the older ones are a pathetic collection of flats where 11 people may live in a single room and share a communal kitchen, water supply and doorless toilets with the residents of an entire floor. These estates provide inexpensive housing for Hong Kong's masses, but they have also exacted a heavy toll in terms of security, social progress and hope for the future. Regularly disrupted by crimes of violence – rape, robbery and murder – many have become breeding grounds for criminals – and rats!

Tokyo; a small leasehold apartment in a "low-rent" district can cost a family more than HK$1 million.

Despite such astronomical and fantastic fees, flats often are sold within half an hour after going on the market (or even months before building designs have been approved or before the first shovel full of dirt has been dug). These same flats may change hands six times before they are constructed, as they are passed profitably from one shrewd speculator to another. Some people here deal every day in such property futures.

Earth Gods in the New Territories: Farmers in the New Territories, Hong Kong's "vegetable garden," are spared most of this urban pain. These rare fortunates have been able to perpetuate a traditional and serene rural life, but legal mastery of the land has often locked even them into a demanding and thankless form of bondage.

It is in the New Territories, however, that Earth Gods still live, attended to by hopeful housewives and farmers who burn joss-sticks and joss-paper before their shapeless clay forms. Here, water spirits still murmur in freshwater springs and ancient agricultural gods are still accorded proper seasonal respects to ensure good harvests. And traditional houses are still there: low and dark with tiled roofs and sporting red banners which guard households from the depredations of negative spirits.

Some New Territories farmers still grow rice in terraced paddies which are fed by water channels running down through an age-old irrigation network. The fields sprawl outside old walled villages – where tiny alleys and streets frame old women in extraordinary black-eaved hats.

Such villagers – male and female alike – chug contentedly on their pipes as the day passes. Some of the walled villages, like Kam Tin – a one-clan place where snarling old ladies charge visitors a few dollars a photo – have, unfortunately, become aggressive "tourist traps" where edible chow dogs patrol flat rooftops and warn their masters when moneyed strangers have arrived. But alas, even in the New Territories you will find "urban" incongruities. Ancient houses now sport television aerials and the rutted pathways called streets accommodate shiny new Japanese cars.

But despite such clashing modernity, some Chinese beliefs never die. Tiny peeping windows, for example, are purposely constructed in these houses to conform to the architectural requirements of *fung shui*, a Chinese geomancy system which maintains harmony and good fortune in a dwelling according to ancient spiritual principles of *yin* and *yang*. These principles, however, are so mysterious and complicated that it takes a well-paid *fung shui* expert (or geomancer) to design a house properly.

Nearly all of the people here are Hakka,

small leathery farming folk hardened by Hong Kong's changeable weather and tough working lives. These farmers' sons and daughters grow up here, but those who can leave for places like London and San Francisco, where they can enjoy a more comfortable and profitable urban existence. However, even though they leave their family farms, once a year, at Chinese New Year, these overseas progeny with their new world money return to their villages in the New Territories and the seemingly deserted and elderly walled villagers spring to traditional life once again for two festive weeks.

The boat people: Distinct from Hong Kong's urban rich and poor and the easygoing New Territories farmers is another great tribe who are part of Hong Kong and yet not. These are the colony's fisherfolk, they who often spend their entire lives on bobbing junks. In recent years these so-called "boat people" have come onshore to live the life of landsmen, but in Aberdeen, Yaumatei and the colony's typhoon shelters, some rarely leave their floating homes. Most of these fishing people come from two main tribes, the Tanka and the Hoklo, the great majority being Tanka.

There is little documented of the origin of the Tanka people. One tale says they are the descendents of a group of people who in ancient times were convicted of treason and were therefore deemed unworthy to live on land. In Canton, according to one explanation, the boat people are the descendents of a general named Lu Tsun, who lived on the island of Honan in 200 BC. He revolted against the emperor and was said to have ruled Canton for 30 years. After his death, his people were overwhelmed and then persecuted by vengeful emperors. During the Tang dynasty they paid punitive taxes and during the Ming dynasty all boatmen between the ages of 18 and 45 were liable to be seized and press-ganged into the Imperial army. However, in 1730 a benevolent emperor, Yung Ching, took pity on these people. He issued a proclamation which allowed them to live on land in villages near the water if they wished to do so. "Why should they be looked down on, simply because it is customary to do so, and forced to keep separate, passing their days floating about in constant jeopardy of their lives?" he asked.

However, despite this edict, the boat people were still despised. They were forbidden to marry landed Chinese, and they were not allowed to take the Imperial civil service examinations.

To this day, they are still regarded by most Chinese as being inferior, and they are still victims of discrimination. Of course, there is no government discrimination against them and in recent years many have "come ashore" to take their place among regular land-dwellers. The boat life is a tough life, and it is often for the future of their children that these people have left the sea. They know that if they remain at sea, their children may remain illiterate, having never stayed in one place long enough to receive a formal education. Besides, many of the boat people find factory work physically easier and much more profitable.

Hong Kong boat people who are still seagoing – an estimated 35,000 of them – are very attached to their religious traditions. The most interesting tradition they uphold is their ancient worship of Tin Hau, the goddess of the sea. She is one of the most popular deities venerated by the sea people, and they turn to her for comfort, solace and hope, particularly during storms. According to local tradition, Tin Hau was a virtuous person who was deified after her death. One of Hong Kong's greatest festivals is Tin Hau's birthday, on the 23rd day of the third moon. It is on this day that the great fishing fleet of Hong Kong sails in all its glory – with banners flying in the wind and flags streaming out behind each vessel – to the most important of the many Tin Hau Temples in Hong Kong – the Da Miao Temple in Joss House Bay.

Apart from such special religious occasions, it cannot be said that the life of boat people is a festive gypsy-like affair. Like most fishing people all over the world, their seagoing work is difficult and often dangerous. It is physically demanding and their on-deck lifestyle is often cramped and squalid. It is no doubt because of this – and also because of new fishing technology – that so many of the boat people have come ashore to stay.

In the past years, fish landings sold through Hong Kong's Fish Marketing Organization have jumped by one third, despite a decrease in the number of working boat people. This is explained by several developments in the industry.

Vanishing sails: One reason is the increased use of diesel engines instead of traditional sail power. Because diesel power is more practical now, those beautiful butterfly wing sails which add such charm to Hong Kong's harbour are now relics of a romantic past. Picturesque though they were – indeed they are a fond symbol of Hong Kong – they limited vessels to the whims of prevailing wind and allowed larger boats to work only in the winter months when the northeast monsoon provided sufficient power for them to tow their trawls successfully. Conversely, smaller sail boats – purse seiners, gill netters and long liners – were unable to risk the gusty winter monsoon and could work only during the summer southwest monsoon when winds were lighter. Today, with diesel power, all vessels and their fishermen work year round. They can also fish longer each day, and machinery cuts the amount of physical effort needed to work. The old fishing gear has gone too, replaced by nets, lines and ropes made from synthetic fibres.

Although all this is officially considered to be for the good, the great capital investment needed these days, plus the greater degree of sophistication required to deal with newer fishing technology, has driven even more poor fishermen ashore. The industry has also become much more competitive, and this may be why a number of junk-operators in the Hong Kong fishing fleet have taken to, or perhaps continued, the colony's old tradition of China Coast smuggling. They have been known to carry consumer goods to China and to bring back gold and silver coins, musk, herbal medicines, and even, on numerous occasions, illegal immigrants who have paid their way out of China to Hong Kong. Whether the poor fishing trade is simply a justification for smuggling is debatable.

It is likely that the end of their fishing life is in sight for many of Hong Kong's "boat people." Many of them, however, are welcoming this return to land and a better life for their progeny. Though it appears to the casual observer on a tour of colourful Aberdeen that this is a free and romantically traditional life, it is really not that great. It's a very trying life, and many of the boat people are only too glad to give it up for government housing on solid land.

Watchful pair at the Peninsula Hotel.

THE URBAN BEEHIVE

Atlantis in reverse: Hong Kong's largely mountainous topography has had much to do with the manner in which the colony's administrators have miraculously squeezed a population of more than 5.8 million people into little more than one-tenth of the colony's land space.

Within the twin urban beehives of Hong Kong Islands' harbour foreshores and mainland Kowloon live half the colony's people. They have less than 9 sq. feet (30 sq. metres) of living space each, and the Kowloon district of Shamshuipo has a population density of 102,300 people per sq. mile (165,000 people per sq. km) – the highest ever experienced by mankind.

Ramshackle development has been another reason for this big squeeze. Lack of planning, decentralisation and housing in past decades forced thousands upon thousands of refugees and immigrants from China straight to the source of Hong Kong's lifeblood, the harbour.

In those times of rampant *laissez faire,* Hong Kong solved part of the problem – the scarcity of new commercial space – by simply creating land where none existed, reclaiming it from the harbour.

Nowadays, so much of this reclaimed land exists – approximately 10 sq. miles (26 sq. km) has been created since the colony was established – that the entire business district on the island harbour-front, from Queens' Road down to the water's edge, now stands where junks, East India-men and tea clippers once rode at anchor. That includes the General Post Office, City Hall, British Forces Headquarters, the Mandarin Hotel, the soaring 52-storey Connaught Centre and the adjacent Exchange Square.

Further along the coast, the Wanchai Reclamation now houses a massive convention and exhibition centre and a dozen office towers.

On the mainland side, Kai Tak Airport runway, the Kowloon-Canton Railway terminus, the Kwai Chung Container Port and the entire Tsimshatsui East development

(which includes four luxury hotels and a dozen commercial centres) have all virtually risen like an Atlantis in reverse from the seabed.

In the late 1950s, the extent of the reclamation works began to worry the colony's planners. So much of the harbour was slated for reclamation that engineers feared that tidal currents might be affected by the changing configuration of the shoreline. A hydraulic research station in England settled the question by constructing a 75-foot (23-metre)

scale model of the harbour with electronically controlled weirs at either end simulating the tides. Tests showed that only a few minor modifications were needed to avoid damaging the colony's most vital asset.

This harbour reclamation always goes on, but otherwise the colony has removed its blinkers and taken a new look at itself, discovering hinterland areas suitable for larger-scale development in the New Territories.

Three sites at Tuen Mun (Castle Peak), Tsuen Wan and Shatin have been turned into vast "new towns," or satellite cities, which will eventually house more than 2 million people, most of them from the densely popu-

Left, laundry day in this high-rise. **Right,** tram beats the jam.

lated concrete jungles of Kowloon. There are also new towns at Junk Bay and Tin Shui Wai. To give an idea of the new residential pressure cookers that have replaced the urban tenements, one public housing complex at Tuen Mun accommodate no less than 90,000 people.

Overcrowding – too little land and too many people – is put forward as a reason for many of the inequities of Hong Kong's society. What it means is that there's not enough *flat* land where immense industrial-residential estates can be built. In fact, much of Hong Kong's hilly regions is unused.

Luxurious speculation: A trip from Central District to the South side of the island, Re-

pulse Bay and then on to Stanley and Shek O reveals large areas of empty, and very scenic landscape – rolling and tumbling hillsides framing some of Asia's prettiest beaches. Towering luxury apartment blocks have been placed in hillside niches, meticulously cut out of the mountain.

But fears of landslides have stopped construction of towering flats in Mid-Levels, above Central District, after the disastrous landslides of 1972.

There is certainly pressure on this land, but not from the industry of the population. The Crown, which owns all land in Hong Kong, is leasing it bit by bit to private developers

for luxury, high-rent residential development – and at a pace which keeps the demand for it at such a fierce pitch that the rents are among the most ridiculous, and pitiless, anywhere in the world.

The government is attacked for its piecemeal land policies which drive up land prices; but this in turn creates surplus budgets for the government, keeping taxes low. It's a no-win situation.

Stanley, for example, a former fishing village on the island's southern coast, now a fashionable residential enclave for expatriates trying to escape the Central District and Mid-Levels rat race, illustrates the general pattern of development in Hong Kong. Luxury houses in the area can reach as high as HK$100,000 per month.

The village is earmarked for redevelopment. The government's plans call for the resettlement of a Chinese squatter village – the squatters will be moved into high-rise public housing estates built on land reclaimed from the bay. Then old homesites will be offered to private developers for luxury residential use.

Another example is Lantau, Hong Kong's little-known "sister" island. Lantau is one-and-a-half times the size of Hong Kong Island. It's beautiful, and it's comparatively untouched.

Yet the first priority of development has gone to local and international consortiums who have been given the island's best locations to develop luxury residential and holiday resorts, the facilities of which only the wealthier citizens of Hong Kong will be able to enjoy. The pressure is even greater on Lantau with the new airport being built off its coast.

People pressure is undoubtedly a nightmare for Hong Kong's planners, as anyone standing in the middle of the island's Causeway Bay area, or Mongkok and Shamshuipo on the Kowloon side, will agree.

But within the principle of *laissez faire* that insists on ruling most of what goes on in Hong Kong, the main bulk of the people are simply being crammed into new pressure cookers, leaving the most attractive land free for speculators.

Role reversals: left, this "ship" appears to be on permanent shore leave while right, a huge community lives on floating accommodation.

On first landing in Hong Kong, visitors may well get the impression that they are participating in a *kung fu* movie; later, that the whole territory is a giant stage-set, being built for a blockbuster Hollywood epic entitled "The Tower of Babel"; and later still, that it is an "anti-health clinic," where people go to get ulcers, fill up on cholesterol and melt down their adrenalin glands.

Hong Kong is, of course, all three. It is also the world's biggest exporter of watches (in quantity terms) and toys, the world's largest

Kong are so crowded, they are wall-to-wall with people. Hong Kong's crowds have a reputation of being the rudest people in the world. There are some, however, who believe that the rudeness tag has more to do with centuries of Chinese superstitions.

It has a government, but nobody knows quite what or where or who it is, or who really "controls" it; and the reality probably is that no one does. *Hongkongians* do have a vote sometimes, for a few members of the Urban Council, but very few people register

drinker of brandy (and nearly all swank brands), one of the fastest-growing economies in the world in real terms, the world's biggest user of telex machines – and it has the world's biggest public housing program per capita.

That's just for starters. It had until recently the world's largest water de-salting plant (water is quite a problem in Hong Kong, because they mix some of it with all that brandy, you see). It has two large and computerised race-tracks, in a place where gambling is illegal except on their hallowed grounds, and the money they take in rivals the government's budget. Some parts of Hong

and vote. However, they are showing more interest in voting lately.

There is even confusion over the name of the place. Well before the beginning of the Sino-British talks drew attention to Hong Kong's precarious status, the word "colony" went out of style; the words "country" or "nation" were too dignified; "territory," though that sounds as if it should be full of Red Indians, is the official designation for most purposes. Hong Kong legally remains a British Crown Colony until midnight on June 30, 1997. It has an executive council assisting the governor and has the power to negotiate international trading pacts.

Virtue as vice and vice-versa: Hong Kong is a "vice-versa" place, that is, all vices elsewhere are virtues here. The visitor should be warned that the accepted description of Hong Kong by some of the "old hands" is quite misleading. They will take a visitor to a great meal and solemnly tell him that Hong Kong is "sheer materialism, old man," a money-grubbing joint with no soul. They will say that it "pulls down all its fine old buildings and erects dead eyesores in their places." Well, the old buildings were not that good, mostly pastiche and fake neo-Romano-Graeco stuff, Brighton Victorian, and poorly finished. The new buildings are not bad – not bad at all; take a look into some of them.

and solvency, both public and private.

• *Luxury:* What you enjoy from hard work and shrewd bargaining. Most of the rich in Hong Kong, a generation or less ago, were beggars, duck-farmers, tailors, dispossessed bourgeoisie and sundry malcontents from all round the region; among the Westerners, a lot were and are night-school students from Peckham and Peebles and Manhattan and Melbourne. They are "self-selected" – that is, they are all refugees from the bloodthirsty cruelties of politics, or from the greediness and incapabilities of governments, from Beijing to Pittsburgh. They came because they wanted to try things out; Hong Kong is a collection of ragged-trousered volunteers.

Yes, Hong Kong has a soul, believe it or not. But it helps if you remember the vice-virtues of Hong Kong. A short guide to them:

• *Materialism:* Another word for hard work, and the ability of individuals and families to take their lumps, accept trouble and fight their way out of it, find new jobs, new incomes, share poverty and prosperity, eat well, drink well, and make do with small pleasures. Materialism means self-reliance

Left, the gold exchange has been frenetic in recent years, but in the big *hong* board rooms, above, business is usually conducted in a more composed manner. .

• *Anarchy:* Another word for freedom. See the description of "government" above. This government of Hong Kong, if it can be identified at all, gives almost no incentives for either work or capital – but, more important by far, it doesn't get in your way, either. You can set up a company within a week; there are no ownership rules, no currency controls, and precious little registration necessary. If you join the anarchy, then you can take all the credit for your successes, but you must take all the blame for your failures. Fair enough?

• *Greed:* Another name for "consumer demand," which is a leading economic virtue. Consumer demand is extremely buoyant and elastic in Hong Kong. Income earners in Hong Kong, somehow, manage to do the impossible – they spend a lot of what they get, and they save a lot, too. See a good economic theorist. Or better still, work in Hong Kong. Taxes are low, by the way.

• *Envy:* The economists call it the "demonstration effect." *Hongkongians* work in the faith that if the other guy can make it up to the Mercedes level, then they can, too. It isn't a question of "keeping up with the Wongs"; the name of the game is overtaking them.

• *Gluttony:* Another name for good taste and enjoyment, the final consumer demand that drives economies forward. All those yachts in the Hong Kong marinas, all those

been condemned by a vocal minority of envious people (usually in very comfortable jobs) who talk about "materialism."

• *Pride:* This is sometimes a virtue, at other times a vice. Hong Kong has no pride in its "traditions." It has no jingo chauvinism; it has no national anthem (it sings the British one when the Royal Family come to call). It has no bloodthirsty harangues about its armed forces and their invincibility – the "armed forces" are a few Gurhkas, a flight of helicopters and a fleet of gunboats.

Instead Hong Kong has pride (which at times come close to arrogance) in its professionalism, its craft, its flexibility, its incredible cosmopolitan clout. Its academic record

television sets, all those cars on the crowded roads, all those packed restaurants – the people devouring those things did not get their money from rich aunts, privileges and sinecures; they got it from screwing the last cent out of every second of time. Here it would be appropriate to quote from Dr. Samuel Johnson, the great guru of the rationalist revolution of the 18th century: "There are few ways in which a man can be more innocently employed than in getting money."

• *Avarice:* Another name for savings, the accretion of capital, which in previous eras has been highly regarded as a virtue. In this century, somehow or other, it seems to have

is almost nil, but its practical record is rivalled only by one or two other small nations, most of which are – guess where? – here on the east side of Asia. When you visit Hong Kong, you are in the middle of a set of countries which have taken their economic fortunes by the scruff of the neck and shaken them into prosperity. No mean feat.

Commerce, sweet commerce: Materialist? Cruelly capitalist? Unthinking, uncaring? No, it's not really like that at all. Oh sure, Hong Kong is no massive government "welfare stage" – but there is that housing programme, one of the biggest in the wide world; there are hundreds of private and public charitable bodies, and a lively voluntary Community Chest. The *Hongkongian* may seem rude and rough when he jostles you on the packed sidewalks; in private, he is generous, cooperative and much given to self-help and clan-help and quiet mutual support.

Oh sure, the city is a busy and sometimes cold place to the newcomer. You have to make your own way, form your own society, bit by bit. But when you have done that, you will find that you have a warm, helpful circle – and what is more, if you want to, it can be composed of all the races on earth. There *is* a Hong Kong society, and it is not the fly-by-night, make-the-money-and-run affair that it is often dubbed; it is complex, and fascinat-

tiny segment of the total society and economy, the tackier side of drugs, hawking and prostitution. It is negligible in the government as such, except perhaps in the field of public works and other construction (and some say the police have weak moments). As for corruption in private-sector commercial life, it boils down to "secret commissions," "finders' fees" and all that jive; commerce is what Hong Kong lives by, and if you think that commerce is a sweet, soft slush fund, then don't come to Hong Kong to do it. Take the corruption stories, like the brandy, with a splosh of water. Hong Kong lives by its wits.

Maybe, one day, the giant stage-set of Hong Kong will be dismantled, and this

ing, and competitive-cooperative, and is based on all those vice-virtues given above.

Corruption? Alas, yes. Although the big syndicates are said by the Independent Commission Against Corruption (a much embattled permanent official body) to have been broken up, corruption still exists.

On the tacky side: A lot of the corruption is still organized and exploited by Europeans, too. It is sad, therefore, but it affects only a

Left, every safe deposit box in the vault at the Hongkong and Shanghai Banking Corporation has a good story to tell. **Above**, a gold merchant admires the soft and rich feel of his bullion.

Dallas-by-the-sea will disappear or disintegrate – which would be a pity. Along with only a few other places, like Singapore, Seoul and Taipei, Hong Kong exemplifies the solution to the world's energy problem. No, not all that hassle over oil and coal and solar heating and nuclear fission – but the energy potential in man, how he makes his way in the world.

Well, Hong Kong's vice-virtues look set to be the parameters of the future... though of course no one can say for sure. To look at Hong Kong in all its frenetic variety is to witness what Alvin Toffler, presciently enough, called "future shock."

There are two diametrically opposed catch-phrases by which people in Hong Kong live their everyday lives: *Anything Goes* and *Don't Rock the Boat*.

Anything goes so far as business and much of one's personal life are concerned. The colony was established on the twin principles of free trade and *laissez faire*, both of which were noble philosophies in an age in which Britain's foreign trade had been monopolized for two centuries by the East India Company.

for limited companies – and there's no limit on the amount of money that can be transferred in and out of the colony. Hong Kong is cosmopolitan, but only in the sense that many people of many different nationalities come here to make money, make it fast, and then get out.

Hong Kong offers quick gratification, normally a return on investment after five years within a framework of minimal government intervention. In one sense, that's all it really does have to offer. Long-term security is still

Hong Kong is still faithful to its founding creeds. Virtually anyone can hang a business shingle here and engage in any business not harmful to human life.

The average Hong Kong industrial worker, earns under HK$5,000 a month, works 6 days a week, and gets as little as 7 days of annual paid leave a year, plus 17 public holidays. That's high by Asian standards, but an embarrassment to anyone who is aware that this is, after all, a British colony where British law and ethics presumably apply.

However, both profit and taxable salaries are low – 15 percent for wage-earners and unincorporated businesses, and 16.5 percent

a question mark, though a short-term boom is expected as local and overseas investment and business try to get in before 1997.

With four seething stock exchanges and as many commodities exchanges, it's a place where the "rugged individualist" can "do business" with the freedom of a Victorian mill-owner, free of any real interfering trade unionism or colonial government restrictions.

It's a place where business takes precedence over every other human pursuit, where success is measured by the number of cars, furs, Oriental antiques and diamonds one owns, and by the height at which one lives on The Peak. It's a high-rolling heaven where expatriates tend to look at life as a series of 3-year banking plans, where shops always seem to be open, bars never seem to close, clubs abound, and servants are an accepted necessity in any household. Acting as a cushion to this affluence and privilege, there are more than 5.8 million people working hard to provide just about anything that one's heart desires. In that respect Hong Kong is an awfully exciting city.

Whilst business is the predominant full-time hobby in Hong Kong, so is it largely the level upon which the colony's two populations, expatriate and Chinese, communicate with one another.

Expatriate perks: An expatriate office worker full-paid leave and travel expenses. Such terms are denied to most Chinese employees: only those who fight their way into the upper echelons of the bureaucracy are rewarded.

This glaring division between the two populations invites consideration of the second of Hong Kong's catch-phrases, *Don't Rock The Boat.* Hong Kong's very survival depends on cheap labour. Also, *laissez-faire* must reign if investment is to continue. *Laissez-faire* reached its prosperous zenith in the late 1960s when much money was salted away in London banks and little was spent locally on housing, health or education. In response to this British habit of saving money for a rainy day, Hong Kong's

at the lower end of the expatriate scale will not work here for less than HK$15,000 a month plus perks. A Chinese office worker is eligible for public low-cost housing and can retire at the age of 60 after 25 years of service on a monthly salary of HK$5,000–HK$10,000.

An expatriate civil servant who signs on for 2½ years, pays only 10 percent of his salary as rent and can look forward to his accrued holiday. There is also a gratuity of 25 percent of his total earnings plus 3 months'

Left, cutting loose in Lan Kwai Fong. **Above**, expatriate pleasure-junkies frolic in Hong Kong's harbour.

Chinese suddenly and violently rocked the boat. Inspired by the fervour of China's Red Guard rampage, a local campaign of riots, strikes and bombings erupted here and hit the colony where it hurt most – its confidence in the colony's future. Money and people fled until Beijing, by confirming again the value it places on this foreign exchange window, helped quell Red Guard passions and restored peace in the colony.

Though the gulf between typical expatriate and Chinese lives is still wide, Hong Kong is now beginning to move into a new phase of social development in which *almost* anything goes.

Having no raw materials that are worth very much, except the most valuable raw material of all, energetic people, Hong Kong lives by trading and organizing, and turning other countries' raw materials and components into final goods; its typical exports are garments, watches, toys, electrical gadgets and a host of plastic items. It also exports some boats and ships. Finally, it is China's main trading port, handling a large and rising proportion of that giant country's rising trade, together with most of the trade of the Portu-

guese territory of Macau next door.

Since it has little local produce, it imports huge amounts of consumer goods – foodstuffs, French wines, Scandinavian furniture, and a whole raft of Japanese consumer whatsits, as well as capital goods like machinery and equipment, and all the raw materials it needs. It is therefore a very good customer for a hundred other countries. Hong Kong makes its income from "value added," in the form of processing, assembly, financing, communications and all the myriad paper-shuffling of commerce, insurance, documentation, shipping, airfreight, fees, commissions, accountancy and other services.

Making money: The economy is extremely flexible, thanks to a general policy on the part of the government to intervene as little as possible in the business process. The establishment of a business is easy and cheap; money and staff freely move in and out; and the government gives some incentives for industry, chiefly involving the leasing of land and the building of specialized accommodation for "flatted factories." There are few disincentives, in the form of controls or niggling regulations: The government assumes that when you start a business in Hong Kong, you know how to make money at it, and that you will be honest enough to declare the taxable income (given the low rates of tax on private and corporate income, it is barely worth spending time and money on avoiding it); so it leaves you alone. There are many chambers of commerce, a Trade Development Council which organizes overseas promotions, many lively trade commissions from many countries, and a lot of legal and accountancy help.

The connections with China are very close, and Hong Kong is Beijing's main source of foreign exchange earnings. In very recent times, China has changed its economic philosophy a great deal, introducing free enterprise elements and a more open economy, some of the Chinese provinces have been given a measure of independent action, and two of these are near Hong Kong – Kwantung (Guangdong) and Fukien (Fujian). Trading and financial links between China and Hong Kong have increased significantly.

Hong Kong has no import or export duties, only some domestic "excises" on petroleum products, tobacco products, wines and spirits and a few other things; these are directed at the domestic consumer for revenue purposes. There are duties and licence fees on vehicles (these have been steeply raised from time to time in an attempt to moderate vehicular traffic, but they have totally failed to do so). There are health and agricultural product regulations on imports and exports, controls to suppress the narcotics trade, and controls on firearms and ammunition.

Hong Kong is thus a free trade area. Attracted by its success, China has now started to develop its own free trade export zones nearby, across the border from both Hong Kong and Macau. These zones are designed especially as sites for mutual business ventures, in which China supplies the land, buildings and labour, while the foreign partner supplies foreign exchange, equipment and know-how. An interesting arrangement is the "compensation trade" method of financing – the foreign partner does not receive profits or interest on the capital, but supplies of the product or service which the joint venture produces (a foreign firm which helps to build a hotel, for instance, gets to sell a proportion of the rooms on its own account, or in the case of a factory producing textiles,

but 70 percent of the land area is mountains and uninhabited islands, so the true "livable-area" density is over 18,000 people per sq. km. One corner of Kowloon called Shamshuipo is alleged to be the tightest-packed mass of humanity anywhere on earth.

The main task of the Hong Kong government is a very obvious one: to arrange and encourage the housing, feeding and employing of this large and accelerating mass of people. In addition to a continuous programme of public housing, the government is building new industrial town areas in the New Territories which were "leased" from China in the last century and will be handed back (with the rest of the place) in 1997.

the foreigner gets a proportion of the output).

Affluence as a problem: Hong Kong had about 5.8 million people in 1991; the population is growing at about 1.2 percent a year as far as natural increase is concerned, but there has been a very large and almost unaccountable number of illegal immigrants from China in recent years, so the total population increase at times may well have reached over 4 percent a year. The place is therefore very crowded. With a land area of only 1,070 sq. km, the density is 5,420 people per sq. km,

When completed, these new urban areas will contain 2–3 million people – a substantial part of the population.

In such a crowded place, with a busy people always on the move (as you will discover the first time you are jostled on the pavements), a lot of government and private expenditure goes into the "infrastructure" – especially modes of travel. The road system is perpetually being extended and improved and the Hong Kong government is committed to spend more than HK$150 billion in public sector construction over the next decade, much of it will be on roads, including a coastal highway along Hong Kong traffic-

<u>Left</u>, two of the more obvious symbols of success. <u>Above</u>, another busy day in Central.

choked north shore. A US$2.2 billion air-conditioned underground railway (the MTR) stretches from Kowloon and the New Territories under the harbour to Central District – some 25 stations spread over 16 miles (26 km). And US$1.2 billion was spent on a Hong Kong Island extension with 14 stations spread over 7.5 miles (12.5 km).

There are two vehicular traffic tunnels under the harbour with three more piercing the mountains into the New Territories, in addition to a cat's-cradle of ferries in all directions round the waters of the territory – from island to island. Hong Kong's airport has got to be unique in the world now – it is in the middle of residential Kowloon! Hong

driven by ambitious small proprietors and professionals, shrewd brokers, bankers and middlemen.

In recent years, Hong Kong's problem has become that of affluence – because of those high growth rates. Money supply has been soaring, ditto consumption expenditure, and construction and property development. Hong Kong receives more than 6 million foreign visitors every year, but 1.5 million *Hongkongians* now travel abroad each year, despite the fact that most of them hold only a shaky document called a Certificate of Identity. The explosion of real incomes threathens to price Hong Kong's goods out of export markets – and *that* would be cata-

Kong also squeezes in a container port, which is so busy that it ranks second in the world in container throughput (after Rotterdam).

The Gross Domestic Product per capita was around US$12,069 by the end of 1990 averaging over 4 percent for the past three years. This is one of the highest growth rates in the world. The GDP per person is about the same as Singapore's, 20 times that of India and about a quarter of that of the United States. The incomes are skewed, with a few rich and a lot of poor – but a large and increasingly aspiring middle-class. It is from this class that Hong Kong, like all capitalist countries, gets its prosperity: the place is

strophic. But the people have a record of being ingenious and flexible in their business, and their challenge is to continuously switch the pattern of their capital and consumption spending around to meet the new demands of each arising situation, to avoid the worst dangers of damaging domestic inflation.

Fiscally, Hong Kong is very conservative indeed. Until 1993, the Hong Kong government had a surplus on every annual budget since the mild recession of the early 1970s. The reasons for the overflow of money are the buoyant tax and land sale revenues, the latter making up some 60 percent of government revenues. But Hong Kong is a crowded place and there are limits to what a government can do in the way of spending – budget expenditures run up against sheer barriers of workspace and workers. Some government departments (e.g. the Post Office) are so efficient that they cover their costs with their income.

More than half the public spending is on public works, schools, housing, health service facilities, etc. In Hong Kong, the utilities are all in the private sector, except the water supply (and that is because a proportion of the water comes by pipeline from China).

Hong Kong lives by foreign trade. Its importance may be judged by the fact that total trade (exports plus imports plus re-

and partly because a group of big banks plus the government Banking Commissioner's Office seem to have looked after the currency with little difficulty. Key interest rates were set for years by a tiny sub-committee of the Hong Kong Exchange Banks Association. But in 1981, the statutory Hong Kong Association of Banks took over. It has obligatory membership for all banks and its chairmanship will alternate between the two note issuing banks, The Hong Kong Bank and The Chartered Bank.

The Association has to consider not only the domestic money flows, but also the general trend of rates elsewhere because money flowing into and out of the place, being subject

exports) is estimated at US$1.3 trillion for 1990 with a total expenditure on Gross Domestic Product of US$46 billion (12.4 percent on 1989). That was the "visible" trade alone; if the "invisibles" were added in, the income from commerce and communications, then in balance of payment terms the total foreign activity would be likely to be three times the GDP.

Hong Kong has no central bank, partly because the public debt has been negligible,

Left, the Port Authority's control tower. **Above**, recreational sailors must learn to avoid Large Floating Objects.

to no controls, can be considerable. The banknotes are issued by two leading banks (under the guidance of the government) and the coins are issued by the government – a typical "mixed economy" arrangement.

The money supply grows by fluctuating percentages each year, depending on the foreign and domestic trade fortunes of Hong Kong – it shrank in two years (1971 and 1973), but has tended to rise steeply again in recent years. The cost of living has not risen to the same degree; even in the grossly inflationary years 1979 and 1980, consumer price indexes rose 12–16 percent a year, depending on the income level. The sharpest increases have been in rents for all sorts of accommodations, and the government bowed to pressure in 1973 to impose limits on rents for residential property, which were lessened in the early and mid-1980s but began to spurt again in 1988.

Hong Kong is extremely well-banked, to put it mildly. As of 1991 there were 165 commercial banks licensed to operate over the counter in Hong Kong, and 151 representative offices. Hong Kong banks are so liquid that when there was a run on the Hang Lung Bank in 1982 (due to false rumours of the bank's connection with a faltering property giant), the Chartered Bank transferred HK$1 billion in cash overnight. Savings

The taxation system is simple, with the rates on both individual and corporate incomes, and with the minimum of rules, allowances, exemptions and all that clutter of calculation that appears on most countries' schedules. Offshore income is, in general, exempted from local taxation, although in the case of some banking activities where a loan borrowed and lent offshore is actually organized in Hong Kong, part of the income is taken into the tax net.

If you are an employer, all you have to do regarding staff pay is to account to the authorities for the total pay of any employee who receives more than the personal allowance; there is no "Pay As You Earn" or

deposits alone have risen 10 times – the savings "habit" goes deep in the society, and at the counters of the lordly banks who accept longer-term deposits, you will see many very modestly-dressed people like hawkers and fishermen. Total time and savings deposits have recently been approaching HK$10,000 per person on the average. Gross domestic savings as a ratio to domestic product are well over 20 percent, which level is taken by economists as a sign of good, capitalist take-off into sustained growth. These figures also indicate confidence in the local economy – otherwise those millions would be fleeing abroad.

withholding tax on individual incomes, but some forms of interest receivable are taxed at source. You can buy tax certificates if you want to pile up your taxes in advance, and get a so-so rate of interest on them.

Licences, where needed – for instance, licences and permissions are required to sell the goods subject to excise, to run a restaurant, to build a new building and to occupy it – are obtained swiftly and usually without corruption; government offices are helpful and efficient.

All land is Crown Land, on various long leases; when a lease falls through, the government usually auctions off the new one (prices for leases of prime sites in Hong Kong have now become the highest in the world).

Harnessing the *hong*: A description of the Hong Kong economy would be incomplete without mention of the big trading houses called *hong*. The four leading *hong* are of British foundation, including Jardine Matheson, Wheelock Marden, Hutchison Whampoa and the Swire Group. There are also two big conglomerates, Sime Darby and Inchcape, which hold significant interests in Hong Kong. But recently, thanks to a very active takeover bid market, mergers and other financial arrangements, British control of the *hong* is waning. New and energetic Chinese

the roll of chairmen and directors of Hong Kong Inc., but it does not change the system – the system under which both public and private enterprise vie to expand and rebuild the economy at an almost frightening speed, but deftly and skillfully.

What is the secret of Hong Kong's fiscal and banking and commercial success? No one is quite sure. Because of this, and because so many businessmen and administrators are somewhat inarticulate on the subject, you will hear some people complain that the "system" is all wrong, and that everything should be done some other way. Experts who come to Hong Kong intending to teach the *Hongkongians* how to run a so-

groups, based on shipping and property and the textile industry, are beginning to build new "empires" and have even taken over one of the British-founded concerns (Hutchison Whampoa). These new entrepreneurs bring to the Hong Kong economy the same businesslike, even buccaneering spirit, that the British once did. They enjoy the same cooperation of the government that their predecessors did, plus the trust and cooperation of the new administration in Beijing. Their arrival on the scene changes a few names on

Left, garments are big business in Hong Kong. **Above**, the objects of their desire.

ciety, almost always go away sadder and more confused than ever.

It all looks like chaos on the outside, but perhaps it is the chaos of the new jigsaw puzzle, freshly stirred on the table-top. Somewhere, every piece fits. But the trouble is that by the time you have fitted all the pieces together, the whole economy has changed, and a fresh box of pieces arrives. Hong Kong is an "organic" entity; it grows from its internal pressures and needs, and is at the mercy of the world of trade and the shifting winds of history. It has to seek a perpetual state of dynamic balance, in a nastily fluctuating world. It abhors rigidity. Flexibility is all.

A spiritual sequence: Would you pay US$641,000 for license plate number 8? An anonymous businessman did just that in Hong Kong on February 13, 1988. He thought the number plate "lucky," because in Cantonese the number symbolizes "living or giving birth."

As of December 1985, Hong Kong's Transport Department has held an average of one auction per month for "lucky" numbers. Number 8 has consistently drew the highest bid. By contrast, the lowest bids allowed

car-owner when in 1970 he drove his dilapidated 1959 Sunbeam Rapier convertible into a petrol station and the station owner offered him HK$2,500 in cash for the "lucky" number 1479 on his car. The car (with the number) had been bought a few years before that encounter for HK$1,000. The car number was (and still is) considered "lucky" because it is also considered an antique. Having been issued chronologically in 1959 well before the big car boom of the 1960s and 1970s, it has no prefix, making it even more valuable.

were HK$1,000 – the reserve price. However, there is one unconfirmed story that a mere HK$250 was once paid for number 913 (whose homophones mean "ever-lasting life"). If true, 913 was one of the best bargains ever bought.

From the time lucky number auctions began in May 1973 until mid-1991, more than HK$120.3 million has been raised for the government's charity lottery fund.

Prior to May 1973, there was already a profitable trade in numbers considered to be "lucky." At that time, the government issued the numbers as they came up in sequence. You can imagine the surprise of a foreign

If it were a three-digit or two-digit or even one-digit license number, it would be worth many thousands of times the amount offered by the superstitious pump attendant.

For ordinary car registration, Hong Kong has an ascending scale of charges. Cars with motors under 1,500 cc can be registered for HK$3,815 while the most expensive registration is HK$11,215 for cars over 4,500 cc. For the official fee, you get whatever number is next in sequence.

The government has designated about 400 "lucky" numbers and carefully restricts their sale at regularly spaced auctions of 15 numbers at a time. Before the auction scheme was started, sought-after numbers were freely traded on the open market and numbers were allotted sequentially with no restrictions. Now, all numbers considered lucky in Cantonese, and prestige numbers in single, double, triple and quadruple digits without prefixes, are reserved and available only through auctions.

Those who possessed "lucky numbers" prior to May 1973, had their car registration books marked "non-transferable," meaning that the number must be returned to the government for auctioning upon death or deregistration. The "lucky" number cannot be transferred to another person – even to a relative – or be made part of an estate. It can

up in sequence (since there are few numbers ever returned). The amount also serves as a reserve price in the auction, and it secures the number's placement in the next auction.

162 – "Easy all the way": Naturally, a black market has developed for the numbers, usually-based around scrapped cars. There is also supposed to be a numbers syndicate which through a cumbersome process of buying and selling vehicles secures "lucky" numbers as they come up in sequence.

Advertisements sometimes appear in the Chinese press offering lucky numbers, though such transactions are illegal and technically impossible. An advertisement in the Chinese press once offered BH8222 (signifying pros-

only be transferred by the owner to another of his vehicles. A lobby effort is now in progress to allow the legal transfer of "lucky numbers" upon death – along with other willed property and possessions.

The Hong Kong government allows "lucky" numbers to be reserved for auction with a deposit of HK$1,000. This allows people to choose their numbers instead of just waiting to see what new numbers come

Left and **above**, license-plate numerals borne by opulent 20th-century carriages are among the colony's most sought-after "lucky numbers." The cars were parked at a movie studio.

perity-easy-easy-easy) for HK$2,500; a real bargain if the deal was actually clinched, because this same number at an auction would fetch three times that sum.

Lucky numbers include: 2 for "easy," 3 for "living or giving birth," 6 for "longevity," 8 for "*baht*" or "prosperity," and 9 for "perpetuity" or "eternity."

Combinations of numbers can also be important. For example, 163 means "live all the way" or "give birth all the way," and 168 "prosperity all the way." This spiritual numbers awareness also has been adopted by nightclubs, boutiques and companies here – all with proper lucky number names.

Hong Kong investors should put their hearts at ease.

—Deng Xiaoping

When those reassuring words from the Chinese leader were spoken during a face-to-face meeting with the British Crown Colony's Governor, Sir Murray MacLehose, in March 1979, Hong Kong's business and financial community heaved a collective sigh of relief. Like men on death row, another reprieve had stayed the colony's precarious life yet again.

Those words were enough to push any thought of Sino-British Agreement into the background. And they were interpreted as an indication that China wanted to continue the lucrative *status quo* under the British. (A solution not without precedent since China did not take Macau back when it was offered in 1974. Rather it retained sovereignty and became a "Chinese territory under Portuguese administration," complete with a Portuguese governor and flag.)

Deng also told Sir Murray that China intended to take over Hong Kong's sovereignty when the time was ripe. This remark was not publicised until December 1982 at which time China and Britain were in acrimonious negotiations over Hong Kong's fate.

Just who ruled Hong Kong is probably no longer a moot point. There was no doubt the British governed this capitalist enclave, having secured that lease-holder's right by virtue of three 19th-century treaties. But since the advent of China's Communist government in 1949, the ruling British and the ruled Cantonese have accepted that Hong Kong's existence is China's whim.

Beijing calling: The Chinese had always called the three treaties "unequal" but were happy to leave things alone, calling the question of Hong Kong an internal one to be settled at China's convenience. That's the way things stood until British Prime Minister Margaret Thatcher's visit to China in September 1982. The Chinese reiterated their stand that they have sovereignty over the

colony because they never recognised the "unequal" treaties. To the sovereignty question, the British, fresh from a victorious battle in the Falkland Islands, responded that treaties are contracts under international law and all discussions must start from there. Talks then began on what would happen when the lease on the New Territories expires in 1997. Since the land under lease comprises nine-tenths of the territory that Hong Kong would never be able to live without, the talks were really about the fate

of the colony as an entrepôt.

The stale cliché – oft repeated and much believed – that Beijing could at any time reclaim Hong Kong with a single phone call to London, only added to the anxiety over Hong Kong's future. Even with the promise of Hong Kong becoming a Special Administrative Region of China – ostensibly autonomous in most things – under a 50-year one-government-two-systems guarantee, uncertainty looms ever ominously. After all, the year 2047 is a long way away.

Pampering the Dragon: If logic were the long guideline, Hong Kong's future, as a Special Administrative Region of China,

<u>Left</u>, mapping out the protagonists in quaint style. <u>Right</u>, eyeing the future?

would be secure as long as it remained an entrepôt, China's window to the commercial world. Under Maoist leadership in particular, Hong Kong had been regarded as less a political entity than a commercial necessity. But chauvinism and nationalism also played an important part in the negotiations on Hong Kong; hence the prolonged uncertainty.

Viewing the Middle Kingdom's turbulent history, the uneasiness that pervades the territory is understandable. Will Hong Kong enjoy another half century of freedom and capitalism under Chinese sovereignty? Will the current Hong Kong government turn into a lame-duck administration as the clock ticks on to 1997? This immediate worry is of

The first direct elections to the Legislative Council in the 150 years' history of the colony based on universal suffrage took place on September 12, 1991. A total of 18 seats – a compromise figure reached between Britain and China – based on geographical constituencies were contested by universal suffrage. The elections for the 21 functional constituency seats followed on September 15.

A very public, and certainly the most acrimonious, power struggle occurred over the new airport.

When China's short-lived pro-democracy movement in 1989 was crushed on June 4 in Beijing's Tiananmen Square, Hong Kong's hopes were shattered. Whatever optimism

greater concern at the moment to the people of Hong Kong than the larger question of their future from 1997 to 2047 and beyond.

In spite of a white paper in 1984 promising direct elections (to teach Hong Kong democracy prior to its 1997 autonomous status) to the Legislative Council in 1985, the government, under pressure from China, postponed them (to 1991), allowing only the 1985 indirect elections for 24 of its 56 seats. These two dozen seats were chosen from Functional Constituencies (representing the professional and various sectors of the economy) and an electoral college made up of members of existing groups (like district boards).

there was over 1997 evaporated with the tanks charging through the square. More than 1 million people took to the streets for organised marches and rallies. Confidence in the colony, both at home and abroad, was low.

With China still preoccupied internally, the Governor, Sir David Wilson, wanted to do something dramatic to restore Hong Kong's confidence. He chose the moribund new airport project, a mammoth HK$80 billion project creating new facilities on reclaimed land off miniscule Chep Lap Kok Island. He added some new containerports, roads, bridges etc. and called it PADS – Port and Airport Development Strategy.

The total price tag for this giant civil engineering project – said to be one of the world's largest – was to be HK$127 billion in 1989 prices. He promised the first planes would be landing in 1997, before the takeover. Private funding was the key to this project.

The Dragon next door wasn't exactly asleep when all this was going on, just not looking. But when it did, the PRC objected that it had no say in a matter which would commit its Special Administrative Region's government to billions of dollars in debt. China, however, agreed with the need for a new airport and the other infrastructure improvements.

The Hong Kong government, in a show of autonomy, parried that China was advised of dence-building project, it became a confidence-destroying one as China widened the argument by stating it wanted more say in how the colony will be governed and financed in the intervening years up to midnight June 30, 1997.

Britain at first took Hong Kong's side while at the same time offering little tidbits of compromise. One of the visitors to Beijing, Britain's Foreign Secretary Douglas Hurd, while speaking in Hong Kong after his visit, hinted the project might be cancelled.

As a last effort, Prime Minister John Major sent his foreign policy advisor, Sir Percy Craddock, one of the men who negotiated the 1984 agreement, to Beijing. Locked out

the various matters. For 20 months acrimonious words were thrown back and forth, and dozens of trips were made between Hong Kong and Beijing.

While the governments were talking, the international finance never materialised – who would invest vast sums in a project like this without China being agreeable – and the Hong Kong government's pet project floundered on the rocks. Instead of a being confi-

Left, Chinese paper money isn't worth much in the colony, but the colony isn't worth much without China's blessings. **Above**, Hong Kong's entrepreneurs have always set their sights high.

of the decision in 1984, Hong Kong was once again locked out in 1991. The resulting Memorandum of Understanding, initialled in July and signed by both Prime Ministers in September – with Major making the trek East of course, not vice versa – became an agreement.

It was virtually a complete capitulation for Hong Kong. China not only received financial guarantees, but statutory positions on the various authorities, something Hong Kong was adamantly against.

Eastern "Emporium of Commerce and Wealth": When Hong Kong Island was first claimed as an offshore base because of its harbour by

British's squabbling "merchant princes" in the mid-1800s, neither China nor the British really wanted it. The man who "possessed" the island for Queen Victoria, the intrepid Captain Charles Elliot, Royal Navy, was told to leave it alone and concentrate on spearheading Britain's trading interests in China's mainland ports. Its first administrator, Sir Henry Pottinger, was forced to take his subordinates to task for launching development against the home government's wishes while he was away fighting the First Opium War against the Chinese.

It took two years for the British Government to actually grant Hong Kong official status as a Crown Colony, and even then the it could not compete with the rich mainland treaty ports like Shanghai and languished for many years as a backwater retreat, opium depot, and a haunt for pirates, smugglers and other less illustrious characters of the British Empire. Its early administrations were peppered with the sort of scandalous characters who have been a familiar blot on successive Hong Kong governments up to the present day – incompetents, exploiters, distressed judiciary, corrupt police and civil servants, and more than a few con-men and outright criminals. 'Tis no wonder that descriptions like "detestable society" and "grotesque anomaly" were pinned to Hong Kong in its early days.

recognition was given with the sort of jaundiced eye with which Westminster has regarded Hong Kong ever since.

The truth is that Hong Kong has never been the Empire's showplace, the "Jewel of the East," that its own administrators and supporters in Britain would have liked it to be. It had always been something of a colonial embarrassment, a disreputable black sheep located sufficiently east of Suez to be largely ignored and left to its devices.

As a trading post it was an immediate failure. Pottinger, the colony's first governor, prophesied that it would become a "vast emporium of commerce and wealth." In fact,

Right into the late 1920s, when piracy was still rife, the colony's main role was that of a staging point for British troops rushed out here to protect the Shanghai concession (where the real political and commercial wheeling and dealing was going on). During the 1930s, the colony had something of a strategic importance as a crossroads for shipping and travel within the eastern sphere of Britain's empire. Other than that, it was simply a haven of British rule and therefore British law for Britons who found themselves in an otherwise alien and often troubled region.

In World War II, Hong Kong's value was

such that no real attempt was made to defend it and it fell quickly to the Japanese on Christmas Day, 1941, after a token, but desperate fight by Hong Kong volunteers, British and Indian Army regulars and a raw, untested expeditionary unit from Canada.

Yet for all its inauspicious history, Hong Kong has survived and indeed flourished. It has outlived the old Treaty Ports and remained a British-administered outpost in the wake of global decolonization, and survives incongruously as a capitalist bastion on the very edge of a gigantic Communist society.

Today it is among the top 20 trading nations in the world and is a manufacturing giant in its own right. It has confounded everyone, even the British, by fulfilling Sir Henry Pottinger's dream of a vast, wealthy Eastern emporium. And it did this not through any real determined struggle of its own, but because the Chinese ultimately wanted it that way.

After China's Communist Revolution of 1949 and the lowering of the so-called "Bamboo Curtain" on the world-at-large, both Hong Kong, and the nearby Portuguese-ruled enclave of Macau, were left intact by the Chinese leadership as convenient windows to the world. They became offshore venues in which the Communists could indulge in capitalist dealings without tainting their domestic ideology or exposing their people to harmful influences. Hong Kong's status hinged (and still hinges) upon just how useful it could be to Beijing.

Milking the money machine: Hong Kong served Beijing well. It was soon acting as its main intake and clearing house, evading Western trade embargoes to the point where China earns about US$6 billion in foreign exchange annually, an estimated 35–40 percent of its hard currency which it sorely needs to pay for its current "modernization" programme.

At the same time, the colony became a dumping ground for Chinese undesirables and was flooded with refugees and immigrants, largely southern Cantonese, who obviously weren't going to be slot peacefully into the Maoist revolutionary scheme. This influx swelled Hong Kong's population from its 1946 level of a mere 600,000 to well over 3.5 million by 1966. It also gave the colony

Left, the impressive I.M. Pei-designed Bank of China building.

a large pool of cheap labour with which to develop its industrial infrastructure based on textiles and electronics. Another 500,000 illegal immigrants from China arrived between 1978 and 1980 alone. Stern legislation, however, has curbed that deluge.

Today, Hong Kong's existence rests entirely upon its ability to make a fast buck. It is a well-milked money-making machine, and as such is looked upon with favour by Beijing – especially since China itself is now turning to capitalist solutions. Meanwhile, Hong Kong's business leaders and colonial administrators now cock their affluent noses at Mother England, that strife-torn, tax-riddled old pensioner on the other side of Suez.

But unlike the British motherland, Hong Kong is not a democracy. It's a contemporary anachronism, a living museum piece of colonial power and economics. A working model of the perfect corporate state. A benevolent dictatorship, if you like.

Parameters of the pyramid: Hong Kong is now ruled by an administrative pyramid topped by a governor appointed by Whitehall in the name of the Sovereign. Below is a 16-member Executive Council of civil servants, the Commander of British Forces which includes 11 "unofficial" members of the public sector, normally taken from the business or financial community, each of whom is appointed by the governor. It is the governor alone who decides what matters the council can discuss.

Policy is passed into law by the 60-member Legislative Council. In 1985 it met for the first time, with elected instead of appointed members (albeit only 24 members and they were indirectly elected through functional constituencies). Though not elected by universal suffrage, this "new look" Legco was the first to challenge the government's decisions and, on a couple of occasions, force the government to back down.

When the Council began its 91/92 session in October, it had a different look and feel again, the results of the September elections. For the first time in the Council's century and a half history, 18 members elected by universal suffrage from geographical constituencies took their seats in Hong Kong's governing body.

The expanded, 60-member Council also has 21 newly, but indirectly, elected members. These are the representatives of the

Functional Constituencies (professional bodies or various sectors of the community). The government is represented by only three "official" members – the Chief and Financial Secretaries plus the Attorney General. There is also the new, non-civil servant post of Deputy President (also appointed). Though the governor remains President of the Legislative Council, the new Deputy presides over the Council full time.

The Hong Kong government, for the first time in its history, does not control the legislative process and must lobby to get its legislation passed. The government must now explain itself to the satisfaction of elected members or see its legislation defeated... a very common occurrence in the west, but a new one to Hong Kong.

Toothless Council: The people of Hong Kong have a direct vote for half the representatives to the colony's 30-member Urban Council, the politically toothless equivalent of a municipal authority in the West. The Council is responsible for keeping Hong Kong and Kowloon running smoothly, that is, collecting garbage, running parks, recreation and culture, and licensing restaurants.

The people of Hong Kong can also vote for about half the members of the District Boards, which the name implies, deal with grass roots problems by area. Another council is the newer Regional Council, a 36-member group with 12 directly elected members and another 9 chosen by the 9 District Boards in the New Territories. This council is similar to the Urban Council, but has, as its bailiwick, the New Territories. All these political activities are aimed at preparing Hong Kong for whatever government it may be that runs the colony after the expiration of the New Territory's lease in June 1997.

Even these modest steps towards free elections by universal suffrage – ironically, to prepare Hong Kong's population for a measure of democracy to be practiced after its handover to a totalitarian country – were objected to by the Chinese government. The ranking member in Hong Kong, Xu Jiatun, head of the New China News Agency, attacked the government in late 1985 for not following the Draft Agreement. Their distrust of the British was rekindled with these elections even though representative government is specifically mentioned in the Agreement.

The head of the Hong Kong and Macau Affairs Office in Beijing, State Councillor Ji Pengfei (the highest ranking PRC government official ever to visit Hong Kong) tried to play down Xu's remarks during his December 1985 visit, but his deputy, Lu Ping, who visited in 1986, reiterated Beijing's displeasure with the way the British are preparing local Hong Kong people for self-government. The Hong Kong government has stated it will consult with the Chinese government before subsequent steps in the process are taken.

This resulted in the first elections to choose members to the Legislative Council by universal suffrage (only 18 out of 60) being delayed until September 1991.

Twin pressures: So far, this archaic system of *laissez faire* government has meant continuing prosperity; the colony's wealth is plainly visible. Unfortunately, constant overt changes in policy have regularly forced Hong Kong administrators to increase social spending on health, education and medicine. More than HK$150 billion was budgeted for construction in the public sector in the 1980s and roads and low cost housing estates were the biggest budgeted priorities along with schools, hospitals, clinics, and recreational facilities. Sadly, there never seems to be enough money available. The twin pressures of an overheated economy (which regularly forces a cut-back in government spending) and the untimely arrival of probably a half million more immigrants in the late 1970s combined to set various housing, medical and educational programmes back by five years or more, in spite of official promises.

Socially, Hong Kong will suffer. Economically, the colony will succeed. The influx of people has again given Hong Kong industrialists a new supply of cheap labour and effectively reversed a labour shortage trend of the late 1970s. Though they are banned, restricted and distrusted by most countries in the world, Hong Kong's Chinese population faces a grim austerity not unlike that from which most fled. But live here they must, regardless of politics, competition and crowding. Their only hope is to acquire enough wealth to make their stay pleasant, and to find an opportunity, somehow, to get out.

Despite the many concerns facing Hong Kong residents, there is still reason to feel upbeat.

At first glance, Hong Kong is everything described in hackneyed epithets – a cement jungle, a bustling port, a capitalist paradise, a British colony. British it still is in status, and anglicised it is on the surface. But underneath this Western facade is a very Chinese mind which stubbornly refuses to change in spite of more than 140 years of British rule.

Chinese attitudes – Chineseness, if there is such a word – remain true to their Oriental traditions, despite colonial rule and the colony's urbane, modern appearance.

The Chinese sense of superiority today does not differ much from that of centuries ago. Chinese are still of the Middle Kingdom, and everyone else is a barbarian. A mulish ethnic pride transcending nationalities has generated a unique tongue-in-cheek approach to all foreigners, including the ubiquitous British colonial.

A Chinese in Hong Kong may *kowtow* to a British lord in public (previously literally, now metaphorically), but behind a self-effacing inscrutable Oriental mask he hides a humorous contempt for all "*gweilo*" ("foreign devils") regardless of race, colour, and nationality. Thus, the modern Hong Kong Chinese will insult the foreigner while nodding humbly, pleasing the unwitting *gweilo* and himself at the same time. Sometimes he is caught out by the handful of *gweilo* who speak his language, but this, surprisingly, is usually taken with good humour on both sides.

On tolerating *gweilo*: An abundance of nicknames for Westerners have developed over the years. The term *gweilo* originated many years ago with the birth of Chinese xenophobia. Originally it was derogatory, but since the Communist riots of 1967 it is quite openly used by both Chinese and resident foreigners. It is slang now, and more commonly used than the more polite term *saiyahn* (Western person). There are, however, other ruder terms used either vehemently or, again, humorously.

Preceding pages: waiting for the action to start at the stock exchange; budding ballerinas share a secret; last-minute rehearsal in front of City Hall. Left, underneath the Western facade is an oriental mind.

Appropriately, when a child throws a tantrum, his mother may call him a "barbarian devil," the same name she uses to deride a foreigner. And the tired Western joke that "all Chinese look alike" is turned around by Hong Kong's Chinese population, especially those not in regular contact with foreigners, to "all *gweilo* look alike."

Yet, this derision of Westerners, which in a way is a form of resistance to foreign domination, also breaks down, and its psychological opposite, the inferiority complex, surfaces. Hong Kong bus drivers, for example, are notoriously rude to foreigners, particularly Caucasians, who make up the racial majority of foreigners who visit and live here. This colonial mentality, however, is changing. As Hong Kong's youthful population drags older generations into the 1990s (at times copying the West in dress or music or style, while simultaneously challenging the West) it is also demanding equality and expressing pride in being sophisticated Chinese.

God Save the Queen?: In general, the Chinese in Hong Kong look upon their British overlords as efficient and political business managers, but with comic tolerance. Theatres, for example, used to blare "God Save the Queen" as a closing finale, but the practice was dropped decades ago because of a lack of patriotic reaction. A few British would stand staunchly throughout the anthem while the Chinese audience shuffled out indifferently, some not even recognizing the tune. When the Queen or some lesser royalty comes to visit, it's a heyday for funseekers and those socially inclined. Chinese school children, who scarcely know who the Queen is, are herded to the airport and stationed along sidewalks to wave little Union Jacks and cheer for a few seconds as Her Highness's royal motorcade races by. To them, the occasion is a delightful break from class. Hong Kong's Chinese leaders and socialites briefly forget their innate Chinese smugness as they, like upwardly mobile counterparts in Britain and the rest of the Commonwealth, vie for invitations to royal functions and dream of seeing their names on the New Year's honours list announcing knighthoods and other, lesser, royal decorations.

In spite of such pretension and feigned royalism, finding a Chinese *truly loyal* (in the British sense of "Queen and Country") to the Queen is perhaps as difficult as looking for a noodle in a haystack. Even civil servants trained in the colonial education system are rarely faithful British subjects at heart. This system deliberately glosses over the history of the Opium Wars. After these wars China ceded Hong Kong to the British as indemnity for losing the battle and to stop British exports of opium into China. Hong Kong's Chinese are basically apathetic. They want simply to be left alone to make money and possibly to emigrate to the West.

Not that they do not take their jobs seriously. They do. But this is more out of an obligation to their families and themselves than to the Crown. Government jobs promise "an iron rice bowl" – a meal ticket for life. If the Sino-British agreement is to be believed, "life" will go on beyond 1997 because the new Chinese government will need administrators and managers too. British rule always appeared the benevolent lesser of other possible evils. To a refugee-minded population, most of whom have escaped Communist China in various waves since 1949, a departure of the British and a subsequent Communist takeover was not a viable alternative. Life under a Taipei government was equally unpopular. True independence was also ruled out due to China's proximity. But with the anachronistic colonial *status quo* under the British ending in 1997, the majority of the population has no other choice but to accept Hong Kong's new status, since they have nowhere to flee.

Though the Chinese in the colony feign a docile submission, sometimes to cover up a deep-seated disdain for their British superiors, the Brits are more or less accepted, even if some of Her Majesty's minions would be only lowly clerks – not managers – back home.

It is this preserved, and at times buried, Chineseness that enables a population of more than 5.8 million to survive on this miniscule dot of territory on China's southeast coast. Despite some squalid living conditions (picture a family of five or more living in one room), the concept of "getting away from it all" simply does not exist for most Hong Kong Chinese. Even escapades to the countryside or beaches are made in throngs. Radio sets are ubiquitous and the

volume is usually turned on high so that everyone can enjoy the din, whether they want to or not.

This immunity to noise and bent for crowds is attributable partly to the gregarious nature of the Chinese character and partly to mental mutation. People born and raised in Hong Kong seem to have developed an inner barrier to cacophony. It is also one of the causes of friction between Western and Eastern mentalities. Europeans are accustomed to a quieter environment and frequently complain about the noise here.

Perhaps the key to understanding the people of Hong Kong is to understand the mechanism which allows the society to func-

tion normally under such closet-like circumstances: they are a people living on "borrowed land" and "borrowed time" in a city constantly in the excited state of a packed stadium during a championship match. A built-in mechanism within each individual – like an automatic valve that shuts when pressure approaches the unbearable – keeps such tension from surfacing. It enables the individual to retreat into an inner sanctuary – perhaps in the hypnotic movements of *tai chi chuan* (Chinese shadow boxing) in early morning hours among the forgetful laughter and concentration of friends; perhaps by the escape of watching a *kung fu* movie; perhaps by gorging on the teatime delights of *yum cha*. This traditional social break in a *cha* house is accompanied by selections of teas, savouries called *dim sum*, and sometimes the chirping of pet birds being "walked" each day. Just about any form of entertainment thrives in the colony: cinemas, restaurants and food stalls, *mahjong* parlours, and fast-talking street hawkers who perform to attract crowds. It seems that for everything in Hong Kong, *a sense of place* is secured only by jostling and pushing. *I push and shove, therefore I exist...*

Mahjong as self-hypnosis: *Mahjong,* a noisy game of tiles played by four, is the national pastime here. It fills a social void. On a Saturday night, buildings verily shake with

may pretend to succeed in curing "barbarian" minds, but could not hope to penetrate a Chinese brain. Here, friends and family are the individual's psychiatrist. "I'd rather talk to a friend about my problems than a stranger who calls himself a psychiatrist," a Hong Kong Chinese will say.

Thus, psychological problems remain unchecked until the psychotic begins chasing people with a meat chopper. There is only one mental hospital for the more than 5.5 million people who live here. It is designed for 1,000 patients but normally houses more than 3,000. And like most "living" situations here, a person has to be highly "qualified" to be admitted. One mentally disturbed fellow

the thunderous clatter of the tiles, and inexhaustible players become mesmerized in the game for days, numb and oblivious to other realities.

People in Hong Kong suffer the usual neuroticism, depression and mental malaise caused by big city life everywhere. But here such problems are aggravated by the public's refusal to recognize them. To the Cantonese, a psychiatrist is a Western quack who

Race fans at Happy Valley, Hong Kong's long popular and profitable attraction, demonstrate varying degress of anxiety as ponies near the finish line. Are the punters winning or losing?

who sought help at the hospital was turned away because the doctors did not think he was crazy enough! It was not until he smashed a television and tried to barge into the Governor's house that the hospital accepted him.

Some of the vagabonds that roam the streets are mental patients ostracized by society. One woman who wanders day and night in Hong Kong's Central business district is rumoured to have come from a wealthy family which disowned her when she became insane. Daffy or not, she survives.

A Beijing puppet?: Up until the agreement settled Hong Kong's future, most people indulged in a happy-go-lucky optimism to make life tolerable. If they were poor they said it was fate; no political power meant no politics and more time for making money. Their lives were sandwiched between the two governments of Britain and China and ruled by a colonial third. They did not even consider rocking the colony's *status quo* because they were so well off economically. The way out of this vicious circle was by wealth, and therefore Hong Kong's population has become one of the hardest working (whether blue- or white-collar) on earth. If money will not get you out of the colony, it will at least make the stay (even under a Chinese government) more pleasant.

The Chinese government wants Hong Kong to remain pretty much as it is, a meeting ground for the world's communists and capitalists, a launching pad for Communist enterprises into the Western world, and vice-versa. One consequence is the 50-year (from 1997) guarantee to keep Hong Kong investments – a guarantee designed to soothe anxiety surrounding the 1997 Agreement. Ironically the conservative Beijing government constantly reined in restive Hong Kong trade unions and other such untolerated dissidents.

Everyone here knows that the riots of 1967 were quelled by a directive from Beijing, not by the iron hand of a British-led police force. Hong Kong Chinese count their blessings; they are better off than the Chinese in Vietnam, or communized relatives in China. They cluck their tongues at low living standards in other Southeast Asian countries. The older generation, who have undergone a lifetime of foreign and civil wars, remind their restless young that life could indeed be a lot worse. And the young have only to look back to recent anti-Chinese riots in Malaysia (in 1969) or in Indonesia (in 1965 and again in 1980) to reinforce the older generation's wisdom. Fierce travel restrictions on Hong Kong Chinese who want to visit other Asian countries are also a constant reminder. The sad truth of the matter is that Hong Kong's Chinese never have had many choices – either in the past under the strange British Crown Colony or now that the territory is to become a Special Administrative Region under the government of Beijing.

Neither did the Hong Kong Chinese have any direct say as the agreement was being negotiated between the sovereign powers of Britain and China. Hong Kong's governor was on the British negotiating team but was forbidden, by protocol, to speak directly to the Chinese side. Neither was the governor nor the people of Hong Kong allowed to comment after the agreement was announced; the two negotiating governments made it clear that the agreement was an all-or-nothing affair – nothing could be changed. It made a mockery of Mrs Thatcher's promise to do nothing unless she first consulted the Hong Kong people. Referendums had been ruled out at the beginning because it was thought they might be too embarassing. Instead, an Assessment Office was established to solicit opinions on something that could not be changed. Britain's parliamentary de-

bate was also a farce since they too could not change anything. In fact, Hong Kong's "Hobson's Choice" was between the Chinese taking over in 1997 with the safeguards in the Sino-British agreement or the Chinese taking over without any agreement.

A close-knit traditional family structure also alleviates the discomforts of living in one of the world's most densely populated areas. Generations live together in low cost, low rental government housing estates, thousands jammed vertically into high-rises. (More than 50 percent of the population is housed in this way). However, the bigger the family, the bigger the labour force, and, of course, the greater the family income. That is why most working class families here can afford televisions, radios, stereos, and other modern gadgets. For if a family consists of four employed members, each contributing HK$3,000 to household expenses, they can afford luxuries seemingly incongruous with their housing conditions. Inside the most dilapidated Hong Kong tenement, teenagers fine-tune blaring stereo sets while housewives plug in electric cookers, television sets, sewing machines and air-conditioners. Hong Kong's newly emerging and affluent middle class uses its wealth to buy things, but remains in public tenement housing because of the colony's horrific land and housing prices (the highest in the world).

Generational differences: Tenement life, however, is not domestic bliss. Clashes among close-living family members are inevitable, especially between in-laws.

Other generational differences further complicate in-house relationships. New concepts of child rearing and nutrition have evolved, and children often become a focus of social discord. Younger Chinese parents, for example, are feeding their children more meat and milk, and infants are now nursed on formula (though breast feeding is regaining popularity). Consequently, new generations are becoming progressively bigger in build, and their modern parents are more liberal and experimental. Grandparents, however, still believe in traditional taboos concerning child rearing and diet; they prefer soybean gruel to formula, and so on. Therefore, they feel slighted when their senior opinions are not heeded; after all, they have raised five, six or seven children of their own. Tensions understandably build-up, but life goes on.

Cramped living (and working) conditions, however, make life difficult for would-be young lovers. Moments alone are rare, and the prying eyes of brothers and sisters, parents and relatives, and colleagues and workmates are not a conducive environment for composing love letters or flirting. Among the colony's few romantic retreats are lovers' lanes, but the all too real threat of being mugged in such places overshadows their appeal. Indeed, young courting couples often band together and form ad hoc security watches. After lights are out in Victoria Park, cooing couples will occupy neighbouring benches, and if one pair runs into trouble, they shout out an "S.O.S." to twosomes nearby.

Dating and marriage are now by free choice. This, however, does not mean that parents do not have a say in marital decisions. Parental approval is usually sought, and the bride or groom-to-be is subjected to the scrutiny of everyone concerned, including close and distant relatives.

Pragmatism versus passion: For economic reasons, the age of marriage in Hong Kong has been delayed. Women generally marry at the age of 24 and men, at 26. The pragmatism of the Chinese character often overcomes passion, and most Chinese are willing to postpone marriage until they have saved a good sum. Besides, Chinese weddings are dear. Banquets for the entertaining of clansmen can cost up to tens of thousands of dollars, and such gluttonous gatherings can be a chore for everyone: for the guests because they have to bring gifts, often in the form of cheques and gift coupons (wedding invitations often are dubbed "blackmail letters"), and, of course, to the hosts.

Concubinage (a form of polygamy) has been outlawed in Hong Kong since 1970, but it has metamorphosed into a more familiar creature. Concubines are now called mistresses, but are still publicly displayed as concubines were – as status symbols. One Hong Kong millionaire buys cars for his five mistresses according to their rank: the first mistress has a Rolls-Royce, the second a Mercedes Benz, and so on.

The older generation of men who took concubines before the new law took effect are allowed to keep them, and their children are recognized and have legal rights to an estate, but such is not the lot of "bastard" children born to modern-day mistresses.

Counting and discounting of "II's": Hong Kong is a land of immigrants and children of immigrants. Most of the older population immigrated from China during the last few decades, but the majority of the total population is young – under 25 – and were born here. The current influx of newcomers ebbs and wanes, depending on Beijing's policy whims. When China started to liberalize its immigration policy several years ago. Hong Kong, already crammed to the sky, took in 1,000 illegal immigrants a day.

Left, your destiny for a price: fortune telling is big business in a city like Hong Kong.

Between the years of 1978 and 1980, some 500,000 illegal immigrants, II's in the vernacular of Hong Kong's officialdom (the figures are an estimate because no one really knows), swam the shark-infested tidal waters along the Sino-British border with nothing more than homemade inflatables, or paddled dilapidated boats, or climbed hills (nearly all under cover of darkness), to come to *the promised land* which is Hong Kong. Ranged against them were thousands of soldiers, sailors, airmen and police. Battalions of China's People's Liberation Army (the PLA) and Chinese coastal gunboats cooperated with British and Gurkha battalions, Royal Hong Kong Police Units, and elements

Southern China, and that Hong Kong television transmissions are clearly received in the same area, encouraged these people.

In the beginning Hong Kong had a liberal, if puzzling, "touch base" policy, whereby an II who ran the gauntlet and arrived in urban Hong Kong – presumably to be reunited with his or her relatives – was permitted to stay. Many were aided by racketeers who serviced a lucrative "underground railway" system. In a departure from strict regulations, no questions were asked when a successful II showed up at the Immigration Department's emergency offices to apply for an identity card. This policy, which was decided upon to prevent the colony's underground and ille-

of the Royal Navy and Royal Air Force, to stop the II's. But still they came in droves.

Initial estimates indicated that for every 10 illegal immigrants who fled from China, half were stopped by the PLA, four ran the gauntlet successfully and Hong Kong forces apprehended one. By 1980, the PLA was catching about six and Hong Kong officials estimated that only one II escaped for every one they caught. They came, of course, for a better life than that available in the communes and fishing villages of neighbouring Kwangtung (Guangdong) Province. The sparkling and tantalizing fact that the glow of Hong Kong is clearly visible for miles into

gal population from mushrooming, was curtailed in 1980. Simultaneously, it was made a crime not to have and carry an identity card at all times, and employers were made responsible for the validity of immigrant employees. Since that law was implemented the frantic flow of II's has been reduced.

A rude dreamland?: In the minds of many in the neighbouring spartan Communist society, Hong Kong's streets are paved with gold. This image has been enhanced by relatives living in the colony, who, thinking that their compatriots are starving under severe Communist rule, scrimp and save to send them money. Hong Kong residents often return to China with truckloads of fabrics, bicycles, televisions, radios and other items that are not easily available on the mainland. And as an ego-inflation exercise, they like to brag about their great life in Hong Kong, to the wide-eyed wonderment of poor relatives in mainland villages.

But the real picture on the British side of the border may not be so rosy; and that on the Chinese side not so gloomy. One Hong Kong worker who sends a good part of his monthly salary to his brother in Canton was surprised to see his brother so plump and pink. While he sweats away more than 10 hours a day in a Hong Kong factory, his brother was enjoying daily hour-long tea breaks.

band of former Red Guards from China. Well-trained in the use of firearms, they managed to pull off the robbery in a few minutes. Police later apprehended the gang, but generally speaking, this sector of the population is hard to trace. Because of such official helplessness, Hong Kong is in the midst of a growing crime wave, much of it perpetrated by disgruntled mainlanders.

China-trained professionals such as doctors, nurses and engineers have to accept menial jobs here because their credentials are not recognized by Hong Kong authorities. A medical board examination has been set up in recent years for the qualifying of non-Commonwealth doctors, but some main-

The disappointment is often bitter once a Chinese refugee sets foot on leased British soil. Their dollar-signed dreams are rudely shattered by the harshness of a highly competitive society which eliminates the economically unfit. In a desperate effort to make it in the world, some resort to crime. The HK$7 million robbery of a bank transport car in 1975, the biggest holdup in the history of Hong Kong at that time, was carried out by a

The *yin* and *yang* of it: cooling herbal teas (left) and pricey French brandies for the hot-blooded (above) are consumed with equal relish by the locals.

land medical graduates feel that the test discriminates against them. The English language test alone eliminates many.

China's recent liberalization policy has also flung wide open the floodgates of legal immigration. (Chinese can travel to Hong Kong on a simple internal travel document and Hong Kong must accept them due to the peculiar political situation here). Consequently, antagonism between new arrivals and local residents is mounting. This population boom also has been aggravated by inflation which has seriously affected social service projects.

There are millionaires of every variety here: some who inherited the family business, some who placed a *right bet at the right time*, and some who lifted themselves by their sandal-straps through sheer effort. Some drive different coloured Rolls-Royces to match their daily attire. Others wear the same old rags for years, and nobody suspects that they have riches stashed away in banks.

Rags to Rolls Royce stories abound in this free enterprise entrepôt, but in this fairy tale many of the beggars-turned-princes remain outwardly humble. A successful entrepreneur may be dressed in a greasy apron, chopping away at roast goose in a restaurant, and another may be hawking noodles and fishballs at a street corner. The owner of the colony's famous Yung Kee Restaurant (his roast goose

residents. Though the official work week is 44 hours, a 70-hour week is not unusual for many. Indeed, other Asian capitalists eye Hong Kong with envy. Laments one Taiwanese toy maker: "Our girls are only half as productive as workers in Hong Kong. Here people take work seriously and don't jabber at work like they do in Taiwan."

Hong Kong is also known for its resilience. One cliché often repeated is that: "despite the hardships Hong Kong faces, it is always resilient enough to bounce back." Little mention is made of the men, women and children who are responsible for such fiscal flexibility. When there is a manufacturing deadline to meet, people work non-

is one of the world's 10 best dishes) started out with such a food stall; he now presides over a multi-storeyed, mega-dollar enterprise – a high-rise golden goose, if you will.

Another industry rich with Horatio Alger Wong stories is the garment business, Hong Kong's major export industry. Many multi-million dollar garment businesses are known to have originated in family workshops employing five workers or less. By hard work, business acumen accumulated after several bankruptcies, and with a bit of good *joss* (luck), they hit the big time.

"Industrious" and "efficient" are some of the catchwords used to describe the colony's

stop for three or four days (and nights) in a row; when business is slack, they switch to other professions or survive through family support; and when demand exceeds supply in a certain field, the business gap is filled overnight. Thus, during the worldwide denim boom of the early 1970s, thousands of little blue jean factories sprouted in Hong Kong. When the market became glutted with the rushed, shoddy workmanship of amateurs, the workshops folded as fast as they were born and owners took their business elsewhere.

The root of this flexibility is a traditional Chinese pride; an additional incentive is provided by the lack of a welfare system in

Hong Kong. If laid off, people cannot afford to wait around for government support; they have to move on to other jobs, even if at a lower status and pay, to survive.

Rapidly changing values: Yet, traditional values are changing. Industriousness and thriftiness often give way to opulence and acquisitiveness. Indeed, humble Hong Kong has broken world records in the consumption of luxury goods. Its residents are proud of being the world's highest per capita consumers of French cognac, and they love being the world's most conspicuous drivers of Rolls Royces. This profligacy has made much impact – especially on Hong Kong youths who seem to have adopted the temporal

China have re-established themselves in the colony, but the threat that their economic mobility may not last forever always hangs over their bank accounts. Speculation concerning 1997, when Hong Kong will be returned – or "liberated" – is a topic of daily conversation in corporate boardrooms and around *mahjong* tables. Meanwhile, the affluent store their money in foreign banks and the middle and lower classes race desperately to enjoy life while they can.

Emigration is a popular way out since the 1984 Sino-British Agreement handing over Hong Kong to China – to the tone of 60,000 of the best and the brightest a year. The price of such security is costly – it means giving up

philosophy of *get it while you can.*

Several factors account for this *nouveau riche* air. One, of course, is the colony's obvious wealth. As its export business grows and industry burgeons, consumer goods loom tantalizingly within reach of a large portion of the population. All the trappings of an acquisitive society emerge.

A second factor, a more subtle one, is a feeling of transience that permeates all strata of Hong Kong society. Many who lost everything when they fled Communist rule in

Left, Yung Kee Restaurant – the goose that laid a golden egg. Above, bird man of Mongkok.

a traditional lifestyle, businesses and friends, and starting out from scratch in an alien country. Some emigrants return to Hong Kong after establishing permanent residence in a foreign country, shuttling back and forth annually to retain their status in both places.

Every summer, thousands of visa applicants flock to the US Consulate and Canadian and Australian commissions. Many are college age students whose scores will not qualify them for admission to local universities. Such applicants have to go through a series of interrogations (at times humiliating) by curt visa officers who want to make sure the students will return home after graduation.

Not unlike its business community, Hong Kong's education is also highly competitive. Parents believe that their child's career is dictated by his kindergarten credentials. For if the child fails to enter a top-rate kindergarten, he cannot get into a top elementary school. This eliminates any chance of going to a top-rate high school, which is a prerequisite to university.

A number of students commit suicide each year because they failed an important examination; many more contemplate this desperate move. Thus, parents make sure that their training starts early. They hire tutors to prepare their children for kindergarten entrance examinations, an ordeal which sometimes requires two hours of testing to determine a child's Chinese, English and arithmetic skills.

Schools teach English and Chinese equally, but the language balance tilts toward English. The colonial government has adopted both as official languages (after many years of recognizing only English as the official language), but the legal language remains English. However, despite this pretence of equal treatment, everyone in Hong Kong knows that mastery of English is the crucial criterion for employment in major banks and corporations. Graduates of Hong Kong University, a British institution that uses mainly English, receive unofficial priority in the job market over those who complete studies at the Chinese-medium Chinese University.

Surprisingly, the average standard of English in Hong Kong is not very high. The alphabet is pounded into little heads at the age of five or less, and children sing *London Bridge* and recite *Run Rover Run*, but they parrot both by rote, with little comprehension of what they are mouthing. When a Shakespearean play covered by the secondary school syllabus each year is announced, it is often literally memorised.

Parochial schools are the most sought after educational institutions. Some parents convert to Christianity so that their children can enter these institutions. The faculty staff comprises a number of foreigners and they impose an awesome presence upon the children – with their looming frames and strangely coloured eyes. To avoid the trouble of learning to pronounce abstruse Chinese names, they christen the students in English. In one school, a British teacher simply goes down the row and arbitrarily names her students John, Mary, Peter, etc. Thus, in every class she teaches, there is a John, Mary and Peter seated in the same order. Some Chinese assume an English name – or simply use their initials – to make their passage into the English world easier.

To many Chinese in Hong Kong, religion is a pragmatic matter. Some get baptized into Christianity for personal gains – benefits from Christian charity organizations, social status, availability of gravesites in Christian cemeteries, and other practical considerations. One old woman born and raised a Buddhist was converted to Catholicism on her deathbed because a gravesite in the Roman Catholic cemetery is much more spacious and cheaper than ordinary "pagan" plots. Land is scarce in Hong Kong, and real estate speculators regularly increase the price of every centimetre of soil, including last resting places. Some gravesites cost tens of thousands of dollars. Therefore, the old woman prayed to Buddha in the morning and took communion from a Roman Catholic priest in the afternoon. By thus covering her beliefs she has assured herself a place in both heavens – and on the earth.

Superstition is perhaps the most appropriate name for Hong Kong's religious bent. Almost every Chinese, be he Christian, Buddhist or atheist, believes in occult forces. He believes that man can control them by arranging his furniture a certain way, by building his home in a divined location, by constructing walls to repel bad spirits, or by consulting a holy book for auspicious dates for major life-cycle events. Moreover, as gambling is a way of life for both rich and poor in this city, it makes a difference whether a person gets off his bed on the left or right side, whether he goes to the bathroom at a propitious time, or whether his wife says the right words to him. The Cantonese word for "book," for example, is poison to a gambler's ears, because that word (*shi*) sounds identical to the Cantonese word for "lose."

Conversely, superstitious people here literally raze mountains to give entombed ancestors a good view in the hope that their pleased grandparents will shower blessings on their earthly lot by guiding them to the right lucky bet.

Superstitious Chinese believe that "lucky red paper" will help to improve their lot on earth.

It has been said that when confronted with something they have never seen before or do not understand, the first impulse of a Chinese is to try eating it. As a result, this canon of Chinese folk philosophy has helped inspire the greatest cooking the world has known.

Standing as Chinese food does on five millennia of uninterrupted civilization, not much has been lost: rather, each generation of Chinese eaters has added great gustatory discoveries of the vast body of eating knowledge that preceded it.

Ancient Chinese cooking bears little resemblance to what you'll savour in Hong Kong today, but certain basic princples remain. Steaming, roasting, smoking and fermentation of meats were practised at least as early as 1000 BC, as was the now-forgotten practice of "scorched" pig roasting without evisceration.

Heavy, ornate, bronze cooking cauldrons and tripods from the Chou dynasty (1122–256 BC) have been unearthed intact. These items were used together as a double-boiler. Recipes of that time were also elaborate: a suckling pig, for example, was stuffed with dates, wrapped with hemp and mint and baked in a shell of clay. After the clay was removed, the pig was deep-fried until crisp, then steamed for three days, thereby producing a layer of fragrant oil.

Rice was steamed in an earthenware vessel that had several holes at the bottom and was lined with bamboo matting. Fish was steamed in a bamboo tube. Meat was preserved by salt curing, by grilling with spices and by fermentation with a yeast and wine mixture.

Early "Barbaric" tastes: Other culinary refinements came gradually as China's developing agriculture provided steady supplies of new ingredients. Each region naturally evolved a distinctive cooking style that reflected its topography, climate, flora and fauna, the temperament of its people, and their contact with outsiders.

Foods of northern and western China, for example, developed apart from the main-

stream of China's southern coastal rice bowl. This northern school, centered on the ancient and present capital of Beijing, was heavily influenced by Mongols who swept into Han China during the late 13th century. When the flat arid plain of northern China fell to these "Outer Barbarians" from the west, the exotic splendour of Chinese "agrarian cuisine" began a "new" taste odyssey.

This newly evolved western Asia cooking – rooted in the hearty flavours of the wintry, simoom-swept steppes – was fine fare, but it

was even further refined by China's indigenous Han chefs.

The Mongols, who founded the Yuan dynasty in AD 1279, were a nomadic tribe. They lived in tents and dressed in furs and their tastes – based on what was available, that is, milk, butter and lamb – were quite different from the native Chinese.

These "uncivilized" wanderers preferred a rough and simple cuisine: whole animals were roasted in stone pits or steamed with rock salt. They made fruit preserves and used pine nuts, rosewater, almond oil and sugar for seasonings; lamb dumplings were made with bean paste and dried tangerine peel; and

Left, noodle making is one of the culinary arts.
Right, self promotion, Chinese-style.

lamb cakes included innards, ginger, gourds, and eggs.

More than three centuries later, China was engulfed by yet another horde – this time by Manchurian warriors from the north who founded the Ching dynasty (1644–1912). Like the Mongols, the Manchus further influenced local Mongol-Han cuisine to suit their unusual tastes. The Chinese adapted well, but not completely.

Indeed, even today, four centuries after the Manchus and Mongols have added new alien recipes to the vast Chinese menu, there are still great battles fought over food preference in China's kitchens. Southern Chinese (mainly the Cantonese, but including sub-

ample, is *sik tzo fan mei* – an expression which literally means "Have you eaten?"

Every Chinese dialect is rich in food symbolism. "You are breaking my rice bowl," wails the Chinese man whose livelihood is threatened. And even to simply learn how to say rice in Chinese, one needs an annotated dictionary. Consider the Cantonese linguistic variables for that common staple: plain rice is *mai*; cooked rice is *faan*; rice porridge (commonly called congee) is *juk*; and harvested but unhusked rice is *guk*.

Eating for the Chinese is also not just a bit of necessary metabolic bother – to be consummated as quickly as possible with great globs of starch three times a day. Granted,

groups such as the local Hunan, Chiu Chow and Hakka people) like to complain that Beijing-based food lacks smoothness and subtlety. Beijing folks, meanwhile, argue that southerners grind, chop and dilute the flavour out of their food.

"Have you eaten?": Whatever their regional and moot food points, Chinese everywhere talk about their food the way Westerners talk about art. This is probably because Chinese cuisine is indeed an art form.

But even if they aren't conscious of their food as a major cultural accomplishment, no Chinese can ever avoid talking about it. The most common Cantonese greeting, for ex-

there has been a sad increase in Western or Western-style "fast food" outlets in Hong Kong, but when eating here, one is still expected to enjoy a measure of entertainment and, most important, a proper and tasty titillation of the palate.

The Chinese concept of a meal is very much a communal affair and one that provides a strong sensory impact. Dishes are chosen with both taste and texture in mind – a stomach-pleasing succession of sweet-sour, sharp-bland, hot-cool, and crunchy and smooth.

In a land which has experienced recurrent hunger and natural disasters, no wastage of foodstuffs is acceptable. Even today children are warned by their parents that if they leave any rice in their bowls they will marry a pock-marked spouse – and the more grains left in the bowl, the more pock-marked their partner will be.

In spite of traditional poverty and privation, or maybe because of it, Chinese nearly always insist on fresh food. It is only recently that refrigeration and freezing methods have been adopted by Asian households. Most traditional Chinese still shop three times a day for fresh meats and vegetables. A Chinese cook does not start a meal with the idea of creating one particular dish like a stew or roast; rather, he or she goes to the market to

Chinese who savours such gourmet fare, many of these delicacies are either banned by law or virtually impossible to obtain. Hence, they are rare and expensive.

Many Westerners also experience difficulty in eating with chopsticks. Small and loose rice grains are a particular *gweilo* ("foreign devils") menace. To accomplish the seemingly impossible, abandon self-consciousness, hold the rice bowl up against your lips in a drinking position and shovel the rice into your mouth with the chopsticks. Scraping and slurping are not considered a *faux pas* here or anywhere Chinese.

One mistake Westerners make, however, is the unseemly swamping of their rice with

buy what is fresh and in season, and then creates the dish.

Monkey's brain and bear's paw: To most Westerners, Chinese food is basically strange. In fact, many dishes considered rare delicacies by Chinese make the Westerner ill. For example, monkey's brain (eaten directly from the skull of a freshly killed monkey), bear's paw, snake, dog, pigeon, frogs, sparrows, live baby mice (good for ulcers) and lizards. Unfortunately for the average Hong Kong

Fowl play: Cantonese favourites include clay-baked chiken (far left) and Peking duck (left). Above, inside a floating restaurant.

soya sauce, a crude act that robs it of its character and function. A meal should include enough spicy and savoury dishes to make the neutral blandness of steamed rice an essential balancing agent.

Chopsticks are thought to have been adopted for eating because of a Confucian distaste for knives – potentially dangerous weapons – on the dining table. In Hunan, China's agricultural rice bowl, curious extra long chopsticks are supplied in restaurants. Stories are told of people who feed each other across the table because the chopsticks are so long they can't manoeuvre the ends into their own mouths!

If chopsticks are impossible for you to co-ordinate, it is perfectly acceptable to use the porcelain spoon provided for soups as a scoop for other courses. And no one minds if you make a mess – it is even permissible to wipe your hands on the edge of the table-cloth. The object is to get the food into your mouth in the most efficient manner.

A typical Chinese meal invariably starts with a cold dish, which is followed by other main courses. Soup – usually clear light broth – may be eaten after the heavier entrees to aid digestion. However, a thick full-bodied soup may be served as a main dish, and a sweet soup often serves as a dessert at meal's end. There are no inflexible rules when it

finest, then judging by popular worldwide demand, Cantonese cuisine just may be the premier regional food of China.

The Cantonese live to eat and, at its most refined level, Cantonese gastronomy achieves a finicky discrimination that borders on cult-ism. Of these decadent gourmets, Confucius once wrote:

For him the rice could never be white enough and minced meat could never be chopped finely enough. When it was not cooked right, he would not eat. When the food was not in season he would not eat. When the meat was not cut correctly, he would not eat. When the food was not served with its proper sauce, he would not eat.

comes to ordering your meal. The main thing is to enjoy the food.

"Die in Liuchow, but eat in Kwangchow": As mentioned, eating and enjoying of Chinese food – given the diversity of foods one can eat in this region – is largely a matter of personal taste. However, since you are in Hong Kong, a colony largely influenced by Cantonese cooking, consider the following oft-repeated Chinese proverb:

Live in Soochow (a city noted for its re-fined manner and beautiful women), die in Liuchow (where teakwood coffins are made), but eat in Kwangchow (Canton).

Indeed, if Chinese cooking is the world's

The gourmet syndrome is found wherever there are Chinese with the means to pursue it, but the Cantonese have pushed it to the extreme with dishes made of bear's paw, shark's fin, bird's nests, duck webs, deer tails, chicken testicles and the aforemen-tioned live monkey's brain.

"Fortune cookies" are a no-no: Visitors to Hong Kong who think they are familiar with Cantonese food soon learn to their surprise that this discipline has little to do with sweet 'n' sour pork – said to have been invented by ever resourceful inhabitants of Canton solely for sweet-toothed foreigners – or *chop suey* – said to have been invented in San Francisco when a customer entered a restaurant at closing time, demanded service and the cooks threw their leftovers into a pot, served it up and in quiet jest called this Oriental goulash *chop suey*. Also, despite Hong Kong's bent for things superstitious, "fortune cookies" do not exist here. They are another romantic *gweilo* invention.

In the Cantonese method of preparation, food is cooked quickly and lightly – stir fried – in shallow water or an oil base, usually in a *wok*. The flavour of the foods is thus preserved, not lost, in preparation. Neither is the original taste of hot, spicy sauces . Many dishes, particularly vegetables or fish, are steamed. This discourages overcooking and

traditional superstition among fishing families, you will seldom see a Chinese diner turn over a fish to reach the meat underneath. He doesn't want a capsized boat and drowned men on his conscience.

Prawns and crabs cooked in various styles – steamed or in a black-bean sauce – are also popular Cantonese seafood dishes. If you hear the term "jumping prawns," this signifies that they are alive (and therefore fresh), but it doesn't mean you are expected to eat them that way! Shark's Fin Soup, golden threads of gelatinous-like shark's fin in a shark broth, is the centrepiece of Cantonese banquets.

Chicken is the most widely-eaten fowl,

preserves a food's delicate and "natural" flavours. Sauces are used to enhance flavours, not destroy them. The sauce usually contains contrasting ingredients like vinegar and sugar or ginger and onion.

A Cantonese restaurant is *the place* to eat fish, steamed whole with fresh ginger and spring onions and sprinkled with a little soy and sesame oil. Cantonese, unlike picky Western eaters, consider a fish's eyes and lips a delicacy. However, in keeping with a

Left and above, street-side stalls have atmosphere aplenty and some of the colony's most delicious offerings.

and in keeping with the Chinese sense of economy and variety, a single chicken is often used to prepare several dishes. Chicken blood, for example, is cooked and solidified for soup, and the liver is used in a marvellous specialty called Gold Coin Chicken (*gum chen kai*). The livers are skewered between pieces of pork fat and red-roasted until the fat becomes crisp and the liver, soft and succulent. The delicacy is then eaten with wafers of orange-flavoured bread.

Cantonese chicken dishes can be awkwardly bony for chopstick beginners, but lemon chicken is prepared boneless with the skin coated in a crisp batter and served in a lemon sauce flavoured with onions, ginger and sugar.

For starters, choose something from the display of barbecued meats in the restaurant's display window. Cantonese barbecuing methods are unrivalled. Try goose, duck or, best of all, tender slices of pork with a gold and honeyed skin served on a bed of anise-flavoured preserved beans.

Also experience the taste sensation of double-boiled soups with duck, mushroom and tangerine peel, and a winter specialty called "Monk Jumping Over the Wall." This is a blend of abalone, chicken, ham, mushrooms and herbs that is so irresistible that monks are said to break their vows of vegetarianism if

are quite often eaten in concert with succulent Shanghai hairy crabs.

Frogs are also found in the rice paddies, and these "field chickens" are often served at banquets in South China. In Hong Kong markets they are sold live in plastic bags, and restaurants prepare them in many delicious ways. The best frog course is deep-fried frog's legs cooked in a crunchy batter mixed with crushed almonds and served with sweet and sour sauce.

Beijing (Peking) Duck: Beijing (Peking) Duck is the most popular northern Chinese dish served in Hong Kong (and it is probably the most popular northern dish anywhere in the world). This duck dish is prepared by roast-

its fragrance is within smelling distance.

Snake is a traditional winter dish, but it is unfortunately a succulent food "misunderstood" by Westerners. Dogmeat is also a winter dish but is legally forbidden here, so special winter eating tours into China, specifically to eat dogmeat, are popular.

"Buddha's Hand": Yet another Cantonese dish to sample in the winter is a casserole of chicken and Chinese smoked pork sausage (*laap cheong*). These sausages are sold in pairs and usually are served steamed on a bed of rice. In autumn, restaurants serve rice birds, those tiny winged creatures which frequent paddy fields at harvest time. These

ing it over an open charcoal fire and slowly basting it with syrup until the skin is crispy brown. In some areas of Hong Kong, you can actually see this meticulous cooking process being performed on the pavement over an earthenware brazier. Patient *foki* (waiters or assistants) slowly cook the duck, over and over again, all afternoon long, in preparation for the evening's repast.

When you partake of Beijing Duck in a restaurant, part of the enjoyment of the meal is the "show" (there really is no other word for it) put on by the chef at your tables as he swiftly carves the duck – *always* with a large razor-sharp chopper (butcher's cleaver) and *never* with carving or paring knives. In delicate cutting motions, performed at your table, the chef slices the skin off for the first of three duck courses with a quick succession of exact strokes, starting at the neck. After the crispy skin is served, the waiter quickly follows with the meat. The skin and meat are eaten with a mild, sweetish soya bean paste mixed with spring onions and cucumber. The duck and sauce are placed on a wafer-thin wheat tortilla that looks like a thin, dry rolled crepe or pancake. This concoction is then rolled up and eaten with the fingers.

The third course from the duck is the soup. Whilst you are busy with the first two courses, the duck's carcass is boiled with a combina-

trace the origins of some dishes. Beijing Duck, for which the traditional recipe ran to nearly 15,000 words, was originally Mongolian, but it's now much more popular in Beijing than in Ulan Bator.

Mongolian hotpot: Mongolian hotpot, called "steamboat" in the Singapore-Malaysia region, is of central Chinese Moslem origins. It is probably the second best known of the northern dishes.

Mongolian hotpot is a winter food, served between November and March in northern-style restaurants. It is probably best described to Westerners as the Chinese version of *fondue Bourguignonne.*

The key preparation utensil for hotpot

tion of cabbage, mushrooms and herbs. Then a duck soup is served. When ordering Beijing Duck, be sure to tell the waiter you want this soup. Some restaurants have been known to take advantage of visitors who do not realize there are three duck courses in a traditional Beijing Duck meal.

Over the centuries, culinary elements from all over eastern Asia have been liberally adapted and absorbed, and it's difficult to

eating is a chafing dish with a small charcoal burning stove built-in underneath and a chimney rising through its centre. A trough around this dish contains soup stock to which is added vegetables, cabbage and herbs. When the soup stock begins to boil, the entire stove is set into a hole cut in the centre of your table (Mongolian hotpot traditionally was a practical way to eat and keep warm at the same time).

Wafer-thin slices of various meats or fishes, previously ordered, are served raw, and you cook the meal yourself in small wire baskets dipped in this hotpot's bubbling broth. A spicy sauce, prepared to your taste by the

Left, prices of shark's fin vary greatly, depending on quality. **Above**, waxed and preserved meats require no refrigeration and are especially popular in the winter months.

waiter, adds to the taste treat. The final course is the remaining soup broth.

Another version of this dish is Mongolian barbecue – a related eating system in which a hot griddle is placed in the same hole in your table. In this variation of the hotpot theme, meats and fish are barbecued instead of boiled.

A surprise for Westerners at their first Beijing meal is that rice is not usually served (unless you request it). Wheat is commonly grown in the north so northerners traditionally eat steamed bread (*pao*) or tasty onion cakes instead of rice.

One of the spectacular treats at a Beijing meal is hand-made noodles (at the table)

of cooking to make them palatable.

For dessert, Beijing restaurants offer toffee apples. These apple treats arrive at your table hot and syrupy and are then dipped in ice-cold water and transformed into a crackling, sesame-coated taste sensation.

Spicy Szechuan: Because Szechuan is one of China's westernmost provinces – and thus much exposed to the spicier delights of food in the Asian subcontinent – the cuisine of Szechuan is renowned for its spicy tastes and pungence.

The ultimate Szehcuan dish is smoked duck, a crisp-skinned specialty with the aromatic flavour of camphor-tea. It is prepared with a seasoning of ginger, cinnamon, or-

called *lie mien*. The best quality vermicelli is produced in Shantung. A fine variety is made from flour dough, drawn out on a frame and dried in the sun. Vermicelli is a symbol of longevity, and so is served at weddings and birthday festivities to ensure long life. Related Western egg noodles are descendents of Chinese noodles and were first introduced to Europe in the 14th century by the explorer Marco Polo.

Bear's paws, another northern delicacy, is an esoteric banquet food found in Hong Kong. However, it is only available in certain restaurants and should be ordered well in advance because the paws require 16 hours

ange peel, coriander and *hwa chiao*, pungent Szechuan peppercorns.

The duck is marinated in rice wine for 24 hours, steamed for two hours, smoked over a charcoal fire sprinkled with camphor wood chips and red tea leaves, fried briefly to crisp the skin, and finally served with lotus leaf pancakes.

Szechuan food is a richly-spiced cuisine with a distinctive chilli sting. Characteristic dishes are succulent prawns seasoned with garlic and ginger, chilli bean paste and wine, garlic-laced eggplant that's mashed and then braised, and *ma-boo* bean curd braised in a powerful chilli sauce.

The latter bean curd dish is a smooth-textured favourite known as "Old Ladies," because it is so soft you can eat it without teeth. It is named after the wife of a 19th-century chef called Chen, and in the Chengtu region of Szechuan, Chen's descendants still operate a famous *ma-boo* bean curd shop.

Noodles or steamed bread are eaten in preference to rice, but Szechuan restaurants do specialise in a crispy rice dish made with the dried scrapings on the bottom of a rice pan. This crispy rice is deep-fried and covered with a rich and delicious sauce of meat, mushrooms and abalone.

Minced beef with vermicelli is known in Chinese as "Ants Climbing a Tree," and

cooling dessert, the perfect dessert to quench chilli fires, is almond bean curd.

Chiu Chow cuisine is also known as Swatow food because this type of cooking originated in the administrative district around the city of Swatow in Kwantung (Guangdong) Province.

Coastal Chiu Chow cuisine: The coastal people of the southeast have an original method of harvesting oysters. They simply push bamboo sticks into oyster beds and the sticks gradually become encrusted with these mollusc. Harvesting is merely a matter of pulling up the sticks, and the cooking part is also just as simple: they hold the sticks over a fire and grill the oysters right in their shells.

steamed Szechuan pork is an expensive winter specialty that combines abalone, pork, chicken, sea cucumber, ham, mushrooms and bamboo shoots. One of the best Szechuan soups is sour pepper soup, prepared with bean curd, chicken's blood and shredded bamboo shoots seasoned with chillies, peppercorns and vinegar.

The tastiest vegetable dish is braised season beans cooked with minced pork and dried shrimps and simmered in soy. And a

Left, the famous floating restaurants at Aberdeen. **Above**, if you don't feel like moving, the "restaurant" will come to you.

In Chiu Chow restaurants the preparation is more sophisticated but equally tasty. Seafood addicts go for oysters fried in egg batter and clams served in a spicy sauce of black beans and chillies. Grey mullet is a favourite cold dish, and pomfret fish smoked over tea leaves and freshwater eel stewed in brown sauce are other highly recommended seafood wonders.

A Chiu Chow restaurant is also an appropriate place to try banquet-style food such as Shark's Fin Soup and Bird's Nest Soup. The dried saliva lining the edible swiftlet's nest provides the magic base for the famous Bird's Nest Soup. The owner of one restaurant in

Hong Kong reputedly rents a mountain in Thailand that is said to harbour the finest collection of swiftlet nests in Southeast Asia. The nest itself is virtually tasteless, but its nourishing saliva linings are believed to rejuvenate the old. This delicacy is also eaten as a dessert flavoured with coconut milk or almonds.

Baked rice birds are a seasonal fowl dish stuffed with chicken liver and served by the dozen. Minced pigeon, meanwhile, is cooked with water chestnuts and eaten wrapped in crisp lettuce leaves spiked with a dollop of plum sauce. Desserts – made from taro, water chestnuts and sugar syrup – are for the sweet-toothed only.

sugar go into a basic marinade. Fresh ginger root and dried tangerine peel are among secondary ingredients added later.

When ordering in a restaurant, it's wise to remember that portions are usually huge and you'll want to try plenty. Start the meal with a cold dish like smoked fish or the famous Drunken Chicken, a delicacy flavoured with Shao Hsing yellow rice wine and eaten cold with a garnish of coriander leaves.

Autumn is the time to sample the hairy crab, a creature prized for its rich golden roe. There's an art to cracking the shell to get at the exquisite centre, and for your first hairy crab eating experience, it's a good idea to go with someone who knows how it's done.

A Chiu Chow meal begins and ends with a thimbleful of "Iron Maiden," an excellent bitter tea drunk to aid digestion.

The Sung dynasty romantic poet and gourmet Su Tung Po invented one of the most satisfying Shanghainese dishes. Su Tung Po Pork uses humble ingredients and simple flavouring, but it's a memorable pork casserole which becomes as soft as bean curd after lengthy cooking.

These slow-braised Su Tung Po dishes are traditionally cooked in earthenware pots to enhance the flavour of the ingredients. The characteristic flavour of such eastern Chinese food is sweet. Soya sauce, rice wine and

Shao Hsing wine traditionally accompanies this hairy-pincered delicacy, and a cup of sweet ginger tea at the end of the meal aids digestion.

Other Shanghai specialties are sweet and sour carp, soya and spiced beef and braised bean curd with minced beef and chilli. Try jellyfish if you're feeling adventurous, or Lion's Head Casserole, which isn't as alarming as it sounds. It's an excellent dish of meatballs cooked with black mushrooms and bamboo shoots. Also recommended is the traditional hot and sour soup, a spicy blend of bean curd and blood, sea cucumber and mushrooms.

The best known dish from Hangchow is Beggar's Chicken. This succulent specialty is available at only a few Hong Kong restaurants, and is served encased in a mud pack that is cracked open with a hammer at your table. In the centre of this mud pack is a delicately baked chicken which has been stewing in its juices for more than eight hours. Though its exact origin is unknown, this gourmet dish can be traced back to the time of the Ching dynasty Emperor Chien Lung (1736–95).

The Hakka – or "guest people," because their long migrant path from the north eventually took them to the south – live in Hong Kong's New Territories. Theirs is a matri-

cause they are peasants, and were thus always on the run from war or famine, the Hakka have created unusual flavours from obvious but generally unused food sources such as braised chicken's blood or pig's brains stewed in Chinese wine. Though the last two dishes might be a bit too much for the average Westerner's palate, he or she should at least try the bone marrow. It has a very delicate taste and is believed to be good for one's health.

Surprisingly, there is only one Hunanese restaurant in the colony, so very few residents and visitors have tried this cuisine. The best known dish in this gastronomic discipline is preserved ham served in a sauce of

archal society and because of this, their women are seen on just about every construction site in the colony. They are easily identified, because they wear black pajama-like clothes (*samfoo*) and wide-brim straw hats with red and black tassles on the brim.

The Hakka main dishes are salt-baked chicken and stuffed duck. To prepare stuffed duck, the duck is first ingeniously deboned through a hole in the neck and then stuffed with a rich assortment of glutinous rice, chopped meats and lotus seeds. Perhaps be-

honey and spices. These thick slices of ham are eaten in a steamed pancake. Minced pigeon soup cooked in a bamboo cup is another specialty.

Southwest Chinese cuisine includes steam pot chicken, a famous Yunnan dish cooked in a specially designed pot with an internal funnel which allows a regulated flow of steam to slowly cook the ingredients. Other Yunnan specialties are peach blossom rice and noodles cooked in chicken broth. The latter dish is called "Crossing the Bridge" noodles. Unfortunately, there are no restaurants specializing solely in Yunnanese food in Hong Kong.

Far left, getting ready for a reptilian repast. **Left**, a busy market scene. **Above**, *dim sum* threesome.

DIM SUM: CHINESE PETIT FOURS

Dim Sum is one of the great unheralded Chinese inventions, ranking with gunpowder and paper. Specifically, it is a Cantonese invention, and to say it is extremely popular with Hong Kong's Chinese population today would be an understatement.

Dim sum to a Cantonese is what whisky is to a Scot or wine to a Frenchman. It is indispensable, and not having one's daily *dim sum* would make life indigestible.

This is not to say that non-Chinese visitors are not encouraged to partake of this taste treat. On

the contrary, the Cantonese take pride in showing off this unique petit cuisine.

Indeed, *dim sum* is so popular that if Hong Kong's tourist business magically declined overnight and nary a Westerner showed up for a *dim sum* lunch, their absence would not even be noticed. Which means that if you want to sample a *dim sum* lunch, you have to make a decision before 10 a.m. and request your hotel to book for you a table.

"Touching the heart": *Dim sum* means "little heart" or "touching the heart" and it refers to food which comes in small portions on equally small plates. The official British word is "savouries," but this ancient fast-food is more reminiscent

of a Scandinavian smorgasbord in reverse. In a *dim sum* house an infinite variety of Chinese hors d'oeuvres comes to you.

The first thing you'll notice about *dim sum* restaurants is how spacious they are. Huge brightly-lit rooms, sometimes floor upon floor, are packed with hundreds of diners eating, reaching, shouting, and gesturing for *dim sum*. The servings stacked on the trolleys are wheeled from table to table on trolleys by girls. If they are true to Chinese tradition, these girls will sing traditional verses of praise about the food as they push the trolleys through aisles jammed with waiters, other trolleys and, of course, anxious customers waiting for already crowded tables to be vacated.

On the trolley trays are steaming bamboo canisters. Visitors rarely understand what the trolley girls are chanting, but don't be shy. It is proper etiquette to take the tops off these canisters and marvel at the contents. Invariably, the girls, when serving a table of Westerners, will take the tops off all the canisters on their tray anyway.

Do's and Don'ts: A couple of *dim sum* points to remember: Try to reach the restaurant for lunch before 12.30 p.m. At that time all the food is prepared and ready to go for early lunchers who come in between noon and 1 p.m. (Official lunch hour is 1 p.m.–2 p.m.) Wait until after 12.30 p.m. and you may lose your table in seconds and suffer a long and hungry wait. Another reason not to eat late is because you may miss out on the day's full range of *dim sum* selections.

Sit on or near a main aisle or intersection (make the request when reserving through phone). Don't sit at the rear because back there it is difficult to attract the attention of besieged serving girls.

Do not be afraid to question waiters who hover around the trolley girls if you need something. Ask them to suggest a delicacy. The waiters might try to feed you a regular dish (out of politeness, thinking you might not like *dim sum*), but stress that you indeed want *dim sum*, not sweet and sour pork or some other Westernised Chinese dish.

Do not ask the waiters to clear your table as the dishes and canisters stack up. In an ordinary Chinese meal, dishes are cleared after each course, but with a *dim sum* lunch, the dishes are usually left on the table until it's time to tally the bill; the waiter merely counts the number of dishes served, and each variably-sized dish is of a certain price. The price can be as low or less than HK$2 for some items.

Lastly, stop by a Hong Kong Tourist Association (HKTA) office before you go for the experience and pick up their *dim sum* brochure which has colour pictures and descriptions of the most popular dishes. Their Chinese names are transliterated into English for your easy pronunciation, and the Chinese characters are also there for waiters' reference.

Yum cha: A *dim sum* lunch provides a daily opportunity (on Sunday it is traditionally a big family outing) to sample this treat, but it is possible to sample some of these dishes at any time of the day. This is made possible via another fabulous invention called *yum cha*, the Chinese version of a tea break.

Yum cha is a snack break featuring tea and *dim sum*. In a *yum cha* haunt, you will notice not only people quietly relaxing in a traditional teahouse setting, but gentlemen out "walking" their pet birds. Bird connoisseurs commonly take their song birds out for a daily airing and stop at their favourite teahouse for a bit of *yum cha, dim sum* and gossip. (The restaurants usually have poles strung across the length or width of their dining area – for hanging the bird cages on, of course.)

To enable you to identify the small delights served at Hong Kong's typical Cantonese restaurant, here is a comprehensive list (Cantonese names and English translations) of the items.

Dim Sum Savouries

Guon tong gau: Steamed dumpling stuffed with minced pork and chicken soup.

Har gau: Steamed shrimp dumpling.

Woo kok: Deep fried taro vegetable puff.

Shiu mai: Steamed minced pork and shrimp dumpling.

Tsing fun guen: Steamed rice flour roll filled with assorted meat.

Seen chuk guen: Deep fried bean curd roll filled with pork, shrimp and oyster sauce.

Lor mai gai: Steamed rice flour dumpling filled with assorted meat.

Chu yuen shiu mai: Sliced pork liver with steamed pork and shrimp dumpling.

Cha siu cheung: Steamed rice flour roll with barbecued pork filling.

Har cheung: Steamed rice flour roll with shrimp filling.

Left, *dim sum* touches the heart and fills the stomach too. **Right**, traditional *dim sum* teahouses allow you to park the bird while you have a bit of *yum cha*.

Au yuk cheung: Steamed riced flour roll with beef filling.

Jar fun gwor: Deep fried rice flour triangle filled with pork, shrimp, bamboo shoots.

Pai gwat: Steamed spare-rib with red pepper sauce.

Fun gwor: Steamed rice flour triangle filled with pork, shrimp, bamboo shoots.

Ham shiu kok: Deep fried rice flour triangle filled with pork, shrimp and vegetables.

Gwor ching chung: Large glutinous rice dumpling filled with duck, preserved egg yolks, mushrooms and wrapped in lotus leaves.

Char siu bau: Steamed barbecued pork bun.

Ho yip fun: Steamed fried rice in lotus leaf wrapping.

Gai chuk: Steamed chicken roll with bean curd wrapping.

Tsun guen: Deep fried spring roll filled with shredded meat, bamboo shoots and bean sprouts.

Dim Sum Desserts

Ng lau jar wan tun: Deep fried dumpling with sweet and sour sauce.

Dun sun: Crisp and sticky sweet cake topped with almonds.

Hung dow sa: Sweet red bean paste soup.

Dun tat: Hot custard tart.

Chien chang go: Thousand-layer sweet cake with egg topping. ∎

It looked like a normal dedication ceremony. Gentlemen in suits, shiny shoes and hard hats, had gathered around a construction site in Hong Kong. The chairman of Hong Kong's then new Mass Transit Railway (MTR) did the earthy honours and broke ground for the US billion dollar venture.

That spade full of dirt would have been the end of dedication ceremonies in most countries, but not in Hong Kong. It was now time for a Taoist priest to beat a gong and say prayers. He had to ensure that the spirits

disturbed during tunneling work done under the construction site would be placated.

Though physically Hong Kong looks like a modern 20th-century city in the best Western tradition, such temporal surface similarities end there. In addition to written regulations and laws about construction of buildings, highways, bridges, tombs, homes and whatever else goes into a modern concrete city, Hong Kong people also honour unwritten spiritual laws called *fung shui* (pronounced *fung soy*). After government departments have completed their building plans, architects and contractors consult a *fung shui* man, a geomancer. His job is to

determine the most auspicious location for not only the building, but also its doors, windows and desks.

Ch'i, yin and yang: *Fung shui* (which literally means "wind-water") is practised with a compass-like device which has eight ancient trigrams representing nature and its elements – heaven, water (the ocean), fire, thunder, wind, water (rain), hills and earth. These elements in turn represent eight animals (horse, goat, pheasant, dragon, fowl, swine, dog and the ox). This Chinese "science" is based on the principle of *ch'i*, the spirit or breath that animates *yin* and *yang*, female-passive and male-active elements. The *fung shui* geomancer's job is to put all these spiritual factors together to make a positive prediction.

Whether non-Chinese people here actually believe in *fung shui* doesn't matter. What is important is that this colony can't be run without Chinese; therefore, the Hong Kong government and private industry heed their ancient beliefs.

The MTR is not an isolated case. One of the most serious of such incidents occurred at the end of 1976 when the colony's major airline, Cathay Pacific Airways, was digging a foundation for a new administration and engineering stores building.

No preliminary *fung shui* ceremony was thought necessary despite the fact that a new air cargo terminal building (located nearby and partially-owned by the same company that owns Cathay Pacific) had observed proper *fung shui* ceremonies on March 4, 1975, well before the building's opening. Employees in the engineering division started to fall ill and word spread that the site's *fung shui* had been disturbed. A *fung shui* ceremony was consequently held, thereby placating the disturbed spirits, and since then no one has been taken ill.

In Central District, at the site where Hutchison House, Bank of America Tower and a multi-storey carpark stand, a mass execution was conducted by Japanese during their war-time occupation of the colony. When Hutchison House reached its full height, a Buddhist ceremony was conducted by the then deputy chairman of that giant conglomerate to appease the spirits of those who had died there.

Across the road, in a government carpark and in government offices on a building's top floors, pencil-pushers in the Transport Department reported seeing ghosts. These incidents of flying spirits became so acute that the dapper Brit who then ran the Transport Department, Brian Wilson, eventually led an exorcising procession of 70 chanting Buddhist monks and nuns through the carpark on February 8, 1974.

Even officers of the law are not immune to the belief in the power of *fung shui*. The Royal Hong Kong Police Force outwardly looks the same as any other law enforcement organization. But when morale dropped severely at the Wanchai Police Station in August 1973, the then new divisional superintendent, Larry Powers, made concerned enquiries among his rank and file.

Powers' men believed the station had bad *fung shui* thrown on it because a building built opposite the station as part of a fair had a low slanting roof with two wooden spirals. Powers called in a *fung shui* expert, and the geomancer concluded that the station's entrance facing the fair was in a bad position and susceptible to omens. His remedy? To keep the "two-horn monster" at bay, he suggested that a pair of old cannons be put on either side of the entrance.

Some people and organizations try to ignore the superstitious and Chinese side of Hong Kong, but such ignorance nearly always leads to trouble.

The Royal Hong Kong Jockey Club is a case in point. Between 1960 and 1965, three jockeys accidentally died during races within 3 yards of the same spot. Initially ignoring this omen that the pariticular spot was jinxed, the austere British gentlemen running the club finally brought in representatives of the Buddhist Association to exorcise that part of the racetrack. So far it has worked and there has been no more deaths.

Hong Kong's Chinese customs affect everyone, even progressive American businessmen. Before the Hong Kong Sheraton Hotel opened in 1974, its general manager, Robert

Hamel, consulted a *fung shui* expert about the hotel's opening date; his local staff was reportedly very pleased.

Another American hotel chain up the street did not do likewise, and it was only after being plagued by bad *joss* incidents did its management call in a *fung shui* expert to set things right.

The Regent of Hong Kong sheathed its lobby and mezzanine in 40-foot (12 metre) lengths of glass on a geomancer's advice. According to a *fung shui* source, the hotel rises at a site where "a dragon enters the harbour for his bath." By designing a see-through lobby, there was no chance of disrupting the dragon's ritual – a mistake which

would have created inexplicable bad *joss*.

Octagonal mirrors or deflectors called *pat kwa* are frequently hung outside windows of large office buildings and apartment houses. It is believed that these deflectors protect their occupants by repelling evil through the reflection of the mirrors.

Westerners might still be curious about the cause of Hong Kong movie star Bruce Lee's death in July 1973. But not Hong Kong's Chinese. They *know* what happened to him. Typhoon Dot, they explain, ripped through the colony shortly before his demise and blew away Lee's *pat kwa*. He then became vulnerable and, naturally, died.

Left, mythical good luck dogs are usually placed at entrances to "guard" the premises. Right, the mirror in the *pat kwa* is meant to repel evil spirits.

Mahjong to the Chinese is not just a game. It is a habit-forming social event, a virtual way of life, which can be as addictive as cigarettes, alcohol or opium.

Mahjong also drives Westerners mad. Not the game, but the noise accompanying it. Mahjong is a game that is virtually impossible to play quietly.

The sounds of mahjong – the clickity-clacking of the tiles rubbing against each other during the shuffle; sharp banging noises as tiles are slammed on the table top with each call; and loud shouts announcing each call – all these seem to pervade much of the normal din which is life in this modern metropolis. Mahjong, besides being a popular social function, is also an opportunity for skillful gambling. Some mahjong fans insist there's as much skill involved in betting during a mahjong game as there is in bridge. And in Hong Kong, where most gambling is illegal, betting on mahjong takes on added significance.

Unseemly behaviour?: A Westerner, who finds himself competing for existence in a mahjong game, is usually aghast at the loud and seemingly "unsocial" (in the Western sense) behaviour that punctuates a typical mahjong game. Westerners do not realize that the cacophony indicates the level of excitement. To a non-mahjong freak, the game smacks of being an antisocial contest instead of a competition between friends. This is a false impression. The Chinese, you'll discover, express themselves in a manner quite unlike a typical Westerner. And indeed, any qualitative judgments should be based on local values, not Western ones. But even if you are an adaptable sort, mahjong games can be intolerably loud.

In Chinese cities, mahjong is played almost everywhere and at any time of the day. At the beach, while children swim, parents set up a table on the sand. At building sites and in factory canteens, workers with the "habit" while away their lunch hour and sometimes their lunch money. Tales abound in Hong Kong of people – from *taitai* (rich housewives) to *amah* (maids) – who have made and lost fortunes in an afternoon's mahjong game.

Mahjong is also ever-clacking at dinner parties, banquets, and wedding celebrations. Bilingual wedding invitations may announce a wedding banquet at 8.30 p.m. in English, but the Chinese side of the invitation often asks the guests to come at 6 p.m. The time differential indicates the duration of a traditional pre-feast mahjong game.

No dilly-dallying: The game originated during the Sung dynasty (960–1279) when it was played with 40 pieces of paper, each with a picture on one side. As the game was played then, each of the four players received eight opening cards, leaving eight for exchanging.

During the Ch'ing dynasty (1644–1912), at the time of the Taiping Rebellion during the middle of the last century, soldiers popularized the game by playing for a flagon of wine. By this time principles of the game had changed and the paper mahjong cards had metamorphosed into more durable bamboo, ivory or bone tiles, some of them elaborately carved.

Mahjong as it is played today in Hong Kong is much more complicated than the original game. The tiles are brick-shaped, about an inch (2.5 cm) long, and are hand-engraved with Chinese characters and patterns. The first time you watch the game, you will be amazed by the speed with which players make moves and bets. There is no dilly-dallying or stalling in mahjong.

To begin play, the leader throws the three game dice. The rolled number is then translated into an exact positioning of the tiles in a square arrangement. The leader takes four tiles, and each player in turn (and in a counter-clockwise sequence, beginning with north) also takes the next four from that position. On the fourth round, the leader takes two and each player one. The leader now has 14 tiles while the other three players have 13 each. The leader then discards one tile (by slamming it on the table, naturally) and play commences counter-clockwise. If north does not want the discarded tile, he chooses another from the tiles still remaining on the table, but only from where the last person left off.

The object of the game is to "go out,"

much as in rummy, by matching up tiles of similar values or suits. The winner is the first player to line up four sets of three tiles (either as three-of-a-kind or as three-tile straights) plus an additional pair (which is the 13th tile plus one picked tile which must fit in to make a pair or, if such a pair exists, form a set), thereby adding up to a total of 14 tiles. (Are you still with us?)

Each player also has a packet of betting chips worth 100 points. Before a game, the players decide what a betting point will be worth – anywhere from one cent to HK$10. When a player "goes out" successfully, he is awarded points based on the combination of tiles he went out with. Each player gives the

to distraction. A typical friendly neighbourhood mahjong game is more like a *kung fu* fight scene than a friendly, social event.

Much of the excitement of the game is due to the pace at which it is played – the faster the moves, the more thrilling the action. Tiles are not merely put down politely on the table and picked up, but are slammed down and grabbed up amidst a great clatter and loud exclamations. As the excitement builds and money changes hands, a sort of frenzy seizes the players and – like the neck-to-neck finish of a horse race – the table appears to be the scene of pandemonium.

Multiply that mad scene by 10,000 or 100,000 and you have a good audio-visual

winner "X" points (chips) and the leader gives double. If the leader wins, he receives double from each of the three players. When a player loses his packet of chips worth 100 points, the game is technically over, unless of course he starts borrowing to prolong it (a fairly common practice). And occasionally, by common agreement, each player starts out with more than 100 points.

Frenetic but friendly: To a Westerner, just about every game of mahjong is "heated," and this is what drives non-mahjong players

Keep your eyes on the *mahjong* hands. The action is frenetic, but relaxing, Chinese-style.

image of Hong Kong on a typical afternoon or evening. Even as you read this story there are mahjong games going on *everywhere* in the colony – in workers' flats, on *sampans*, in tea shops, in mansions, in factory canteens, at the seaside – everywhere!

The game of *mahjong* appears to be anything but a game of leisure and relaxation. But that, of course, is exactly what it is. Mahjong also is used as a conclusive Chinese test of a stranger's mettle. Indeed, an old Chinese saying advises that if one wishes to find out what kind of man his daughter is going to marry, the best way to find out is to invite him over for a "friendly" game of mahjong.

The people of Hong Kong live two lives. One is lived according to the Western solar calendar, which brings them the benefits of annual holidays such as New Year, Easter and Christmas. The other is according to the Chinese lunar calendar, which involves a series of traditional family get-togethers throughout the year. On lunar holidays family members also visit temples and ancestral graves to make offerings to deities and fore-fathers. It is therefore not unusual for those who attend Easter services also to observe traditional ceremonies with strong overtones of Chinese beliefs and customs.

Various festivals mark the passing of the four seasons. They follow the lunar calendar with its 12 months of 30 days each. An additional month occurs during leap years to make up for the uneven number of days in non-leap years. Because ancient Chinese civilization was agriculturally based, the lunar calendar was "naturally" calculated to suit agrarian realities.

It is believed that this calendar was first developed by one of China's legendary sage kings, Emperor Yao, who in the third millennium BC ordered his astrologers to accurately determine the solstices and equinoxes so that farmers would know when to plant their crops.

In addition to such ancient associations with the seasons, Chinese festivals also celebrate legends and historical events. Whatever the origins of these Chinese festivals, it should be noted that contemporary and practical considerations have influenced the nature of some traditional celebrations.

For example, fireworks, formerly an integral part of such festivals as the New Year and the Ching Ming spring celebration, have been forbidden by law in Hong Kong since the colony's Red Guard political riots of 1967. As a result, devil spirits have to be scared away by other means, much to the celebrants' chagrin. On the other hand, papier-mâché Rolls-Royces, jumbo jets and television sets are burned as offerings to enrich the well-being of those in the afterlife.

The faithful flock to pay their respects at festival time.

Chinese New Year is the most important holiday on the calendar. Legend has it that in prehistoric time, when the Chinese had already settled in the basin of the Yellow River, their peaceful life was disrupted one wintry night when a mysterious monster attacked the citizens and destroyed their crops and homes. According to sages of the time, the appearance of this monster occurred after the sun had shown 365 times. It was found that this ferocious creature, called *Nien,* was afraid of three things: noise, illumination and the colour red.

Thus, on the 365th evening, vigilant Chinese had their houses brightly lit and made sure that 100 solid objects had been painted red. In addition, they struck drums and gongs and performed lion dances. As a result of these precautions, the monster disappeared. This tradition of celebration, now essentially a gesture of thanksgiving, has since been faithfully observed by Chinese on the 365th evening of every lunar year.

"Kung hay fat choi": Traditionally, celebration of the New Year lasts 15 days. In some homes it is still fully celebrated, but modern-day responsibilities have caused it to be limited, in many Chinese families, to three days.

Some old Chinese customs, deliberately discarded or simply forgotten during the rest of the year, are revived during the New Year days. For example, the emphasis on respect for one's elders is manifested on New Year's Day when the younger generations offer tea to their elders.

It is customary for married couples to give *lai see,* a red envelope containing lucky money, to children. The amount is theoretically insignificant, because it is the act of giving that is important. It is a gesture believed to bring luck and prosperity to both the giver and receiver. The traditional Chinese New Year Cantonese greeting is *kung hay fat choi,* meaning "wishing you prosperity," and it is heard reverberating through homes and streets at this time.

Two systems are used in naming and determining the character of every new year. The first system names each new year after an animal. There are 12 animals represented in the scale. In recurring chronological sequence the names of the years are: Rat, Ox, Tiger, Rabbit, Dragon, Snake, Horse, Ram, Monkey, Rooster, Dog and Pig. This perpetual or cyclical system is called *kan tse*.

The second system which determines the character of the new year is based on astrology, the *I Ching* (a complicated system of fortune telling), and on the Chinese view of heaven and earth.

The New Year festival is a happy time. Children run around with bright red packets of *lai see* – lucky money – and salaried people are happy because they have just received a year-end bonus which, in some cases, represents two or three months' pay. Shop assistants and waiters, *foki*, are treated to a year-

New Year's debts equal bad joss: It is bad *joss* to begin the year with outstanding debts, so this is an important time to settle accounts. However, Chinese pragmatism occasionally causes problems. The crime rate is always higher at this time of year because some Chinese will steal enough money to pay off their debts in order to begin the new year with good *joss*. Of course, modern Asia has proper billing procedures in business and a good accountant is usually careful enough not to let accounts mount up.

Another custom is the buying of peach blossoms (which bring good luck in male-female relationships), kumquat trees and narcissus flowers. These are indispensable

end feast by their bosses, *lo ban*. This feast is rich in food and symbolism. Chicken is always the main course and, in the manner of a good host, the boss serves his employees with his own chopsticks. If a *foki* receives the most succulent part of the chicken, it means he is being treated as a guest, not as part of the family, and is therefore out of a job for the coming year.

On the 16th day of the 12th moon (the last month), businessmen close their accounts and thank the three gods of wealth – Kuan Ti, Tusan Tan Shang Ti and Ts'ai Shen – for a prosperous year (if it has indeed been one) and wish for another such year.

decorations at this time of the year. Gardeners work hard year round pruning leaves and buds so that these plants will bloom virtually overnight on New Year's Eve.

Sweetened lips: New Year's celebrations actually begin about a week before New Year's Eve. This period is known as "Little New Year," and it is said that the "God of the Kitchen," Tsao Wang departs from his domain then for a yearly journey to heaven to report on all Chinese families.

It is of course desirable that Tsao Wang tell only good things about the family or report as little as possible, so Chinese families guarantee that he bears good tidings by preparing a special sticky-sweet candy, *tang kwa*, which is smeared on the god's lips so that they are sealed or so only sweet words will be spoken. Naturally, most of the sweets find their way into the hands and mouths of the youngsters in the family.

Wine is also offered, and paper money burned, to assure Tsao Wang a comfortable journey. During his absence in heaven, the family turns his image around to face the wall and burns a caricature of him. Before he returns on New Year's Eve, the house must be thoroughly cleaned and each family member must help (if he or she wants to remain in Tsao Wang's good graces). Following this New Year's cleaning, the image

"opportunities," chicken is "the phoenix," kumquat is "gold luck," pig's tongue is "profits," dried oysters are "splendour," melon seeds are "silver," and pig's trotters are "good luck in gambling."

Two traditional foods made especially for New Year are *gin tuy* and *yau kok*. The former looks like a softball; the latter has a triangular shape. Both are fried and made with glutinous rice flour; *gin tuy* has sesame seeds sprinkled on the outside, *yau kok* is stuffed with a filling of crushed peanuts, coconut shreds and sesame seeds. If you sense the urge to try either of these, buy them at the nearest Chinese grocery store. They also serve as proper gifts if you are calling on

is turned back around or a new image of Tsao Wang is placed above the stove. A feast is prepared to greet him after his long journey, and door gods are set up for the new year.

"Silver ingots": As one would expect in any celebration where a kitchen god is honoured, food plays a big part in the Chinese New Year. Indeed, a virtual feast is prepared in the house to usher in the year. Certain foods are even renamed. Translated from the Chinese, eggs become "silver ingots," mushrooms are

Left, Chinese New Year is a frenetic time for all. **Above**, participants in the dragon dance require lots of skill and stamina.

someone. Cognac, however, is also an acceptable "modern" offering.

Tradition lives on and on. No one goes to sleep on New Year's Eve, and little children are discouraged from dozing off, in the belief it will shorten their lives if they are not awake for New Year's Day. After the new year has arrived, the head of the family presents all the children and juniors with *lai see* so they will have good fortune for another 12 months.

On New Year's Day ancestors are honoured at family altars, and red scrolls inscribed with characters signifying happiness, prosperity and long life are pasted on the walls. A basket of food is placed in the centre of the living room to guarantee that there will be enough to eat in the coming year, and knives and scissors are hidden away so that no one will cut luck's continuity.

The second day is known as *Hoi Nien* or "The Opening of the Year." The most important event of this day is a banquet-style dinner. The third day is commonly regarded as one which might induce quarrels, so social visits are avoided. The seventh day is called *Yan Yut* or "Everybody's Birthday." Though now observed only in a modified way, it is a day on which smiling faces are expected.

Honouring Chu Yuan: The Dragon Boat Festival (*Tuen Ng* in Cantonese, *Tuan Yang* in Mandarin) has been celebrated on the fifth day of the fifth moon (early June) for the past 2½ millennia. Its exact origin is unknown, but legend notes that this festival commemorates the tragic death of the honest and learned minister of state, Chu Yuan, who died in 288 BC in the ancient Kingdom of Ch'u during the time of the Warring States (403–221 BC).

At that time, Chu was the true and dedicated power behind the throne; he was a wise man who advised the ruler correctly for the good of his people. Other envious advisors, however, didn't appreciate Chu's influence, so they encouraged his disfavour with the king. Consequently, the king's *joss* failed him because he took bad advice (which resulted in his losing a war to his neighbour). To make matters worse, the old king was captured during the fighting.

To express his concern for the old ruler, Chu Yuan wrote a poem called *Li Sao*, the classical Chinese version of a political speech. (Because of the poem, the festival is sometimes called **Poet's Day** or **Patriotic Poet's Day**.) This angered the new king who ordered Chu Yuan's exile. But instead of leaving, Chu Yuan jumped into the Mi-Lo River, a river in the present Hunan Province. Today's dragon boat races symbolize the vain attempts of friends who raced to this spot to save unfortunate Chu.

Another tale has Chu Yuan despairing that his good counsel was being ignored. While wandering alone one day he composed *Li Sao* and then became so disgusted at the human world of intrigue and deceit that he committed suicide.

In mourning for their honest statesman, the people threw rice in the river to feed his ghost. One bright day Chu Yuan's ghost (or spirit) appeared to the people on the river bank and said: "You made offerings to me for which I am thankful, but the rice was all devoured by turtles and fish. I hope you will offer me rice again, but this time, please wrap it in bamboo tubes, close the openings with leaves and bind them with different coloured thread so that the turtles and fish will not dare to eat it."

Yet another version of this honourable Chu tale has him instructing that silk be used (not bamboo) and that the silk rice packets be bound with fine threads, each of a different colour. Such rice packets are now the standard offering made during this festival.

A dragon boat is like a huge war canoe with a dragon's head carved at the bow and a dragon's tail at the stern. Depending on their size, they are manned by 20 to 80 paddlers accompanied by a drummer at mid-canoe who sets the timing of oar strokes with a huge drum.

There are half a dozen Hong Kong sites where these day-long races are held. These venues change occasionally, but Tai Po and Yaumatei usually host the biggest dragon boat events. Stanley Village is another popular site. (Check the newspapers, your hotel or call on the Hong Kong Tourist Association to find out the exact sites and times.)

"Lady dragon-boaters": Various organizations, both European and Chinese (such as the police, firemen, army, embassies, bars, restaurants, clubs, Boy Scouts, welfare groups, and even the local journalists' union) enter teams. Elimination heats are held and the final championship race is run by the three fastest boats. For the past 2½ millennia it has been exclusively a man's sport, but in 1971 Hong Kong's first women's team entered these races; now, ladies' teams are quite common.

Each race site is crowded with people who watch from the shore and from the decks of every conceivable type of boat. The course itself is usually surrounded by hundreds of junks of all sizes, each one covered with bunting indicating team affiliations. Pleasure boats, warships, police launches and ferries are also gathered nearby.

A gunshot signals the start of a race and immediately an unbroken cadence of drums aboard the dragon boats and the clanging of cymbals aboard spectator junks (to ward off evil spirits) fills the harbour with noise.

This holiday has also developed over the

years into another celebration – this one dedicated to the Goddess of Heaven (*Tin Hau* in Cantonese and *Matsu* in Mandarin). Though this goddess has her own special day, she is *the* goddess of fishermen and, by logical watery extension, also a patron of swimmers, lifeguards, sailors and, in the case of this holiday, dragon boaters.

A glutinous rice concoction, called *ch'un tse* in Cantonese or *tsung tzu* in Mandarin, is sold during this festival. In North China and Taiwan, the *tsung tzu* are triangular shaped, but in the south they are square.

About a week after local dragon boat races, special **International Dragon Boat Races** are held in which teams from all over Asia,

minded Chinese of old. The union of man's spirit with nature in order to achieve perfect harmony was the fundamental canon of Taoism, so much so that contemplation of nature was a way of life.

This festival is also known as the **Moon Cake Festival** because a special kind of sweet cake (*yueh ping*) prepared in the shape of the moon and filled with sesame seeds, ground lotus seeds and duck eggs is served as a traditional *Chung Chiu* delicacy. Nobody actually knows when the custom of eating moon cakes to celebrate the Moon Festival began, but one belief traces its origin to the 14th century. At that time, China was in revolt against the Mongols. Chu Yuen-chang,

and some from as far away as the United States, compete.

Moon cake festival: A Mid-Autumn Festival (*Chung Chiu*), the third major festival of the Chinese calendar, is celebrated on the 15th day of the eighth month. This festival corresponds to harvest festivals observed by Western cultures (in Hong Kong, it is held in conjunction with the annual **Lantern Festival**).

Contrary to what most people believe, this festival probably has less to do with harvest festivities than with the philosophically

Above, digging in with intensity at the annual Dragon Boat Race.

and his senior deputy, Liu Po-wen, discussed battle plans and developed a secret moon cake strategy to take a certain walled city held by the Mongol enemy. Liu dressed up as a Taoist priest and entered the besieged city bearing moon cakes. He distributed these to the city's populace. When the time for that year's *Chung Chiu* festival arrived, people opened their cakes and found hidden messages advising them to coordinate their uprising with the troops outside. Thus, the emperor-to-be ingeniously took the city and his throne. Moon cakes, of course, became even more famous. Whether this sweet Chinese version of ancient Europe's "Trojan

Horse" story is true, no one really knows.

The moon plays a significant part in this festival. In Hong Kong, any open space or mountain top is crowded with people trying to get a glimpse of this season's auspicious full moon.

First lady on the moon: It is generally conceded that Neil Armstrong, the American astronaut, was the first man on the moon (he made that historic landing in 1969). But that's not necessarily the truth to Chinese, who believe that the first person on the moon was a beautiful woman who lived during the Hsia dynasty (2205–1766 BC).

This somewhat complicated moon-landing story goes like this: A woman, Chang-O,

Another version of this story notes that Chang-O, the wife of the Divine Archer, shot down nine of ten suns plaguing the world and received the Herb of Immortality as a reward.

Whoever the hero was, Chang-O grabbed the pill (or the herb) and fled to the moon. In some versions it is uncertain whether she ever actually got there, because Chinese operas always portray her as still dancing-flying towards the moon.

When Chang-O reached the moon, she found a tree under which there was a friendly hare. Because the air on the moon is cold, she began coughing and the Immortality Pill came out of her throat. She thought it would be good to pound the pill into small pieces

was married to the great General Hou-Yi of the Imperial Guard. General Hou was a skilled archer. One day, at the behest of the emperor, he shot down eight of nine suns that had mysteriously appeared in the heavens that morning. His marksmanship was richly rewarded by the emperor and he became very famous. However, the people feared that these suns would appear again to torture them and dry up the planet, so they prayed to the Goddess of Heaven (*Wang Mu*) to make General Hou immortal so that he could always defend the emperor, his progeny and the country. Their wish was granted and General Hou was given a Pill of Immortality.

and scatter them on Earth so that everyone could be immortal. So she ordered the hare to pound the pill, built a palace for herself and remained on the moon.

This helpful hare is referred to in Chinese mythology as the Jade Hare. Because of his and Chang-O's legendary importance, you will see – stamped on every mooncake, every mooncake box, and every Moon Cake Festival poster – images of Chang-O and sometimes the Jade Hare.

The old man on the moon: There is a saying in Chinese that marriages are made in heaven and prepared on the moon. The man who does the preparing is the old man of the moon

(Yueh Lao Yeh). This old man, it is said, keeps a record book with all the names of newborn babies. He is the one heavenly person who knows everyone's future partners, and nobody can fight the decisions written down in his book. He is one reason why the moon is so important in Chinese mythology and especially at the time of the Moon Festival. Everybody, including children, hikes up high mountains or hills or onto open beaches to view the moon in the hope that he will grant their wishes.

To celebrate this sighting of the moon, red plastic lanterns wrought in traditional styles and embellished with traditional motifs are prepared for the occasion. It is quite a sight to

ogy, the butterfly is the symbol of longevity and the lobster the symbol of mirth. Star-shaped fruit is the seasonal fruit in the autumn, and the carp is an old symbol of the Emperor, personifying strength, courage, wisdom and, of course, power.

Tin Hau observances: On an island such as Hong Kong, it is natural that legendary deities related to the sea should figure prominently, at least among the boat people, in traditional observances.

The **Festival of Tin Hau** (also spelled T'ien Hou), dedicated to the Mother-Goddess of the Sea, takes place on the 23rd day of the third month, when fishermen make offerings to their popular protector.

see Victoria Park in Causeway Bay, or Morse Park in Kowloon, alight with thousands of candlelit lanterns. These "Lantern Carnivals" also occur spontaneously on most of the colony's beaches.

The lanterns are made in such traditional shapes as rabbits, goldfish, carps, butterflies, lobsters and star-shaped fruits. However, in modern Hong Kong you will also see lanterns in the shape of missiles, airplanes, rockets, ships and tanks. In Chinese mythol-

Left and above, the Lantern Festival, held to celebrate the sighting of the moon, is especially popular among children and the young at heart.

Tin Hau's origins are nebulous. However, it is said that she was the sixth and youngest daughter of a Sung dynasty (AD 960–1279) mandarin who lived in the fishing village of Pu Tien in Fukien Province. She was born Mo Niang in the eighth year of Emperor Yuen Yan's reign (1098). Even as a child she was adept at forecasting the weather, a talent which endeared her to fishermen.

She is said to be able to walk on water if supplied with a straw mat. Tin Hau also calms the waves, helps fishermen make bountiful catches and protects them from shipwreck and sickness. Her apotheosis took place during early days of the Ch'ing dynasty (AD 1644–1912) when the Emperor K'ang-hsi beatified her by edict and conferred upon her the title of Heavenly Queen.

Tin Hau festivities begin at dawn when junks, *sampans* and lighters, all gaily bedecked with streaming multicoloured pennants and crammed with people, fill Hong Kong's water-ways as they head for one of the many temples. The biggest Tin Hau temple – and festival – is at Joss House Bay in the New Territories.

Cheung Chau's "Bun Festival": Hong Kong's Cheung Chau Island is a living picture postcard of a quiet fishing and rural community, but during the four days of its annual **Bun Festival** it is inundated with thousands of

areas where they wanted to build houses. To allay any misfortune that might occur here – and to placate the spirits of the dead whose remains and resting place they were about to disturb – three prominent Taoist priests were brought in for consultation with gods and the island's elders. Though nobody was certain who the remains belonged to, it was thought best to have a spirit-placating festival to rid the site of bad *fung shui*.

This observance is commonly referred to as the "Bun Festival" – which is an English nickname, not a translation from the Cantonese – because of the grand finale.

At midnight between the third and final day of the 4-day festival, there is a free-for-

visitors. This festival begins on the eighth day of the fourth moon (usually early May).

The Bun Festival is not a traditional Chinese celebration. Rather, it is a *ta chiu* or spirit-placating observance. Depending upon whom you hear the original story from, this festival commemorates the victims of a plague which swept the island some 75 years ago, or it commemorates the hundreds of brutally slain victims of pirate Cheung Po Chai, who ruled Cheung Chau and its surrounding waters before the British presence. It is his temple which is the focal point of the festival.

The actual festival began after Cheung Chau residents discovered human bones in

all, quaintly described as a race, for symbolic offering of buns, or *pao*, which are mounted on bamboo towers that rise some 60–80 feet (18–24 metres).

The object of this free-for-all is to grab as many buns as you can once a signal has been given. He who accumulates the most buns and/or buns from the highest points on the towers will enjoy the best *joss* during the coming year. Recently, due to a series of gang fights during over-enthusiastic climbs up these towers, this bun-tower climbing ritual has been abandoned. (The buns are perfectly edible and are not unlike the type the Chinese eat with tea for breakfast.)

Presiding over this 4-day Cheung Chau festival are three deities: Shang Shaang, the red-faced god of earth and mountains: To Tei Kung, a household god who brings good luck; and Dai Sze Wong, the God of Hades. Effigies of these three gods are built and villagers pay homage to them.

The third day of the festival is highlighted by a grand procession. Near the end of the procession come colourful parade floats borne on long support poles by lines of bearers. Usually each village street or organization on Cheung Chau enters a float. They depict the various vices and virtues of mankind. The key characters on these floats are always portrayed by children, who wear colourful, traditional costumes and kneel, stand or balance themselves on their hands.

Graveside picnics: The **Ching Ming Festival** – "The Clear and Bright Festival" – is related to the solar calendar. This seasonal festival marks the beginning of spring and is held on the 106th day after the winter solstice and is celebrated here in April.

On this day observants customarily visit ancestral graves where traditional rites and offerings are made to honour one's ancestors. This unusual ancestral observance is related to the traditional Chinese need to receive blessings from previous generations at the onset of a new undertaking. The event, however, has the atmosphere of a picnic because the offered food is eaten at the various gravesites. It is not a solemn occasion, but rather, a time for happy communion with one's forefathers.

Feeding the hungry ghosts: The **Festival of Hungry Ghosts** occurs on the 15th day of the seventh moon, and is the closest Chinese equivalent to the Christian's All Souls Day.

Taoists and other Chinese religious sects (as well as superstitious people from the Chiu Chow region of Kwangtung Province) take this festival seriously and actively participate in it. Depending on individual preference, donations from the human world may or may not benefit the ghosts; however, in the human world one group that benefits greatly from this holiday are papier-mâché craftsmen. They fashion complete wardrobes, cars, airplanes, furniture, money and other neces-

sities of life, out of paper, and these folk art forms are all burned as offerings during the Festival of the Hungry Ghosts. The act of offering gifts to the ghosts by burning such paper replicas generally takes place on the pavements and is quite a colourful scene.

Cheung Yeung mountain-climbing: The **Cheung Yeung Festival** is observed on the ninth day of the ninth month (in October). This festival is related to a disastrous incident that occurred during the Han dynasty (206 BC–AD 221). According to legend, a gentleman, upon the advice of a soothsayer, sought to avoid calamity by taking his family to the mountains for 24 hours. Upon returning to his village, the gentleman found that

disaster had indeed struck. Thus, a custom of leaving one's home and going off to a higher location continues today, and roads up to Victoria Peak are jammed at this time as modern-day doomsdayers follow that ancestor's example.

To the boat people, Tam Kung, a local boy-god capable of raising and quelling tempests, is the most important deity after Tin Hau. Therefore, a **Tam Kung Festival** in his honor is held on the eighth day of the fourth month in the district of Shaukiwan on the eastern tip of Hong Kong Island in an area known as Ah Kung Ngam or "Ancestor's Rocky Hill."

Left, scrubbing the ancestral remains is an annual ritual. **Right**, offering a prayer to the gods at Chinese New Year.

Much as Hong Kong's modern life-style offers continual diversification and variety, religion remains an unchanging, integral part of the life of its people. Even though practically every denomination of the Christian faith – as well as Judaism, Islam, and other Oriental religions – are represented here, the bulk of Hong Kong's people still practice traditional forms of Chinese religion.

Hong Kong's homes, streets and countryside are dotted with literally hundreds of small to huge Confucian-Taoist-Buddhist temples and shrines, and by numerous other religious structures maintained by Middle-Eastern and Western religious faiths. All practice their religions freely here – with little or no interference, intolerance or discrimination.

In countries which are substantially nurtured by only one faith – such as Italy by Catholicism or Saudi Arabia by Islam – the multi-religious practices tolerated here must verge on sacrilege. Hong Kong Chinese, however, take for granted an eclectic worshipper who goes into a Taoist temple to burn incense after having attended Sunday services in a Christian church.

Chinese religious ways: Specifically Chinese customs, superstitions, cultural preferences and traditional ways of life here are not necessarily results of strict religious beliefs, but are dependent on a number of external factors. In the case of China – and by extension, Hong Kong – they are integrated with religion, whether indigenous or imported, to such an extent that it may be hard to identify the subtle differences.

Confucianism was originally a way of life; its essence was based on the concept of propriety in human relationships. This involves a pious attitude toward one's superiors, and respectful behaviour towards living parents. Confucian doctrine is basically coloured by social overtones. Therefore, it encourages hierarchism, both metaphysical and spiritual, and its natural outcome is evidenced by the elevation of Confucianism in China to the status of religion.

A monk offers daily prayers at the impressive Po Lin Buddhist temple on Lantau Island. Po Lin is Chinese for "Precious Lotus."

Taoism, on the other hand, is introspective; its ideal aims at perfection through complete conformity with *The Way*, or principle (*Tao*), of nature. For a sage to understand his own nature, an understanding of the nature of all things is very important. Hence, unity with all things in a pantheistic identity of spirits becomes the goal. Assuming such unity is within human reach, a search for immortality through the use of alchemy and a search for harmony with all living things are its guiding principles.

Most Taoist gods, therefore, are legendary figures whose earthly existence is considered to be worthy of imitation. The jurisdiction of their spiritual powers is directly related to special or outstanding aspects of their former earthly forms. Visual evidence of this phenomenon are specific attributes associated with each deity. The God of Literature, *Man*, for example, always holds a brush. Much as Taoist canons are philosophically based, Taoist religious practices are coloured by mythology and pantheism.

Foreign Buddhism: Unlike China-born Confucianism and Taoism, **Buddhism** is a "foreign" religion imported to China from India during the first century. The branch of Buddhism which thrives in China is known as the Mahayana School. This is a Buddhism which focuses on the achievement of enlightenment in order to reach *nirvana*, or the state of extinction of self, as exemplified by Gautama Buddha, a historical figure who lived in the 6th century BC in northern India. Buddhism involves gaining release from the sufferings of physical existence and attaining the Buddhist goal of *nirvana*.

A peculiar and interesting aspect of Chinese religious practices is the recognition and acceptance of deities historically foreign to the basic tenets of a particular religion. Kuan Yin (the Goddess of Mercy), for example, is a Buddhist deity worshipped in Taoist temples. This cross-pollination spiritual device is often used to overcome the competition different temples face in attracting faithful followers. The idea is to appeal to as wide an audience as possible.

The following prominent temples and shrines are only samples of Hong Kong's innumerable "Chinese" places of worship, but each should provide the casual visitor with fascinating insights into Chinese people and their multi-faceted faiths.

Patron of police and criminals: The **Man Mo Temple**, on Hollywood Road, near "Cat Street," is the colony's oldest existing temple, dating back to 1842 or 1847. It is also the colony's largest. This temple is dedicated to the god **Man** (born Cheung Ah Tse in AD 287), who is the God of Literature. Man also controls the destinies of civil servants (mandarins) who in ancient times were the hierarchy of the Chinese intelligentsia.

The temple is also dedicated to the God of Martial Arts or War, **Mo**, who was born

shake the bamboo sticks inside a *chim* (a canister) until a number is chosen, then go to the adjacent **Litt Shing Kung (All Saints) Temple** to consult a soothsayer. He will read your number and predict the future. The principal goddess here is Kuan Yin.

Tin Hau Temple: The grandest, most spectacular celebration dedicated to **Tin Hau**, the colony's popular Goddess of the Sea, takes place at **Da Miao** ("**The Green Temple**") in Joss House Bay when tens of thousands of people aboard hundreds of junks and public ferries converge on the hilltop temple to the accompaniment of gongs and drums. It's a memorable experience to see this colourful fleet assembled off the remote Fat Tong Mun

Kuan Yue in AD 160. (He is also known as **Kuan Ti** or **Kuan Kung**.) Mo is best known for the protection he gives people from the deprivations of war and is said to be a favourite of members of Hong Kong's underworld. Ironically, he is also found in virtually every police station. The police worship him for the same reasons that criminals do. Mo is also a patron of pawnshops and curio dealers.

Guarding the temple are **The Eight Immortals** and inside are two sacred brass deer, each about 3 feet (1 metre) high. They symbolize longevity. Inside is also a smaller shrine to **Pao Kung**, the God of Justice. If you choose to have your fortune told here, you

Peninsula in the New Territories.

The entryway to this temple is painted with a pair of **door gods** whose task is to guard against any mischief-making evil spirits who might attempt to enter. Legends indicate that this pair of gods represents two generals of the T'ang dynasty (AD 618–906), **Chiu Shu-pao** and **Hu Ching-tai**, who were able to protect the Emperor from demons by posting themselves outside the palace gates.

The main part of the temple (which houses statues of the guardian gods) is separated from an antechamber by an open court. Of particular interest here is a statue under a canopied shrine representing the god **Wong**

Tai Sin. He is one of the most popular gods in Hong Kong because he is known to generously grant the wishes of his many devotees.

The **Tin Hau Temple** in Aberdeen, meanwhile, dates back to 1851 when the present temple site was still on the seashore. Its last renovation was in 1898, but it is still in good condition. Like most traditional Taoist temples, its rooftop is bordered by miniature figures from Chinese legend and mythology.

The central shrine contains two statues of Tin Hau. The smaller one is carried in processions on festival days. This duplication of the principal deity is a common practice in Taoist temples. Numerous statues here, representing a pantheon of minor deities, illustrates the flexibility of Taoism and reflects the diverse needs, both material and spiritual, of Hong Kong's true believers. Each demigod is responsible for answering a specific request. A wrestler, for example, would be praying at the wrong door if he sought the help of a demigod known as **The Unpredictable Ghost** (whose main function is to escort souls to the underworld and is usually shown carrying gold or silver). One of the **T'u Ti**, or **Local Gods**, most of whom are related to the soil or earth, might be a more suitable benefactor. Such a patron would be specifically empowered to ensure that the wrestler experiences a soft landing when thrown to the ground.

Merciful Kuan Yin: The incorporation of gods of different faiths under one roof is also illustrated by the presence of **Kuan Yin**, the merciful goddess who is able to deliver people from misery by granting them one of her compassionate glances. A large screen, known as the **spirit screen**, blocks the way from the main entrance to the central shrine and functions to keep evil spirits out of the temple. Because it is believed that such spirits can only move in straight lines, their negative presence here is thus deflected by placing a spirit screen at strategic locations in a temple (or home). Another notable object within this temple is a drum and a bell (cast in 1726).

The temple-keepers here wear rich red robes and black silk hats as they lead worshippers from one altar to the next and call out incantations and prayers.

There are five large altars. The goddess herself is at temple centre, flanked by four large ceramic figures. One holds a large pen, supposedly to record people's good or bad habits. A second holds the goddess's gold seal. The other two characters are known as "**Favourable Wind Ear**" and "**Thousand-Li Eye**."

On a side wall are three shelves holding 60 tiny figures known as **Tai Sui**. They are the **Gods of the Year**. The Chinese calendar has a 60-year cycle and, appropriately, when people worship they pray to a god that corresponds to their age. Parents bring newborn infants (who are considered to be a year old when they are born) to worship at the **Number One God**. On Chinese Lunar New Year, everyone becomes a year older, so the same child, after New Year festivities, will be presented to the **Number Two God**, and so on. Being 60 years old is a great honour; to live through the entire 60-year cycle and start a second round is quite an achievement.

The City God: Next door (to the left) is the temple of **Shing Wong**, known as **The City God**; he is a spiritual magistrate who is expected to dole out rewards or punishments to every city dweller – an onerous task, considering the several million people who live in this city. He is also responsible for those who have already died, so Shing Wong has the needed assistance of **Ten Judges of the Underworld**. Anyone who dies has to pass the judgement of these Ten Judges, who decide whether one should be punished for wrongs done. Some of the grotesque penalties meted out are graphically depicted on the wall murals.

Next to Shing Wong is the **Fook Pak Temple** (on the far left as you enter the complex) where **To Tei (The Earth God)** and **Kuan Yin** share the places of honour. Gods of justice, war and happiness are also present. There are lots of shiny brass and redolent clouds of incense here. Out in a courtyard, under a palm tree, is an unusual icon. It is small and simple, a square-cut stone with a few carved figures near it and a box of sand for the placing of joss sticks. This is **The District God**. It attracts many worshippers, who unburden their hearts here.

Another important deity is **Kam Fa, The Goddess of Pregnant Women**. With her are 12 assistants, each of whom has a special power related to the raising of children.

The temple to the right as you face the Tin Hau Temple is the temple of **Shea Tan**, a shrine dedicated to the local community. By the entrance of this temple are sketches of a palm and a face which remind worshippers that this particular temple is for the deliverance of oracles. The shrines inside this temple belong to **Shea Kung**, a local earth god, who is a "landlord" charged with the safe-keeping of districts, villages, towns and other residential zones. Shrines are also dedicated to **The God of Wealth**, **The Unpredictable Ghost**, the 60 **Tai Sui**, **The God of War**, **The God of Literature**, **The Goddess of Mercy**, **The God of Justice** and another local deity, **Wong Tai Sin**.

A supernatural tipster: One of Hong Kong's newest temples is Kowloon City's **Wong Tai Sin Temple**, built in 1973. The first temple on the site dates only to 1921, and for its first 50 years it was private. This temple was erected in honour of **Wong Tai Sin** who has the best reputation of all the Taoist gods for the best of all reasons: he grants advice to devotees about useful horse-racing tips and he cures illness.

At the **Temple of Ten Thousand Buddhas** are literally thousands of 12-inch (30-cm) high, gold and black buddhas that line this temple's 45-foot (14-metre) high walls from base to ceiling. According to one source, there are 12,800 buddhas in the temple. Dedicated to Kuan Yin, this temple's main complex was built in 1950. Located in what was once the tiny New Territories fishing village of Shatin (now the site of the government's "new towns" housing 100,000 people), this temple is located on a hillside and is reached after climbing more than 400 steps.

There are four other temples in this complex, but they are located another 60 to 70 steps up the hill. The temple at the extreme left is dedicated to **The Jade Emperor**, the highest of all Taoist gods. The next temple has a large statue of **The God of War** and in the next shrine is a statue of Kuan Yin.

Ching Chuen Koong Temple at the 21 milestone on Castle Peak Road in Castle Peak in the New Territories comprises a Taoist temple complex and a home for the aged. Its main temple was built in 1853 and is dedicated to **Lui Tung-pin** (also known as **Lui Tung Bun** and, in Cantonese, **Liu Shui**), one of **The Eight Immortals** of Taoism.

A brief history of Taoism's spread to Hong Kong and a record of its two branches under **Chung Yuen** and **Chung Chuen** is recorded in writing on pillars in this temple.

Other notable features of this temple compound are large murals depicting various Taoist deities such as **Wong Mo** or **The Mother of the Jade Emperor**. Outdoors, stately archway, lily-ponds, willows and rock gardens frame a gracious and traditional Chinese garden. And a library here documents the 4,000-year history of Taoism.

Ching Shan or **Castle Peak Monastery** was originally established in AD 428, but the present monastery was founded by a Buddhist monk in 1918. Of particular interest here is a **fish tomb** which signifies the Buddhist belief that no form of life should be destroyed. A stone inscribed with the characters *Ko Shan Tai Yat*, "The Best Among High Mountains," rests on a peak that rises above the monastery.

Ling Tou Monastery is situated on the northern slope of Castle Peak. It is nearly 1,500 years old, but the present buildings in the Ling Tou complex are only about 200 years old.

On outlying Cheung Chau Island, the **Temple of the Jade Vacuity** is a place of note. It was built in 1783 in grateful homage to the god **Pak Tai** who drove a plague away.

Pak Tai was a Chinese prince who practised perfection nearly 3,000 years ago. When he died he was invited to become a god and was appointed **Commander of the Twelve Heavenly Legions** to fight against The **Demon King**. The most impressive feature of this temple is its characteristic Chinese roof of green concave tiles and circular ridges. It is the main rallying point during Cheung Chau's annual Bun Festival.

Po Lin Monastery on Lantau Island has perhaps the colony's most imposing traditional Chinese architecture. Its 60-foot (18-metre) high main temple establishes a tone of beauty and serenity and reigns architecturally in this monastic compound, living up to the name of the monastery, *Po Lin*, which means "Precious Lotus." The monastery's main attractions include the marble sculptures of 500 *lohan* followers of Buddha, and the icons which relate the life story of Buddha.

Petite brass deer, traditional paper lamps and bright fluorescent fixtures glow in the fine old Man Mo Temple on Hollywood Road, Western.

Chinese opera is an integral part of Chinese cultural entertainment and originates from China's earliest folk music and dances. Historically, the form of modern day Chinese opera – a definite story put to music and dance – emerged during the Sung dynasty (AD 960–1279). During the 18th century, Chinese opera came to be associated with festivals and state occasions at the Imperial Court in Beijing. But this does not mean that Chinese opera was enjoyed only by royalty and the intelligentsia.

operas, due to its development under imperial patronage. Beijing opera is characterized by the court's official dialect, Mandarin.

Shrill falsettos: The backbone of Chinese opera is the actor-singer. Not unlike Western opera stars, Chinese operatic singers undergo many years of intensive training. To achieve a proper high-pitched falsetto requires strenuous discipline and relentless dedication.

Singing artistes are in turn accompanied by a traditional Chinese orchestra. Musicians playing percussion instruments occupy

On the contrary, its very form explains its popularity among common folk. This custom survives so well in Hong Kong that during any important festival on the Chinese calendar, a performance of Chinese opera is obligatory.

Performances of Chinese opera are usually held in informal bamboo and mat theatres temporarily erected in public areas (in keeping with a tradition of building such mat-shed structures in the large patios of old Chinese homes).

Chinese opera have many cultural and regional variations. Cantonese operas, for example, are quite different from Chiu Chow

one side of the stage while others responsible for wind and string instruments sit on the opposite side, leaving the main area of the stage clear for the performers. To the novice Westerner, Chinese music seems incomprehensible, partly because little obvious melody seems involved in the instrument-playing, and also because the actors' shrill vocals usually dominate the performance. As in Shakespearean theatre, there were no actresses during Chinese opera's early development. The stage was regarded unsuitable for women, so female roles were portrayed by male actors. As in the West, however, that tradition has died.

Makeup, movements, props and specific costume colours identify an actor's age, sex and personality the moment he or she appears on stage. Actors in Beijing operas wear extremely heavy makeup, a cosmetic style derived from the use of painted masks in older operatic forms.

Cantonese and Chiu Chow operas do not feature such heavily painted faces, but makeup is still very important for dramatic effect and role identification. In Beijing opera a white patch on the nose indicates a comic character of low rank; a completely white face suggests an evil and treacherous character; a red face identifies a courageous but dim-witted man; and a black-faced actor

painted scenery background panels are usually used. And though intricately carved furniture is sometimes used, a great deal of the enjoyment of a performance is left to the audience's imagination. For example, an actor taking measured steps behind two squares of embroidered silk is indicating that he is seated on a sedan chair.

Purple for barbarians, yellow for emperors: The colour code is important – each colour identifies the rank, status and personality of the different operatic roles. Yellow is the colour of emperors, green represents a person of high rank, and purple is the mark of a barbarian general.

As in Western operas, Chinese ones incor-

is a normal, thinking person.

Headdresses are also a vital part of the Chinese opera costume: the more important the character, the more elaborate it is. There are no less than 18 types of opera beards, each symbolizing a different personality. Costumes are understandably very exaggerated in style. Though based on historical dress, they are created to achieve as great a theatrical effect as possible.

Props are normally sparse, but brilliantly

Left, getting ready for a performance in the opera is a lengthy and elaborate process. **Above**, all set for the stage.

porate a lot of mime, dance, sword-playing and acrobatics. And, for the principal artists, gesture, movement and attitude are all as important as vocal lines. Folklore, legends and historical incidents are the dramatic sources from which Chinese opera's vast repertoire is drawn.

It is perfectly acceptable for audiences of Chinese opera to arrive late for a performance, leave early, walk around and chat, or even eat during a show, which may run anywhere from 3 hours to a whole day. However, performers of Chinese opera do line up on stage to acknowledge applause at the end of a performance.

Hong Kong's nightlife image is perhaps best personified by author Richard Mason's famous character, Suzie Wong. In spite of the fact that "The World of Suzie Wong" has undergone drastic changes since the 1950s when the book and subsequent movie twitted the outside world's romantic imagination, Mason's now stereotypical image of a gentle Chinese bar girl still attracts the bachelors.

These days, however, a more accurate local nightlife image might be a Japanese businessman being teased by a topless hostess

brothels, pubs, nightclubs, and restaurants that dot these neon nightscapes.

Suzie Wong may be pushing 40, even 50, but her female heirs are young and nubile. You often have to chat and drink your way through to find her, but that Chinese girl flashing long white legs through a slit *cheongsam* is still out there.

In spite of its "Suzie Wong" reputation, Hong Kong does have enough nightlife to please anyone. From straight in-and-out porn and hardcore girlie bars – to pleasant pubs

in a pseudo-plush but very expensive Wanchai or Tsimshatsui gawk-bar.

Hong Kong tomcatting is an expensive proposition these days, but the high prices seem to be ignored by the platoons of sailors, soldiers, airmen and marines from many nations who still march into the "The Wanch" – as Suzie's world is endearingly called by residents. Gone are the heady R&R days of the Vietnam war when whole fleets would sail into "Fragrant Harbour" for a brief and raucous visit, but The Wanch, and her Kowloon sister, Tsimshatsui, are still attractive haunts. Somehow, both visiting GIs and civilians manage to find a respite in the bars,

and discos to which you could even take your mother – they're all here.

Suzie Suzuki bars?: Hong Kong not only has a variety in kind, but in price. There are only a few bars where you can quietly nurse a beer for under HK$50, while on the other side of the same street a "Japanese-style" club can set you back 10 times as much for that same amber bottle of San Mig. In the former, you can either choose to be alone or invite a "luverly" to join you for about the same price per drink. But in the Japanese clubs (Suzie Suzuki bars?) you'll pay HK$250 or more for a quarter hour of a hostess's company, *plus* the cost of her quickly quaffed drink.

The following is an after-hours survey of some of the more popular places, identified according to categories:

Girlie bars can be divided into two types – topless or non-topless, and (*á la* Suzie Wong) where you pay hostesses by the quarter hour, or where you don't.

In case you imagined that because times have changed in Wanchai there are fewer bars – fear not. Stand on Lockhart Road any evening, look through that avenue's neon collage of innumerable bar signs, and you'll find whatever or whomever your Asia dream may be, and then some; indeed, Wanchai is still alive and Suzie Wong-ing.

"True" girlie bars offer beer for about oldest "true" girlie bar on the circuit. It is not. But it looks like it is, probably because the luverlies there have not changed since the bar opened. If you are a connoisseur of bar scenes, a trip to the Red Lips is a must. To complete this trip into the colony's sensual past, also visit the **Red Lion** and **Four Sisters**. They are also "old," but their "girls" are a bit younger – reminiscent perhaps of Hong Kong in the 1950s and 1960s.

The best, most popular (with women as well as men) and oldest topless bar is the **Bottom's Up**, where four hexagonal and interconnected bars are connected by mirrors (so you are never quite certain whether you are coming or going). Topless barmaids

HK$100 and girls' drinks will cost about the same. Good examples are the **Pussycat**, the **New Makati** and **Crossroads**, both with Filipino girls in Wanchai, which are not topless; and the **Suzie Wong**, **Panda** and **Popeye** which are. Across the pond in Kowloon, meanwhile, the **Red Lion**, **Four Sisters** and **Red Lips** are also not topless.

The aging Red Lips: There are some Hong Kong hands who say the Red Lips is the

sit in the middle of these six-sided "bars" on very large swivel stools that look more like sunken swivel-beds. Others in this genre include the **Kismet** and the **New Lido**. But be warned that most of the topless bars located in Kowloon, perhaps with the exception of the Bottom's Up, are designed with the rich Japanese businessman's pocketbook in mind.

The hostess clubs are definitely aimed at big spenders, which means the majority of their patrons are Japanese. Indeed, many of these even have Japanese names, such as the **Ginza** and **Kokusai** (both located in Kowloon). The **Copacabana**, **New Playboy**

Left, a swanky hostess club in Kowloon – this one previously had the same name as a well-known Swedish car maker, who was not at all amused. **Above,** a hospitable barmaid at Mad Dogs.

and **Latin Quarter** are somewhat more universal in appeal, as are Hong Kong's **Mitoro Fujiya** and **Dai-ichi**. The **Korea Palace** – with Korean hostesses – is a favourite hangout for both Japanese and Korean businessmen.

The two biggest hostess clubs in Hong Kong are **Club B Boss** and **China City Night Club**, each with nearly 1,000 girls. Other clubs include the **Mandarin Palace Night Club, Club Metropolitan, Caesar's Night Club, Club Cabaret** and the **New Tonnochy**. As you would imagine, Hong Kong has not escaped the karaoke invasion and most clubs feature it. Two places specialising in it are **Club Karaoke** (China

Old China Hand and **Horse and Groom**. Two other Hong Kong taverns are the **Shakespeare**, and **Mad Dogs**.

Back across the harbour are the **Cutty Sark** (one of the most expensive), the **China Coast Pub** (Airport Meridien), the **White Stag** and the **Blacksmith's Arm**, plus three distinctively Aussie pubs – **Ned Kelly's Last Stand**, the **Stoned Crow** and the **Kangeroo Pub**.

Filipino dance bands are standard fare here, as they are throughout Asia, but beyond such *mabuhay* sound spots, there are only a few bars in Honkers where you can hear live rock or jazz. These few, however, should not be missed. The **Dicken's Bar** in the Excelsior Hotel has jazz, mostly on Sundays (on other

Merchants Hotels) and **Kara Karaoke** (New World Harbour View Hotel).

Pre-fab pubs: One of the more pleasant nightlife changes in Hong Kong has been the rebirth of more pubs or taverns for those who prefer a type of conviviality which was previously only available in more expensive and subdued hotel bars. That's probably because a group of pre-fab pubs have hit Hong Kong and have set the colony's newest getting-pissed style. The first of these were the **Bull and Bear** and the **Jockey**, both in Central. It was just a matter of time until a pub or tavern hit The Wanch and within staggering distance of each other are now the

days it's a proper pub). **The Godown** is one of the first clubs to schedule folk and jazz nights. In Kowloon, **Ned Kelly's Last Stand** swings from folk to jazz and rock, while **Jazz Club** (Lan Kwai Fong) is the place to hear foreign musicians; while **Hardy's** in Wanchai is known for its folk music. For wine bars, try **Brown's**; for champagne, the **Champagne Bar** (Grand Hyatt).

Piano bars, discos and dancing halls: True cocktail lounges and piano bars exist here too, but virtually all are in hotels. Some of these bars are pure piano bars; others have a husky-voiced female vocalist accompanied by a small combo or solo guitarist. All are pleasant and quiet places to meet a friend or simply be left alone. Recommended are the **Lobby Lounge** in the Marriott Hotel and **Cyrano's** in the Island Shangri-La Hotel, **Great Wall** in the Sheraton, the **Inn Bar** in the Holiday Inn-Golden Mile, **Royal Falcon** in the Royal Garden, **The Flying Machine** in the Airport Meridien, the **Chin Chin** in the Hyatt Regency and the **Gun Bar** in the Hong Kong Hotel. All are in Kowloon. The **Dragon Boat** in the Hilton, **Captain's Bar** in the Mandarin, **Yum Sing** in the Lee Gardens, **Lau Ling** in the Furama Kempinski Intercontinental, and the **Oasis** in the New World Harbour View Hotel are, likewise, all in Hong Kong.

97 (in Lan Kwai Fong) and **J.J.'s** (Grand Hyatt). Hong Kong discos, however, can be expensive boogie experiences. Entrance fees (which include two drinks) range from HK$50 to HK$100.

There are not many Western-style supper clubs left. In fact, the **Pink Giraffe** in the Sheraton is one of the few left. However, the Hilton often hosts special dinner theatre shows in their ballroom, so keep an eye on nightlife ads to find out what's scheduled there. There are also a few Chinese supper clubs still operating, but these are usually not very popular with Western tourists. Likewise, Chinese ballrooms, in which you buy tickets to taxi-dance with painted and pow-

And what would Hong Kong's nightlife be without a pulsing disco scene? Hong Kong's rather late answer to Studio 54 or Regine's is **Canton** where the "chic seek to meet" as the saying goes. Vying for the colony's best boogie bar title are **Hot Gossip**, **Manhattan** and **Apollo 18**, (complete with a robot greeter). Disco records also spin eternally at **Inn Place** (Holiday Inn-Golden Mile) and **Hollywood East** (Regal Meridien), **Nation**

dered ladies, can be a language problem. You'll be amazed at how much lighter your pocketbook has become when you leave such establishments.

Another pleasant diversion are the colony's floating supper clubs. Entertainment isn't great, but the scenery from these air-conditioned nightclubs that cruise through the harbour is superb, making for a memorable and romantic evening.

Common sense rules: The same prudent rules of common sense apply in Hong Kong's bar as they do in any other fun-loving country. Don't flash all your cash. Perhaps it is even wise to leave most of it in a hotel safe

Far left, pumping up the volume at Hot Gossip.
Left, J.J.'s at the Grand Hyatt is definitely "in."
Above, Lan Kwai Fong has more than its share of choice spots.

deposit box with your passport. Though most bars have credit card decals, you'll find it is difficult to pay with them because cashiers will keep saying things like "cash discount." A little perseverance, and plastic payments should work.

Though there is a saying referring to yachts that "if you have to ask the price, it isn't for you," that advice could also be applied to women. However, it will save you a lot of hassle if you know the score before you tuck in. Most Wanchai/Tsimshatsui bars have a sign posted somewhere advertising the cost of drinks for you, and for her, plus the escort rental time and fees. Look for this sign or ask, to avoid later arguments over your bill.

bars, and can be higher than HK$5,000 in classier hostess joints. If you are considering a "buy out," you might consider sleeping during the day so you can leave with the girl after work hours, and after serious negotiation, of course.

Which leads us to the subject of guest houses. Some of the conservative hotels don't allow a man to toddle in with a rent-a-bird in the middle of the night. But as you can imagine, there are plenty of "cheap guest houses" in both Wanchai and Tsimshatsui which will cater to your every impetuous need. These places usually rent rooms by the hour, or two, but an all night price can be negotiated during low-occupancy periods.

Beware of piling on drinks (unless you can afford it, of course) when a hostess brings her lovely friend over to your table. It is good for the ego to be surrounded by caressing women who laugh at your bad jokes, but the clock is ticking doubletime and you can't plead later that "I didn't ask for her, and her, and..."

In the topless bars, the local rule is "no touchee," unless of course you have an inspired gift of gab – and grab. A hint: barmaids usually do not have drinks bought for them, because they are not, strictly speaking, hostesses. But they rarely refuse the gesture.

On "buying out": A "buying out" fee may top HK$500 in some of the cheaper girlie

The best "guest houses" are in Kowloon Tong and easily found by taxi from Tsimshatsui. Here, depending on your pocketbook's bulge, you can rent anything from a straight room to one with a heart-shaped vibrating bed surrounded by mirrors – by the hour or all-night. Your choice.

The biggest problems for foreigners out on the town are encountered in Chinese ballrooms. Some are straight, but many are "controlled" by alleged local triad heavies. Therefore, any argument which develops is quickly subdued by efficient "enforcers." Girls who join your table and with whom you dance (to abbreviated dance numbers) cost about HK$100 for a 10-minute long tête-à-tête.

Customer drinks cost about the same as in other bars. Dance hostesses make their money by time, not by the drinks they sell, so they often drink along with their customers, at the same price. Local intelligence indicates that ballroom girls are an easier "buy out" than those in other bars, but the buying-out fee is still exorbitantly high in the swankier ballrooms (and language may prove to be a problem).

If you *really* get into Hong Kong's nightlife, you may be offered a chance to experience a hush-hush "floorshow" in a "private club." These clandestine shows feature simu-

about HK$500 an hour on a 5-hour minimum companionship.

Rent-a-bird: If you drop by an escort agency, you can thumb through photo books there and choose the lady of your dreams. If not, it is potluck escort affair. Rent-a-birds come in all shapes, sizes and nationalities so that Europeans can fulfill their fondest cross-cultural fantasies with Asians, and vice versa. Officially, of course, you are just hiring a woman for her charming conversation, good looks and to accompany you to dinner or a party. Any other conquests are subject to negotiation.

If you have visited Bangkok or Manila and the word "massage" brings back idyllic fan-

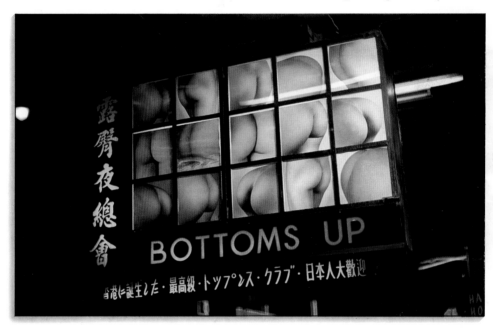

lated sex, and their cost is relative to their eroticism. However, the shows are quick (usually about 20 minutes) and you pay HK$100 or more per act. Drinks are extra, of course. These shows, however, are said to be not nearly as good as those staged in some other parts of the Wicked East.

For nighthawks who can't be bothered with a bar, club or restaurant ambience, female company is but a phone call away. There are a dozen or so escort agencies which will supply you with a companion for

<u>Left</u>, kara is okay if you sound like Sinatra – or had a few too many. <u>Above</u>, a Hong Kong institution.

tasies of kneady Thai or Filipino establishments, Hong Kong will certainly be a rude awakening. Most of the colony's massage "parlours" are mobile – meaning the lasses come to you.

However, by making a modest reservation, you can still get your tired and harried bod back on the right path *chez vous*. A massage costs about HK$300 for 1½ hours and usually includes a bath. It seems fairly easy for the masseuse to gain entrance to hotel rooms during the day. And for a straight sauna and massage, most Hong Kong hotels have good health club facilities which are excellent.

PLACES

Queen Victoria's consort must have offered a right royal chuckle when a messenger delivered the news that Hong Kong was to be added to their Empire.

"Albert," tut-tutted the Queen, "is so much amused by my having got the island of Hong Kong, and we think Victoria ought to be called Princess of Hong Kong in addition to Princess Royal."

Her Majesty couldn't have been criticized for lack of prescience, as Hong Kong Island has little to recommend it: the coastline is rugged, there isn't a single river, not much arable farmland, and no engineer has ever found a trace of mineral on this once-desolate tropical isle.

All that Hong Kong was ever good for – according to the opium merchants who took it as booty – was 17 sq. miles (45 sq. km) of the best deepwater harbour in the area. Her harbour could shelter ships from any storm, be they torrential typhoons or the emotional outpourings of an obstreperous Chinese emperor.

But Hong Kong Island is only a part of the Crown Colony. True, until World War II, it was the most important part, politically and economically. But like Julius Caesar's Rome, all of Hong Kong can be divided into four parts – Hong Kong Island, Kowloon, the New Territories, and the colony's numerous outlying islands.

The "**island**," as it's popularly known, is 29 sq. miles (75 sq. km) of topsy-turvy real estate. The earliest British settlements were established here, so consequently Queen Victoria's little "joke" (and the place her Foreign Secretary, Lord Palmerston, called a "barren island with hardly a house upon it") is now dominated by great banks and counting houses, enormous futuristic buildings, opulent hotels, splendid residences on Victoria Peak, fine beach resorts, and the colony's oldest Chinese communities.

Across Hong Kong Harbour – 2 minutes by the underwater Mass Transit Railway, 7 minutes by the venerable Star Ferry and less than 10 minutes by car through the two tunnels – is the mainland town of **Kowloon**, a residential-industrial complex packed into 3.75 miles (6 km). Kowloon was ceded to the British in 1860 (under the Treaty of Peking) so the insecure Brits could better defend the harbour. Most tourists see only the tip of Kowloon, the **Tsimshatsui** district, which is Kowloon's trading venue and the site of her many hotels, bars and posh shopping centres.

This land parcel, on the southeastern tip of mainland Asia, was originally developed as the terminal for a railroad which in the old days would carry colonial passengers through China and Czarist Russia all the way to Paris, the west coast of France, and ultimately, back to London. A second purpose was for godowns to store goods being ferried to the island. The third, less savoury reason, was that Kowloon was a convenient place for prosperous British merchants

Preceding pages: big city skyline on Hong Kong island; owning a boat in Hong Kong is one way of saying that your ship has come in; Tin Hau temple in Causeway Bay; pretty maids all in a row – children at Cheung Chau's Bun Festival. **Left**, a bird's eye view of some of the most expensive real estate in the world.

to house their mistresses. The government didn't sanction either mistresses or brothels on the island, but they hardly could control the mainland.

North from Tsimshatsui along Nathan Road are the **Yaumatei** and **Mongkok** districts. The latter has the dubious distinction of being listed in the *Guinness Book of Records* as the place with the densest population concentration on earth: 165,000 residents per sq. km!

East of Mongkok is **Kai Tak Airport**. To the north are numerous resettlement areas and **Boundary Street**, perhaps the most important "separation point" in the colony.

Boundary Street marks the demarcation line between Hong Kong colony, granted to the British in "perpetuity" (but which will be given up to the Chinese in 1997), and the New Territories (NT), which don't belong to the United Kingdom but instead were leased in 1898 by the Convention of Peking for a 99-year period (which ends in 1997).

The NT used to be called "unspoiled." A century ago, when it was known as "The Emperor's Rice Bowl" for its fine arable land, it must have had a verdant beauty. Today, though, its towns house countless factories that are hardly beautiful in an 18th-century unspoiled sense. "Progress" and population pressures have caused the government to instigate "new town" projects. "Little" market towns like **Tsuen Wan**, now has a population of 700,000, and a once-tiny pirate port like **Tuen Mun** is fast expanding to house 600,000.

However, still in the NT are the colony's spacious Chinese University, some quaint walled villages and traditional rural architecture. The main old towns of the NT include **Shatin** with its new racecourse and university, the northern settlements of **Tai Po** and **Fanling** (with its championship golf course), **Sheung Shui**, and, near the last train stop before China, the border town of **Lo Wu**.

Recently, the border hasn't really stopped there; Beijing (government) authorities have allowed the district of **Shum Chun (Shenzhen)** to be used as a duty-free export area; consequently, many Hong Kong businessmen commute over the border on an almost daily basis, joining farmers who have done so since a border was drawn.

Most of the latter towns are near **Tolo Harbour**. Tolo Channel on the east goes up to **Mirs Bay** and China, while the harbour's northern reaches flow towards the still somewhat unspoiled district of **Sai Kung**. To the west are farms, and **Tai Mo Shan**, the highest mountain in the colony, at 3,142 feet (957 metres). The westernmost sector is called **Castle Peak**. And due north is **Deep Bay**, on the China border.

Along with the New Territories, British Hong Kong has leased 234 islands which will also revert to China in 1997. (The exceptions are little Stonecutters Island and Hong Kong Island). Few of these islands are inhabited, and they are probably reminiscent of what Hong Kong Island itself looked like more than a century ago.

Hong Kong's spectacular success is a reflection of the sheer determination and single-minded approach of its people.

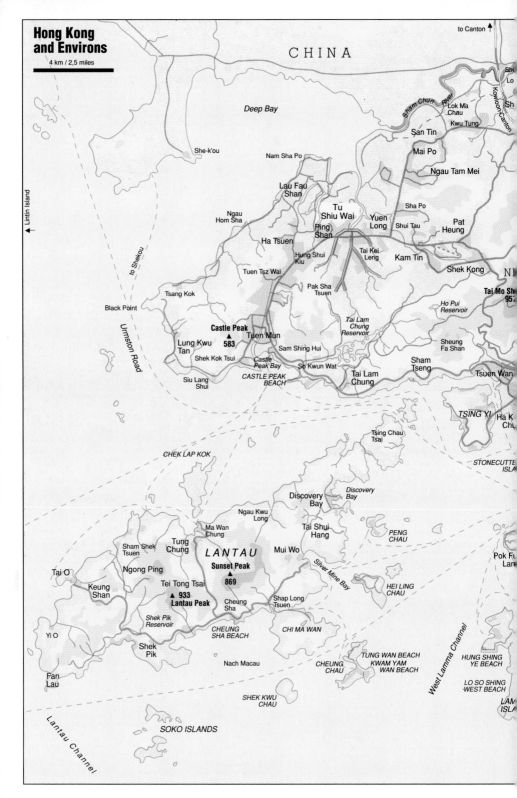

Hong Kong and Environs

4 km / 2,5 miles

CHINA

to Canton

Deep Bay

She-k'ou

Lintin Island

to Shekou

Black Point

Urmston Road

Lung Kwu Tan

Shek Kok Tsui

Siu Lang Shui

Tsang Kok

Castle Peak ▲ 583

Tuen Mun

Castle Peak Bay

CASTLE PEAK BEACH

Sam Shing Hui

So Kwun Wat

Nam Sha Po

Ngau Hom Sha

Lau Fau Shan

Ha Tsuen

Tuen Tsz Wai

Hung Shui Kiu

Tu Shiu Wai

Ping Shan

Pak Sha Tsuen

Tai Kei Leng

Yuen Long

Shui Tau

San Tin

Mai Po

Ngau Tam Mei

Sha Po

Pat Heung

Kam Tin

Lok Ma Chau

Kwu Tung

Kowloon-Canton

Sh Lo

Sh

Sham Chun River

Shek Kong

Tai Lam Chung Reservoir

Ho Pui Reservoir

Sheung Fa Shan

Sham Tseng

Tai Lam Chung

Tsuen Wan

N
Tai Mo Sh 95

CHEK LAP KOK

Tsing Chau Tsai

TSING YI

Ha K Chu

STONECUTTE ISLA

Discovery Bay

Discovery Bay

Ngau Kwu Long

Ma Wan Chung

Tai Shui Hang

Mui Wo

PENG CHAU

Pok Fu Lan

Tai O

Keung Shan

Yi O

Fan Lau

Sham Shek Tsuen

Tung Chung

Ngong Ping

Tei Tong Tsai

▲ 933 Lantau Peak

Shek Pik Reservoir

Shek Pik

LANTAU

Sunset Peak ▲ 869

Cheung Sha

CHEUNG SHA BEACH

Nach Macau

Shap Long Tsuen

Silver Mine Bay

CHI MA WAN

CHEUNG CHAU

HEI LING CHAU

TUNG WAN BEACH
KWAM YAM WAN BEACH

West Lamma Channel

HUNG SHING YE BEACH

LO SO SHING WEST BEACH

LAM ISLA

SHEK KWU CHAU

SOKO ISLANDS

Lantau Channel

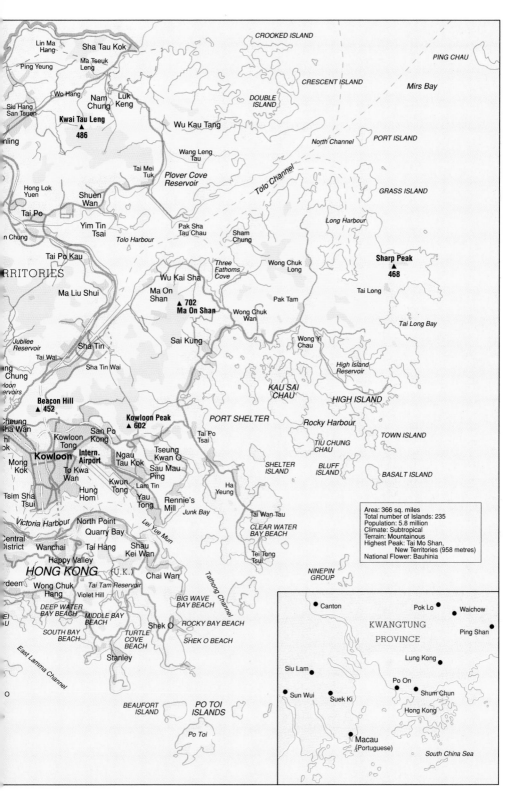

CROOKED ISLAND

PING CHAU

Lin Ma Hang
Sha Tau Kok
Ma Tseuk Leng
Ping Yeung
Siu Hang San Tsuen
Wo Hang
Nam Chung
Luk Keng
Kwai Tau Leng ▲ 486
nling
Wu Kau Tang
CRESCENT ISLAND
Mirs Bay
DOUBLE ISLAND
Wang Leng Tau
Tai Mei Tuk
Plover Cove Reservoir
North Channel
PORT ISLAND
Tolo Channel
GRASS ISLAND
Hong Lok Yuen
Shuen Wan
Tai Po
Yim Tin Tsai
Pak Sha Tau Chau
Sham Chung
Long Harbour
n Chung
Tai Po Kau
Tolo Harbour
RRITORIES
Ma Liu Shui
Wu Kai Sha
Three Fathoms Cove
Wong Chuk Long
Sharp Peak ▲ 468
Ma On Shan
▲ 702 Ma On Shan
Wong Chuk Wan
Pak Tam
Tai Long
Tai Long Bay
Jubilee Reservoir
Sha Tin
Sai Kung
Wong Yi Chau
Tai Wal
ng Chung
loon rvoirs
Sha Tin Wai
High Island Reservoir
Beacon Hill ▲ 452
Kowloon Peak ▲ 602
PORT SHELTER
KAU SAI CHAU
HIGH ISLAND
heung ha Wan
hi ok
Kowloon Tong
San Po Kong
Tai Po Tsai
Rocky Harbour
TOWN ISLAND
Mong Kok
Kowloon
Intern. Airport
Ngau Tau Kok
Tseung Kwan O
TIU CHUNG CHAU
To Kwa Wan
Sau Mau Ping
SHELTER ISLAND
BLUFF ISLAND
BASALT ISLAND
Tsim Sha Tsui
Hung Hom
Kwun Tong
Lam Tin
Ha Yeung
Yau Tong
Rennie's Mill
Victoria Harbour
North Point
Junk Bay
Tai Wan Tau
Central District
Quarry Bay
Wanchai
Tai Hang
Shau Kei Wan
CLEAR WATER BAY BEACH
NINEPIN GROUP
Happy Valley
HONG KONG (U.K.)
Chai Wan
Tei Tong Tsui
rdeen
Wong Chuk Hang
Tai Tam Reservoir
Violet Hill
BIG WAVE BAY BEACH
DEEP WATER BAY BEACH
MIDDLE BAY BEACH
ROCKY BAY BEACH
EI U
SOUTH BAY BEACH
TURTLE COVE BEACH
Shek O
SHEK O BEACH
Stanley
East Lamma Channel
o
BEAUFORT ISLAND
PO TOI ISLANDS
Po Toi

Area: 366 sq. miles
Total number of Islands: 235
Population: 5.8 million
Climate: Subtropical
Terrain: Mountainous
Highest Peak: Tai Mo Shan,
    New Territories (958 metres)
National Flower: Bauhinia

Canton
Pok Lo
Waichow
KWANGTUNG PROVINCE
Ping Shan
Lung Kong
Siu Lam
Po On
Sun Wui
Suek Ki
Shum Chun
Hong Kong
Macau
(Portuguese)
South China Sea

171

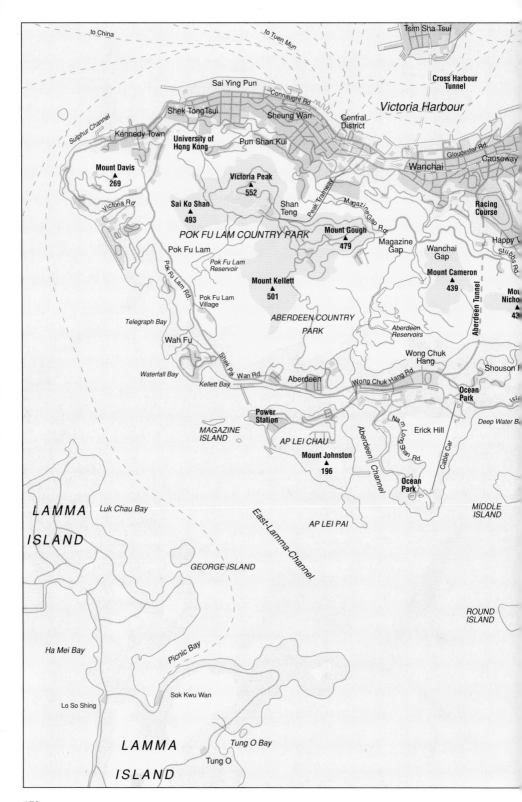

to China

to Tuen Mun

Tsim Sha Tsui

Cross Harbour Tunnel

Victoria Harbour

Sai Ying Pun

Connaught Rd

Shek Tong Tsui

Sheung Wan

Central District

Gloucester Rd.

University of Hong Kong

Pun Shan Kui

Wanchai

Causeway

Kennedy Town

Sulphur Channel

▲ Mount Davis
269

Victoria Rd

Victoria Peak
▲ 552

Shan Teng

Racing Course

Peak Tramway

Magazine Gap Rd

Happy V

Stubbs Rd

Sai Ko Shan
▲ 493

POK FU LAM COUNTRY PARK

Mount Gough
▲ 479

Magazine Gap

Wanchai Gap

Mount Cameron
▲ 439

Mou
Nicho
▲ 43

Pok Fu Lam

Pok Fu Lam Rd.

Pok Fu Lam Reservoir

Mount Kellett
▲ 501

ABERDEEN COUNTRY PARK

Aberdeen Tunnel

Pok Fu Lam Village

Telegraph Bay

Wah Fu

Aberdeen Reservoirs

Wong Chuk Hang

Shouson H

Waterfall Bay

Shek Pai Wan Rd.

Aberdeen

Wong Chuk Hang Rd.

Ocean Park

Isla

Kellett Bay

MAGAZINE ISLAND

Power Station

AP LEI CHAU

Na m Long Shan Rd.

Erick Hill

Cable Car

Deep Water B.

Mount Johnston
▲ 196

Aberdeen Channel

Ocean Park

MIDDLE ISLAND

LAMMA

Luk Chau Bay

ISLAND

AP LEI PAI

East-Lamma Channel

ROUND ISLAND

GEORGE ISLAND

Ha Mei Bay

Picnic Bay

Lo So Shing

Sok Kwu Wan

LAMMA

Tung O Bay

ISLAND

Tung O

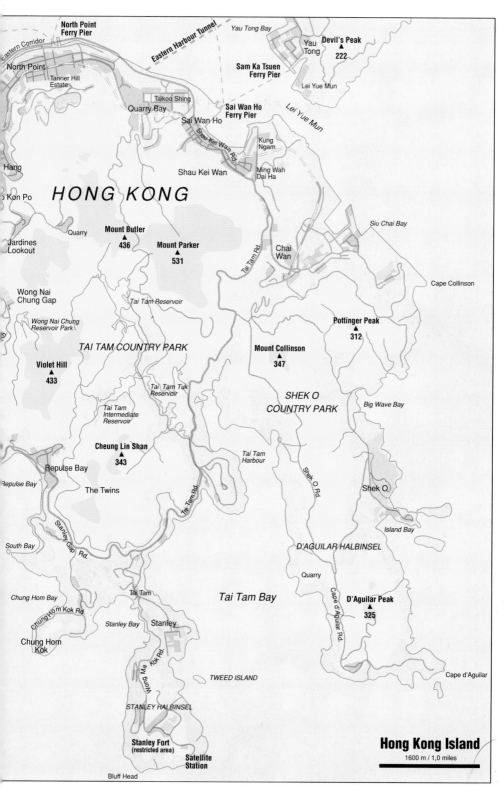

North Point
Ferry Pier

eastern Corridor

North Point

Tanner Hill
Estate

Eastern Harbour Tunnel

Yau Tong Bay

Yau
Tong

Devil's Peak
▲
222

Sam Ka Tsuen
Ferry Pier

Lei Yue Mun

Taikoo Shing

Quarry Bay

Sai Wan Ho
Ferry Pier

Sai Wan Ho

Shau Kei Wan Rd.

Lei Yue Mun

Hang

Kung
Ngam

Kon Po

Shau Kei Wan

Ming Wah
Dai Ha

HONG KONG

Quarry

Mount Butler
▲
436

Mount Parker
▲
531

Siu Chai Bay

Jardines
Lookout

Tai Tam Rd.

Chai
Wan

Cape Collinson

Wong Nai
Chung Gap

Tai Tam Reservoir

Pottinger Peak
▲
312

Wong Nai Chung
Reservoir Park

TAI TAM COUNTRY PARK

Mount Collinson
▲
347

Violet Hill
▲
433

Tai Tam Tuk
Reservoir

SHEK O
COUNTRY PARK

Big Wave Bay

Tai Tam
Intermediate
Reservoir

Cheung Lin Shan
▲
343

Tai Tam
Harbour

Repulse Bay

Tai Tam Rd.

Shek O Rd.

Shek O

Repulse Bay

The Twins

Island Bay

South Bay

Stanley Gap Rd.

D'AGUILAR HALBINSEL

Quarry

Chung Hom Bay

Tai Tam

Tai Tam Bay

Cape d'Aguilar Rd.

D'Aguilar Peak
▲
325

Chung Hom Kok Rd.

Stanley Bay

Stanley

Chung Hom
Kok

Wong Ma Kok Rd.

TWEED ISLAND

Cape d'Aguilar

STANLEY HALBINSEL

Stanley Fort
(restricted area)

Satellite
Station

Bluff Head

Hong Kong Island

1600 m / 1,0 miles

HONG KONG, "THE ISLAND"

Wall Street, Fifth Avenue, the Bourse: However barren it was a century ago, nobody standing in the middle of Hong Kong Island could ever imagine it as anything but a great metropolis and an entrepôt to the world's third largest port. Its highrises pop up everywhere, with a futuristic look. Fifty-storey buildings are more common than 10-storey buildings. And the colony's old grey bank image is quickly being superceded by mirrored, metallic and white-slick office structures. The **Central** business district is a combination of Wall Street, Washington, Fifth Avenue, the Bourse, The City and an architectural merry-go-round.

Yet for all its urban pull, this Central vortex serves the same purpose it did nearly 150 years ago. The port, with its 7,000 visiting ships a year, was the colony's *raison d'etre*; along the old harbourfront were all her important business and banking houses, and her residents were housed in squalid and opulent suburbs around Central, where they still live today.

True, nobody realised then how much reclamation would transform the city. (Originally, Queen's Road formed the port area.) And it wasn't until relatively recently that the south side of the island was utilized extensively. Consequently, that area is still the most pleasant place in all Hong Kong.

To see the north side of Hong Kong island (the side facing Kowloon) at its best costs only HK$1 aboard one of the ancient double-decker trams which rattle along – certainly one of the great travel bargains in the world. Incidentally, Trams Tours are available as well as a special Hong Kong innovation – the private Tram Party.

Climbing the Peak: The island is dominated by **Victoria Peak** (known simply as "The Peak"). As long ago as 1860, the Governor of the colony suggested that more affluent Europeans should take up residence on the cooler Peak. This is still where the richest members of the colony live.

Mystical and mythical Central: The centre of any great world capital is dominated by its government offices (usually of austere Roman-granite architecture), and perhaps a statue to a great past ruler in an adjoining park.

Hong Kong's **Central District** is no exception. Except that the *real* government of Hong Kong is its banks. So when one exits from the **Star Ferry** underpass, looking ahead at the great concrete vista to the south, he or she sees the spires of two of Hong Kong's three main banks – the modernistic US$1 billion Hongkong Bank (reputedly the most expensive building in the world), and to its right, the Standard Chartered Bank. Let your eye wander past the old Bank of China Building to the left of the Hongkong Bank to the gleaming 1,209-foot (368-metre) high Bank of China Tower, opposite the Hilton Hotel on Garden Road, with its pair of chopsticks pointing upward from the roof. (Behind it is Citibank Plaza.) The Bank of China's sharp angles point directly at the other financial institutions, a bad (or good depending which side you're on) *fung shui* omen. And the park in the foreground, once graced with a statue of Queen Victoria, today frames only a **statue of Sir Thomas Jackson**, a chap who managed the Hongkong and Shanghai Bank for 30 years at the end of the 19th century.

For all its hard-boned, materialistic, economic, business and capitalistic realism, there is something mystical about Central District. After all, a century ago nearly all of this hard ground was under water. And reclamation here has been astonishing, making up virtually all Central.

There are few truly historic buildings to give real character to Central. The blue-and-white **Hong Kong Club** was demolished in 1981 and has been replaced by a modern skyscraper. But the colonial-style **Supreme Court Building**, once evacuated in mid-session because its foundations were undermined by the construction of the MTR (the underground railway) running in the

*acific Place
s a huge
ood,
hopping and
ntertainment
omplex.

area, is now repaired and houses the Legislative Council.

The money of Central is mythical. So complex is the business of buying and selling land and property here, and so incestuous are the corporations which trade with each other, that at one auction in September 1980, a record high of HK$26,245 per sq. foot was the price realised to purchase land for a new office building site. Office space in Central was renting for HK$27 and up per sq. foot in January 1981, and selling for an average of HK$4,500 per sq. foot. So all-consuming is the business of doing business here that the "government" itself is shunted to the sidelines. The Governor lives fairly isolated on Upper Albert Road at **Government House**, which dates from 1855 and is not accessible to the public.

Colonial crumbs: The Victorian-Gothic **St John's Cathedral**, inaugurated in 1849 and the colony's oldest Anglican church, is tucked away behind the Hilton Hotel on Battery Path Road. The red brick **French Mission Building**, now housing government offices, is one of two other modest examples of 19th-century architecture, but is hardly worth the climb up the hill in the heat. The other is **Flagstaff House**, home to the **Museum of Tea Ware** (enter from Cotton Tree Drive) and is reputedly Hong Kong's oldest surviving building. It was once the residence of the British commanding general, when the area was known as Victoria Barracks.

Today, that vast expanse is **Hong Kong Park**, and houses, among other things, aviaries and botanical gardens. That object looking like the tower of a mosque is an observation tower, and a great place to photograph the area – if you can make it up the steps. You can enter the park from Cotton Tree Drive or through Pacific Place on Queensway.

But these buildings are aberrations. More to the Central style is **The Landmark** (they don't even call it a building), a structure opened in 1980 on Des Voeux Road on the site of the old Gloucester Hotel (which was demolished for the New Gloucester Building, which in turn

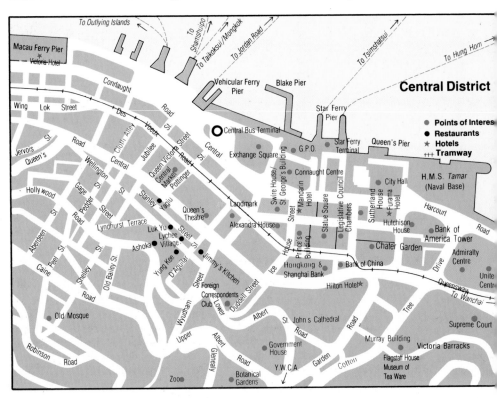

Central District

Points of Interest
Restaurants
Hotels
Tramway

was destroyed to make way for The Landmark). Five floors surround a vast 20,000-sq.-foot (6,000-sq.-metre) atrium with 100 shops. The fountain in the middle has been constructed with a cover above it to form a stage.

The best place to begin one's Central tour is at the **Star Ferry Terminal**. Blinking at the right of the Hong Kong piers is the unmistakable polka-dotted **Jardine House**, whose distinctive round windows have inspired the Chinese to nickname it the "House of a Thousand Orifices." The **Hong Kong Tourist Association's** (HKTA's) **Information & Gift Centre** dispenses handy pamphlets and has a good supply of souvenirs in the basement shopping arcade. Hong Kong's Filipino community gathers in strength here and in Statue Square at weekends.

Just behind this holey wonder is the **General Post Office** (GPO) and the **Government Information Service Bookshop**. Across the street to the west from the GPO and Jardine House are the shiny towers of Exchange Square, one

of the most modern office complexes in the world and the home of the Hong Kong Stock Exchange. The shopping arcade there is called **The Forum**. Even further west is the **Outlying District's Ferry Pier** where *Hongkongians* hop a ferry, to escape to one of the more peaceful outer islands, and the **Macau Ferry Terminal** and **helipad**, both in the **Shun Tak Centre**. All can be reached by an overhead walkway from the Star Ferry.

To the left is **City Hall**. This complex houses a concert hall and theatre, a number of offices and most important, billboards which advertise cultural programmes for the month – an obvious necessity for tourists searching for something artistic.

Across Connaught Road Central is an open space full of fountains and things that look like benches for bus stops. This is **Statue Square**, Central's "green" lung and gathering place for the thousands of Filipina maids on Sundays. Adjacent to the East is the art deco former **Ritz-Carlton Hotel**, next door

On work days, Central's streets are clogged with humanity (below), but there's still room for a tai chi session (right).

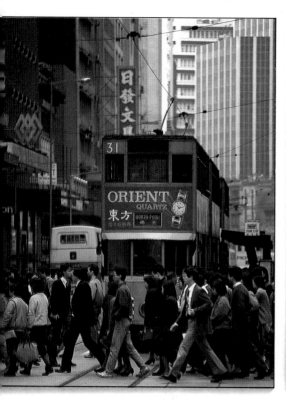

to the **Furama-Kempinski Hotel**. Across Murray Road, lined up along the very short **Lambeth Walk**, best known for the **Bull 'n' Bear Pub** are Hutchison House and Bank of America Tower, from whence you can connect to the overhead walkways East to the buildings on Queensway and the Admiralty MTR station.

Upon emerging from an underpass which fronts the Star Ferry Terminal, one finds oneself on Connaught Road Central. To the right, the swank **Mandarin-Oriental Hotel** is connected by walkway over the Chater Road to **Prince's Building** and its shopping mall, which in turn has a walkway over Ice House Street to Alexandra House. From Alexandra House, a system of walkways leads to the Landmark and Swire House, which is interconnected to World Wide House (over Pedder Street) and Jardine House (over Connaught Road) and beyond to the General Post Office, the Star Ferry, Exchange Square and West to the ferry piers. Don't panic. It is easier to walk than read. To the left of Connaught Road Central is **Statue Square**, with its war memorial and a statue of Sir Thomas Jackson.

Behind this pedestrian pivot point on Des Voeux Road, the colony's great new buildings begin their grand sweep. Queen's Road was the original "Main Street," but a little footpath in front of the Queen's Road godowns and counting houses was later turned into Des Voeux. Central has also spread east along Queensway. The walkway from the Murray Road Carpark, which you can get to from the aforementioned Bank of America and Hutchison House, leads you to the packed shopping arcades of **Admiralty Centre** and **United Centre**, with the Admiralty MTR station below.

There is also a walkway from the Hilton Hotel's Garden Road side, across Queen's Road, along the other side of the Murray Road Carpark ending up in a strange looking building, Bond Centre, from which there is a walkway to the **Supreme Court**. Normally, visitors would not be interested in Hong Kong's law courts but in this case, they are

The lobby of the posh Landmark building.

located next to one of Hong Kong's finest shopping and entertainment sites, **Pacific Place** on Queensway. (You can also get to Pacific Place by a walkway from Admiralty).

Don't let the instructions put you off (you'll welcome the walkways in the rain), they are easy to follow. At the end of the walkway is the Hong Kong Island up-market version of Kowloon's all-in-one Ocean Centre/Ocean Terminal/Harbour City complex.

This vast, air-conditioned concrete expanse contains shops, restaurants, bars, cinemas and three hotels (the Marriott, Conrad and Island Shangri-La – each with their own restaurants and shops). You could "visit" Hong Kong without ever leaving its confines.

A chic chandlery: Up on Queen's Road is the new site of **Lane Crawford**, the single most famous luxury department store in Asia. Founded in the mid-1850s by a sea captain who wanted to outfit visiting ships, Lane Crawford today hardly poses as a ship chandlery. But to the west, along Queen's Road, are dozens of *real* ship chandleries, on the same site where, decades ago, ships did dock and take on stock.

Befitting its role as the site of "original" Hong Kong, Queen's Road beyond this point becomes less grandiose and has traditional crafts shops on its Western district flank. Here are shops making kitchen utensils like knives and *wok*, tea merchants, swallows' nest merchants (one of the largest is at 331 Queen's Road Central), calligraphy suppliers and silversmiths.

While in "**lower**" Central, one should also explore some of the side streets between Queen's Road and Des Voeux Road. Just west of the D'Aguilar Street are two interesting little streets – **Li Yuen Street East** and **Li Yuen Street West** – which have stalls and shops that sell clothing, look-alike high fashion accessories and fabrics galore. Bargaining is expected here. Another popular "cloth alley" is the one closer to Western, on Wing On Street just west of the **Central Market**.

On Queen's Road looking south, one realizes why Hong Kong was considered basically worthless when first taken over. The original island, before reclamation, was simply a huge mountain. Behind Queen's Road, the old waterfront road, is a hill which rises precipitously from sea level. Climb up **Ice House** or **Wyndham** streets till they meet. That old, triangular-shaped ice storage building (circa 1911) is now the house of **Foreign Correspondents** and the **Fringe** clubs. Wyndham is lined with shops.

Another worthwhile climb is D'Aguilar Street with its fascinating boutiques. Stanley Street, just off D'Aguilar, has some excellent restaurants, a few antique shops and camera shops. Continuing up D'Aguilar, cross Wellington Street and proceed through the tiny flower market. On the right is **Wo On Lane** with its fun shops. Farther along, two lanes open off at both sides. The one on the left is the "L"-shaped **Lan Kwai Fong**, a street which is also referred to as an "area" in Hong Kong's jargon. Lan Kwai Fong is the centre of Hong Kong's "trendy" nightlife. Here chic restaurant mix with equally chic bars and discos, which in turn mix shoulder to shoulder packed pubs and tiny snack shops – everything from pizza to noodles – for those wanting a nibble at 4 a.m. or 5 a.m.

These side streets wind up to **Hollywood Road** (*see Western District*), with its plethora of antique, furniture, rattan and used bookshops. Along here is **Lyndhurst Terrace**, a pretty little place with shops that sell Chinese opera costumes. Lyndhurst Terrace curves down into **Wellington Street**, an avenue well-known for its *mahjong*-makers and framers.

Going up and following Hollywood Road, doing as much window-shopping as possible, one eventually reaches Possession Street. Possession Street marks the border between Central and the down-to-earth old Chinese section of Hong Kong called **Western District**.

WESTERN DISTRICT

Go Chinese in Western: If one was foolish enough to try to identify the "real Hong Kong," one would think inevitably of **Western District**, which begins at Possession Street, and sprawls west to Kennedy Town. More practically, Western's atmosphere emerges around **Central Market**, near the fringes of the busy Central district. The best time to visit the market is at about 6 a.m. when all meats, seafood, poultry, fish and vegetables are unloaded and are ready for sale and distribution.

Western was the very first district to be settled by the British. They soon moved out, however, after malaria epidemics had decimated their numbers. Its mosquitos were left to Chinese immigrants who came pouring into the colony after 1848. Today, there is virtually nothing British about this area; it is now a traditional Chinese urban society at its purest: not especially pretty, perhaps, but undeniably colourful.

For one thing, Western is known as a last refuge of the Hong Kong Chinese artisan. Unfortunately, the world of the Chinese artisan in his natural habitat isn't seen by many visitors, but here one can marvel at *mahjong*-makers who cre-

ate *mahjong* tiles that range in function and form from low-priced plastic to high-priced hand-carved husks. Here also is the Chinese herbalist, with his fabulous aromas of snake musk, herbs, ginseng and powdered lizards. All are part of intriguing pharmacopoeia potions that date back 4,000 years.

Surprises at every corner: In Western, too, are the chop-makers who carve name stamps along **Man Wa Lane**. This is a great Chinese art. Perhaps only the Arabs have as much respect for calligraphy as the Chinese. And watching a Man Wa chop-carver sculpt a man's name out of stone, ivory, jade or wood is quite an experience. (Bear in mind that there are male and female calligraphic styles: when background material is carved out, the chop is male; when the characters are gouged out, it's female.)

Western is also a home to jade-carvers, opera costumers, fan-makers, pottery-shapers and eggroll-bakers. There are Chinese surprises on every corner.

A good place to begin pottering around Western is at the **Chinese Merchan-**

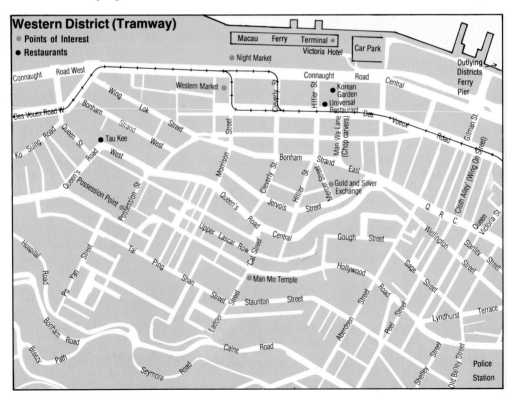

dise Emporium, located opposite Central Market. Four floors of goods from China are sold here more cheaply than in China's own **Friendship Stores**. These stores, which import their merchandise from the mainland, are owned by Beijing's Hong Kong representatives.

Western Market: On Morrison Street, stands a red brick Edwardian-style building – the Western Market. It was opened in 1906 and was used for more than 80 years as a food market. Recognised as a historical landmark, its elegant architectural features were preserved and restored; and in 1991, it was converted into a cultural and shopping complex. Dubbed as Hong Kong's version of London's Covent Garden, it sports a diversity of handicrafts, fabric and souvenir stalls. The Tin Bin, one place to look for antique toys, and the Fook Ming Tea Shop for traditional, home-style Chinese food are housed here.

A little lane leading to the ferry pier's right side between Queen's Road and Connaught Road is Man Wa Lane, the aforementioned street where chop-makers make and ply calligraphic stamps. At right angles to this, between the continuation of Queen's Road (Bonham Strand) and Des Voeux Road is colourful **Wing Lok Street** with its shops selling herbs, odd medicines, preserved seafoods and tea.

You will now reach **Possession Street**, which has great patriotic significance for the colony. It was around here that the British formally annexed Hong Kong in 1841. At that time the island extended only as far as Queen's Road. However, land here has been vastly reclaimed over the years, so no monument marks the exact annexation rites site. The only memento to the *HMS Sulphur*, whose crew was the first to step ashore officially, is **Belcher Street**, west of here, which was named after the *Sulphur's* captain. As for atmosphere, Possession Street looks like a reversion to the 19th century, as no vehicular traffic is allowed. Rather, sounds and ambience here are generated only by people. Here, too, are fortune-tellers, and on **Fat Hing Street** is a line of shops which

Belcher Bay fronts Kennedy Town in Western.

specialize only in traditional baby goods.

Just one block above Bonham Strand is **Jervois Street**, another "specialty" street, this one devoted entirely to snake restaurants and Chinese wineshops.

As one probes deeper into Western, it's easy to forget "colonial" Hong Kong. The district past **Bonham Strand** (a marvellous street for printing shops) looks more like a set for an old *Fu Manchu* movie. City planners have classified this area as a slum, but architecturally this district – with its old 4-storey buildings with ornate balconies and carved balustrades – is more colourful and convenient than the colony's more modern housing estates. And every little street has its own "exotic" specialities: ginseng and birdnests, shark's fin and jade, funeral wreaths and snake wine, fortune-tellers and calligraphers, and ivory and stone carvers.

Western District is for walking, for poking into little alleys and getting lost on improbable side streets. Try, however, to avoid the early morning hustle and bustle of the harbour unloading.

Walking one's bird: Hang Wen, at 119 Queen's Road Central, is a "bird restaurant," where early morning tea-drinkers bring their ornately-caged pet birds together for a group sing. On the corner of Bonham Strand and Cleverly Street is another such birdshop. And only a few blocks away, rice merchants meticulously blend a dozen varieties of rice.

Look for the key-cutters, tinkers, carpenters, cobblers and barbers in any alley. Their miniature factories operate in about 20 sq. feet (6 sq. metres) of space. Booths may be simple upended crates, and the materials of their trade are stacked outside. Bow-drills are of ancient design and timeless utility, as are other tools. Rope-laying factories, alive with another old Chinese craft, go about their business in the open air. Here you'll discover a veritable carnival of teashops, handicraft factories and restaurants where tourists rarely go.

Minibuses and trams clank along the main streets, but walk as much as possible, all the way to Western's end, at **Kennedy Town**, where you'll find one

Many interesting discoveries awaits the adventurous on Hollywood Road.

of the colony's oldest Chinese settlements. Still very crowded, it has a Portuguese-style *praia*, a road which curves along original footpaths bordering **Belcher Bay**. Past this are some uninteresting slaughter-houses and squatter shacks – but an unparalleled view of the waters leading to Macau. Looming in the foreground is **Green Island**. This is "**lower**" **Western district**.

Portuguese architecture: The hilly upper region of Western (which is actually part of Mid-Levels) is totally different; here the architecture is less Chinese than Portuguese – with tiled pitch roofs, stucco walls and projecting balconies. Here also are a few fine houses, the **University of Hong Kong**, and – as usual – splendid views of the harbour.

If one decides not to go all the way to Kennedy Town, be advised that it's easier to reach Western and Mid-Levels via Western Street off Queen's Road. Otherwise, when in Kennedy Town, travel up Smithfield Road to Pokfield Road, then backtrack toward the University. Pokfield turns into Pokfulam

Chinese vintages at the local wine shop.

Road, then passes by Belcher Gardens into the University of Hong Kong (which opened in 1911, though some buildings there date to 1886). Some of the architecture is interesting here. The **Anatomy Building**, the **Government Bacteriological Building** and the **Vice-Chancellor's Lodge** were all built before World War II.

Antiquities, real and fake: For tourists, the most interesting place may be the **campus museum** which houses a good collection of pottery and porcelain. Nothing especially rare, but well preserved pieces. The **University Press** has a number of very interesting titles for scholars who appreciate such things.

Coming back to Central district via **Bonham Road** can be an exhilarating experience. There is nothing of distinctive tourist interest en route, but the occasional views are grand (especially the numerous peeks at lower Western District). The old but fast-disappearing architecture of schools and mansions en route is also a fascinating glimpse into Hong Kong's colonial past.

Past Bonham Road and Caine Road, a detour north a block to Robinson Road was the austere **Ohel Leah Synagogue**. Now demolished following a bitter battle, it will be replaced by a replica and a high-rise housing the club. Jews have been in Hong Kong since its founding, but this building wasn't opened until 1901. It was financed by Hong Kong's prominent Sassoon family. The building was in Spanish style, with two towers, an imposing porch and elaborate interior carvings. The outside landscape is quite pleasant.

While returning to Central, don't miss a cruise down one of the most fascinating of all local shopping areas: **Ladder Street**. This road zig-zags down steep inclines from Caine Road down to Hollywood Road and Queen's Road Central. Nobody knows when its broad stone steps were constructed, but old records say that this 118-foot (65-metre) "street" was built so sedan chair bearers could more easily carry their human cargo from Hollywood Road to residential Caine Road. On Ladder Street (not to be confused with the "ladder streets" in

Central) are some of Hong Kong's earliest houses, including old shuttered buildings with wooden balconies and elaborate carvings.

Where Ladder Street meets Hollywood Road is the area's so-called "**Thieves Market**" (also known as "Cat Street," perhaps because it was once the middle of a red-light district). The lanes here are filled with bric-a-brac, real and fake antiques, and more stalls than one can ever browse through. Bargaining is the rule here – whether for a safety pin, shoelace or (if you should be so lucky) a Tang dynasty horse.

You can continue down to Queen's Road, or continue to explore the latter-day wonders of **Hollywood Road**. Here are dozens of antique shops, furniture shops, rattan shops, and places selling blackwood chests, snuff bottles, porcelains and antiques. Don't look in, but *go in* and explore. Look in the dark corners, where owners sometimes hide their best pieces.

While on one of these zig-zagging ladder streets, pause a moment and consider the following impressions of this area penned by the lady traveller Isabella Bird Bishop who was here during the great Hong Kong fire of 1878:

Escaping from an indescribable hubbub, I got onto a bamboo chair (and was borne up) streets choked with household goods and the costly contents of shops... Chinamen dragging their possessions to the hills; Chinawomen carrying children... making a scene of intense excitement.

God of Civil Servants: At the corner of Hollywood Road and Ladder Street is **Man Mo Temple**, built around 1842 on what must have been a little dirt track leading up from Central. Tourists regularly throng through Man Mo – but this doesn't inhibit the temple's regular worshippers who animatedly create thick and redolent clouds with their burning joss offerings.

Man is the God of Civil Servants and of Literature. (Within Mandarin society, civil servants were, by definition, the most well-educated and sophisticated.) Mo is the God of Martial Arts and War, and is more popularly known by his worshippers as Kuan Ti or Kuan Kung. Guarding the temple are the legendary Eight Immortals. Inside are two solid brass deer (believed to represent longevity), and a colourful wooden carving. Near the altar are three sedan chairs encased in glass. Years ago, when the icons of Man and Mo were paraded through Western on festival days, these chairs were the ones on which they were transported.

If the atmosphere looks vaguely familiar, it is because this area was once used as a set in *The World Of Suzie Wong*, the popular Hong Kong-based film which starred Nancy Kwan and William Holden. Apparently, this corner of Central and Western was more "Wanchai-looking" than the Wanchai District where the film supposedly took place. After this cinematic pause, one can either walk back to Central or take a taxi to the Peak Tramway.

It's now time to leave this very crowded, colourful and chaotic part of Hong Kong for a place of solitude, snobbishness and sophistication.

Left, Man Mo Temple and **right**, looking down Ladder Street.

THE PEAK

Victoria Peak – *The* Peak to those who have made it to society's top – wasn't always regarded with such awe. "Although beautiful in the distance," a travel writer once quoted, "it is sterile and unpromising upon more close examination." Indeed, during the first six years of the colony's history, hardly anybody travelled to those inhospitable heights.

In 1847, the Colonial Surgeon, William Morrison, recommended The Peak for reasons of salubrity. And in 1860, the Governor, Sir Hercules Robinson, recommended that Europeans go to The Peak to get away from the unhealthy malarial climate in the lower regions. But it wasn't until 1888, when the **Peak Tramway** (actually a funicular railway) was opened, that The Peak became *the* Peak. Everybody who was (and is) anybody longs to live on The Peak. Before the tramway, sedan chairs transported lucky colonials to the top. Such coolie-powered transportation died long ago, but palanquins are still used during charity races staged to benefit Matilda Hospital once a year.

The most affluent residents up there compete for the best chefs and stage the colony's most sparkling dinner parties. Its best flats and houses are rented out by the government – as Peak perks, if you will – to the colony's senior civil servants; or earmarked by the *hong* (Hong Kong's massive trading conglomerates) for their top executives. Swimming pools have been installed in lieu of verandahs, and bungalows now dot the area's greenswards, but the area's wilderness beauty adjacent to stately homes, graciously survives.

Walks around The Peak abound for the nature-lover. On a clear day, one can wander through forests of bamboo and fern, stunted Chinese pines, hibiscus, and vines of wonderfully writhing beauty. Ornithologists still go up there to log sightings of blue magpies, crested goshawks and kites.

The best way to see The Peak in all its bucolic glory is by walking around

Lugard Road, which begins just opposite the Peak Tram's upper terminus at 1,305 feet (395 metres) above sea level. Just to the right is the **Peak Tower Restaurant**, which offers magnificient views, if clouds haven't smothered them.

Walking to the right of this mini-shopping centre, one can marvel at some of the world's finest vistas – scapes which sprawl all the way to China and Macau. Going around Lugard Road to where it intersects with Harlech Road, one sees first the harbour, then Green Island and Peng Chau to the north, Lantau and Macau to the west, Cheung Chau further west, Lamma Island to the southwest, and finally the great masses of junks and *sampans* at Aberdeen to the south. This hike takes about two hours from the Peak Tramway and back again.

For the really energetic, Mount Austin Road leads one to the gardens of a building which was once the summer residence of the Governor. This building was destroyed during World War II by the Japanese, but the walk about its former grounds is still stupendous.

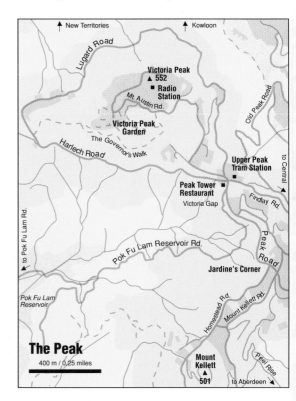

Strolling out to the edge of Mount Austin Road on The Peak's barren hillsides at sunset, one is again treated to astonishing views of the colony. And up here – at The Peak's very peak – you will be 1,805 feet (547 metres) above sea level.

On Peak Road, before the Peak Tram Terminus is the elegant **JK's Restaurant**, part of the Jimmy's Kitchen Group.

Descending by the steep Peak Tram, you realize that the Tram is not just a "tourist attraction," no matter how many tourists crowd it. No, this is as much a local commuter vehicle as New York's IRT or London's Tube.

The Tram runs from 5.40 a.m. (rush hour; not a tourist in sight) to 1 a.m. and hasn't had a single accident since its opening in 1888. As at the beginning, it still has two cars which carry 72 passengers and one driver, and is pulled up and lowered by 5,000-foot (1,500-metre) steel cables wound on drums.

While descending on the tram, you can stop at **Barker Road** and indulge in some of the finer views and footpaths through the Peak forest. This road leads to exclusive **Plantation Road**. The next stop is **May Road**, where the Tram negotiates one of the steepest passenger vehicle gradients in the world. The stop on **Bowen Road** has one of the better views of **Wanchai**. Joggers run here day and night, and it's said that wild monkeys can sometimes be seen in the trees.

The following two stops, **Macdonnell Road** and **Kennedy Road**, each lead to the entrance of the colony's **Zoological Gardens** and **Botanical Gardens**, which house good collections of flora and fauna. An aviary here has about 700 birds of 300 species. The best time to visit is dawn, when locals are engrossed in *tai chi chuan* exercises. This rather curious exercise, which looks like a slow-motion ballet, is a shadow-boxing exercise which dates back to the time of Confucius, utilizing movements and breathing inspired by Buddhist meditation forms.

The tram's lower terminus is just up from the Hilton Hotel on Garden Road – far below the upper echelons of Hong Kong society.

Stunning view from The Peak.

WANCHAI

In the celluloid version of *The World of Suzie Wong*, the *very* snobbish Sylvia Sims, at one of her Peak dinner parties, embarrassed the late William Holden to no end by speaking about the unfortunate denizens of **Wanchai**.

At that time, in the mid-1950s the contrast must have been juicy. Many Peak-dwellers went slumming in Wanchai, much as 1920s flappers would love going to Harlem for flippant fun. But Wanchai nightlife was not meant for the Peak's *taipan*. In the late 1940s, it was a hangout for sailors. Writer Harold Stephens recalls that in 1949, there weren't more than four bars in the area, but they were crowded. During the 1960s, Wanchai helped give rest, recreation and succour to thousands of American, Australian and New Zealand soldiers and sailors on R&R (Rest & Recreation) from Vietnam, as well as thousands of merchant marines from

hundreds of countries. Then, as now, Hong Kong was a popular port-of-call.

Not the same old Wanch: Today, Wanchai lives on its reputation. Like an old prostitute, aged to the point where she's now the madam of a brothel, Wanchai now slouches more than she slinks. A bit shabby these days, she's seen it all, and has good stories to tell, but it takes extra energy to put life into the old girl.

As for the Wanchai girls, they still stand around bar-doors and give a perfunctory "pssst" to potential customers. But these days they're sadly overwhelmed by newer and more palatable and exotic nocturnal delights.

Wanchai's "red light district" now plays second fiddle to more liberated nightlife venues: gaudy big hostess clubs, topless bars, discos, and raucous English-style pubs (where the dartboards usually get more action than the women across the street).

There are also peculiarly Eastern forms of entertainment. Like Chinese ballrooms, which rarely see foreigners. Good reason too, as the places are dingy, alcohol is almost never served, and all that one can do is sit in semi-darkness and wait for a hostess to make pleasant conversation in Cantonese or Chiu Chow.

The "Wanch" is *the* place for night people (some bars never close) and night-strolling. Here are brightly-lit fruit markets, souvenir shops, second-hand bookshops, and tailors open until midnight. (Warning: tailors here vary from tacky to svelte – and a suit made in 24 hours can unravel just as quickly.)

The Wanchai area is also host to some superb restaurants: **Rigoletto** has some of the best Italian food; a seat by the window of the **Fenwick Street** restaurant is *the* place for Wanchai people-watching: **Perfume River**, next to the **New Harbour Hotel** and the **Saigon** on Lockhart Road have minty fresh Vietnamese food; **SMI** reeks of marvellous curries reminiscent of the Straits down south. **The Chilli Club** on Lockhart Road is an example of the dozens of restaurants offering spicy Thai food. As for Chinese restaurants, Wanchai has literally thousands, as well as endless outdoor noodle stands. On Lockhart

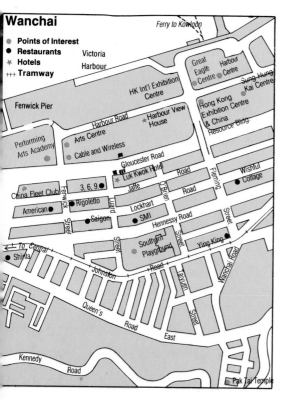

Wanchai

- Points of Interest
- Restaurants
- ✳ Hotels
- ┼┼┼ Tramway

Road, Wanchai's "Main Street," are bars for old-time *Hongkongians* – the **Old China Hand** and **Horse And Groom** – which perpetuate a dartboard atmosphere favoured by UK blokes in addition to the expected plethora of girlie bars. The up-market crowd heads to **Joe Bananas** for eating, drink and music.

Cultural Wanchai: Nobody thinks about Wanchai for culture, but it does harbour the **Hong Kong Arts Centre** on its Harbour Road. Opened in 1977 with contributions from the public, the Arts Centre has 15 floors of auditoria, rehearsal rooms, theatre workshops, and the offices of numerous cultural organizations. On any given night, the centre may be presenting a Shakespearean play, a Japanese *kabuki* ensemble or a Humphrey Bogart and Marlene Dietrich film. Across the street is the **Academy for Performing Arts** (**APA**), the territory's newest cultural addition. Its theatres could also be staging anything from a Broadway show to a ballet while its classrooms turn out Hong Kong's future actors, dancers, directors and cameramen.

Fenwick Pier, where the warships disgorge their sailors on R&R is just up Harbour Road, behind the APA. This section of Harbour Road (called Wanchai North) has the HK$3 billion **Hong Kong Convention and Exhibition Centre**, a vast centre which includes the **Grand Hyatt** and **New World Harbour View Hotels**, as well as Hong Kong's tallest building, **Central Plaza**, which at 1,228 feet (374 metres) is the fifth highest in the world. And for those who want to stay those extra days the **Immigration Department** is in Immigration Tower, cunningly located just behind **Wanchai Tower**, through which you walk to get there. There is a also a walkway from the Wanchai MTR Station on Lockhart Road which takes you directly to the Immigration Department's Building.

Larger ensembles are featured at the other end of Wanchai, in the **Queen Elizabeth Sports Stadium**, on Oi Kwan Road. Opened in 1978 at a cost of HK$50 million, it has a seating capacity of 3,500 and hosts anything from Sad-

Cultural showcase: the Academy for Performing Arts.

dler's Wells Ballet to basketball games. Nearby, on Gloucester Road, is the **Government Sports Stadium**, the scene of regular football matches.

Wanchai is well-known for night-time shenanigans. "Night-town" glows along the main east-west artery of **Lockhart Road**. By day, The Wanch's atmosphere is totally different. Due to the high rents in neighbouring Central, many businesses have spilled into Wanchai, creating a ready clientele for better restaurants and shops.

Lucky mirrors: Two blocks to the south of Hennessy Road is a far more "Chinese" section of town, **Queen's Road East**. Here are famous Chinese furniture-makers working right out on the street, where they fashion camphorwood chests and hardwood tables and chairs.

Here also are two well-known Chinese temples. On **Stone Nullah Lane**, to the right off Queen's Road East, is **Pak Tai Temple**, home to a 10-foot (3-metre) copper image dating to 1604. Closer to Central is Tik Loong Lane, which leads pilgrims to **Chai Kung Woot Fat Temple**, the **Temple of the Living Buddha**. Here, visitors who have overcome illnesses leave offerings in the form of mirrors with lucky inscriptions. Thus, the temple interior is dazzling.

Between Queen's Road East and Hennessy is Johnston Road, bisected by Southorn Playground, a place where Chinese opera is often presented at night. Parallel to Hennessy Road to its north is Lockhart Road, Gloucester Road and finally Harbour Road.

On Gloucester Road, is the **Luk Kwok Hotel**, the infamous "short-time" hotel where the fictional Suzie Wong lived, loved and worked. Today, the redeveloped Luk Kwok is rather posh, so gone is the quaint little place with a big dance floor and a wonderful series of balconies and shaky staircases you saw in the film. The Luk Kwok is now a modern hotel but should you look behind it, avoiding the bright lights of discos, you may still catch a few glimpses of old Wanchai in the alleys – though they shall soon pass to dust under jackhammers and cranes.

Gearing up for business at this night market.

HAPPY VALLEY

Western District was the first Hong Kong suburb occupied by Europeans, but they soon deserted it and moved to a spot which seemed healthier. Optimistically, they named this second living area **Happy Valley**. It was relatively distant from the sea, somewhat deserted and, most important, didn't have as many "unhealthy" and malaria-ridden rice farms in its vicinity. (By the late 1840s anti-malaria laws had been passed which banned farming on the island.)

Playing the ponies: In 1841, shortly after Happy Valley was settled, the colony's residents created the greensward and edifice which has made Happy Valley world famous. This is the Royal Hong Kong Jockey Club's **Happy Valley Racecourse**. Until a few years ago, this horse-racing oval was the only one in the colony. It's less than one mile long, but during the October-to-May racing season, it attracts thousands of race-goers (about 35,000 a running). Night-racing here is very impressive, and if you'd like to experience this, visitors' badges and information can be obtained from the Hong Kong Tourist Association. (Racing tips are published in all the English-language newspapers, and are broadcast on television for the benefit of serious pony-players.) There isn't a spot anywhere in Happy Valley which doesn't give visitors at least a partial view of the race track. And indeed, the name of the district has become synonymous with the sport. Curiously, Happy Valley is also a favourite shopping zone.

Geographically, Happy Valley's would-be happiness begins on Queen's Road East, at the corner of long winding **Stubbs Road**. To savour her best views, though, one should zigzag to the top of Stubbs Road, to Peak Road. Here squats a beautiful 4-storey house built by a Chinese merchant in traditional Chinese chauvinist style (with a different storey for each wife). A few blocks down is another Chinese-style house, this one

A day at the races: Hong Kong is a colony of punters.

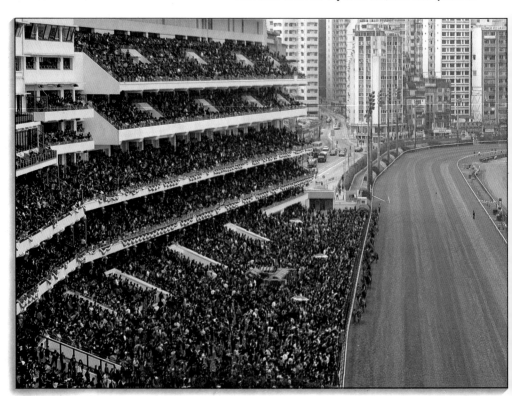

with a green roof (green signifying that the owner was wealthy and wanted to flaunt the fact). Film buffs might be interested to know that this was the movie home of Clark Gable and Susan Hayward in *Soldier of Fortune*, one of Gable's last film roles before he died.

Just above the intersection of Tai Hang Road with Stubbs Road is an official **rest garden** and **lookout point** which frame an unimpeded view of the harbour, the Kowloon promontory and, of course, the race track. Nearer Stubbs Road's bottom, at the corner of Queen's Road East and Stubbs Road, is a fine **Sikh temple**, dating to the last century.

Celestial kitsch: Travelling east on Queen's Road one will find five segregated cemeteries. First is the **Muslim Cemetery** near a mosque. Next to that lies a **Catholic Cemetery**, established in 1847. The largest final resting place here is the **Colonial Cemetery**, first occupied in 1845. Lovers of epitaphs won't find this historical place as interesting as Macau's literate Protestant Cemetery, but it does have many interesting old headstones which were placed over the remains of early missionaries, soldiers and sailors. Its most famous inhabitant is Lord Napier, who opened up trade with China and died at Macau in 1834.

Beyond these three cemeteries is the **Parsee Cemetery**, circa 1852. And on nearby Shan Kwong Road is the **Jewish Cemetery**, consecrated in 1855; its oldest surviving tomb is dated 1859.

Like Stubbs Road, nearby **Wongneichong Gap Road** also offers superb views of the city. (One mustn't confuse Wongneichong Gap with Wongneichong Road, which is adjacent to the race course.) Also on this road, which leads to Repulse Bay Beach, are **tennis courts** and the venerable (founded, 1851) **Hong Kong Cricket Club** which moved here from Central in 1975.

A Chinese Disneyland: Outside of its race-course, Happy Valley's second most well-known attraction is a place which looks like a hallucinogenic vision of a Chinese Disneyland. This is the **Aw Boon Haw** (formerly Tiger Balm) Gardens on Tai Hang Road. The 150,000-sq. foot (45,000-sq. km) amusement park stands in celestially kitschy splendour – sort of a garish Chinese "Disneyland." This zany site has terraced grottos which are profligate with bizzarre stone sculptures and garish reliefs from the most awesome and awful tales of Chinese mythology. Garish is not *exactly* the right word… ostentatious, gaudy, psychedelic… call it what you will. The sculptures say something about the Chinese mind, but we leave the visitor to deduce what that might be.

However, there will be no questioning of good taste after one visits the mansion at Aw Boon Haw Gardens. This estate houses one of the finest jade collections in the colony. Permission is needed for entering; seek assistance from the Hong Kong Tourist Association.

While on Tai Hang Road, you can see on nearby hillsides hundreds of little shacks; these are the temporary homes of squatter refugees who are awaiting resettlement by the government. Further up and due right is one of the larger resettlement estates, **Lai Tai**.

Proper decorum is observed by sartorial types.

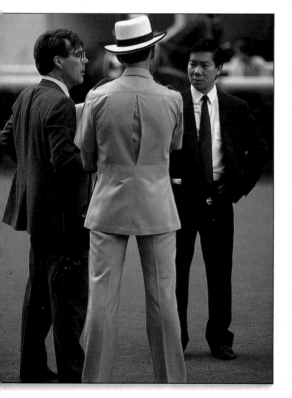

CAUSEWAY BAY

Cruising down from Tai Hang Road to King's Road, opposite **Victoria Park**, you enter a fascinating modern sector of the island: **Causeway Bay**. (The area can also be reached more directly by tram, bus or a taxi from Central.)

Causeway Bay is bounded on the east by Victoria Park, on the west by Canal Road, on the south by **Caroline Hill** and Leighton Road, and on the north by the harbour. Causeway Bay really was a bay until the 1950s when the bay disappeared into a great land reclamation project. (What was then Causeway Bay is today Paterson Street.)

Sunset by *sampan*: The present-day "bay" is occupied by the **Royal Hong Kong Yacht Club** on **Kellett Island** (which also was once a "real" island), and the **Typhoon Shelter**. To get there, cross Victoria Park Road in front of the **Excelsior Hotel**. At sunset hour, you will immediately be besieged by a gaggle of women. Don't get the wrong idea. All they are offering is a chaste ride in one of their "floating restaurant" *sampan*. No hanky-panky is ever suggested. Besides, there is no room for hanky-panky because the deck is filled beam to boom with tables and chairs. Bargain for the *sampan* before you get on. The price should be about HK$60 to HK$100, depending on the *sampan*'s size.

Your *sampan* will weave its way through the crowded sea lanes of the typhoon basin by paddle power, a-bobbing while dodging other restaurant *sampan*, fishing junks, pleasure yachts, and large passenger ferries. The place is alive with water traffic. Bring your own wine if you wish, because the bar *sampan* (which buzz your craft moments after it clears land) add offshore markups to the price of their booze. Cold beer, however, is reasonably priced.

Kitchen *sampans* pull up next, vying for orders and showing off their fresh prawns, crabs and fish. Seafood, noodles, congee, omelettes – just about anything edible – can be prepared before you in the precarious floating kitchens.

Music is provided by a live band-*sampan*. But be warned that by popular colonial opinion, this floating combo is considered to be the worst, most out-of-tune band in Hong Kong, or perhaps the world. A "song menu" is passed over for your consideration and it usually includes two selections. No other music is played, and the band's favourite and standard tune is – would you believe – "The Yellow Rose of Texas." This floating musical repertoire has not changed in a decade. Cost: HK$25 per tune.

Though they hardly serve Chinese haute cuisine, restaurant *sampan* are a fun experience, and the food is fresh, tasty and filling.

Going to the toilet on these little restaurant *sampan* is also an experience not to be missed, especially by the ladies. A tiny cubicle in the stern is curtained off when you make appropriate anxious gestures. Some actually have a pot (which empties directly into the bay) and others just an open hole you squat over. If such arrangements are unacceptable, or if her ladyship is not an

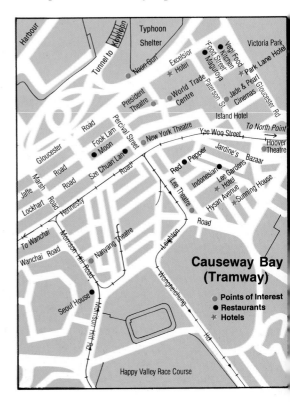

194

able contortionist, don't give up. Make even more proper and disgusted gestures, and your *sampan* lady will scull over to a luxury yacht where, for a modest tip to the boat boy, you may relieve yourself in grander and more civilized comfort.

This part of Hong Kong's waterfront also features a unique genuflection to the musical genius of Noel Coward: the **Noon-Day Gun**. Nobody knows for sure why the gun is fired at noon everyday, but according to a century-old legend, this ritual, now a Hong Kong tradition, began one day in the mid-1800s when one of the Jardine's opium boats sailed into the harbour and a willing minion gave the boat a 21-gun salute. The Hong Kong governor was incensed that a mere purveyor of "foreign mud" should receive the same greeting as an official figure, so – as penance – he ordered that the gun be fired at noon everyday in perpetuity. Ergo, Coward's lyric: "In Hong Kong, they strike a gong and fire a noon-day gun, to reprimand each inmate who's in late."

Guess what time it is.

The legend may not be true – the penance sounds too Greek, almost Promethean. The real truth is probably that the Jardine's managing director got a reprimand in the Royal Hong Kong Jockey Club. Whatever the rascal reason, Jardine's doesn't regret the story. Every New Year's Eve, Jardine's executives, in their fanciest bib 'n' tucker stand by the gun and ceremoniously fire it at midnight to the discreet applause of a small colonial gathering.

"Modern" Causeway: Causeway Bay's "modern" history began in 1973 when the Cross-Harbour Tunnel was opened. This underwater freeway is one of the largest tunnels in Asia. Its four lanes cross 1.25 miles (2 km) of harbour water between Hong Kong and Kowloon.

With this tunnel came the inevitable: Causeway Bay was transformed into a thriving little city. Deluxe hotels like the **Park Lane** and the **Excelsior** opened. Next door to the Excelsior is the **World Trade Centre**, a 42-storey complex chock-a-block with plush offices, restaurants and night clubs. In the same

building is the **Palace Theatre**, a posh cinema.

Street blocks behind the Excelsior have shopping outlets which sell goods at prices cheaper than similar stores located in Central or Kowloon. Big department stores (**Daimaru**, **Matsuzakaya**, **Sogo**, all Japanese; and branches of **China Products** and **Lane Crawford's**), movie theatres and literally hundreds of little hi-fi and camera shops crowd into Hennessy Road and continue west down to Canal Road. Most are open until 10 p.m. each night.

One block to the east of Paterson Street, at right angles to the Plaza Hotel and Victoria Park, is **Food Street**. In Food Street's tow blocks and 80,000 sq. feet (25,000 sq. metres) of space are 28 diverse dining places, more than 200 chefs and menus listing some 2,000 dishes. More than 100,000 people gorge themselves here each week on Peking duck, Punjabi *dahl*, American beefsteak, Cantonese congee, Japanese *teppanyaki*, and garlicky Szechuan eggplant – among innumberable other dishes. The quality varies, but Food Street is good fun; its fountained and canopied lanes are worth a good half hour of nighttime.

Due east two blocks is the aforementioned Victoria Park, which is busy about 20 hours a day. Around 4 a.m. *tai chi chuan* and jogging exercises begin. Later, tennis players on 14 different courts begin playing. And by mid-morning, football players, kite-fliers and swimmers are exercising.

Each December, the park plays host to a **Hong Kong International Karting Prix**. And during the Chinese New Year and the Autumn Lantern Festival, the park is aglow with flower displays – of peach, orange and narcissus blossoms – and hundreds of candlelit lanterns; it's one of the colony's most beautiful annual sights.

Across from Victoria Park is **Tin Hau Temple Road**, whose temple dates back to 1747. On Tunglowan Road, near the **Park Theatre**, is **Queen's College**, the oldest Anglo-Chinese school, founded in 1862. And on the northern side of this street is the **Causeway Bay Magistracy**. Daily courtroom sessions, conducted in English, are open to the public.

So much for "modern" Causeway Bay. "Old" Causeway Bay has existed since the beginning of Hong Kong. The first Jardine godowns were on **Yee Woo Street** (*Yee Woo* is Jardine's name in Shanghainese) which is a short continuation of Hennessy Road. In this sector is **Jardine's Bazaar**, a marketplace which also dates back to those "foreign mud" and buccaneering days. Today, Jardine's Bazaar and nearby **Jardine's Crescent** are equally fascinating.

Indeed, each street in this area has special shopping wonders. **Pennington Street** is known for its shops making paper effigies for funerals, Chinese medicine shops and old-style pawn shops (where the chief pawn-broker sits high up in a judgement seat like the Lord of Justice himself). At an herbalist teahouse, for HK$1 a bowl, you can enjoy "24-flavoured Tea," a brew prepared with different seeds, lichen, grasses, roots, stems and fungi. On nearby **Irving Street** are soya sauce and wine shops. And on **Fuk Hing Lane**, century eggs and earthenware pottery venue, you can pick up a *wok*, Chinese all-purpose cooking pan.

This maze opens up to Hysan Avenue, where there are many boutiques, and more "ethnic" restaurants than anywhere else in the colony.

A 5-minute walk and you will discover Vietnamese, Indonesian, Russian, Cantonese, Shanghainese, Malaysian, Indian, Korean, Chiu Chow, Italian, Japanese, and good old European and coffeeshop food, all at very reasonable prices.

Turning to the east, head up Leighton Road to Caroline Hill. Here is the colony's largest orphanage for girls, **Po Leung Kuk**, founded in 1880 to aid girls who in years past had been kidnapped into slavery. The nearby **Morrison Hill Sports Club** hosts numerous sporting activities.

On the way to Causeway Bay's main artery, Hennessy Road, (due west) is Canal Road. Here, Causeway Bay meets Wanchai. Facing west and across the street to the left are traditional Chinese butcher shops with fresh meat.

NORTH POINT, QUARRY BAY, SHAUKIWAN AND CHAIWAN

East of Victoria Park, Hong Kong becomes a shabby industrial area, where more and more highrises sprout with every new joint venture.

However, the best way to explore the four major sections of eastern Hong Kong – **North Point**, **Quarry Bay**, **Shaukiwan** and **Chaiwan** – is by tram. Sitting on a tram's upper deck, you can say bye-bye to Victoria Park, and cruise and relax for 45 minutes.

Red stars at the Sunbeam: The first eastern Hong Kong district is **North Point**, which has a few movie theatres, a couple of good department stores, and a ferry service to **Kwun Tong** on the Kowloon side.

Continuing due east, one's tram lurches past the **Hong Kong Funeral Home** the largest mortuary on the island. Opposite

Tramming is a good way to see Hong Kong.

are dozens of convenient wreathmakers. You are now in **Quarry Bay**, with the harbour to your left, and bare green hills to your right. Continuing along **King's Road**, you come to **Taikoo Shing** on the left, one of the new vertical cities that have sprung up. The main interest for visitors is **Cityplaza I & II**, the shopping and entertainment complexes. Located here are hundreds of shops, ice and roller skating rinks, bowling alleys, cinemas, **Tivoli Terrace** – an excellent sidewalk cafe run by Jimmy's Kitchen (one of the colony's most venerable eating establishments) – and the Italian delicatessen, **Vini & Salumi**.

Across King's Road from Taikoo Shing is another giant residential/commercial complex – called **Kornhill** – within which is the **Grand Plaza Hotel**.

A bit past the main part of Shaukiwan town, just off the main road, is the interesting **Tam Kung Temple** on A Kung Ngam Road. Tam Kung isn't a character usually found in Chinese mythology text, because he made his late spiritual debut during pre-British Hong Kong years. He is a boy-god who predicts the weather and is thus a favourite patron of fishermen. On Tam Kung's birthday, on the eighth day of the fourth moon (around May), fishermen sail here from other parts of the colony to pay their respects with dragon-dancing, spirit medium rituals, incense burning and colourful processions through Shaukiwan's busy streets.

To continue on to the far eastern end of the island, board a local mini-bus.

The next settlement in this direciton is **Chaiwan**, which squats around **Leiyuemun Bay**. Chaiwan has a few parks, housing estates, a huge Chinese cemetery, and an old English fort.

The road that forks to the right leads to Shek-O Beach, which is on the south side of the island.

There isn't much to do in Chaiwan. During the windy season, some photographers like to go out to a nearby hillock and photograph the sprawling Chinese cemetery. Following such breezy weather the cemetery is blanketed by colourful kites which have escaped from their owners.

SOUTHSIDE: SHEK O, STANLEY, REPULSE BAY, AND OCEAN PARK

"Unofficial" visitors cannot continue due east from Chaiwan town because this road leads to the sensitive military intelligence base of **Little Sai Wan**. But by backtracking a bit, and turning right down **Shek O Road**, one travels directly to the south side of Hong Kong Island – and a totally different world.

Southside Hong Kong is a region of rocky coasts and smooth white beaches; of little fishing villages and unhurried markets. Neither an office building nor factory is anywhere in sight. But on summer weekends, every office, factory and farm worker in the colony seems to descend on the southside's shores.

Of Hong Kong's 36 gazetted beaches, the southside of the island has 14. A few, like **Rocky Bay** on the road to Shek O, have virtually no facilities, save an unparalleled view and an uncrowded beach. Others, like Repulse Bay, feature busloads of tourists, a McDonald's hamburger stand, and about as much peace and quiet as a carnival.

Shek O and Big Wave Bay: Shek O Beach is somewhere at middle ground. The road from Chaiwan skirts **Mount Collinson** on the left, and **Tai Tam Harbour** to the right. At a fork in the road, you can go left about 4 miles to **Big Wave Bay** (a beautiful beach, but with absolutely no public transportation to the beach). The Shek O beach and village, about the same distance from the fork, can be reached by public bus and Big Wave Bay's beach is a 30-minute walk from Shek O.

The marketplace at Shek O Village caters almost entirely to bathers. What the market and beach hide, though, is the site of some truly luxurious homes. Following paths at right angles to the beach, you can wander through lane after lane of high-walled mansions owned by some of Hong Kong's most affluent citizens.

Stanley Village hugs the rugged coastline.

Past the village, stroll out to **Shek O Headland**, facing the islands of **Tai Tau Chau** and **Ng Fan Chau**. To the right is the southernmost point of the island, **Cape D'Aguilar**. It was from Shek O Headland and this peninsular that almost nightly appearance of Vietnamese refugee boats could be seen in recent years as they drifted listlessly, looking for a safe harbour and freedom.

A good 18-hole golf course is on the road just before the beach, but you must be a member of the **Shek O Country Club** to dig divots there.

Trekking at Tai Tam: After the first turn-off to Shek O, the road from Chaiwan continues in a curve to one of the most well-trodden hiking spots on the island: **Tai Tam Reservoir**.

This was the first reservoir erected in Hong Kong, its earliest section completed in 1899. The 2-hour walk in lovely areas surrounded by mountains, begins on **Tai Tam Road**, skirts around the different reservoirs, and ends at **Wongneichong Gap Road** near the **Hong Kong Cricket Club**. Boaters can also enjoy the scenery by renting boats out on the water run-off areas below **Tai Tam Bridge**.

The most strenuous trail goes not only around the reservoir but continues on a little catchwater path to the top of a hill, along the whole southern coast and on past **Deepwater Bay** and **Stanley Village**. There is nothing difficult about this path, but hiking down to the lowlands requires extra effort.

Once **Repulse Bay** is sighted, the gradient steepens and, indeed, unwary climbers have experienced serious accidents by trying to take a shortcut to the road. The best plan is, ironically, to reach the gully by literally breaking into a prison.

After Deepwater Bay and Repulse Bay, the hill curves down into Stanley Village. But the path here leads directly into **Stanley Prison**, one of the colony's security establishments for malefactors. To the surprised looks of guards, you'll be descending *into* the prison. Simply shrug your shoulders and walk on an outside path to the exit.

Stanley's clothing stalls are always good for a bargain or two.

Stanley: That's the most unusual way to get to Stanley Beach. The more usual route from Tai Tam is to take public transportation or a car past Tai Tam Reservoir along the coast to **Turtle Cove** then to Stanley Village Road and the village itself.

Despite Stanley's English-sounding name (it was named after Lord Stanley, the 19th-century Secretary of State for the Colonies), Stanley was a thriving Chinese capital long before the British set foot here. In fact, a **Tin Hau Temple** here documents that the town was founded in 1770 by a pirate, Chang Po Chai, who captured the island.

Once one of the colony's best-kept shopping secrets, today **Stanley Market** attracts thousands of visitors on weekends, though it's open every day. Here, a few steps from New Street, is a large area with shops selling fashionable clothes (usually over-runs or seconds), rattan, fresh food, ceramic jugs, budget art, hardware, brass objects, Chinese products, vases – practically everything.

Eating used to be a second-rate experience in Stanley. But in 1979, **Stanley's Restaurant** opened along the main street facing the harbour and began to serve French food at fair prices. Along this street are also the **Beaches Restaurant** and two pubs **Lord Stanley** and **Smuggler's Inn**, should you need a respite from shopping. Other small restaurants are dotted around, including the pizza parlour/Italian restaurant, **Il Mercato**.

There are several institutions of interest here. The **Hong Kong Sea School**, for example, is a unique institution. It accepts only boys from underprivileged environments, about 550 a year. Each pays a small sum (if they can afford it), and they are then trained to join the ranks of Hong Kong's most advanced seamen. Modelled on the UK's National School of Seamanship, it imposes a spartan regimen on the boys, but also trains them in all the basic and advanced techniques of seamanship.

Down the road is Stanley Prison, and to the right of this is the **Stanley Military Cemetery**, a quiet and fitting reminder of the part which Stanley played in World War II. It was in Stanley – at both the prison and at nearby **St Stephen's College** – that the Japanese interned British prisoners-of-war. Near the cemetery is **St Stephen's Beach**, a cleaner and more pleasant place than Stanley's main beach.

Crowds and chic: From Stanley, you may travel to the "capital" of the south side, **Repulse Bay**, directly on Repulse Bay Road. The 15-minute trip (which doubles in time on jammed summer weekends) leads to **South Bay** and **Middle Bay** beaches, which are usually less crowded than the madness which haunts Repulse Bay Beach on weekends.

Repulse Bay Beach, now widened several times its original size and improved, has everything except peace and quiet. It had one of the finest resort hotels in the East, **The Repulse Bay Hotel**, now replaced by a pastel coloured commercial/residential complex with a big designer hole in it called **The Repulse Bay**. (Depending on whom you speak to, the hole is either part of the design, for *fung shui* or wind control purposes.) If you think it all looks a bit

Throngs hit the beach at Repulse Bay.

familiar, the terrace/verandah section, complete with stairs, fountain and lawns, is a replica of the old Repulse Bay Hotel. Interesting restaurants – **The Verandah** (a replica from the hotel), **Spices** (serving mixed Asian foods), **Hei Fung Terrace** (a Cantonese restaurant), **The Bamboo Bar** (a partial replica of the old hotel's famous bar) – and outdoor barbecues can be found here. It also has hamburger and noodle stands, thousands of blaring transistor radios, luxurious high-rises, and a beach which gets filthy on weekends (due to an invasion of some 25,000 bathers).

Unfortunately, the hills remind one of a very sad story. It was over those same hills that invading Japanese came pouring at the end of 1941, determined to make the grand Repulse Bay Hotel just another building in "The Captured Territory of Hong Kong." The hotel at that time was a military target, because British and Canadian troops used it as a headquarters (to keep open the road betwen Stanley and Aberdeen). After three days of fighting, the hotel was

Seaside apartments in the bay.

taken, and Commonwealth prisoners were marched to **Eucliffe Mansion** (this castle has also been demolished) to the right of the hotel and about 0.25 miles (0.4 km) away. Here, most of the prisoners were executed, and survivors were put into the **Stanley Internment Camp**.

Two questions are always asked about Repulse Bay. (1): What is "repulsive" about the bay? Except for the Monday morning garbage cleanup, nothing. It was named after the battleship *HMS Repulse*, which took an active part in the thwarting of pirates who plundered here in the early days. (2): What is that huge statue just to the right of McDonald's and fronting the life-saving club? She's the most popular of all goddesses in Hong Kong, **Tin Hau**. She is the Queen of Heaven, but – most important – she is the protector of fishermen and anybody engaged in seafaring activities.

Southside attractions: From Repulse Bay, the coast road curves westward over some of the colony's most beautiful scenery – to Deepwater Bay, Ocean Park and Aberdeen. (If going by bus,

you must sit on the top deck to soak in this ride's magnificent vistas.)

Deepwater Bay has some very beautiful mansions (including the house where *Love Is a Many-Splendoured Thing* was filmed). It also has a good 9-hole golf course managed by the **Royal Hong Kong Golf Club** (open on weekdays to tourists). Farther along is the more exclusive **Hong Kong Country Club**.

Nearby is a street which leads to the **Police Training School** and one of Hong Kong's biggest tourist attractions: **Ocean Park** and the adjacent **Water World** (May to October only).

Opened in 1977, Ocean Park cost HK$150 million. It is owned and subsidised by the Royal Hong Kong Jockey Club. Located on 170 acres (69 hectares) of land, it is the world's largest oceanarium. The Park actually consists of two sections: a **Lowland** site with 40 acres (16 hectares), and a **Headland** site of 130 acres (52 hectares). The two sectors are linked by a 0.9-mile (1.4-km) **cable car** bridge.

On the Lowland are a number of gardens, parks, and a children's zoo (including a remarkable trained-bird show). But it's the Headland, at the end of a spectacular cable car ride which overlooks the South China Sea, which has the most interesting exhibits.

The **Ocean Theatre** here is the largest marine mammal theatre in the world, with a seating capacity of 4,000 and a pool fit for dolphins, killer whales, and occasional visiting diving shows. **Wave Cove**, nearby, simulates a rocky coastline, with a special machine that generates waves up to 3 feet (1 metre) high. At two different levels, sea lions, seals, dolphins, penguins and sea birds may be seen diving or skimming along the cove's surface. There is an Atoll Reef with more than 300 different fish species and about 30,000 swimming specimens. It is the largest aquarium in the world, containing 500,000 gallons (2-million litres) of seawater. One can view this aquarium from three different levels.

Close to the Atoll Reef is the walk through **Shark Aquarium**. Opened only

Having a ball at Ocean Park.

202

in December 1990, 50 well-fed sharks belonging to 20 species (no Great Whites, though) can be seen lazing around and being hand-fed.

On the headland is also the amusement park with various rides including The Dragon, one of the world's longest rollercoasters at 2,484 feet (840 metres), which seems to whip out over the beautiful South China Sea at each pass.

Anyone who ventures up to the headland can attest to the magnificent views. The 231-foot (70.5-metre) **Sky Tower** should add a grand dimension to the word "viewing". Its total height is about 627 feet (200 metres) above the Lamma Channel – and no, you will not have to walk. A revolving cabin capable of holding 72 people will do the honours.

The **Japanese Garden** next to the Aviary are two more attractions in addition to three **Greenhouses** and a **Butterfly House**.

One different aspect of the Ocean Park is the living museum, **Middle Kingdom**. Opened in 1990, this is a 12,000-sq. yard (10,000-sq. metre) reincarnation of 5,000 year of Chinese history through seven dynasties dating from Xia (2205 BC) to the last one, the Qing (Ching), which was overthrown in 1911.

Tickets to Ocean Park (including Middle Kingdom, rides, avaries etc.) cost HK$130 for adults, HK$65 children (6–17; under 6 free). Call 555-3554 or 873-8555 for information.

In 1984, the adjacent **Water World** section was opened as a separate attraction. This is a water play park with dozens of different activities including water slides and a lovely beach. It is only open from late April through October. The cost is HK$60 for adults, HK$30 for kids (6–17; under 6 free), with special low evening prices. Call 555-3554 or 552-0293 for information.

The main road, **Wong Chuk Hang**, proceeds left towards Aberdeen and soon passes by the Grantham Hospital (on the right) which treats heart diseases exclusively. Also near here is the Aberdeen Trade School, run by the Catholic Church to educate the children of Aberdeen's boat people.

Getting around in the park is half the fun.

ABERDEEN

Aberdeen has a character unlike any other town in the colony. Its charm, though, is questionable because this naturally ideal typhoon anchorage is home to about 20,000 of Hong Kong's 70,000 "boat people" and their 3,000-odd junks and *sampans*.

"Egg people": The term "boat people" has two meanings. One refers to Vietnamese refugees who came pouring into Hong Kong during the late 1970s, causing a momentary population-plus panic. (The panic was soon allayed when manufacturers realized that the Vietnamese were an ideal source of cheap labour.) The more traditional boat people are those who have been living on local waters for thousands of years.

The latter group of boat people consists of two main tribes: the Tanka (literally the "egg people," because they used to pay taxes in eggs rather than cash) and the Hoklo. Other Chinese have never accepted them (pre-Communist China wouldn't even permit them to settle on land), but Hong Kong is encouraging them to leave their boats. Schools for their children are opening up, housing estates are being constructed for them, and as land is gradually reclaimed from the harbour, the fishing people are being lured to work in factories.

Romantics might bemoan this loss of "traditional life," but these hot metal-roofed boats are really a "floating slum" and an obviously inconvenient lifestyle. Nobody, however, is forcing the boat people to leave their lifestyles: they make their own choice.

"Little Hong Kong": At any rate, tourists are still seduced by the colourful 30-minute ride through Aberdeen Harbour (for about HK$100). They still enjoy the chaotic atmosphere, the incredible collection of sea life and the dynamism of this city upon the water. They also enjoy the opulent Chinese **floating restaurants** (take a *sampan* there), which are not in Aberdeen Harbour proper anymore, but in the "yacht basin" of

Aberdeen's typhoon shelter is home to many "boat people."

Shumwan, across from the Aberdeen Boat Club and the Aberdeen Marina.

What, though, does the southern Hong Kong town of Aberdeen have to do with that Scottish town of the same name? Only that the village wasn't named after the Scottish city, but for the Earl of Aberdeen, the 1848 Secretary of State for the Colonies. To the Chinese, Aberdeen is still called *Heung Keung Tsai*: **Little Hong Kong**. And like "big" Hong Kong, Aberdeen hardly lacks for wealth. Perhaps most of the wealth has come through smuggling instead of legitimate enterprises, but **Main Street** here has quite a few banks, countless jewellery shops and the feeling of a bustling financial district.

To see this area best, begin with the town's **Tin Hau Temple** built here in 1851. The temple is rather shabby most of the year, but during April's Tin Hau Festival, it is alive with ceremony and thousands of gaily-decorated boats converge on Aberdeen's shores. It's an event not to be missed. Along Aberdeen's Main Street is a good **China Products Emporium** and an interesting **Fisherman's Hall** where wedding receptions and elections are held.

The four side streets between Aberdeen's Main Road and Chendu Road all have their own character. Northernmost **Lok Yeung Road** has a little shop selling pet food – not only for fish and birds, but also for caterpillars! And street barbers still cut a mean head of hair here.

At **Wu Pak Street** there are a few good general markets. Finally, at **Wu Nam Street**, one can take a ferry four times a day to **Sok Kwu Wan**, a tiny settlement on **Lamma Island**, to sample that isle's good seafood. Why so good? Because the ferry is managed by the progressive Sok Kwu Wan Fisherman's Society. They should know!

Another good ferry ride (optional because a bridge now links the mainland to that destination – is the one to **Apleichau Island**. This island, just 2 minutes away from Aberdeen, houses the colony's great boat-builders. They make ferries, sloops, cruisers, speedboats, yachts and steel lighters, as well as traditional *sampan* and junks. For the latter, it takes only 3 months to make an 80-foot (24-metre) junk from teak logs, a traditional task they complete using no blueprints. An innate sense of knowing what's right takes the place of formal plans. Usually somebody in the yards speaks English.

Near the island's landing is a shrine to its local god, Hung Shing, a legendary weather forecaster. Few people pay homage at this **Hung Shing Shrine**, because Tin Hau is more popular.

On the outskirts of Aberdeen is the **Holy Spirit Seminary**, which overlooks the town. This seminary, built in 1931, welcomes visitors.

Jade Palace Restaurant at 2 Wah Fu Road houses five floors of an extraordinary collection of eating places: French, Cantonese, Shanghainese, Pekinese, Hong Kong's only Hunanese restaurant and a proper nightclub.

Up the hill towards Pokfulam is **Chi Fu Fa Yuen**, another huge housing development with its own shopping centre which includes the Chi Fu village, a "traditional" Chinese village.

Tin Hau, the Goddess of the Sea.

THE STAR FERRY

Hong Kong, which in Cantonese means "Fragrant Harbour," provides a spectacular venue for the double-ended double-decker green and white Star Ferries which ply a route of 0.85 nautical miles every few minutes (that adds up to an average of 455 crossings per day) between the piers at Hong Kong Island's Central and Kowloon's Tsimshatsui. They run so frequently that one of the Star's senior coxswains has reportedly logged a million miles on the cross-harbour route.

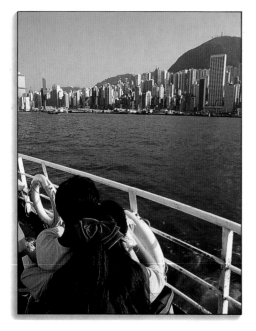

On board the Star Ferry, residents and tourists can be easily differentiated. The tourists are normally toting cameras and are understandably agog at the harbour's charming panorama of junks, lighters, *sampans*, freighters, tankers, motor-boats, ferries, and warships which are constantly maneuvering through this confined waterway. The colony's jaded residents, meanwhile, are tucked into a newspaper or, if it's racing season, a scratch sheet giving tips and odds on the day's nags. Indeed, the Star Ferry is so vital a part of life in the colony that a late 1950s fare increase of HK$0.05 was enough to spark a riot.

The Star Ferry Company traces its origin to 1870 (only three decades after the founding of the colony) when a Grant Smith initiated a first cross-harbour ferry service with a twin-screw launch. Eighteen years later, an Indian resident, Dorabjee Nowrojee, introduced the colony's first steamboat ferry service. In 1898, Nowrojee was bought out by the Star Ferry Company which a year later replaced his older boats with two coal-burning double-decker ferries, the *Morning Star* and the *Guiding Star*.

A paltry sum of HK$0.10 at the turn of the century entitled you to a first class one-way trip. And Chinese peasants who used the lower deck paid only HK$0.01 per crossing. In those first years, the average annual passenger traffic was about 600,000. By 1904, three more vessels had been added to the Star Ferry's fleet and fares were increased to HK$0.15 and HK$0.10 for first and economy classes.

At the turn of this century, piracy was still rampant here, but thanks to their lucky stars, a Star Ferry was never pirated. The only serious peacetime accident happened in April 1937, when the *Meridian Star*, approaching Hong Kong Island with what was later diagnosed as a faulty steering gear, struck a sister craft, the *Night Star*, amid ships. The *Night Star* returned to the Hong Kong pier to allow its passengers to disembark, but continued to sink while tied at dockside. At the last moment, her crew slipped lines and it sank next to the pier. She was later recovered.

The fleet consists of a dozen green and white, double-bowed vessels which can take 580 passengers and a 10-men crew each. The Star Ferry Central to Tsimshatsui (Kowloon) runs daily (except during the typhoon season) from 6.30 a.m. to 11.30 p.m. (the Central-Hong Kong Service runs 7 a.m. to 7.20 p.m.). The Tsimshatsui (Kowloon)-Wanchai service runs from 7.30 a.m. to 11 p.m.

All told, the Star Ferry is one of the world's greatest travel bargains. Its first-class one-way fare is only HK$1.20 (the lower deck second class fare is HK$1). The company also runs harbour tours and water/land tours in conjunction with Hong Kong Tramways.

Slowly the kaleidoscope that is Hong Kong's urban theatre passes by: Hong Kong Island's north shore appears during abrupt stops and starts as the ancient vehicles jerk through some of the world's worst traffic.

Hong Kong's trams (or streetcars, if you prefer the American term) are an intriguing aspect of life in the colony. Though they serve as a prime form of transportation for many of Hong Kong Island's 1.5 million residents, they are also one of the best ways to enjoy a charming do-it-yourself tour of the island – at the amazingly low price of only HK$1 per journey, regardless of distance travelled.

a tram. Unfortunately, there are no trams in Kowloon. You'll have to come across to Hong Kong Island to experience one.

A word of warning: the trams have a seating capacity of 28 on the upper deck and 20 on the lower deck. But about another 100 people can be stuffed – and are stuffed – into one during rush hours. Thus, it's no fun travelling by tram during rush hours. Not only is it uncomfortably crowded, but outside traffic is jampacked too. Aside from those two times during the day, and when

The normal tour of Hong Kong Island as packaged by travel agents usually consists of a bus trip up to The Peak, then to North Point and the Aw Boon Haw (formerly Tiger Balm) Gardens, on to Repulse Bay and Aberdeen on the south side of the island, and the journey back.

For a truly unique experience – one that can accommodate any pocketbook – hop on

there are major sporting events or horse races, the trams are fairly uncrowded. All trams require exact fare change.

The trams are regularly spaced, one arriving every few minutes. Once you board a tram, head upstairs and, if possible, sit up front. The view up there, as you might imagine, is a scape of real life in the colony.

The Hong Kong Tourist Association (HKTA) has an excellent fact sheet on trams which, incidentally can be part of a posh dinner tour or, believe it or not, hired out by the hour for rolling cocktail parties. It can also be part of a water-tour in conjunction with the Star Ferry.

__Left__, on the ferry to Central. __Above__, a cheap way to watch the world go by.

Some say they are a social embarrassment. Others feel they are an integral part of Chinese life in the Orient generally, and Hong Kong specifically. Regardless of where you stand on the matter, the rickshaw (or *jinriksha*) still survives in this British Colony.

Clustered around the Hong Kong and Kowloon entrances to the Star Ferry are the remnants of a once vast fleet of rickshaws that, as recently as post World War II, numbered about 8,000. Rickshaws then, as in the 19th century, were an important form of Hong Kong transportation.

Today they number under 20 and owe their existence almost entirely to the tourist trade. Hong Kong's rickshaw "boys" – average age about 60 – show a complete disdain for traffic signs and regulations, pulling their landcrafts in straight lines through pedestrain subways, onto pavements and going in the wrong direction.

Naturally, in a bureaucracy like Hong Kong, you need an annual license to own a rickshaw and a second license to pull it. However, the Hong Kong government issued its last rickshaw license in 1975 when there were about 80 left in the colony. They don't intend to issue any more.

Though rickshaws were once commonly used as taxis, they were also used by wealthy families and businesses that needed or wanted a private and inexpensive form of transport. The last private or commercial license, held by a stationery company in Central District, expired in 1967.

These popular vehicles, known as *sze ka che* (which is also the Cantonese term for any private transport), have always been considered a snug and romantic travelling mode. Indeed, local records show that in 1917, 60 of Hong Kong's 1,750 registered rickshaws were run by brothels.

Sedan chair on wheels: The rickshaw dates back to the 19th century when an ingenious American Baptist missionary, Jonathon Goble, reportedly designed a rickshaw for his wife. It seems Mrs Goble was reluctant to ride in a sedan chair carried by coolies, and she was determined to do something to relieve their difficult labour. Hence the Reverend Goble's rickshaw – a sedan chair on wheels.

The name comes from Japanese words: *jin* (man) *riki* (power) and *sha* (carriage). In modern Tokyo there are less than 100 *jinriksha* still operating, compared with about 170,000 a century ago.

By 1863, some 22 years after Hong Kong was claimed by Britain, the colonial government introduced Ordinance No. 6 – a statute pertaining to the licensing of public vehicles and chairs, drivers, bearers and horses – was passed. By 1895, there were about 700 licensed rickshaws and more than 8,000 regis-

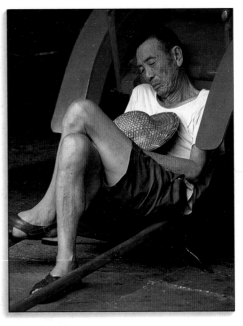

tered pullers.

By 1924 there were 3,411 rickshaws registered. In that year a rickshaw could be rented for HK$0.28 and a puller could expect to net about HK$1.50 in a 12-hour day. But in those days a bowl of fish balls noodles cost HK$0.03 and a labourer could support both a wife and concubine on HK$18 a month.

No more rickshaws?: The rickshaw's decline began with the advent of the motorcar. There were only 218 rickshaws registered here in 1938 just before the World War II started. There was a brief resurgence of popularity in 1945 when the number of rickshaws shot up past 8,000 due to a lack of vehicles, parts and fuel. But as soon as Hong Kong recovered from the depression, the final decline of the rickshaw started.

Believe it or not, there are legally "no" rickshaws now operating in Hong Kong because no annual licenses have been issued for the past eight years. The latest operator's fee was HK$50 per year – which allowed a rickshaw boy full run of Hong Kong Island and the Kowloon Peninsula. For an extra dollar he could add the entire New Territories to his service area. This rule means that those rickshaws you see lined up daily on both sides of the harbour by the Star Ferry terminals do not legally exist because the Transport Department, under whose aegis

then try to charge HK$100–HK$150 for a short ride. A quick run into Central or Tsimshatsui from the Star Ferry terminal should probably cost a good bargainer about HK$20–HK$50.

Sometimes a bit of levity is inserted into the arduous life of a rickshaw-puller. During the 1970s, R&R (Rest & Recreation) invasion by allied troops fighting in Vietnam, rickshaw races between inebriated members of the various countries' armed forces visiting here were run in the middle of the night down Lockhart Road through the Wanchai "Suzie Wong" bar district on Hong Kong Island, or from the Star Ferry to a favourite bar in The Wanch. Much to the amusement

rickshaws operate, has no record of them.

The Hong Kong Tourist Association, however, notes in its *Facts and Information Booklet* that the cost of a rickshaw ride in the colony is HK$100 per 5 minutes. In reality, bartering is the key. In fact, rickshaw boys seem to make most of their money these days by posing for tourists who want a souvenir photo. That price is also negotiable, and can run as high as HK$20–HK$25 a snap. However, beware of rickshaw pullers who skip away with an unsuspecting passenger and

Left, catching a few quick ZZZs. Above, "Take me to the harbour, my good man!"

of rickshaw-pullers, the soldiers would sometimes trade places with a puller and race away madly to the cheers of his mates.

The Rickshaws Derby or Sedan Chair Race are fun projects for charity which attract crowds. At one such event, two Europeans convinced the Transport Department to "issue" them rickshaw licenses on the condition that their rickshaw would be auctioned off for charity. The request was granted.

Rickshaws even managed to survive a period a few years ago when they became an "*in*" gift for the person who has everything." They were literally being bought off the streets for about US$100–US$150 each.

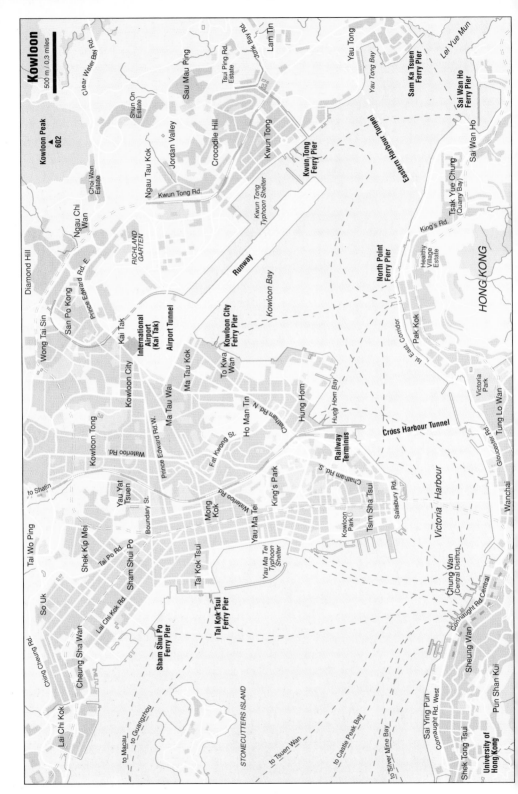

Kowloon

500 m / 0.3 miles

Clear Water Bay Rd.

Kowloon Peak
▲ 602

Shun On Estate

Sau Mau Ping

Jordan Valley

Crocodile Hill

Lam Tin

Yau Tong

Sam Ka Tsuen Ferry Pier

Lei Yue Mun

Sai Wan Ho Ferry Pier

Sai Wan Ho

Junk Bay Rd.

Tsui Ping Rd. Estate

Yau Tong Bay

Kwun Tong

Kwun Tong Ferry Pier

Eastern Harbour Tunnel

Choi Wan Estate

Ngau Chi Wan

Ngau Tau Kok

Kwun Tong Rd.

Kwun Tong Typhoon Shelter

Tsak Yue Chung (Quarry Bay)

Diamond Hill

Wong Tai Sin

San Po Kong

Prince Edward Rd. E.

RICHLAND GARTEN

Runway

Kowloon Bay

North Point Ferry Pier

King's Rd.

Healthy Village Estate

HONG KONG

Kai Tak

International Airport (Kai Tak)

Airport Tunnel

Kowloon City

Kowloon Tong

Kowloon City Ferry Pier

1st East Corridor

Pak Kok

Victoria Park

Tung Lo Wan

to Shatin

Waterloo Rd.

Ma Tau Wai

Ma Tau Kok

To Kwa Wan

Ho Man Tin

Hung Hom

Hung Hom Bay

Gloucester Rd.

Wanchai

Prince Edward Rd. W.

Chatham Rd. N.

Fat Kwong St.

Cross Harbour Tunnel

Tai Wo Ping

So Uk

Shek Kip Mei

Tai Po Rd.

Yau Yat Tsuen

Boundary St.

Mong Kok

Waterloo Rd.

King's Park

Railway Terminus

Chatham Rd. S.

Salisbury Rd.

Victoria   Harbour

Ching Cheung Rd.

Cheung Sha Wan

Lai Chi Kok Rd.

Sham Shui Po

Yau Ma Tei

Tai Kok Tsui

Yau Ma Tei Typhoon Shelter

Kowloon Park

Tsim Sha Tsui

Chung Wan (Central District)

Connaught Rd. Central

Sheung Wan

Lai Chi Kok

Sham Shui Po Ferry Pier

Tai Kok Tsui Ferry Pier

STONECUTTERS ISLAND

to Macau

to Guangzhou

to Tsuen Wan

to Castle Peak Bay

to Silver Mine Bay

Sai Ying Pun

Connaught Rd. West

Shek Tong Tsui

Pun Shan Kui

University of Hong Kong

KOWLOON, "NINE DRAGONS"

Kowloon, though geographically a part of the Chinese mainland, is politically British soil, having been ceded to Britain in 1860 under a Treaty of Peking which was negotiated as a Chinese concession at the time of the so-called Opium Wars. This was the second of three treaties that created the present Royal Crown Colony of Hong Kong.

The name Kowloon is made up of two Chinese words, *gau*, meaning nine, and *lung*, meaning dragon. Tradition says that a boy emperor who once lived here noticed there were eight hills so he called them the "Eight Dragons." A servant pointed out that an emperor is considered to be a dragon also; therefore, the eight hills plus the boy emperor were the nine dragons – *gaulung*. This was transliterated to English as "Kowloon."

Since the government's answer to the colony's shortage of usable land is to grind down mountains and push this earth into the sea, a visitor can no longer count eight dragons, let alone nine. However, there is a little park near Kai Tak Airport where the boy emperor, Ping, and his minister died. They had been driven by Mongol invaders to the edge of the land and, to avoid their being captured, the chief minister took the young emperor into his arms and jumped into the sea, thereby ending the Sung dynasty. Ping was the first and last Chinese emperor ever to live in what is now Hong Kong. In that park is a rock inscribed *Sung Wong Toi* which means the "Sung Emperor's Terrace."

Shopper's "paradise": Kowloon is a mere 3¾ sq. miles (10 sq. km), but it is this small area that most people remember after a visit to Hong Kong. Kowloon is *the* "shoppers' paradise" most visitors aim for, and also the site of most of the colony's big hotels that cater to tourists and businessmen.

At the tip of the peninsula, **Tsimshatsui**, is the **Star Ferry concourse**, and the **Ocean Terminal/Ocean Centre/Harbour City complex**. Then

comes *the* "**Golden Mile**" with its myriad shops and hotels, and Kowloon's answer to the Suzie Wong style of nightlife. Next to Tsimshatsui is the Yaumatei district where people live aboard junks and barges.

The **new railway station** that has replaced the old **Kowloon-Canton Railway Terminal**, where people used to board steam-powered trains for travel to Europe, is in **Hung Hom** on the other side of the "tip." In Hung Hom, next to the railway station, is the Hong Kong Coliseum, a massive indoor stadium which easily seats more than 12,000.

Just beyond is **Kai Tak Airport**, actually a legal part of the New Territories, but looked upon as being in Kowloon. Flights land and lift off from Kai Tak on an average of one every 2½ minutes during peak hours.

Nearby is the famous (in Hong Kong) **Kowloon City Market**, an incredible concentration of outdoor and indoor stalls centered on **Lion Rock Road**. A short walk away lies the spot where the infamous **Walled City** once stood.

Farther east, in the middle of a huge housing estate, is the **Lei Cheng Uk Tomb**, discovered in 1955 during excavations for a housing estate. "The tomb was built during the Han dynasty, when Kowloon was under the administrative district of Tung Kun, in the Wu Kingdom which took control of South China (including present-day Hong Kong) in the period immediately following the collapse of the Han empire." It dates back to between AD 100 and AD 200 and comprises three rooms where you can still see shards of crockery and other relics from those ancient days.

On the border of the New Territories is the largest privately-financed housing project in the city, **Mei Foo Sun Chuen** and nearby is the **Laichikok Amusement Park**. The park has rides and games, a house of horrors and a rink for ice-skating.

There is also the **Sung Dynasty Village**, a complex which holds traditional performances and demonstrations on incense-making. Hungry visitors can stop by at its food outlet for snacks.

Electronic items are usually a good buy.

TSIMSHATSUI, "THE PENINSULA"

When exploring Tsimshatsui, start at the **Star Ferry**. It's no longer the only starting point, because you can now drive through the **Cross-Harbour Tunnel** from Hong Kong Island, or whiz under the harbour on the **Mass Transit Railway**. But for a century, the only way from the island was the faithful Star Ferry, and the reason for going there was to catch the train to Europe. Where the old clock tower stands was "this end" of The Orient Express, the Far East terminus of the rail journey to and from London. Nearby is the **Peninsula Hotel**, where people stayed before boarding the train.

At the **Star Ferry concourse** are some small shops, news vendors, who hawk many overseas newspapers, and a wharf for the harbour's tourboats.

Next to the Star Ferry wharves is **Star House**, which contains the first of the shopping arcades. There is the large **Chinese Arts and Crafts** store, where everything from garments to expensive porcelain may be purchased.

Adjoining the **Star House/Hong Kong Hotel complex** is the **Ocean Terminal/Ocean Centre/Harbour City complex**, on Canton Road, one of the largest air-conditioned and interconnected shopping centre in the whole of Asia. Adjacent to that complex is **China Hong Kong City** which houses the **China Ferry Terminal**. A walkway connects to Kowloon Park. Across Canton Road is Silvercord, another huge shopping centre.

A short walk from the Star Ferry takes you past the old **YMCA** (with modern additions, including a swimming pool) and the venerable (1928) Peninsula Hotel. Across the street is the egg-shaped **Space Museum**, **Planetarium** and **Space Theatre**.

Next to it is the **Hong Kong Museum of Art** and the **Hong Kong Cultural Centre**, a theatre complex capable of staging anything from grand opera or intimate theatre.

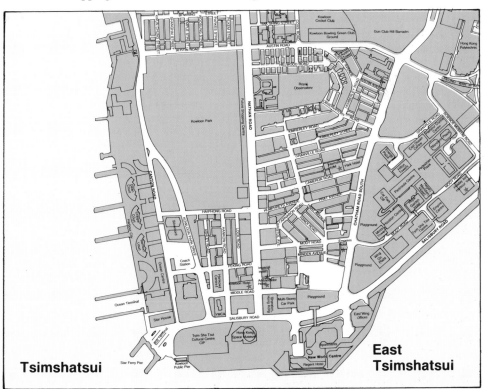

Tsimshatsui

East Tsimshatsui

A walkway along the waterfront runs from the Star Ferry, past the aforementioned, the Regent Hotel and the New World Hotel and Centre onto the Tsimshatsui East waterfront – a pleasant walk if it is not hot and humid or raining.

Nathan Road: Across **Nathan Road** – the start of Hong Kong's famous Golden Mile tourist belt – is the **Sheraton Hotel**, new compared to **The Pen** but now a part of the scene. Across Chatham Road from the Sheraton is **Regent Hotel**, famous for its 40-foot (12-metre) high, glassed-in lobby. Built on the reclamation, it looks across the harbour to Hong Kong Island and lofty Victoria Peak.

Here, at the bottom of Nathan Road, one's overall impression of Tsimshatsui is tall buildings and advertising signs and shop shingles stacked one atop another as far as the eye can see. For a grand commercial impression, stand at this same spot after dark and enjoy the dazzling brilliance of neon-upon-neon.

Nathan Road was named after Sir Matthew Nathan, a major in the Royal Engineers who built the road and later became Hong Kong's Governor (in 1904). During Nathan's time this road was a meandering track lined with banyan trees (some of which can still be seen near the **Miramar Hotel**). Citizens used it to drive out to the countryside in horse-drawn buggies for Sunday picnics. Nathan's futuristic notion that Nathan Road would one day be part of a big commercial centre seemed so laughable then that his road was called "Nathan's Folly."

Today there are glittering jewellery shops, camera stores and hi-fi outlets, thousands of them, crammed to the sky. Indeed, those technological playpens and numerous Oriental crafts shops which crowd Nathan Road and its cross-streets are what most visitors to Hong Kong remember when they return home. Gold, diamonds, jade, pewter, ivory, watches, cameras, rugs, carpets, carvings, candelabras – speciality and sundry shops here stretch on and on.

Looking for food? Restaurants also exist all along Nathan Road and its sidestreets. Formal dining rooms and coffeeshops are easily spotted in the major hotels, and there are innumerable others outside. At least five types of Chinese cuisine – Chiu Chow, Pekinese, Shanghainese, Cantonese and Szechuan – are available in addition to Korean, German, Hungarian, French, Malay, Indonesian, Italian, New York kosher, and others.

Kowloon's Tsimshatsui is also the heart of Hong Kong nightlife. In addition to Chinese opera and traditional theatre, there are glittering international chorus line-cabaret acts in the major hotels. And for gentlemen with hours and dollars to kill, acts of even more universal appeal are performed in the numerous topless bars situated on side-streets off Nathan Road, particularly Peking Road. You can still find girlie-bars that retain the flavour of halcyon R&R days of the 1960s and 1970s. (One of the oldest haunts is the **Red Lips Bar** on Lockhart Road.) There are also many pubs and bars including **Ned Kelly's**, **Mad Dogs**, **Kangaroo** and **Stoned Crow** if you or your pocketbook want a respite from the hustling bargirls.

Bar City: Most of the vintage servicemen's bars have been peacefully overshadowed by the more recent "topless bars," the most famous being the **Bottom's Up** on Hankow Road.

Because the colony is always at the forefront of modern efficiency, Hong Kong also offers packaged joy in the form of frenetic tours of **Bar City** in the **New World Centre**. Here are three bars in one venue – including cowboy-style hooting at Country 'n' Western watering holes and acrobatics at a Japanese disco.

The shoreline swings to the east after Tsimshatsui East, forming Hung Hom Bay. That strange looking up-side down pyramid is the **Hong Kong Coliseum**, a 12,000-seat indoor stadium which has featured everything from the Ice Follies to pop concerts and basketball. Across from it is the red-bricked **Hong Kong Polytechnic**. Beyond that is **Whampoa Gardens**, the centrepiece of which is a giant cement boat which houses the area's shopping arcade and cinemas.

Hung Hom is also the site of **Kaiser Estate**, the venue for many, many factory outlets, mostly selling clothing.

Architecture in balance: Victorian clock tower and post-modern cultural centre.

TAILORING TIPS

Made-to-measure items are still consistently at the top of every Hong Kong visitor's shopping list, and tailoring is a very important part of the touristic economy.

The problem for most shoppers, regardless of destination, is time. There is just not enough of it. Therefore, if first-rate made-to-measure clothes are anywhere on your shopping list, move that must do item to the top of the list. Yes, you can probably find a tailor willing to sell you a 24-hour suit, but like most things done in a rush, it would no doubt prove to be a shoddy and disappointing production – if not today, then next week when the buttons fall off and threads begin to unravel.

Give yourself plenty of time for tailoring by immediately getting on with the laborious task of choosing a tailor. The difficulty is not with physically finding a tailor shop – Hong Kong boasts more than 4,000 – but with finding one that has quality materials and proven suit-building skills. Shop location and, of course, price, are also among important considerations. If you have a reliable business or social contact in the city in which you are planning to buy something, by all means consider their advice.

Everybody in the colony, of course, has a favourite tailor but a visitor should seriously weigh his choice after considering the proximity of the tailor's shop to his hotel. True, you may find a tailor who's slightly cheaper or even better on the back streets and you might even have the address of one recommended by somebody who was here 5 or 10 years ago; but before you make a decision, remember the hassle of travelling to an out-of-the-way shop. Time, money and convenience factors may inspire you to patronize a shop closer to where you live or perhaps in your hotel arcade.

Sewing down a deal: All tailor shops will ask for a down payment and here you can put the *first* rule for tailor shops into practice: "The amount of personal service received is inversely related to the down payment." In other words, the smaller a down payment you can get away with the more attention you will receive at the end of the project.

"Be explicit in your directions," says Sam of the famous Sam's Tailor, dresser to royalty and the commoner alike. In most cases, the salesman who has taken your measurements and to whom you are meticulously rattling off your specific instructions is not the tailor. Most tailor shops give the cloth to members of the tailors' union, who then do the final cutting and sewing. Obviously, it is at this transfer point that there is miscommunication. Perseverance is the key. It is your suit and those specific details you requested are important. Obviously, if you go to a shop with its own in-house tailor, you are ahead of the game. However, in most shops the tailor is not on the premises.

Most tailor shops will try to get by with one fitting. It is easier for them. Demand as many fittings as you desire, but remember that a minimum of 3 days within a 3-to-5 day period is the norm: one when the material is basted up, one when it is partly finished, and a final fitting.

"It's a good idea to reiterate any special requests (number of pockets, flaps, etc.) during these fittings, because the tailor himself will usually do these fittings, in consultation with the sales clerk," adds Sam. If the tailor is not there to fine-focus your fitting, complain. One last word of warning: tailor shops in Hong Kong are hospitable – sometimes too hospitable. Remember, alcohol often complicates this made-to-measure exercise.

If you are going back to a colder climate (like Europe), you might consider advising the tailor to leave the waist a little bit looser, because it is likely you'll put on more weight in the colder climate. Alternatively, you might ask him to leave a little extra material in the waist or crotch so that you can easily have the trousers let out later if necessary.

Mail order: All tailors keep records of clients' measurements, so it is theoretically possible to re-order by mail. Just bear in mind – and body – how many fittings it took when you were last in the shop. If the shop outfitted you right off, maybe you can chance an order via mail. But if it took them a week to make a presentable suit when you were physically here to inspect the work, that problem will only be aggravated when dealing via post. ∎

"Pants are troublesome because they are deceptively easy to fit." As our sage advises, be wary of the tape.

YAUMATEI

Heading north on Kowloon's Canton or Jordan roads, you will surge with the peninsula's traffic into the **Yaumatei District**, an area known for its large typhoon shelter where Hong Kong's famous boat people anchor their floating homes.

Bobbing brothels: It has been said that some citizens of Yaumatei's boat city live a lifetime without setting foot on shore. Inhabitants can get a haircut, medical aid or attend a church service – all without going ashore. And their children can attend floating schools.

Yaumatei typhoon shelter is also famous for its infamous floating brothels – one-girl *sampan*s that don't guarantee privacy. A passionate customer may find that while rocking in his little love-boat he's creating waves and disturbing neighbours who are playing *mahjong* or watching loud television to port and starboard of his busy aft. This is grand

Left, the airport approach is one of the most difficult in the world.

watersport, but amorous love-boaters should be warned not to *sampan*-hop alone in this area at night.

Just inland from the teeming waterfront is **Shanghai Street**, a matrimonial avenue well-known for its traditional shops selling old-fashioned gold ornaments and other such items for a Chinese bride's trousseau.

At the junction of Kansu and Reclamation streets is the colony's famous **Jade Market** which has hundreds of stalls selling jade ornaments. If you plan to visit the market, opt for a morning trip and avoid the afternoon crowd. The closest MTR station is Jordan Road, where dealers offer jade in every sculptable form – from large blocks of the raw material to tiny, ornately-carved chips. Some jade pieces here are priceless; others are almost worthless. It's open from 10 a.m. to 4 p.m., and most of its customers are Chinese, so you know it's not a typical tourist trap.

In the **multi-storey carpark** at Yaumatei you'll find practitioners of an age-old Chinese craft, professional letter-writing. Here a calligrapher will transcribe a letter in pen (or brush) and ink, or he'll bash it out on a typewriter, whichever you prefer. They handle love letters and business correspondence with equal ease.

Famous temples: Yaumatei's **Temple Street**, originally famous for its temples, is now renowned for its **night market** that lights up after the sun goes down. Here, between Jordan Road and Kansu Street you'll find a riot of colour and activity, with an endless array of market goods.

In the Temple Street area are four temples, grouped together in **Public Square Street**. The colony's main **Tin Hau Temple** was built on these shores more than 100 years ago. Land reclamation has forced it to move inland, but Yaumatei's boat people hike to it regularly to worship sea gods, particularly Tin Hau, the protector of fisherfolk. Also in this district are fabulous temples built to honour **Shing Wong**, a spiritual magistrate, and temples dedicated to **Tei** and **Kuan Yin**, the Chinese gods of earth and mercy.

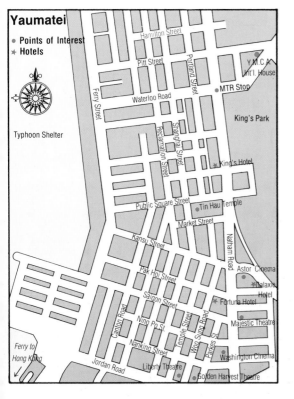

Yaumatei
- Points of Interest
- Hotels

Typhoon Shelter

Hamilton Street
Pitt Street
Portland Street
Ferry Street
Waterloo Road
Y.M.C.A. Int'l. House
MTR Stop
King's Park
Shanghai Street
Reclamation Street
King's Hotel
Public Square Street
Tin Hau Temple
Market Street
Nathan Road
Kansu Street
Pak Hoi Street
Astor Cinema
Galaxie Hotel
Saigon Street
Canton Road
Ning Po St.
Woo Sung Road
Temple Street
Parkes St.
Fortuna Hotel
Majestic Theatre
Nanking Street
Jordan Road
Liberty Theatre
Washington Cinema
Golden Harvest Theatre
Ferry to Hong Kong

Mongkok, Sanpokong and Kwun Tong

Hong Kong is well-known as the most densely populated place on earth. And within Kowloon is a district with the highest population density of Hong Kong – **Mongkok**. Here alone live an estimated 165,000 people per square kilometre.

Wong's Corner: Many stories are told of how Mongkok got its name. In the first place, the word or name does not exist in any Chinese dialect. The "kok" part of it means "corner" in Cantonese, and one popular hypothesis notes that the name was supposed to be Wongkok, meaning "Wong's Corner," but a sign painter inadvertently stenciled the "W" upside down, thus making it Mongkok instead. The shops along this stretch of Nathan Road boast many bargains not found on the lower and pricier end of the "Golden Mile."

Sanpokong, one of Kowloon's first manufacturing areas, is located just opposite Kai Tak Airport in a crowded and dirty jumble of streets bordered on one side by Choi Hung Road and on the other side by Prince Edward Road. Businessmen who visit the colony's factories know the place well. For tourists, the only reason to go there would be to browse through **factory outlet stores** on Tai Yau Street and on sidestreets such as Ng Fong, Luk Hop, Pat Tat and Sheung Hei. Pay attention to the barrow men who may also be wheeling and dealing.

Kwun Tong is considered part of Kowloon administratively but is actually part of the New Territories. It houses numerous industrial facilities and therefore is one of the colony's newer centres for manufacturing, industry and housing estates. It is important enough to be serviced by new four-lane highways (rare in Hong Kong) and ferries from Central, plus it is the final stop on the Mass Transit Railway.

Again, there is not much of interest to tourists except a few factory outlet shops

No-frills shopping in a factory outlet.

and a fascinating **Temple of the Monkey God**, located at **Saumauping Road** in the Saumauping housing estate.

A celestial rascal: The Monkey God in Chinese religion is known and loved by children. He is an Oriental Santa Claus, Charlie Chaplin and Mickey Mouse reincarnated into one. Chinese children are raised on stories of the Monkey God, a rascal who raised so much hell on Earth that he was sent to Hell.

It is a well-known but difficult-to-find temple (the only way is to ask any area resident or the local taxi driver). However, you will soon find a fine shrine dedicated to the Monkey God in his most-exalted form as *Chai Tin Dai Sing*, or the "Great Sage Equal to Heaven." According to some of the stories told of him, he was more than equal to Heaven, which is why he was banished.

Worshippers at this temple seek health, peace and happiness. There is a medium here who speaks for the Monkey God, and an interpreter relays his messages to the faithful because the medium uses a language unknown to anyone except himself, the interpreter and, of course, the Monkey God.

If you happen to visit in the last week of September you can experience a show here that can only be described as a "happening." It's the annual birthday celebration for the Monkey God, and worshippers produce a show worthy of Barnum and Bailey at their most bizarre. The medium first prays until the Monkey God takes over his body and proceeds to use the medium's body to prove his supernatural powers. For openers, the medium will plunge his hands into boiling oil without any burns or discomfort being inflicted upon himself. Thus, the demonstration continues, eventually ending with a grand feast.

The Mass Transit Railway (MTR) makes access to Kwun Tong easy these days. From that stop it's just a short taxi ride to the village of **Leiyuemun**, a tiny fishing village at the eastern entrance of the harbour called **Leiyuemun Pass**. Here you can buy a "jumping" (live) fish and take it to a nearby restaurant for immediate cooking.

Below right, tenement in Mongkok.

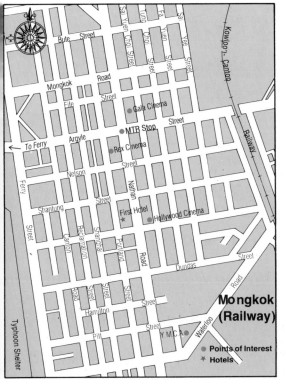

KOWLOON CITY

The **Kowloon City Market** is centred on **Lion Rock Road**. Here you'll find anything from bananas to barbecues, shoes to swine, *cheongsam* and entire sets of porcelain dinnerware – up for sale at prices much less than in the regular "tourist-oriented" districts.

The **Wong Tai Sin Temple** sits a few yards from the MTR station of the same name. The temple is situated on Lung Chung Road amidst modern towering skyscrapers. Like many Chinese temples, this one is not merely a place of worship, but also a centre for community affairs.

From a distance your eye is attracted to Wong Tai Sin's bright yellow roofing tiles, which were brought from Kwantung Province across the border. Much of the temple's stonework was likewise imported from the same Chinese quarries that have supplied temple builders in China during the past centuries.

Favourable *fung shui*: One of the most important icons at Wong Tai Sin was brought to Hong Kong by a family in 1915. It was a painting they had worshipped in a temple in China called Sik Sik Yuen. It was first placed in a small temple in Wanchai, but was later moved to this new Kowloon site. Backed by the powerful Lion Rock, and fronting the sea, geomancers agreed that this new site had favourable *fung shui*.

The temple was completed in 1921 and served for 50 years, before it was again rebuilt.

For its first 35 years, until 1956, the temple was completely private, but then it was opened to the public at an admission fee of HK$0.10. Proceeds went to charity, and so far about HK$4 million dollars have been raised this way. In addition to admission, the temple's donation boxes raised so much money that the old temple was pulled down and a new one constructed.

The current HK$4 million edifice was opened in 1973. More fund-raising is evident as you approach the temple.

Crowded day at Wong Tai Sin Temple.

Here are a series of little fortune-tellers' booths. Each fortune teller pays a monthly rental for his stand. The temple's current earnings, averaging about HK$250,000 a year, go to hospitals and schools.

As you approach Wong Tai Sin you may hear the shaking of a *chim*, a wooden cup full of prayer sticks. The *chim* is shaken until a stick falls out. The number of the stick is then carefully noted, and later, the worshipper will have his stick-fortune interpreted by a seer at one of the rented stalls.

Messages of fortune: If you see somebody shaking out another stick from the cup, and then another, it doesn't mean he's increasing his odds of getting a good fortune told. Rather, he's shaking a stick for each of a number of relatives or friends. He'll collect a message for each of them and report their fortunes when he gets home.

The rear of the temple's main altar is carved to show, both pictorially and in calligraphy, the story of the great god Wong Tai Sin. Originally a poor shep-

herd boy, Wong Tai Sin was one day blessed by an immortal who showed him how to refine cinnabar (vermillion, a red mercuric sulfide, HgS) into an immortal drug.

After doing this, he secluded himself for 40 years and remained alone until his brother found him. The brother (ever practical) asked him what he'd done with the sheep he was supposed to be guarding. The immortal Wong Tai Sin took him to a spot where there were many white boulders, and instantly turned them into sheep.

Kowloon's answer to the "short time" hotels of Wanchai and Causeway Bay is found in **Kowloon Tong** where they are known locally as **blue motels**. They are an economic anomaly in today's Hong Kong, having somehow escaped the so-called "Rent Spiral." In a city where small apartments are advertised for sale at HK$5 million, and where a flat can cost HK$50,000 a month to rent, it seems strange that a trysting couple can have one of these little rooms for only HK$200 an hour.

Below and right, temple devotees wish for good luck in the new year.

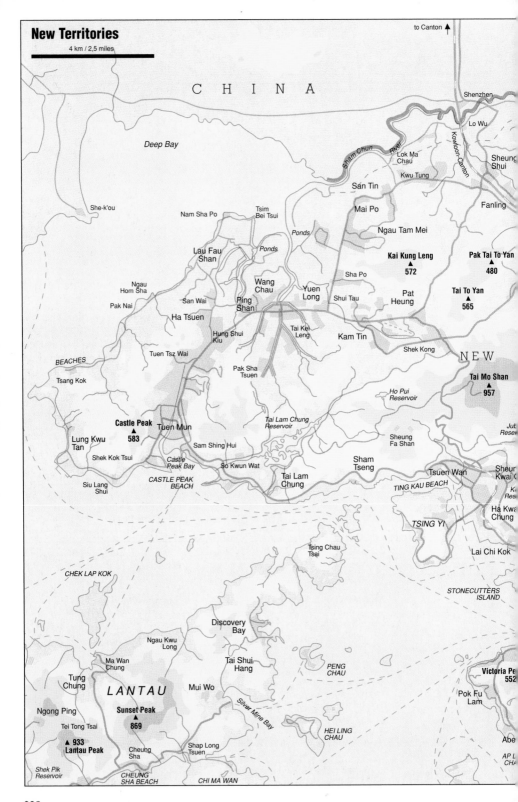

New Territories

4 km / 2,5 miles

to Canton

C H I N A

Shenzhen

Lo Wu

Deep Bay

Sham Chun River

Lok Ma Chau

Kwu Tung

Sheung Shui

She-k'ou

San Tin

Mai Po

Fanling

Nam Sha Po

Tsim Bei Tsui

Ngau Tam Mei

Ponds

Lau Fau Shan

Ponds

Kai Kung Leng
▲
572

Pak Tai To Yan
▲
480

Ngau Hom Sha

Wang Chau

Yuen Long

Sha Po

Pat Heung

Tai To Yan
▲
565

Pak Nai

San Wai

Ping Shan

Shui Tau

Ha Tsuen

Tai Kei Leng

Kam Tin

N E W

Hung Shui Kiu

Tuen Tsz Wai

Shek Kong

BEACHES

Tsang Kok

Pak Sha Tsuen

Tai Mo Shan
▲
957

Ho Pui Reservoir

Castle Peak
▲
583

Tuen Mun

Tai Lam Chung Reservoir

Sheung Fa Shan

Jul
Rese

Lung Kwu Tan

Sam Shing Hui

Shek Kok Tsui

Castle Peak Bay

So Kwun Wat

Tai Lam Chung

Sham Tseng

Tsuen Wan

Sheur
Kwai (

Siu Lang Shui

CASTLE PEAK BEACH

TING KAU BEACH

K
Res

Ha Kwa
Chung

TSING YI

Lai Chi Kok

Tsing Chau Tsai

CHEK LAP KOK

STONECUTTERS
ISLAND

Discovery Bay

Ngau Kwu Long

Tai Shui Hang

PENG CHAU

Victoria Pe
552

Ma Wan Chung

Tung Chung

Mui Wo

Silver Mine Bay

Pok Fu Lam

LANTAU

Ngong Ping

Sunset Peak
▲
869

HEI LING CHAU

Abe

Tei Tong Tsai

▲ 933
Lantau Peak

Cheung Sha

Shap Long Tsuen

AP L
CHA

Shek Pik Reservoir

CHEUNG SHA BEACH

CHI MA WAN

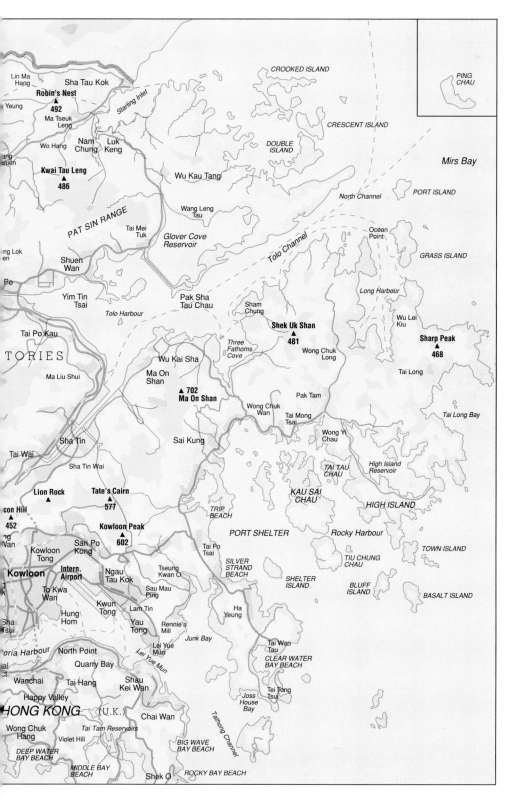

Lin Ma Hang

Sha Tau Kok

Robin's Nest
▲
492

Yeung

Ma Tseuk Leng

Wo Hang

Nam Chung

Luk Keng

Starling Inlet

CROOKED ISLAND

PING CHAU

CRESCENT ISLAND

Kwai Tau Leng
▲
486

Wu Kau Tang

DOUBLE ISLAND

Mirs Bay

PAT SIN RANGE

Tai Mei Tuk

Wang Leng Tau

Glover Cove Reservoir

North Channel

PORT ISLAND

Shuen Wan

Yim Tin Tsai

Pak Sha Tau Chau

Tolo Channel

Ocean Point

GRASS ISLAND

Long Harbour

Wu Lei Kiu

Sham Chung

Tai Po Kau

Tolo Harbour

Shek Uk Shan
▲
481

Wong Chuk Long

Sharp Peak
▲
468

Three Fathoms Cove

Tai Long

T O R I E S

Wu Kai Sha

Ma On Shan

Ma Liu Shui

▲ **702**
Ma On Shan

Pak Tam

Tai Long Bay

Wong Chuk Wan

Tai Mong Tsai

Sai Kung

Wong Yi Chau

Sha Tin

Tai Wai

Sha Tin Wai

TAI TAU CHAU

High Island Reservoir

Lion Rock
▲

Tate's Cairn
▲
577

KAU SAI CHAU

HIGH ISLAND

con Hill
▲
452

Kowloon Peak
▲
602

TRIP BEACH

PORT SHELTER

Rocky Harbour

TOWN ISLAND

g
Van

San Po Kong

Kowloon Tong

Tai Po Tsai

TIU CHUNG CHAU

Kowloon

Intern. Airport

Ngau Tau Kok

Tseung Kwan O

SILVER STRAND BEACH

SHELTER ISLAND

BLUFF ISLAND

BASALT ISLAND

To Kwa Wan

Sau Mau Ping

Lam Tin

Hung Hom

Kwun Tong

Yau Tong

Rennie's Mill

Ha Yeung

Sha
sui

ria Harbour

North Point

Junk Bay

Lei Yue Mun

Tai Wan Tau

CLEAR WATER BAY BEACH

Quarry Bay

Wanchai

Tai Hang

Shau Kei Wan

Tei Tong Tsui

Happy Valley

HONG KONG (U.K.)

Chai Wan

Joss House Bay

Wong Chuk Hang

Tai Tam Reservoirs

Violet Hill

DEEP WATER BAY BEACH

MIDDLE BAY BEACH

Shek O

BIG WAVE BAY BEACH

ROCKY BAY BEACH

Tathong Channel

THE NEW TERRITORIES

Many visitors to Hong Kong see only a small fraction of this unique British colony. Most concentrate on bargain-hunting in Central and Tsimshatsui, sometimes interrupting their shopping sprees with a water tour of Aberdeen or an obligatory bus trip to the top of The Peak. Other more adventurous folks book a ferryboat trip to either Lantau, Cheung Chau or Lamma Island, where they get to see an easier-going part of Hong Kong.

All of these usual excursions are good fun, but even if you take in some of the outer islands, you would have missed out on more than 88 percent of Hong Kong's 412 sq. miles (1,070 sq. km). Indeed, a Hong Kong visitor is short-changing himself if he doesn't spend at least one full day exploring the colony's **New Territories**.

The New Territories include the area right down to Boundary Street in Kowloon, but most people here say you're not really in the New Territories until you've travelled beyond Lion Rock Tunnel, Kowloon's Walled City and Laichikok. Actually, the Li Cheng Uk Tomb, the Walled City, Kwun Tong, and Kai Tai Airport are all part of the New Territories lease, but they are popularly considered to be in Kowloon, or "New Kowloon."

You can start your New Territories tour by heading out toward **Castle Peak** (*see map*) or towards Shatin and Taipo. Alternatively, you can travel on Clearwater Bay Road which leads to the **Sai Kung Peninsula**.

On the Castle Peak side of the Kowloon peninsula is **Laichikok Amusement Park** which has been entertaining people for decades and is one of the world's few places where you can enjoy Chinese opera and ice skating in the same compound. Another attraction, the **Sung Dynasty Village**, is a recreation of part of a village that existed in China 1,000 years ago. Everything in the place has been made exactly as it was in olden times, from the wineshop to the "bank" (the same kind in which the first paper money in the world was used). The village's impressarios stage special performances for visitors that include a traditional wedding ceremony and *kung-fu* demonstrations.

Just around the corner from Laichikok is **Kwai Chung**, the complex of five container terminals, and the industrial community of **Tsuen Wan**, a good example of Hong Kong's "New Town" developments. It is the end of one MTR line and when you look at the skyline of this city with a projected population of a million people, it is difficult to imagine its romantic, often violent, and essentially rural past.

The Tsuen Wan area has been inhabited since time immemorial, but the recent Chinese presence seems to have begun about the 2nd century AD. In the 13th century the Chinese empire stretched to this area simply because the Chinese Emperor was being driven south by invading Mongols. In 1277 he and his entourage arrived in Tsuen Wan. Later, between 1662 and 1669, when the Formosan pirate Koxinga was building his empire, the Manchu government ordered a mass evacuation of coastal areas to save the populace from that marauder. Koxinga's forces demolished the vacated settlement of Tsuen Wan and it was not repopulated until the late 17th century.

In the country: In 1898, at the time the New Territories were leased to Hong Kong's colonial government, the total industry of the Tsuen Wan area consisted of 24 factories. These factories produced incense powder, and were powered by waterwheels turned by streams running down the mountainside. The population then was about 3,000. The year 1919 saw completion of **Castle Peak Road**, and by 1961 there were 250 industrial enterprises employing about 24,000 of the New Territories' residents.

The container terminals you now see were built entirely on reclaimed land. Leases have been granted on **Tsing Yi Island** to industrial enterprises such as tank farms, power stations and other ventures that require only initial access by water. When land access was needed, the government contributed to the cost of the bridge you now see spanning **Rambler Channel**.

From Tsuen Wan, heading out toward Castle Peak, you suddenly, surprisingly, find yourself in the country! If you take the **Tuen Mun Highway**, you will race along a modern motorway with few views of the countryside, except for glimpses of gardens sliced by modern clover-leaf interchanges and flyovers. You end up in the new town of Tuen Mun, which is connected by a Light Rail Transport system to the old market town of Yuen Long.

From this road you'll see more of the New Territories' agriculture, mostly produce grown for the urban market – such as lettuce, cabbage, carrots, and other items familiar to Western visitors. There is still plenty of evidence of traditional Chinese farming; people plant rice by hand, and till their fields with plows pulled by water buffaloes.

Indeed, while on this road one begins to understand why the oldest of the New Territories' walled villages, Kam Tin, was given a name which in literal translation means "Embroidered Fields."

Gurkhas and gardens: A little farther on is the headquarters of the colony's **Gurkha Regiment**, those world-famous Nepalese fighters who have for so many years supported the armed forces of the British Commonwealth.

About 13.5 miles (21.8 km) along Castle Peak Road is **Dragon Garden**, where occasionally, by special arrangement, group tours are accepted at a small fee per person.

This is a traditional Chinese garden, built by a wealthy Hong Kong businessman, and comprises grottoes, ponds, **a neo-imperial mausoleum** and a 50-foot (15-metre) sculpture of a dragon lying half submerged in a pond. Many of the plants in this garden were imported from China.

Near Castle Peak itself, adjacent to the LRT station, is a huge temple called **Ching Chuen Koong**, and it is unusual in several ways. For one thing, it is home for aged people who have no relatives or means of support. Secondly,

Traditional cake making at the Sung Dynasty Village.

it is a repository for many Chinese art treasures, including lanterns more than 200 years old and a jade seal more than 1,000 years old. There is a library of 4,000 books, which document the history of the Taoist religion.

The interior of the main room is as ornate as in ancient temples, with red and green rafters under a roof and beams painted in a green and yellow pattern.

This temple is dedicated to Lui Tung Bun, one of the so-called Taoist Immortals. He was born in AD 789 and became a Taoist missionary after he was inspired by a dream known in mythology as the "Rice Wine Dream." Whatever caused his inspiration, it set him on the path of good works and he spread the works of the Taoist faith rapidly, ridding the earth of many evils.

He also had the help of magic weapons, such as a **devil-slaying sword** and **magic fly-switch** that you'll see displayed alongside his statue in the temple. At the front of the altar is a **1,000-year-old jade seal** kept in a glass case. The altar is protected by two statues that

Monastery in Tuen Mun.

were carved from white stone about 300 years ago for a temple in Beijing.

Inside the temple you'll see room after room of small photographs of people who have died. Their relatives pay the temple's keepers to have these pictures placed in special numbered slots, and forever after, living progeny can visit to pray for their ancestors.

"Cup Fairy Hill": Near Tuen Mun, on the slopes of **Castle Peak**, is a much smaller, but just as interesting temple. Though it is fairly high up the slope, there is a paved road that runs almost to its entrance.

This small **Pei Tu Temple** is dedicated to a character of Chinese mythology who was a monk, but not a totally honest one, and was forever getting into trouble. One night he stayed with a family and in the morning took off with a prized golden statue.

His perturbed host and friends pursued him on horseback to a bend in the river. The monk then called upon one of his magic skills, took out his wooden bowl, stepped into it, and pushed off across the

stream. All the horsemen could do was watch. They couldn't risk their horses or lives in the deep, fast river. From that time on the rascal monk was known as the "Cup Ferry," which in Chinese is *Pei Tu*. When he was finally driven south as far as Castle Peak, then called "**Green Mountain**," he stopped running and established his monastery on this hillside. Hence it is called *Pei Tu Shan*, which means "**Cup Ferry Hill**."

On one side of the gateway of the Pei Tu Temple is an inscription stating: "There is no gate in this gateway because we do not want to keep people out." On the other side of the gateway is another message saying that the temple is always clean because no one ever leaves any trash lying around – a gentle hint for visitors and worshippers.

A must on any trip around the New Territories is **Lau Fau Shan**, a huge fishmarket near **Yuen Long**. Here you'll find a restaurant with an entryway and walls decorated with thousands of oyster shells, each about 5–6 inches (13–15 cm) long.

A "street" much too narrow for an automobile passes by dozens of restaurants, both small, open-air affairs and smart, air-conditioned places. Here are sellers of dried fish and salted fish and many places hawking live shrimp, prawns and larger fishes. Look at the fishes swimming around in the tanks, pick one out, pay for it, then take it to one of the nearby restaurants and have it cooked. However, don't eat the sometimes contaminated raw oysters.

At the end of the street is a **fishmarket** where boats unload the previous night's catch and where the day's weighing and bidding activity cause a deafening hullabaloo. There are mountains of empty oyster shells and live oysters 4–5 inches (10–13 cm) big. Out on the dock you can see China just 2 miles (3 km) away. Many illegal immigrants from China have swum to the bay here.

Yuen Long is another redevelopment project. It began as a traditional market town set in the middle of the largest flood plain in the New Territories. Its population, before redevelopment, was 40,000, and that is expected to grow to 1 million when all the residential and commercial land in this area has been developed as planned. Formerly a centre for privately-run marketing, the town is rapidly taking on a labour-intensive, light industrial role which is expected to absorb up to 20 percent of this area's work force.

North of Yuen Long is a new housing development, beside the **Mai Po marshes**, that is a marvel for all visitors from North America. Upon completion of its first phase, the **Fairview Park** housing project gave North American visitors the eerie feeling that they had somehow slipped through a time and location warp into a small town in the American Midwest of the late 1940s. Here are perfectly straight streets, prim two-storey houses of only three varying designs, white-picket fences, little gates, and a pair of young trees planted in each home's green lawn.

Walled villages: Fairview Park, which is populated almost exclusively by Chinese families, is a true meeting place of East and West. Happy throngs of mostly

High-rises in Tsuen Wan.

young people enjoy modern, light, airy homes with little of the noise and industrial pollution of other parts of Hong Kong. Here, there is sunshine and fresh air, and soon there will be industry nearby, and on-site facilities for recreation and entertainment. At the back of the estate is a sort of "environment wall." On the other side are the Mai Po marshes, as they always were, supporting wildlife. It's a great spot for bird-watchers.

Also near Yuen Long are the **walled villages** of **Kam Tin**. The most popular for visitors is the **Kat Hing Wai village** (which is often mistakenly referred to as the Kam Tin Walled Village).

There are 400 people living at Kat Hing Wai, all with the same surname, Tang. Built in the 1600s, it is a fortified village with walls 18 feet (6 metres) thick, guard-houses on its four corners, arrow slits for fighting off attackers, and a moat. The "authenticity" may seem spoiled by some of the modern buildings inside, complete with television aerials peeping over the old-time fortifications, but there is still only one entrance, guarded by a heavy wrought iron gate. You can enter the village for a nominal admission fee, but in ancient times, that gate was used to keep out undesirables. Something else that's only allowed by permission, and payment, is the taking of pictures of the elderly folk sitting around the gateway. Only after coughing up a couple of dollars can you snap away. The commercialism continues inside, where at least one street is lined with vendors.

Kam Tin also has a small "Suzie Wong" bar scene, well known to British soldiers stationed in the NT, but virtually unknown to most residents and visitors alike.

An exciting next stop is near the **Lok Ma Chau Police Station**. There, you can stand on a hilltop and gaze at a lot of flat land parted by a meandering river. That river is the **Shum Chun**, and it marks the **Chinese border**.

Unless you plan to take a China tour, this is as close as you'll ever get. That can be quite a thrill, even though China has opened its doors to visitors. Before

Sorting out oyster shells in Lau Fau Shan.

1978, this was as close as most people could get to the Celestial Kingdom.

If the visitor happens to be a business person, he or she will enjoy an added thrill there, something to gladden the heart of any entrepreneur who deals in light manufacturing or assembly of products. In keeping with the many other changes of attitude on the part of the now-progressive Beijing government, China has opened a section of land just across the border in **Shum Chun** for industrial purposes – to encourage joint ventures between overseas investors and Chinese communes. There are already more than thousands of joint ventures operating in this **Special Export Zone**.

Patience may be required for some of the intricacies of the negotiations, but the bottom line results in many cases have been deeply satisfying, particularly for manufacturers who crave low operating costs and unskilled labour. One factory owner, faced with a rapidly-increasing wage bill at his factory in Hong Kong, suggested to Chinese authorities that he pay commune work-ers 20 percent less than what he had paid in Hong Kong. The Chinese negotiator said he thought commune labourers would be pleased with 50 percent less. As it turned out, the workers were more than pleased to sit all day in an air-conditioned building and assemble gadgets than to labour for a pittance in nearby paddy fields. For many Mainland Chinese it is an unexpected introduction to the modern world. Otherwise, they would have to swim to escape from China.

In spite of the so-called "new towns," and the modernization of China across the border, it is in the New Territories, in the vicinity of Yuen Long, that you see aspects of traditional Chinese life that do not exist even inside China itself.

Choice burial sites: You'll see clusters of what appear to be huge pickle jars, with wooden lids, sometimes six or eight parked on a hillside. These pots contain the bones of dead Chinese. These people died and were buried long ago, but several years later, their bones are ex-humed and placed in jars here to await **Farming near Kadoorie.**

236

consignment to their final resting place. This process takes a long time, because the exact arrangement of a grave is tremendously important and may take a long time to ascertain.

The graves, shaped like concrete armchairs, are sometimes huge. You can see them on hillsides, and if you stand by one you can usually view the sea or a pleasant valley. The *fung shui* (wind and water) placement of a grave is important. The departed relative is going to be stuck on that hillside forever, so to keep him happy his descendants bury him where he can enjoy a good view and favourable breezes – conditions which are increasingly difficult to find even for the "living" in Hong Kong. The other reason for the long wait before a proper burial is that these graves cost a comparative fortune, and it may take a hardworking family many years to save up enough money to purchase a well appointed tombsite.

Twisting and turning on Route Twisk: And speaking of construction, there's plenty of it going on in the New Territo-

The distinctive costume of a Hakka woman.

ries. You will see women working along with men here. Here are hardworking **Hakka women** dressed in *samfoo* (black pajama-like suits) their faces framed by black curtains around the brims of their wide coolie hats. They come from a mysterious and very traditional matriarchal society and think nothing of labouring at jobs that Westerners consider to be for-men-only.

Proceed with caution if you are tempted to photograph these women. They dislike photographers, and will literally chase a shutterbug across a field. So, use a zoom lens, or be prepared to shoot and run.

From Yuen Long and Kam Tin you can take a scenic route via **Shek Kong**, which is the big **British military garrison** and **airfield**. From Shek Kong, **Route Twisk** begins, and takes you on one of the best scenic drives in Hong Kong. Within minutes you are high up in forested mountains, apparently far from all human habitation. Route Twisk twists and turns for miles and then suddenly plunges right into the techno-industrial age of modern **Tsuen Wan**.

Before turning into Route Twisk, you can continue on Lam Kam Road to **Pak Ngau Shek** in the **Lam Tsuen Valley**, where the **Kadoorie Experimental and Extension Farm** is located. Aside from the farming, this area is much like a landscaped garden in a rural setting.

Another scenic rural route takes you from **Shek Kong** to **Fanling**, where there are three fine **golf courses**. Also nearby is **Luen Wo Market**, the region's traditional marketplace.

Fanling and nearby **Sheung Shui** are undergoing a redevelopment plans to make another "new town" that will accommodate 170,000 people, the bulk to be housed in Sheung Shui. The area near the **Fanling Railway Station** will be a public housing development for 20,000 people plus a residential and commercial development for another 4,000 people, to be privately developed.

Tai Po – "Buying Place": Just around the corner from the Better 'Ole, but by no means easy to find, is one of the New Territories' least visited temples. It is called **Fung Ying Sin Koon**, a name meaning "paradise." There is an intricate system of pathways and steps leading to the altar and its grounds include many waterfalls and shady benches suitable for meditating.

Tai Po is a place name meaning "buying place," and the town certainly lives up to its name, serving as it has for many years as a place for farmers and fishermen to meet and exchange goods. But, like much of the old market towns, it too has been redeveloped.

The old town lies at the northeastern end of **Tolo Harbour** where the highway crosses the **Lower Lam Tsuen River**. On the northeast side of the river is the famous **Tai Po Market** which includes a huge fish market and dozens of vegetable stalls.

Fu Shing Street will give the visitor a good idea of market town life in the New Territories; it is packed with shops selling everything from rattan furniture to thousand-year-old eggs.

The **Hong Kong Railway Museum**, complete with vintage stock, is housed in the former Tu Po Market KCR station. Not far away, but with its own railway station, is **Tai Po Kau**. From here, or from the train, you can see the departure and return of the fishing fleet. Like all the "new towns," Taipo is undergoing the transition from an old market town to a modern city; its former population of 30,000 is expected to rise to 220,000!

To the east, **Mirs Bay** is largely undeveloped because it's well off the beaten track, its population of islanders cling to traditional employment forms such as fishing and vegetable-growing.

Recently, the bay has achieved dubious fame as a watery escape route for illegal immigrants swimming for Hong Kong. Reports of illegal immigrants being apprehended – and the sighting of the bodies of numerous persons who have drowned in the attempt – are everyday news. There were early-1980 reports of marine police beefing up their forces to stop vicious racketeering in illegals. Opportunists bought high-powered speedboats on a time-payment basis, then made just one overnight run to

Life in the walled village of Tsang Tai Uk.

pick up illegals off Mirs Bay's China shores and run them back to the urban part of Hong Kong. The fees paid by a half dozen grateful illegals more than covered the cost of the down payment on the boat. Today, police also chase smugglers, who transport goods including videos and stolen luxury cars in high-speed boats.

Just to the east of Tai Po on Ting Kok Road is the famous **Tai Ping Carpet Factory**, where you can see all phases of Chinese carpet-making. South of Tai Po, about halfway to Shatin, is the **Chinese University**. Across from the University is the lovely **Yucca da lac**, an outdoor restaurant with superb views.

Whether you enter **Shatin** by road or rail, you'll be amazed to find a bustling metropolis in the middle of the agricultural New Territories. Massive housing projects occupy fields where just a few years ago the greatest activity was water buffaloes pulling plows in rice paddies. The New Town Plaza is a massive shopping and entertainment complex, while Riverside Plaza Hotel along the banks of the Shing Mun River is another modern addition.

Shatin's 12,800 Buddhas: The **Shatin Valley** has several places of worship, of which three are worthy of note:

First is the **Temple of 10,000 Buddhas**, which can be reached by climbing 431 steps up the hillside above the **Shatin Railway Station**. There you will find a main altar room with 12,800 small Buddha statues on its walls. The temple is guarded by huge, fierce looking statues of various gods, and by just as fierce watchdogs which are chained up in the daytime. Also in the complex is a **nine-storey pagoda** of Indian architectural design, commemorating a Buddha who was believed to be the ninth reincarnation of Prince Vishnu.

A farther 69 steps up the hill is the **Temple of Man Fat**, where you can meet the man who created this temple and pagoda complex – even though he died a long time ago. Called **Yuet Kai**, he was a monk who spent a lifetime studying Buddhism and living a meditative life. His greatest concern was to achieve immortality.

When he died he was buried, but, according to Chinese custom, his body was later dug up to be reburied in its final resting place. However, the body was found to be perfectly preserved and radiating a ghostly yellow glow. Since there was obviously something "supernatural" about Yuet Kai, it was decided to preserve his body in gold leaf for posterity.

From the Temple of 10,000 Buddhas, you can see, across the valley, the famous **Amah Rock**, which looks like a woman standing with a baby on her back. Legend has it that a local fisherman once went to sea and did not return with the fleet. His wife waited patiently for his return day after day, but he did not appear. After a year the gods took pity on her and turned her into stone. These days the rock is a place of worship for faithful Chinese women.

From either of these two places of worship you can look down on a third place of worship, one much more in tune with the present day spirit of Hong Kong. This shrine is dedicated to Instant

Tai Ping carpets are coveted worldwide.

Wealth, or The Fast Buck, and is called the Royal Hong Kong Jockey Club's **Shatin Racecourse**. Thousands of punters (the grandstands hold 75,000) persistently go there every October through May horse-racing season to bet money on the ponies and then pray for good fortune.

There is really only one winner in every race, however, and that is The Royal Hong Kong Jockey Club. After every race, hundreds of thousands of crisp Hong Kong dollars flutter into the Jockey Club's coffers. But as with those earned at Happy Valley racecourse, the winnings from these races are spent on charitable projects.

The modern Hong Kong Sports Institute, funded by the RHKJC, is just beyond the racehouse. It exists to train the territory's athletes for international competitions like the Olympics.

Another place of interest is the **Tsang Tai Uk** (Mr Tsang's Big House), a **walled village** built in the mid-19th century by a wealthy quarrymaster. As you emerge from the **Lion Rock Tunnel**, the village is on your right, just a stone's throw from the motorway.

Actually, most of Tsang's progeny have moved elsewhere, and the fortress is now rented out to more distant relatives of his family. However, this remnant of the colony's opulent early days will be preserved despite the usual pile-driving march of high-rise development.

This village is rarely visited by tourists (mainly because of difficult access) but the people here are hospitable, pleasant and the village less commercial than the more frequently visited Kam Tin walled village.

A tour of Hong Kong's New Territories and the Hong Kong Tourist Association's **The Land Between** tour are some of the best tours. Both provide the visitor with a good look at Chinese traditional life, but at the same time there is evidence everywhere of the urgency of modern development. A great relief from this mad rush into the use-of-space age is afforded by a separate trip to another part of the New Territories called the **Sai Kung Peninsula**.

Beyond Kai Tak Airport follow Clearwater Bay Road past some new developments, then turn off onto **Hiram's Highway** which takes you to **Sai Kung Village** (slated for redevelopment, but not yet touched by it) and you'll be in an area preserved as a **country park**. The park is not open to private motor vehicles. It is one part of Hong Kong where you can put on your boots and backpack and go trekking into the woods for several days.

If you stayed on Clearwater Bay Road, you would find a different scene: luxurious villa set among lush hills, and Hong Kong's answer to the Hollywood of the 1940s and 1950s. This is the **Shaw Brothers Movie Town**. Here, many a mini-epic has been committed to celluloid, and all the stars are Celestials. The only Occidentals present are language-dubbers, so don't be surprised if you see a Mandarin film and the mighty warriors have Pittsburgh accents or a trace of Strine.

Beyond Shaw's the drive is scenic with almost a Mediterranean flavour. There is the posh **Clearwater Bay** country and villas that look down on beautiful beaches and at impossibly green islands which cluster like jade in the expanse of deep blue water. An extra indentation in the shoreline of Clearwater Bay is **Joss House Bay** which really comes alive once a year on the birthday of the sea goddess Tin Hau. Hundreds of junks and *sampans* head for the **Tin Hau Temple** here to pay their respects to the Queen of Heaven, who is also commonly known as the Goddess of the Sea.

This temple was built by two 11th-century brothers who allegedly were saved by Tin Hau after their junk was destroyed by a typhoon. While they were lost at sea, the brothers held onto a statue of Tin Hau, prayed for her help, and eventually they reached **Tung Lung Island** alive.

In 1012, after they had gone into business and become wealthy, they built a temple on the island and dedicated it to Tin Hau. Later, another typhoon wrecked the temple, but descendants of the two brothers built its replacement in 1266 at this site.

Wooden tablets with names of one's relatives are placed in the ancestral shrine.

HONG KONG'S OUTLYING ISLANDS

It is regrettable that so few visitors make time to go to the outlying islands, for it is here that the real magic of Hong Kong is uncovered, an inheritance which brings Hong Kong in line with its apparently more traditional neighbours.

On the islands are ancient villages, little fishing communities, monasteries where for centuries man has contemplated the foolishness of worldly concerns, and natural amenities central Hong Kong seems short of: grass and trees and quiet moments and long empty beaches. Most of these places are only an easy ferry ride away from the Hong Kong most people know.

Although the British Crown Colony of Hong Kong is just short of 150 years old, archaeologists have ascertained that man has been living around this area for close to 6,000 years. Whether Hong Kong's original inhabitants were the forerunners of those here today, no one

really knows. The ancient tribes who left their marks on Hong Kong – in the form of rock carvings found on Lantau, Po Toi, Tung Lung, Cheung Chau, and Kau Sai Chau islands – have probably long since travelled further. Scholar William Meecham, in his book *Rock Carvings of Hong Kong*, has related these early residents to the Yeuh tribes, whose closest living descendants are probably the Vietnamese people.

Apart from these ancient stone carving residents of Hong Kong and its islands, in the last thousand years those who have made their homes on the islands have mainly been the area's traditional fisherfolk and farmers – the Hoklo, the Tanka, and the Hakka. Older descendants of these agrarian tribes have managed to maintain their traditional lifestyle, but their children are now among the greater number of contemporary Chinese who have gone overseas to live and work. In some families every member of the "younger generation" has gone to work in London's Soho district or San Francisco's Chinese restaurants (from where they send money back to their parents to enable them to maintain their satisfying but fast-dying lifestyle).

"Progress" is ending ten centuries of pastoral life here as roads are paved and telephone and electricity services are installed. A large power station is already being built there, two live-in resorts (one with a deluxe resort hotel) are in the offing.

Soaring property values have also brought land developers to the islands – those who want to build big luxury housing developments, and those who have a stake in the visitor industry. They understandably want to get tourists out of the shopping districts so they will spend more time – and money – in the colony.

As in any resort area, there are two sides to this kind of development: on the one hand, it brings a share of prosperity to those who would otherwise miss out on some of Hong Kong's more charming areas. Conversely, the coming of money and a "modern age" signals the ruin of traditional lifestyles.

Preceding pages: home on the range. Left, rock with a view. Below, temple tower on Lantau.

MISTY LANTAU, "BROKEN HEAD"

Of all the outlying islands, the greatest in size, and perhaps in atmosphere, is **Lantau**, which has a land area twice that of Hong Kong Island. In some ways it is still not too late to experience, on Lantau, rural village lifestyles which have endured unchanged (except perhaps for television sets) since the fall of emperors, colonization and the decay of kingdoms and of the colonial empire.

In Cantonese *Lantau* means "Broken Head," perhaps because its rugged dignity is dominated by the ragged and two part **Lantau Peak** that rises 3,086 feet (935 metres) high at the heart of lizard-shaped Lantau.

Lantau has been very much in the news these days because the new airport is to be sited off the north coast on reclaimed land and a tiny island called Chep Lop Kok. Despite new bridges and roads connecting the airport to Kowloon and Hong Kong, Lantau proper is to be cut off from some of the intrusion – though housing estates are planned – to leave most of the island in its rural state.

Follow the Wind: The island is cobwebbed with wandering pathways and dusty trails which spiral up, down and around her scenic mountains.

A particularly good opening trail circles the blue **Shek Pik Reservoir**, on the west slopes of Lantau Peak. This 5,500 million gallon (20,900 million litre) reservoir gathers most of the freshwater carried from Lantau's heights by rushing streams and rivulets.

Because Lantau is twice the size of Hong Kong Island, but supports a population of only about 15,000 inhabitants, the sense of space and peace here is the opposite of that on the more populated island (provided, of course, that you avoid busy weekends when many of the colony's more urbane residents flock here for a respite from their workaday freneticism). It is because of this peace and the sheltering serenity of the island that there are so many monasteries here, both Christian and Buddhist.

For those who land at **Silver Mine Bay**, Lantau's main visitor point, regular buses travel from there along Lantau's southern resort coast to the brightly painted red and gold **Po Lin Monastery**. This popular monastery is set on a steep hill due north of the Shek Pik Reservoir and is home to the world's largest outdoor bronze statue of Buddha. Here, in a large visitors' dining house, you can enjoy a good vegetarian lunch served by Po Lin's resident monks.

West of Po Lin, in the direction of **Tung Chung** on Lantau's north coast, is an excellent walking path that traverses mountain ridges, small canyons and over rushing streams en route to Lantau's **Yin Hing Monastery**, a haven rich with traditional Buddhist paintings and statues. This monastery sits on a slope and commands a fine view of the surrounding mountains, farming country and the blue South China Sea.

For those who would like to break up their Po Lin area tour with a local-style high tea hour, there is a proper tea plantation and teahouse called the **Lantau Tea Gardens** just a short walk away from the Po Lin Monastery compound. The teahouse has rooms for rent, barbecue facilities and a free camping area.

On Lantau's northeast coast, meanwhile, is a meditative spot with a decidedly different aura. This is the **Trappist Haven of Our Lady of Liese (Joy)** at **Tai Shui Hang** which is looked after by a closed Christian order sworn to silence.

Because the Trappist monks are protective of their privacy, they do not welcome casual visitors to their inner sanctums. Until recently, they did allow visitors to stroll through their grounds.

The Trappists also serve a simple fare to hungry travellers; and it is possible to spend an evening in their simple dormitory or a two-room guest house. The best way to reach the monastery, besides hiking there overland, is to catch a ferry to nearby **Peng Chau Island**, then hire a *sampan* to take you across the narrow channel between Peng Chau and Tai Shui Hang on Lantau, or catch a ferry (from Peng Chau).

Lantau is also a fine place to observe the "living" traditional lives of the colony's fast-disappearing "boat people."

Lantau monk.

In the popular arrival point and small fishing village of **Silver Mine Bay** (also known as **Mui Wo**), boat people will be seen crowded aboard numerous junks and *sampans* in that protected waterway.

Anyone who has seen a junk close up has to marvel at the fact that such a rough and tumble collection of timber, barrels, poles and rough-hewn planks can cope with Hong Kong's typhoon-ridden seas. But they do – and when a nasty storm hits the colony, the biggest of these junks go out to sea to do battle there with nature, rather than risk being battered into splinters near shore.

Semi-land dwellers: In Lantau's principle town, **Tai O**, on the west coast, the island's Tanka boat people have turned semi-land dwellers. Some of their larger junks have been turned into three-storey "permanent" living structures that have been gathered together into a seaborne slum. Farther up at Tai O creek, they have also built rickety homes on stilts over parts of the creek where waters rise during tide changes.

Another fine place to study these sturdy old seagoing horsecarts is at **Penny's Bay** on Lantau's north coast. One of Hong Kong's best-known shipmakers is based there. His shipbuilders make not only traditional junks, but also modern cruising craft.

While on the northern side of Lantau, try to visit **Tung Chung**, an old fortress and bay that curves around the pointed southern tip of little **Chek Lap Kok Island**, now devastated by work on the new airport project.

On a hill overlooking this little harbour you'll spot an **old fort** which was built in 1817. This fort's thick ramparts still stand, as do six old cannons, much as they did during the last century when they guarded this town and bay from smugglers, pirates and unexpected "Outer Barbarians."

Another hideaway which beckons persons interested in peace and quiet is the **Lantau Mountain Camp** at about the 2,538 feet (769 metres) elevation of **Sunset Peak** (2,868 feet/869 metres). This camp consists of 20 small stone houses which were built before World

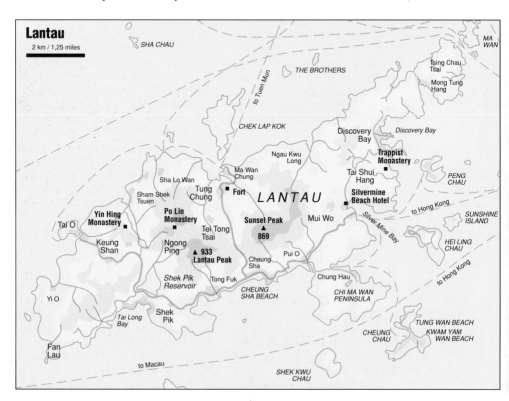

War II as a rest haven for the colony's Christians and Christian missionaries on leave from China. They can also be rented by laymen who book in advance.

Expansive Lantau is also understandably famed for its many long, smooth and often empty beaches. The finest sandy sweeps are on the southeast coastline that arcs from **Cheung Sha** south of Silver Mine Bay to **Tong Fuk**.

The most popular and crowded beach (probably because it is the easiest one to reach) is **Silver Mine Bay Beach** and a resort of the same name near the Silver Mine Bay ferry landing. From Silver Mine Bay you can travel by good road to the afore-mentioned Tai O village. It is an old, somewhat grubby place, but truly ethnic in the complete Chinese sense.

The bus route from Silver Mine Bay to Tai O passes through **Pui O Village**, a nondescript seaside village whose main claim to fame is the **Tong Fuk Provisions Store**. This out-of-the-way store not only stocks ample provisions of cold wine and beer, but is also a restaurant serving both Chinese and Western food. It is nicknamed " Charlie's" because the owner is a retired chef from the Hong Kong Hilton Hotel.

Off-the-beaten-track Tai O can also be reached by ferry from Central. En route to Tai O the Central-Tai O Ferry puts in at Tung Chung, the northern shore fortress village, so by planning your day in advance you can enjoy both Tai O, Tung Chung and a fine cruise.

A major development, isolated from the rest of the islands, on Lantau is **Discovery Bay**, a housing/resort complex that includes a golf club. It is one of the most pleasant places to live in Hong Kong, right by the beach in a well-planned, uncrowded community.

The **Sea Ranch Development** on the southernmost tip of **Chi Ma Wan Peninsula** is another project. It too has apartments in a lovely environment.

Discovery Bay is served by hoverferries which run from Blake Pier in Central. And notwithstanding, Lantau remains a good place to escape from the hustle and beep of urban Hong Kong.

Lantau provides city folk the chance to enjoy its wide open spaces.

LOVELY LAMMA, "STONE AGE ISLE"

The third largest of the outlying islands, and somehow less well-known both to visitors and to local people, is **Lamma Island**. It is nicknamed "Stone Age Island" because of its archaeological association with some of the earliest settlements in Hong Kong; and perhaps also because it is reasonably free of high-rise buildings, cars and factories.

Though it is just over 5 sq. miles (8 sq. km), Lamma is rich in green hills and beautiful bays. And – because it's mountainous – there is a very small area of cultivation. Eroded mountain tops dominate the island's grassy lower slopes.

Lamma is an island totally devoted to fishing and has a small population, less than 6,000 people (which includes a surprising number of Europeans who want to "get away from it all" and commute to urban Hong Kong daily for work). Although Lamma has a regular ferry service, it has remained relatively undiscovered – much to the joy of those who have moved out to its peaceful ambience.

"Weekend Admirals": The nearest Lamma village to Aberdeen – from where a round trip by privately-chartered *sampan* will cost about HK$100 – is **Sok Kwu Wan**, which lies on the eastern shore of a long fjord-like inlet known as **Picnic Bay** and is the haunt of Hong Kong's "Weekend Admirals" or "Saturday Sailors," the nautical names given to the colony's pleasure-junk captains.

Its quay is lined with excellent fresh seafood restaurants – the **Lamma Hilton** (no relation), **Lamma Regent**, **Lamma Seafood Fortune**, **Peach Garden**, **Fu Kee** and **Chow Kee** seem to share most of the business – so treat yourself to a bargain repast while you are here.

It is possible to walk the entire length of the island to Sok Wan's sister town of **Yung Shue Wan** at the north end of Lamma. This village, popular with expatriates trying to get away from the bustle of Hong Kong, sports many restaurants as well as bars. This trek follows a gentle hilly track up and down dividing valleys and treats hikers to a spectacular view across the sea to the Chinese **Lemas Islands**. The entire journey can be negotiated in a couple of hours, thereby leaving time for a fine Lamma seafood meal.

Vegetable farms: Both towns here offer the best of many Chinese worlds to the curious onlooker. Not isolated, yet underdeveloped, Yung Shue Wan has an excellent street market and the air is pungent with the smell of dried fish. Vegetable farms stretch up behind the village. At Sok Kwu Wan, visit the lovely **Tin Hau Temple**. The road which connects these two towns leads a walker first through neat patches of paddy and an occasional cluster of brightly-painted houses, then along **Hung Shing Ye Beach**, a long clean beach.

Farther along, the road gives way to narrow dusty tracks. A gentle climb along the sides of the hills reveals breathtaking scenery below and, eventually, an aerial view of Sok Kwu Wan, distant Hong Kong, Cheung Chau and Lantau.

Left, applying the finishing touches.

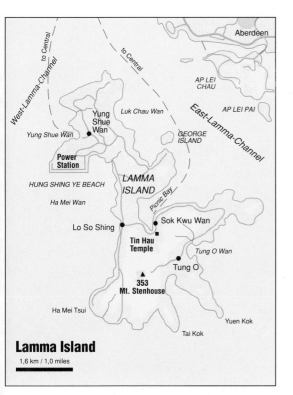

Lamma Island

1,6 km / 1,0 miles

CHEUNG CHAU, "OLD CHINA" ISLE

Cheung Chau is different. It is much smaller than Lantau, for one thing, and it is urbanized in a rather charming "Old China" way with the distinctly Chinese junks and *sampan* crowding Cheung Chau's curving little harbour.

This dumbbell-shaped isle – with hills at either end and a village nestled in a connecting rod of land – is narrow enough that you can walk from **Cheung Chau Harbour** on its west side to **Tung Wan Harbour** on the east in a just a few minutes.

Cheung Chau is a fishing island, with a few farms in its more distant reaches, and its main town is a tangle of alleyways. There are no cars, a Hong Kong phenomenon which gives the island an automatic serenity.

Cheung Chau's sense of community is strong, but it does not exclude the visiting stranger. People here are friendlier than the hurried city dwellers in Hong Kong's Central District. Many Europeans have moved here "to get away from it all."

The island was once the haunt of pirates. One of the greatest pirates of all, **Cheung Po Chai**, used to hide out on this island when he was in danger and fearing for his life. His tiny **cave retreat** can still be explored.

Once a year the whole island community comes together for a big **Bun Festival**, which is a celebration held to exorcise wandering and malicious ghosts who have been unable to find rest in this world.

The festival, known as *Ching Chiu* in Cantonese, originated many years ago after the discovery here of a nest of skeletons, probably the remains of people killed by pirates.

After this discovery the island was plagued by a series of misfortunes, and the islanders eventually called in a Taoist priest who recommended that they should placate the restless spirits of the murdered people by making offerings to them once a year.

Ever since then the island has held an annual four-day Ching Chiu Festival between the last 10 days of the third moon and the first 10 days of the fourth moon which is usually in late April or early May.

During this time, Cantonese operas are staged, along with other street entertainment; and finally a great festival day on which bamboo towers covered with edible buns are dismantled.

These specially inscribed buns are given to the thousands of bystanders, to bring them good fortune throughout the coming year. The principal Bun Festival rites are held in the **Temple of the Jade Vacuity**, Cheung Chau's oldest temple.

There are excellent beaches to be found on Cheung Chau. They can be reached either by walking on the peak road across the island through the little homesteads where vegetables are grown and chickens raised, or by hiring a small *sampan* for a modest fee.

The main beach, but not the nicest, is across the Cheung Chau Harbour on the other side of the narrow isthmus.

Left, children take centre stage at Cheung Chau's Bun Festival.

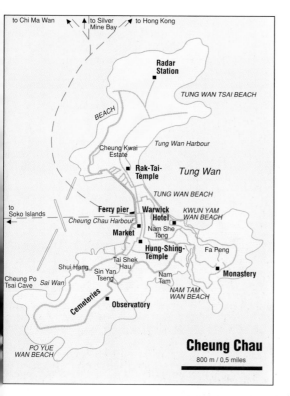

Cheung Chau
800 m / 0,5 miles

OTHER ISLANDS

Some of the more distant outlying islands have even more elusive charms, though occasionally the charm is slightly melancholy because these islands are more or less deserted.

A **"ghost island"**: Out at Mirs Bay northeast of Kowloon, is **Ping Chau**, one of the colony's most remote isles.

Years ago this island had a population of 3,000. Now, only two men live there full time. Other islanders return at weekends and on public holidays to open hostels and basic restaurants. The majority of Ping Chau's native sons and daughters have gone to work in Chinese restaurants in London. The exodus first began in 1969 when the islanders emigrated and left behind their charming stone-built houses, some of them very much like the traditional homes that are found in Kwangtung (Guangdong) Province. Their many courtyards and winding passages have been left behind to howl empty in Mirs Bay's wind and rain.

"10,000-Layer Cake Rock": Just beyond Ping Chau are the misty hills of China's **Po On District**, a rather intriguing sight that inspires the visitor to head straight for Mainland China instead of returning to Ping Chau's docking place at Emperor Point. On Ping Chau there are long white beaches of smooth sand scattered with seashells, starfish, and spiked sea urchins. Coloured rock which forms the base of the island and descends into Mirs Bay waters is called **"10,000-Layer Cake Rock"** by the Cantonese, after a cake of the same name found in most local bakery shops. Other delightful names are the **"Seashell Cave,"** so-called because the sea has honed its wall to a finish as smooth as glass. Also fascinating are **"Dragon Fall Hill," "Breast Cave"** and **"Hard-to-Get-Over-Water."**

Passing through Ping Chau's virtually deserted village, the visitor will be able to see how the villagers have used shale, stone and shingle to roof their cottages. Because this "ghost island" is so close to China, it was a favourite

Buildings on Ping Chau are strictly low-rise.

target in recent years for "freedom swimmers" who swam across these waters in attempts to escape from their Communist motherland. Nowadays, Ping Chau is little more than a picnic place for those who take the ferry from Ma Liu Shui, near the University KCR station. But it's a fine picnic place, with charms exceeding those of many other islands. Quiet beauty and the slight melancholy of her deserted village add an extra dimension to a visit here.

Probably the best Ping Chau beach for a picnic is **Lai Tau Wan** with its attractive white sand and clean sea – amenities which are becoming increasingly rare in Hong Kong. The entire island is only about half a square mile in area, so it is easily travelled. Also in Mirs Bay is **Tap Mun Island** with its thriving fishing community. The only access to Tap Mun is by ferry through the **Tolo Channel** from **Ma Liu Shui**.

Tap Mun – fisherfolk haven: The island is well worth visiting, as it is an important base for Hong Kong's fishing folk. It has, in common with most of the other out-lying islands, a **Tin Hau Temple** dedicated to the goddess of the sea. This temple is frequented by fishermen, even those from Shatin and Tai Po, because it's the last Tin Hau temple en route before junks and *sampan* head for open sea. Therefore, fishermen make a special point of visiting the temple to make offerings and pray for a safe return from their voyages.

The Tin Hau Temple is more than 100 years old and both it and the one village on Tap Mun have risen around an inlet which forms a natural harbour for fishing boats. The harbour is usually busy with fishing and work boats, and along the edge of the inlet is a line of cheek-to-cheek old cottages. It is a central exchange point for fisherfolk from all over this region. There is one odd thing about this particular Tin Hau temple. When East winds roar, their sounds can be heard in a crevice under the altar. This eerie howling is interpreted by fishermen as a warning of storms to come.

On the other side of the island, the eastern side, is the **Tap Mun Cave** where the sound of temple drums and

gongs being beat inside the distant Tin Hau Temple can be heard. Local people believe that this cave runs underground the island from one side to the other. This picturesque island is a favourite with the colony's more adventurous picnickers; there are shops and restaurants on it to cater to visitors who do not bring along picnic lunches.

Kat O Chau – ancient ambience: A lovely Tap Mun neighbour is **Kat O Chau**, or "**Crooked Island**," a richly green island thick with butterflies, wild flowers and a summer chorus of frogs and cicadas. Kat O is larger, but it's a rather sleepy island with an atmosphere reminiscent of ancient China. The houses here are built of traditional brickwork and tiles topped with ceramic tile eaves. The inevitable Tin Hau Temple here is decorated with perfectly preserved blue and green glazed ceramic friezes.

Kat O's people number about 2,000 Hoklo fishermen, who usually are dressed in the traditional black costumes of the Hoklo tribe. They spend their days catching, drying, selling and eating fish. The island is renowned for its abalone, squid and mussels, so make plans to eat them before catching a ferry back to Hong Kong.

There are many other islands that are not easily accessible by public transport, but they can be visited if you have access to a private boat. Other islands which are well worth a visit and are accessible by ferry are **Ap Chau**, **Po Toi** and **Ma Wan**.

Ap Chau's true believers: Ap Chau is another fishing island with one unusual feature about it: the 500 fishermen and their families are all members of the True Jesus Church, headquartered in Taiwan. In 1965, the whole island clubbed together to build a **True Jesus Church** and they have regular meetings where the 80 families communicate in strange tongues and shake in ecstasy during their services. The only other notable characteristic about zealous Ap Chau is that it has no electricity supply.

Po Toi is a tiny island inhabited by some 200 people. It has a **haunted house** and some curious **rock carvings** which

Below and right, fishing is the main activity of the outer islanders.

might possibly be the epitaph of an emperor who is rumoured to have died on or near Po Toi. An even smaller island, 215-acre (87-hectare) **Ma Wan**, is notable only because it was once the site of a Ching dynasty **custom station**.

Tung Lung Island: Tung Lung is a small, sparsely populated island lying off the southern tip of the Clearwater Bay Peninsula, to the east of Hong Kong Island. Its main features of interest to visitors are a renovated fort, and huge cliffs. To reach the fort, walk left from the hamlet at the ferry pier. The path soon leads over the rolling, open landscape of northern Tung Lung. The fort, perched on a low headland in the northeast, is soon visible. During the 18th century, and until it was abandoned in 1810, the fort guarded the approaches to Canton and Hong Kong. It fell into disrepair, was excavated by archaeologists, and its interior is now preserved, showing the bases of partitions between rooms. Nearby is an information hut (closed on Tuesdays).

There are fine views from the fort, northwards across the Clearwater Bay Peninsula, eastwards across sea and island, and south to the dramatic cliffs of Tung Lung's east coast. A rough path leads up alongside the cliffs; there are also paths onto headlands with sheer drops into narrow ravines – if you follow these, take care. The island is reached by a ferry (at weekends only) or small boat – called a *kaito* – from Sai Wan on Hong Kong Island.

Sek Kwu Chau: Sek Kwu Chau, a small island near Cheung Chau, is not open to casual visitors as it is now given over to **SARDA**, a private body which runs the heroin rehabilitation centre there. Heroin addiction is a major problem in Hong Kong and most forms of treatment are fairly ineffective in that they may remove the lifestyle of the addict with nothing more fulfilling. Therefore, the rate of re-addiction is heavy. On Sek Kwu Chau, however, the addicts come voluntarily but must agree to stay for at least six months. They, in fact, stay for an average of a year and many for up to 18 months.

THE "LATIN ORIENT"

Macau has also been hit by the speculation about its future as its neighbour Hong Kong, but as its then governor Rear Admiral Vasco Almeida de Costa explained: "Macau is not a colony." Portugal's constitution defines Macau as a "Chinese territory under Portuguese administration. The present status... serves the interests of Portugal, China and the population of Macau." Nevertheless, Beijing began negotiations with Macau in 1985 with a view to sorting out that territory; probably by Hong Kong's 1997 deadline.

After nine months of non-acrimonious negotiations – compared with two years of oft-times very acrimonious discussions between Beijing and London – a Sino-Portuguese agreement was signed on April 13, 1987. As with the Hong Kong agreement, this one guarantees the "one country, two systems" principle for half a century from December 20, 1999, about 2½ years after its British neighbour's reversion to the People's Republic of China on July 1, 1997. (Of course, with Macau's agreement, some wags are calling it the "one country, three systems" principle.) Macau will be given the status of a Special Administrative Region and its existing economic and social systems, sights and liberties will be guaranteed for 50 years.

With the lure of her casinos and hotels, Macau now has a large infrastructure – which will soon include an airport and port – which has converted the sleepy "Latin Orient" image into a high-rolling "Las Vegas (or Monaco) of the East" lifestyle, while keeping a bit of the Iberian charm.

As befits the oldest European settlement on the South China coast, Macau's antiquity is there to be seen. Most Macau tourists see only a tiny part of this 6.1-sq. mile (15.5-sq. km) territory (without its neighbouring islands of Taipa and Coloane, Macau is only 2.1 sq. miles/5.2 sq. km). And most of what they "see" races by the windows of an air-conditioned bus.

Forget about "official tours" for the moment. One of the best (and quickest) ways to see Macau is by hire car or taxi. Guides-cum-drivers accost visitors as soon as they clear immigration at Macau's Ferry Terminal. Generally, the hiring of a knowledgeable guide is a matter of luck, but some of the local drivers are quite good. They've collected most of the free visitor pamphlets published by the Department of Tourism and are suprisingly knowledgeable. The cost of a tour is Ptc 150–300 per person for about 60 to 90 minutes; unless you want to lounge about, this is about all the time you'll need to cruise the greater Macau area.

Preceding pages: the 17th-century Guia Lighthouse is the oldest on the China coast. **Left**, Portuguese beauty.

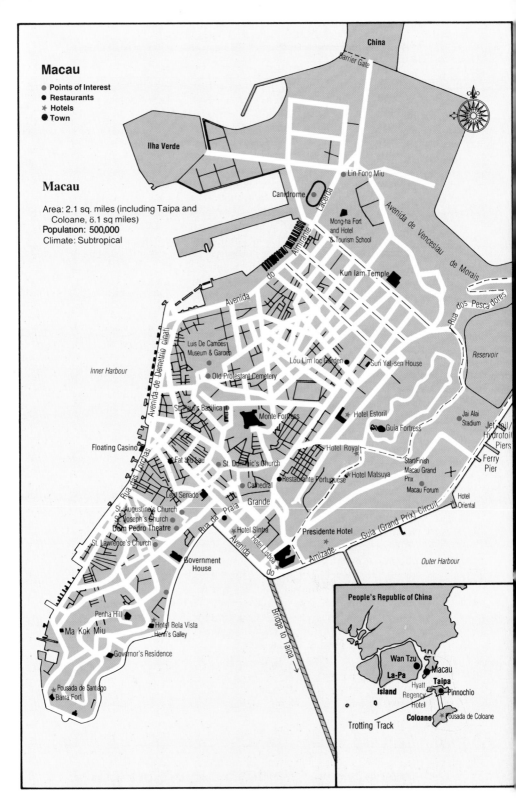

Macau

- Points of Interest
- Restaurants
- Hotels
- Town

Macau

Area: 2.1 sq. miles (including Taipa and Coloane, 6.1 sq miles)
Population: 500,000
Climate: Subtropical

China

Barrier Gate

Ilha Verde

Lin Fong Miu

Canidrome

Laceda

Mong-ha Fort and Hotel & Tourism School

Avenida de Venceslau de Morais

Kun Iam Temple

Avenida

do Almirante

Rua dos Pescadores

Avenida de Demetrio Cinatti

Inner Harbour

Luis De Camões Museum & Garden

Lou Lim Ioc Garden

Sun Yat-sen House

Reservoir

Old Protestant Cemetery

St. Paul's Basilica

Monte Fortress

Hotel Estoril

Jai Alai Stadium

Jet foil/Hydrofoil Piers

Floating Casino

Fat Siu Lau

St. Dominic's Church

Guia Fortress

Hotel Royal

Ferry Pier

Rua das Lorchas

Leal Senado

Cathedral

Restaurante Portuguese

Hotel Matsuya

Start/Finish Macau Grand Prix

Macau Forum

St. Augustine's Church

St. Joseph's Church

Dom Pedro Theatre

Grande

Rua da Praia

Hotel Sintra

Presidente Hotel

Hotel Oriental

St. Lawrence's Church

Government House

Avenida do

Guia (Grand Prix) Circuit

Amizade

Outer Harbour

Penha Hill

Hotel Bela Vista
Henri's Galley

Ma Kok Miu

Governor's Residence

Pousada de Santiago

Barra Fort

Bridge to Taipa

People's Republic of China

Wan Tzu

La-Pa

Island

Macau

Taipa

Hyatt
Regency
Hotel

Pinnochio

Trotting Track

Coloane

Pousada de Coloane

HISTORIC MACAU

The first stop is usually **Penha Hill**, atop which stands the magnificent **Bishop's Palace**, unoccupied for many years now but partly open to the public. From one vantage point there, you can see across the **Old City** to Macau's **Inner Harbour**, and less than a mile farther, China. From another point, you can see **Outer Harbour** approaches and the island of **Taipa** which is connected to the peninsula by a bridge. In case you are wondering why tiny Macau has such a huge Bishop's Palace – larger than anything in this area outside the Philippines – the answer is that at one stage in early Eurasian history Macau was *the* Asian seat of Roman Catholicism. Bishops here controlled all of the church's missions from Goa to the Moluccas and Nagasaki.

Macau was also the training and publishing centre for Roman Catholic missionary efforts in this part of the world.

The Bishop's Palace complex also houses **Penha Church**. Though the present building dates only from 1935, the first chapel here was dedicated in 1622. It has been said that peninsular Macau has more churches per square mile than Vatican City, and if you try to visit just the ones mentioned here, you will probably agree.

Perhaps the most striking Macau church is the towering facade of **St Paul's** with its impressive grand staircase. Historians call it the finest monument to Christianity in the Far East.

Unfortunately, the site must have had bad *fung shui* (if taking into account both Chinese Taoism and Portuguese Christianity). The first church at this site was destroyed by fire in 1601 and construction of a new one was begun the following year. The classical facade you now see was added before 1630. In 1835 another fire (in the church's kitchen) spread and eventually destroyed St Paul's adjacent **college**, a **library** reputed to be the best east of Africa, and, again, the church. In 1904 efforts were made to rebuild the church, but, as you will note, little was done. Today the grand facade of St Paul's remains as Macau's most enduring visitor symbol.

If you are touring by taxi, the driver usually races on to one of the colony's Chinese temples, but ask him instead to take you to **Monte Fort (St Paul's Fortress)** which overlooks the facade (look to the right as you face the facade and you will see the fort's massive stone walls above). This fortification was built in the early 1620s. When Dutch ships attacked and invaded Macau in 1622, the then half completed fortress was defended by 150 clerics and negro slaves. A lucky cannon shot by an Italian Jesuit, Geronimo Rhu hit a powder keg being carried by the invaders and the badly injured Dutch were defeated.

A-Ma, Ma Kok Miu, Macau: Tours here always include the Chinese temples of **A-Ma**, for which Macau is named, the **Kun Iam Temple**, famous for its table on which the first Sino-Lantau American treaty was signed in 1844, and the **Lin Fong (Lotus) Temple**.

The Temple of the Goddess A-Ma

squats beneath **Barra Hill**, at the entrance to Macau's Inner Harbour. It is the oldest temple in this Portuguese Territory, said to date back 600 years to the Ming dynasty. It certainly was there in 1557 when Macau was ceded to Portugal. The original temple was said to have been erected by Fukinese fishermen and dedicated to Tin Hau, the patron goddess of fishermen. It was then called Ma Kok Miu (Ma Point Temple). The Chinese named the area A-Ma-Gao or the Bay of A-Ma and the arriving Portuguese picked up on the name.

The oldest surviving part of this temple is a lower pavilion to the right of its entrance. There is a multi-coloured, bast relief stone carving here said to be a rendering of a Chinese junk which carried A-Ma (who is Tin Hau in Hong Kong) from Fukien Province through typhoon-ravaged seas to Macau, where she walked to the top of Barra Hill and ascended to heaven.

The second temple complex of Kun Iam (which in Cantonese is pronounced Kuan Yin) is dedicated to Buddhism's Goddess of Mercy. Some sub-temples in this complex are dedicated to A-Ma. The present temple dates back to 1627 and was built on the site of an earlier 14th-century temple. Foreign visitors, particularly Americans, will be pleased to know that at a **stone table** in this temple's courtyard, the first Sino-American Treaty was signed on July 3, 1844, by Ki Ying, China's Viceroy in Canton, and Caleb Cushing, a lawyer and former congressman from Massachusetts who was US President John Tyler's "Commissioner and Envoy Extraordinary and Minister Plenipotentiary" to China.

The third temple, the Lin Fong (Lotus) Temple, built in 1592, is quite near Macau's 19th-century **Portas do Cerco** ("Border Gate"). In the old days it served as a guest house for mandarins travelling between Macau and Canton. Its most recent restoration took place in 1980, but it is still an excellent example of classical Buddhist architecture. Clay friezes over its entrances are some of the best examples of Buddhist art in this region. An image of the sea goddess Tin

The old section of town has many reminders of the colonial past.

Hau stands tall over the main altar, beautifully garbed in silk robes and an opulent headdress.

The nearby Portas do Cerco, Macau's main border gate, was built in 1870. Just a few years ago the gate was closed to foreigners (though Chinese passed through it in each direction daily) and visitors were forbidden to photograph it. Today the gate is open from 7 a.m. to 9 p.m. to accommodate those going into China to resorts across the border. And you can now snap away here to your camera's content.

"The Father of Modern China": Most tours make a quick visit to the **Dr. Sun Yat-sen Memorial House**. Dr. Sun – the "Father of Modern China" is revered in both Beijing and Taipei. Though opened after he died, the Memorial is near where he practiced medicine at nearby **Kiang Vu Hospital**. (He was one of the first Western-trained Chinese doctors in this area.) His birthplace is across the border in China's **Cuiheng Village**. If you are wondering why the memorial is not as old as you'd expect,

Charming facade of St Miguel Church.

this is because in the 1930s it was used as an explosives depot and accidentally blew up one day. What you are looking at is a new structure built near the original monument site.

Another "classic" is the **Leai Senado** ("Loyal Senate") building on Macau's main square. This building was dedicated in 1784 and its facade was completed in 1876. It was restored in 1939 and more internal restoration was recently completed. The title "Loyal" was bestowned on the Senate on May 13, 1809 by Portuguese King John VI (who was Prince Regent at the time) as a reward for continuing to fly the Portuguese flag when the Spanish monarchy took over the Portuguese throne.

An inscribed tablet here grants Macau its sacred title: "City of the Name of God, There is None More Loyal." The original tablet dates from 1654, and was placed here by Macau's Governor and Captain-General then, Joao de Souza Pereira. Half the offices on ground floor have been converted into a beautiful gallery for special exhibitions.

Head up the Senate's staircase to the fine wrought iron doors and beyond. Admire the beautiful Portuguese tiles on the walls, absorb the scene of the beautiful garden below, and run your fingers over the Senate's belltower. The **library** and **council chamber** here include beautiful examples of Old World woodwork.

Kwangtung pottery: Two other areas often missed by quickie tours – but very accessible by walking or taxi – are the **Camões Garden** and the **Dom Pedro V Theatre**. Named after Portugal's most famous poet, Luis de Camões (1524–80) the renovated 18th-century building now houses the Orient Foundation though it was once the residence of the president of the select committee of the East India Company, the all powerful firm which for centuries "ruled" the area from India to the South China Sea. The completely-restored theatre is tiny – about 350 seats – but charming.

An interesting, contrasting episode in Dom Pedro V's long history ended in 1985 when the Crazy Paris Show, a titillating French strip extravaganza moved to larger premises in the Lisboa Hotel after five years of bounding that ancient stage with sexy routines.

Don't miss seeing many of Macau's old churches; you shouldn't, because most of the intrigue and history of this colony's past 400-plus years took place behind their sanctified walls.

St Dominic's Christian-Oriental motifs: The church of **St Dominic** is one of the oldest and most famous, dating from the 17th century. (Spanish Dominicans had a chapel and convent on this site as early as 1588.) To gain entry, ring a bell to the right of the facade. When you get inside, you will note that many of the Christian motifs are of an Oriental style.

The baroque-style church of **St Augustine** is the largest in the region. The present structure dates from 1814, and its ornate facade from 1875, but Spanish Augustinians founded a first church there in 1586.

Just near the Dom Pedro V Theatre is **St Lawrence's**, another church which dates from the 16th-century, but which was rebuilt in 1803, 1846 and then again

1892. It is one of the most elegant of Macau's religious edifices and is now open to the public. Its double staircase, iron gates, towers, and crystal chandeliers are European, but the roof is made of Chinese tiles. It overlooks the pastel pink government administration buildings next to it.

Perhaps the starkest proof of the recent deterioration of both Macau and her once mighty Roman Catholic presence is the **church and seminary of St Joseph**. Its beautiful chapel is now open to the public. This Jesuit seminary was dedicated in 1728 and its sole purpose was to establish religious missions in China, a task it performed admirably.

Today its vast halls, classrooms and living quarters are empty, but renovation is in progress. It is the home of Msgr. Manuel Texieira SJ, Macau's oldest Portuguese (he arrived in 1924) and foremost historian. Even he has not managed to salvage all the valuable books, maps and drawings in random storage here.

The church of St Joseph's (circa 1746) is reached through the seminary, or through the street if the front door is open. The church is now used only once a year on New Year's Eve to celebrate a special Mass. Though the sacred relic – a 6-inch (13-cm) piece of bone from the left arm of St Francis (ardent Macanese and Portuguese Catholics believe the relic protects the city from natural disasters) – has long been moved to the Chapel of St Francis on Coloane Island, the statues in the lovely chapel were salvaged from St Paul's in 1835.

There are a couple of other places nearby that are not on the usual tourist route. One is the **Barra Fortress** which has been turned into the deluxe **Pousada de Sao Tiago**, a new hostelry that was developed within the walls of this 17th-century fort.

The oldest Lighthouse: The **Guia Fortress and Lighthouse** (there is also a chapel) is the first thing you see when you approach Macau by sea. This 17th-century landmark stands atop **Guia Hill** guarding coastal approaches. This Western-style lighthouse is the oldest on the China coast. It is now open to the public

T-shirt design gets the message across effectively.

and even houses a small art gallery. There are also some interesting tunnels underneath.

Protecting the other approach to the city is the 19th-century fortress of **Mong-Ha**, built to provide a defense vantage to guard the Portas do Cerco. It too is now a small government inn. Other buildings (new and old) house the Macau Hotel and Tourism School.

"Las Vegas of the East": Sleepy Macau is also vicarously known as the "Las Vegas of the East," or, if you are a European, the "Monaco of the East." Indeed, gambling is the main reason over 6 million visitors each year – 80 percent of them Hong Kong Chinese – make the 40 miles (64 km) sea cruise across the Pearl River Estuary to this Portuguese territory.

Lady Luck – who lurks in nine casinos, dog-racing and trotting tracks – thieves on gambling mad Chinese.

Macau's casinos, each one virtually packed every day, feature Western and Chinese games of chance. If you tire of conventional craps, roulette, baccarat (*chemin de fer*) or blackjack, you can try your hand at Chinese *fantan*, *sik-po* (*dai siu*) and *pai-kao*. Also popular are Keno and slot machines.

These casinos are located in the Lisboa, Mandarin, Hyatt-Regency, Kingsway and Westin Oriental Hotels, the Macau Jockey Club (race days only) on a permanently moored floating barge in the Inner Harbour called the Casino de Macau (or the "Floating Casino"), and at the Kam Pek on Travessa A. Novo (just off Avenida Almeida Ribeiro). The latter formerly specialized only in Chinese gambling games.

For those unfamiliar with Chinese games of chance, here's a rough guide:

Fan-tan is played with buttons. An unknown number of buttons are put under an inverted cup and then counted out in groups of four. You bet on how many buttons will be left in the last group counted out – one to four.

Sik-po (also known as *dai siu*) is a dice game in which three dice are shaken and their numerical value tallied. Bets are made on Small (*siu*), that is any

number from 4 to 10, or Big (*dai*), 11 to 17, rolls. You can also bet on specific numbers – singly or in combinations.

Pai-kao is Chinese dominoes.

There is no such thing as a miracle book that will help you win at any gambling game, but there are instructions available at the casinos that explain Macau's gambling games in detail and, hopefully, lead you in an auspicious direction.

Taipa Trotters: Despite – or perhaps because of – numerous rumours of trackside fixing and other foul play, greyhound racing seems to attract the Pearl River's hardest core gambling crowd. "Mr Bigs" abound in Macau's dog-racing venue, the Canidrome on Avenida General Castelo Branco.

On good nights the Canidrome roars with money madness of the purest sort. Even in jaded Macau, this place is quite a scene. Ironically, this high-energy gambling place is situated only three quarters of a kilometer away from the straight-laced People's Republic of China.

The Canidrome's regular 14-race cards begin at 8 p.m. on Saturday, Sunday, Monday and Tuesday. Admission is Ptc 2 to public seats, Ptc 5 member's stand, Ptc 25 for VIP rooms, and Ptc 80 for six person boxes. Off-course betting centres can be found at the Lisboa Hotel and the Kam Pek Casino.

Another running attraction in Macau's varied world of gambling is a horse-racing track, the Macau Jockey Club, located on Taipa Island. Founded in 1980 as a trotting track, the MJC now offers flat racing.

The Macau Grand Prix: Asia's Monaco wouldn't be complete without an annual motor-car race. So, like its glittering Mediterranean sister, Macau each year (on the last weekend in November) cordons off a twisting, through-the-streets grand prix race course that starts and finishes on Avenida da Amizade near the ferry piers. Racing drivers from around the world race Formula III cars for 32 laps around this 3.8-mile (6-km) Guia Circuit.

The Macau Grand Prix begins at 2

Highrollers' neon beacon above the Casino Lisboa.

p.m. on race Sunday. When this race was first run in 1954, the winner took 4 hours, 31 minutes and 19.1 seconds to complete 51 laps. He posted an average lap speed of 49 mph (79 kph) in his Triumph TR2. Today, average lap speeds are over 90 mph (145 kph), with cars sometimes hitting 140 mph (225 kph) on the waterfront straightaway. The official lap record is 2:20.64 (for a lap speed of 97 mph/156 kph) set in the 29th Grand Prix in 1982 by the winner, Brazilian Roberto Moreno. (Masahiro Hasemi clocked 2:20.48 in practice but that does not count.)

This racing weekend also features another international grand prix, a secondary race for motorcycles that has been run since 1967. Also held during this fast moving grand prix week are production car and endurance races.

Screeching tires, sunshine and gambling tables draw a well-heeled, thoroughly hedonistic crowd to Macau's Grand Prix Week. During this week, Macau is inundated with some 50,000 racing aficionados, and this otherwise quiet territory swings with pre- and post-race parties.

If you don't make hotel reservations well in advance it is next to impossible to find a room in Macau at this time.

The "Other Macau": The "Other Macau" is not on the peninsula that is generally regarded as Macau, but consists of the two islands of **Taipa** and **Coloane**. Previously, access to these islands was by small ferry boats which, in the case of Coloane, could only be approached at high tide. Today, Taipa is connected to the mainland by a beautiful arching bridge. Access these days is as simple as getting into a taxi or climbing aboard a local double-decker bus.

Taipa and Coloane's cobble-stoned villages have grown a bit, but they are still tiny, rural and charming – a cross between out-of-the-way Iberian villages built around a central plaza and surrounded by typical old Chinese farming communities.

Taipa was also at one period (1717–23), the busy centre for Western trade with China when an Imperial edict

The bridge to Taipa.

banned English and French ships at Canton and insisted they moor at Taipa instead. The major industries on Taipa in the old days were junk-building and the manufacture of firecrackers.

Taipa's development started slowly. The trotting track, now the Macau Jockey Club offering flat racing, opened in 1980 followed in 1981 by the University of East Asia, now the University of Macau. Hyatt-Regency Taipa Island Resort was the first major hotel on the island, opening in 1983. And Taipa Village itself has now become a venue for some of Macau's finest eateries, attracting locals and visitors alike to its wide variety of restaurants. Further development is in the offing as Macau's steps from the drawing board into realty.

Taipa's "Latin Orient" ambience, however, still lives. Indeed, the small *praia* just below Largoda Carma rivals its larger and more famous predecessor on the Macau peninsula for beauty, elegance and romance. To preserve this 19th-century ambience, a **Casa Museu** (house museum) has been created (completed with period furniture) out of one of the five old houses, the first step in what will be a cultural complex.

Coloane, too, seems to have been forgotten for many years, but is now bursting back into prominence because of its **beaches**. Coloane is almost twice as big as Taipa – 2.6 sq. miles (6.5 sq. km) in area compared with Taipa's 1.4 sq. miles (3.8 sq. km). It is so close to China you can see quite clearly and easily a Chinese fishing village that sits only a quarter mile beyond a strip of water. And with a strong pair of binoculars, you can see the villagers meandering about, doing their Communist things.

One of Coloane's beaches, **Kao Ho**, is the site for Macau's deepwater port. Situated on the northern end of the island, it was a traditional haven for South China Sea pirates. Most of the islanders patronized piracy, which apparently was their main source of livelihood. But the pirates overstepped their watery bounds. After a mass kidnapping of Chinese children from Canton, and a subsequent refusal of outrageous ransom demands by Coloane's buccaneers, Portuguese authorities went after the pirates and defeated them in a two-day battle in July, 1910. A memorial to this incident is set into a tiny square in front of the Portuguese **Chapel of St Francis Xavier**. This tiny chapel houses a relic, a 6-inch piece of bone from the left arm of St Francis, plus the revered bones of Vietnamese and Japanese martyrs who were slaughtered because of their religion in centuries past.

Except for race fans who frequent Taipa's track, Coloane is probably the more popular of these two Macau Islands, usually because of the **Pousada de Coloane Roman NOBR** on **Cheoc Van Beach** and the Westin Resort, with its golf club (members only), at **Hac Sa Beach** area. Coloane is connected to Taipa by a causeway. At Hac Sa Beach, there is a park of the same name with a swimming pool and sports-facilities. Cheoc Van Park, on the beach of the same name, also has pool facilities. Coloane Park is a combination walk-in aviary and gardens with barbecues, restaurants and walks.

Below, the Chapel of St Francis Xavier. Right, courting couple get cuddly.

TUNG NGAI
DUTY FREE SHOP
東藝免稅店
DUTY FREE
TUNG NGAI
KENG NGAI
DUTY FREE SHOP
京藝免稅品店
LARGO DA COMPANHIA DE JESUS

TRAVEL TIPS

GETTING THERE

The colony is served by more than 30 airlines, plus another dozen charter and cargo airlines.

Kai Tak is one of the few airports still located virtually within a city – about 3 miles (5 km) and about 10 minutes away from Kowloon's Tsimshatsui hotel district, 20 minutes from Causeway Bay and about 25–30 minutes from Central District (both on Hong Kong Island).

Managing an airport that handles more than 12 million passengers a year is no fun. Kai Tak has been expanded – and expanded – but at times when a half-dozen 747s are arriving and departing at the same time, the runway and skies are like an airborne cattle yard. However, Hong Kong maintains one of the world's most efficient runway-to-hotel gauntlets.

The terminal building doesn't win architectural awards, but recent massive renovation efforts have eased many former traffic bottlenecks. Upon arrival, jumbo aircrafts park alongside modern passenger bridges. Immigration, customs and baggage check points are all within a short walking distance, and free baggage carts are available. You can push your carts past customs, or hire a porter (they are free, but a tip of HK$3 per piece of baggage is normal). A Hong Kong Hotel Association's reservation desk is available to assist travellers as are foreign exchange facilities. Free phones are in the buffer hall immediately past customs. There are well-marked, but still confusing, exits: left is the greeting area if you are being met; straight ahead are hotel buses and city-bound tour coaches.

Security: Security is very rigid at Kai Tak. Nearly all the airlines X-ray all baggage before it is checked in. All hand carry items are either X-rayed or manually inspected. The X-ray machines at Kai Tak do affect film. Amateur and professional photographers should always take their exposed and unexposed film out before they go through the X-ray machine because though one particular machine might not harm the film (assuming the warning sign is correct and the machine functions correctly), the cumulative effect of X-rays on film can damage photographs.

Announcements: Silence now reigns supreme, so check flight boards or ask ground hostesses about flight times.

For those with plenty of time and very ample means, a half-dozen cruise lines include Hong Kong on their "Exotic East" or "Round-the-World" grand tours. Most have recently added a Chinese port – but few give enough time in any one place for more than a cursory view. Among the current fleet that tie up at Ocean Terminal (Hong Kong's well placed and serviced passenger wharf) are ships from **Norwegian America Line**, **Royal Viking Line**, **Holland-America Line**, **Cunard** (very occasionally in the sleek form of the *QE2*) and of course **P&O**, whose steamships once ruled the England-to-Far East run.

Only slightly more direct and less expensive are passenger-carrying freighters. **American President Lines** (San Francisco) and **Glen & Shire Lines** (London) are the only ones that make anything like frequent Pacific or European runs, stopping as well at various ports along the way. Either the *ABC Shipping Guide* (available at most libraries) or one of the several "freighter travel" services can often pinpoint others. There is, of course, always the possibility – fairly slim in most places – of talking tramp skippers into taking extra crew. Shipping pages of newspapers selling on newsstands in Asia or in any major port city, are the best places to start.

Finally, on the American West Coast, around the Pacific and in most ports in Asia, even marginally experienced sailors can sometimes pick up an empty spot on a private sailing boat. In Hong Kong, the best places to ask are the **Royal Hong Kong Yacht Club** (at Kellett Island, Causeway Bay, across from the Excelsior Hotel) and various anchorages in Stanley and Deep Water Bay.

TRAVEL ESSENTIALS

Most visitors need only a valid passport to enter Hong Kong. Also, in keeping with recent trends worldwide, vaccination certificates for cholera are waived except for arrivals from officially declared "infected areas." Youthful and visibly less well-heeled arrivals will probably be asked to show onward tickets, "sufficient means" or references in the colony, but few bona fide tourists are ever turned away.

Visitors are not allowed to take up employment, paid or unpaid, to establish or join any business, or

THE NOBLE TIME

JUVENIA

— 1860 —

Mystere ®

C O L L E C T I O N

STEEL - STEEL/GOLD - 18KT GOLD AND WITH PRECIOUS STONES

to enter school as a student. And except in unusual circumstances, visitors are not allowed to change their citizenship status after arrival.

Without a Visa: The maximum stay varies according to nationality: 6 months for British subjects (United Kingdom passport holders only); 3 months for other British passport holders (Commonwealth countries) and citizens of Andorra, Austria, Belgium, Brazil, Chile, Colombia, Denmark, Ecuador, Eire, France, Israel, Italy, Liechtenstein, Luxembourg, the Maldives, Monaco, the Netherlands, Norway, Portugal, San Marino, Spain, Sweden, Switzerland and Turkey; one month for citizens of Bolivia, Costa Rica, Dominican Republic, El Salvador, Finland, Germany, Mexico, Morocco, Nepal, Nicaragua, Pakistan, Panama, Greece, Guatemala, Honduras, Iceland, Paraguay, Peru, Tunisia, the United States, Uruguay, and Venezuela; 14 days for citizens of Thailand and 7 days for other nationals.

Must Have a Visa: Visitors from the categories listed below always require a visa: (1) Nationals of Afghanistan, Albania, Argentina, Bulgaria, the People's Republic of China, Cuba, Czechoslovakia, Hungary, Kampuchea, Laos, Mongolia, North Korea, Poland, Rumania, Russia, Vietnam and (North) Yemen; (2) holders of Taiwan passports; (3) all "stateless" persons; and (4) holders of Iranian and Libyan passports.

Applications for Visas: If a visa to Hong Kong is required, apply at the nearest British Embassy, Consulate General or High Commission (in Commonwealth countries), or write directly to the Immigration Department, Immigration Tower, 7 Gloucester Road, Hong Kong (tel: 824-6111). Allow at least 8 weeks for an answer.

MACAU-CHINA TRIPS

If admitted into Hong Kong with a multiple-entry visa, you will not need another Hong Kong visa to return from Macau or China. With a single-entry visa, you will need a re-entry visa (obtainable from the Immigration Department) to come back.

TRANSITS

Visas are not normally required for transit stays if valid onward booking (by air) is held and travel documents are in order, or if onward or return bookings (by sea) are held for the same vessel, travel documents are in order and the carrier accepts responsibility for removal of passenger. (In other words, you can get off your cruise ship when it is in port.) Sea/air or air/sea transits are governed by normal visa regulations.

PASSPORT PHOTOS

Need a quick passport photo? Though there are many photo shops which provide half-day or one-day service, you will soon discover there are handy coin-operated photo machines at most major Mass Transit Railway Stations. The three most well-known ones are in the Transport Department (Murray Road, Hong Kong), the Immigration Department, and the YMCA Salisbury Road (near the Star Ferry, next to the Peninsula Hotel), Tsimshatsui, both in Kowloon. Price: HK$18 for four photos.

MONEY MATTERS

The financial arts are Hong Kong's stock-in-trade. Because it's a strategic centre for international transactions, the colony has banks of every description and there are no local restrictions whatsoever on the import, export, purchase or sale of foreign currency. Anything from credit cards to "black" or "hot" cash can be handled – but there are clearly better and worse ways to go about such money dealings.

Businessmen and tax fugitives notwithstanding, most visitors need not get too bogged down in the esoterica of floating exchange rates. Though the Hong Kong dollar fluctuates, its value is usually around HK$7.80 to US$1. Hotel cashiers are handy, often open 24 hours, and as a rule they change either traveller's cheques or major foreign currencies, usually at a slightly higher rate than financial institutions or money changers.

LEGAL TENDER

The Hong Kong dollar has a singular distinction: it is the world's last major currency issued not by a government but by local private banks. With unflagging free enterprise, the two leading financial houses here – **The Hongkong and Shanghai Banking Corporation** and **The Standard Chartered** – issue all the colony's paper money, emblazoning notes with grandly stylized views of their own headquarters. The British Queen is confined to coins and one cent notes. The Hong Kong dollar (HK$) is divided into 100 cents. There are seven standard bills. Each bank uses a different motif, but all share similar denomination colours: $1,000 (gold), $500 (brown), $100 (red), $50 (blue), $20 (orange) and $10 (green). There is also a small and rarely seen one cent (1¢) note that's only slightly larger than a subway ticket. They are blank on one side and make unique souvenirs. Coins include 10¢, 20¢, 50¢, $1, $2 and $5.

EXCHANGE RATES

Many licensed money changers, usually open from 9 a.m. to late at night, will often accept more obscure foreign notes – at a substantial markdown. Nevertheless, their traveller's cheque and banknote rates are considerably better than those offered by hotels. For large transactions – US$250 or more – exchange rates usually can be negotiated to even greater advantage.

TRAVELLER'S CHEQUES

They are sold here by foreign exchange dealers and banks. European or Japanese traveller's cheques are as acceptable as US dollar cheques. Many small merchants here prefer traveller's cheques to credit cards or hard currency, so hold out for more than the going bank rate during any negotiations involving traveller's cheques.

PERSONAL CHEQUES

These will be of little use here, even at a local branch of the issuing bank back home (unless prior arrangements have been made). There are some shopkeepers who won't let such paper complications stand in the way of a good sale, but most will probably laugh.

OVERSEAS REMITTANCES

Receiving money from overseas is a minor but sometimes unavoidable hassle. The simplest, fastest and surest money transfer agents here are the major international banks – preferably one from the traveller's home country, and ideally one where a regular current or savings account is maintained (see the "Commercial" phone book's yellow pages). Your bank's local staff can explain various options, but the best procedure is to have a friend or relative make a deposit in your home bank and instruct that institution to relay funds to a particular bank or related bank branch in Hong Kong. To avoid delays, your full name, passport number and address should be included with the transfer document. You also should know to which bank the money is coming and should inform the bank of your pending cash transfer. If you accept all or part of your money in Hong Kong dollars, and the rest in traveller's cheques, you will get a better deal than if you receive all the money in foreign currency. (A minimum surcharge of HK$25 is usually charged for the latter.)

HEALTH

Hong Kong's once well-deserved reputation as a "Whiteman's grave" went out with pirates and the end of the opium trade. Standards of health and medicine today compare fully with the West, and aside from the obvious, travellers need take no particular precautions.

INOCULATIONS

For travellers heading off to more exotic locales, two Port Health Inoculation Centres give any and every shot at bargain prices: at 2nd floor, Centrepoint, 181 Gloucester Road, Wanchai, Hong Kong (tel: 572-2056); and Room 905 Government Office Bldg, 393 Canton Road, Tsimshatsui, Kowloon (tel: 368-3361). Hours are 9 a.m.–1 p.m. and 2–5 p.m.

Monday through Friday, and 9 a.m.–1 p.m. Saturdays. (There is also a centre at the airport.)

GASTRIC UNREST

In hotels and main-line restaurants (including all those named in these pages), health standards hold up well against any in the world. Order what you like, and worry more about the various glutton's maladies than some indescribable Oriental dysentery. Off the beaten path, things predictably become more problematic – but rarely exceed even the newest China hand's powers of discretion. Assuming one conquers the obvious oddities (the shirtless chef, the shoeless waiter, the chicken gizzards et al), an obvious question arises: how much local colour is too much? The buzz of a hundred flies is one standard bad sign, as is food served tepid rather than steaming hot. Lack of a refrigerator means nothing in itself, because most Chinese prefer "warm" (freshly killed) meat. A quick glance at the raw ingredients never hurts. As more positive steps, go where the locals seem to go, do as they do by rinsing chopsticks and bowls in hot tea, and drink either more hot tea or anything from a bottle – without ice. Fruit – with the usual tropical caveat about avoiding pre-peeled items – is fine for dessert, but the cautious might stick to ice cream.

In the end, though, getting sick results more from bad luck than from anything one does or doesn't do. The hapless – and most travellers to most places seem doomed to this at some point – can minimize debilitation by:

1) Eating nothing solid for 24 hours, then starting slowly on soups and noodles;

2) Drinking copiously (bland liquids only) to stave off dehydration; and

3) Going as easy as it seems reasonable. For persistent diarrhoea or vomiting, obviously seek medical attention.

DRINKING WATER

The true colonial prefers stronger stuff, the Chinese stick with tea, and many (possibly nostalgic) Western residents insist on boiled or bottled water. Nevertheless, both officially and in fact, straight from the tap is perfectly harmless. It's still not a good idea to ask for a glass of water at a street stall in the New Territories, but several decades have passed since hotel guests had to brush their teeth with gin.

USEFUL DRUGS

Hong Kong has recently tightened up its former laissez-faire approach to prescription drugs. Although birth-control pills and the sometimes-crucial lomotil diarrhoea pills can still be bought over the counter anywhere, things like Valium and tetracycline will require a bit of persuasive talking – and bargaining – at one of Wanchai's "medicine

NO MATTER HOW FAR YOU ARE FROM
CASH FROM 150,000 ATMS WORLDW

GlobalAccess

GlobalAccess means just what its name says: instant access to your money, wherever and whenever you need it. 24 hours a day. In over 60 countries around the world.

At HongkongBank's ATM network throughout Asia and the Middle East, you can conduct all your usual ATM transactions. You can also withdraw cash and make balance enquiries at Midland Bank ATMs in the UK, and Marine Midland Bank ATMs in the USA. Simply look for the GlobalAccess logo. And, of course, you can get cash from the Plus ATM network worldwide.

It's easy, it's instant and it's fast becoming indispensable for anyone who travels.

For more details on GlobalAccess contact your nearest HongkongBank office. Then you can keep in constant contact with your cash, no matter how far you are from home.

HongkongBank

The Hongkong and Shanghai Banking Corporation Limited

companies." Otherwise, Watson's (various locations), Mannings (various locations) and Victoria Dispensary (Theatre Lane, next to Queen's Theatre, off Queen's Road Central, Hong Kong) are among the more complete and easily accessible pharmacies.

WHAT TO WEAR

Clothing should follow seasons not unlike those in the American Deep South. Dank winter months (January and February) require sweaters, heavy jackets or even a light topcoat. A fickle, cool-to-warm spring (March and April) is best handled with adaptable, all-purpose outfits. High, emphatically tropical summer (May through September) demands the lightest cloths, umbrellas (traditional local models are superb, raincoats a steamy washout) and some sort of protection against fanatic air-conditioning. Much-favoured and dry and temperate fall (October through December) is best suited by middle-weight clothes with perhaps a sweater for cool nights during the later months.

Style of dress is happily more a matter of personal taste than public acceptability. The odd habits of visiting "barbarians" long ago ceased to startle residents, and shorts, sandals and haltertops are as popular locally as they are, for most of the year, practical. Obvious opulence, on the other hand, will impress hotel room-clerks – and inspire pajama-clad merchants to new heights in "tourist" pricing. Any semblance of skirt or coat-and-tie mollifies the handful of hotel restaurants requiring "formal dress."

As in most of the world, working businessmen in Hong Kong wear business clothes. Short-sleeved, perm-press "safari-suits" have taken up some of the slack left by the decline of the rumpled linen suit, but otherwise a crisp, cravatted globetrotter look is – sometimes sweatily – de rigueur.

ANIMAL QUARANTINE

No animals are allowed into the colony without first spending a minimum of 4 months in private or government guarantee kennels.

The problem does not usually affect short-term visitors. All queries or pleas should be posted to the Agriculture & Fisheries Department, Canton Road Government Offices, 12–14th floors, 393 Canton Road, Tsimshatsui, Kowloon, tel: 733-2142.

CUSTOMS

Though Hong Kong is a well-known duty-free port, arriving non-resident visitors still face the usual limitations on consumable luxuries: 200 cigarettes, 50 cigars or 250 grams of tobacco; a quart of liquor or spirits; and cosmetics "in reasonable quantities for personal use." The only import duties levied here are on petroleum products and alcohol products (both grog and perfumes). Everything else is duty-free. (The allowances for returning residents is half

that of non-residents – 100 cigarettes or 25 cigars or 125 grams of tobacco – plus one bottle of still wine, i.e. no liquor or spirits.)

Hong Kong is also a free money market, so there are no restrictions on the type or amount of money brought in or taken out. (Warning: the next countries you visit might have special monetary rules, so check their restrictions before you leave Hong Kong.)

Airport customs officers take a very active interest in drugs and firearms. The worst most tourists can expect is a very stern glance and a few pointed questions, but this interrogation frequently includes full-scale searches, particularly of suspicious young arrivals from Thailand or India. Prescription medicines should always be carried in their original containers. Firearms, live ammunition, knives, spears, bows and arrows must be declared immediately and left in customs custody until departure.

PORTER SERVICES

Porters are available at the airport arrivals area, and are at your service whether you arrive privately or by hotel transport. Though this service is free, they do appreciate a gratuity, normally about HK$3 per piece of baggage.

EXTENSION OF STAY

It is extremely rare for a person on a visitor's visa to change his or her visa status category without first leaving the colony. However, visa extensions are usually given freely provided you have the means to stay here (without working) and onward ticketing. Address all queries to the Immigration Department, Immigration Tower, 7 Gloucester Road, Hong Kong, tel: 824-6111.

ON DEPARTURE

DEPARTURE TRANSPORT

Hotels and travel agents offer regular airport transportation services. Any metered taxi will also gladly make the run to Kai Tak. (See "Getting Around" for charges.) An airport bus service stops every 10 to 20 minutes at major hotels in Central District and Causeway Bay (on Hong Kong Island) and at Tsimshatsui in Kowloon. Some hotels are reluctant to dispense airport bus information because it is the cheapest way of getting to the airport and would interfere with their own airport transportation services. On airport buses, however, there are no individual luggage racks (just a communal baggage bay) and the buses' steps are steep. Travellers with a lot of baggage would probably prefer a taxi or hotel service, because there is no porter service from the curbside bus stops. Route A1 serves Kowloon and the fare is HK$8. Routes A2, A3 and A5 serve Hong Kong Island and their fare is HK$12 (exact change only). For more information, call 745-4466.

CHECK-IN

Though most airlines at Kai Tak Airport have computerized booking facilities, they still request check-in at least two hours before flight time because of the airport's burgeoning crowds. Cathay Pacific has a City Check offering complete check in, same day services at Pacific Place II, 88 Queensway, Hong Kong, tel: 747-1788. The hours are 8 a.m.–8 p.m. You can check in and receive your boarding pass (no luggage) at United Airlines, 29th floor, Gloucester Tower, Landmark, Pedder Street, Central, Hong Kong, tel: 810-4888. Normal office hours. Most airlines begin their check-in 3 hours before flight time, but Jardine Airways, which handles quite a number of flights (see airlines listing), allows a same-day check-in from 3.30 p.m., which means you can drop your bags off and receive a boarding card any time during the day at your convenience.

DEPARTURE TAX

The airport's departure tax is HK$150 for adults and youths over 12 years old. Travel agents may include this in your ticket price. If not, you pay at check-in and a receipt is attached to your ticket.

UNACCOMPANIED BAGGAGE

Overweight duties charged for accompanied baggage are quite expensive. At Kai Tak Airport, however, there is an Unaccompanied Baggage Service in the Passenger Terminal and near the check-in counters. This service will forward your excess baggage by air freight. (Or take it to the Air Cargo Terminal – about a mile from the Passenger Terminal – or leave it with a commercial air freight forwarder.) Arrive at Kai Tak long before your normal check-in time, because it takes time to complete the various airway bills. Payment for such services is required in advance and credit cards are accepted. Your bags will not accompany you on your flight but should arrive at your destination 24 hours later. If you want the bags to be on your flight, to avoid two trips to the airport, go to the airport at least 24-48 hours before your flight to make such arrangements. Note: Your bags, regardless of when you send them are collected in the Air Cargo Terminal, not in the passenger baggage collection area.

HAND-CARRY BAGGAGE

The size of hand-carry items allowed on aircraft is more strictly controlled in Hong Kong than at most other airports. As you go into immigration security sectors, uniformed personnel will inspect hand-carry items. There is a box there measuring 22 x 14 x 9 inches (56 x 36 x 23 cm) and all your baggage must fit into it (with the exception of garment bags.)

Additional "hand baggage," however, can be purchased in transit area duty-free shops.

If you have items that cannot be checked as baggage – such as baby bags or strollers or large camera bags, etc. – ask for the airline's supervisor. (The check-in girl will call her.) They are strict but fair and often will either escort you through customs or give you a red baggage exemption tag.

GETTING ACQUAINTED

TIME ZONES

The International Dateline puts Hong Kong resolutely ahead of most of the world. There is no daylight savings here so Hong Kong remains GMT +8 all year. Go back or forward the specified number of hours to determine standard time (and in some cases today's date) in other places:

Auckland	+4
Athens	-6
Bangkok	-1
Buenos Aires	-11
Cairo	-6
Dacca	-2
Europe	-7
Honolulu	-18
Jakarta	-1
Johannesburg	-6
Karachi	-3
Kuala Lumpur	same
Lagos	-7
London	-8
Macau	same
Manila	same
Mexico City	-14
Moscow	-5
New Delhi	-2½
Ottawa	-13
Peking	same
Rangoon	-1½
Singapore	same
Seoul	+1
Sydney	+2
Taipei	same
Tehran	-4½
Tel Aviv	-6
Tokyo	+1
USA (East)	-13
USA (Pacific)	-16

Example: If it is noon in Hong Kong, in New York it is midnight the previous evening (-12 hours) in summer, or 11 p.m. in winter (-13 hours).

CLIMATE

A historian recently noted that Hong Kong's weather is "trying for half the year." Foreign residents might agree, but few visitors stay long enough for the weather to become truly oppressive. In meteorological terms, the climate is tropical (just barely) and monsoonal. Two seasons dominate the year – one consistently hot, wet and humid (the **Southwest Monsoon**, corresponding very roughly to spring/summer), and the other cool and dry (the **Northeast Monsoon**, corresponding to fall/winter). The colony can, however, experience great variations in this general pattern – notably in periods between successive monsoons – and dramatically during **typhoon season**. The word "typhoon" is derived from Cantonese *dai fung* which means "big wind." It is Asia's version of a Western hurricane.

TYPHOONS

If you are unlucky enough to be here when a full-scale typhoon sweeps in from the South China Sea, you will find out first-hand why it was named *dai fung*, or "big wind," in Cantonese. There is not much you can do except slink back to your hotel and have a typhoon party, which is precisely what many Hong Kong residents do in their homes during these Asian hurricanes.

The **Royal Observatory** is modern enough to have early-warning computers and a weather satellite ground station, so no longer does the weatherman stand out on the RO's lawn to see which ways the clouds are moving. When a typhoon or "**Severe Tropical Storm**" (which may escalate into a typhoon) comes within a 400-mile radius of the colony, storm signal #1 goes up. The populace is quite blase about a number one signal. A #1 signal can remain aloft for days – sometimes during beautiful pre-storm weather, or be quickly changed to the next important signal #3. Number 3 is the first real alert because it signifies that winds are reaching speeds of 22 to 33 knots with gusts up to 60 knots.

Never Underestimate a Typhoon. Too many visitors, mostly from the United States and the Caribbean, probably do because they have seen so many hurricanes. They tend to think typhoons are nothing more than severe rainstorms. A few statistics for the disbelievers. Typhoon Hope in 1979 left 12 dead and 260 injured. Severe Tropical Storm Agnes in 1978 left 3 dead and 126 injured, and Typhoon Rose, which left the harbour a shambles, claimed 130 lives, 80 on a capsized Hong Kong-Macau ferry. Typhoon Ruby in 1964 killed 120 and Typhoon Wanda in 1962 killed 138.

For information about a typhoon, call the **City & New Territories Administration's Typhoon Emergency Number** (835-1473), but do not ring the Royal Observatory, the police or the first brigade, who are all on full alert. To find out if the airport is closed, phone 769-7531, but rest assured that individual airlines will regularly update you on the details of their own typhoon-disrupted flights.

DRY MONSOONS

The dry monsoon season begins sometime in September, and brings 3 months of warm (rather than hot) days and usually clear blue skies. Nights are cool, humidity low, and day-to-day temperature changes are slight. The best months to visit are October and November; the colony is predictably chock-a-block with visitors during this period. From December through early January, it is still sunny during the day and cool at night. This period

Average Temperatures and Rainfall

	Average daily Maximum °F/°C	Average daily Minimum °F/°C	Average monthly Rainfall (in./mm)
January	64/18	56/13	1.2/30
February	63/17	55/12.5	1.8/45
March	63/17	60/15.5	2.8/70
April	75/24	67/19.5	5.3/133
May	82/28	74/23	11.4/285
June	85/29.5	78/25.5	16.0/400
July	87/30.5	78/25.5	14.5/363
August	87/30.5	78/25.5	14.4/360
September	85/29.5	77/25	10.9/272.5
October	81/27	73/22.5	3.9/98
November	74/23	65/18.5	1.7/43
December	68/20	59/15	1.0/25

For temperature (and time) dial 18501

signals a gradual shift to less predictable weather. Beginning with Chinese New Year – late-January to mid-February – the temperature and clear and dry skies alternate with longer spells of cold wind and dank mist that can run unbroken for weeks. Mountaintops occasionally show night-time frost (the appearance of frost is always a headline story in local tabloids), and beaches at this time of the year are largely deserted.

Hong Kong's rainy season arrives in earnest about the middle of March, when the temperature rises, humidity thickens and trees grow green. Skies can be consistently gray, and heavy afternoon rainstorms become increasingly common. Though quite changeable, this "spring" season generally stays cool enough to be agreeable with most visitors.

Mid-May to September is high summer, and also the unpredictable typhoon season. Punctuated by cloudbursts, intense tropical sunshine scorches open land and broils even well-tanned skin. Humidity rarely falls below 90 percent, but temperatures rarely top 90–93°F (32–34°C). Airconditioning eases this steamy torpor, so much so that sweaters are sometimes required indoors.

CULTURE & CUSTOMS

One would think that a territory immersed in the diplomatic business of selling would realize the importance of being polite. The reverse, unfortunately, is often true. Hong Kong deserves its dubious reputation, as "the rudest place on earth." The Hong Kong government is aware of this protocol problem and constantly exhorts (through media campaigns) its 150,000 plus civil servants to be polite. The Hong Kong Tourist Association is also concerned.

TIPPING

Though a 10 percent gratuity is added to most hotel and restaurant bills, you are still expected to tip. If the service has been bad, however, collect every penny from the change tray. If the service has been abominable, go up to the restaurant manager and demand that the automatic 10 percent service charge – in your case, non-service charge – be deducted from your bill. Most Chinese restaurants add on a service charge, but some of the smaller, traditional ones do not.

Bellboys, porters and doormen usually receive about HK$20 per piece. Cloakroom and lavatory attendants, HK$1. Taxi drivers, barbers and hairdressers, about 10 percent. Tourist guides – if good – may get HK$30–$50. It is not necessary to tip cinema usherettes or petrol kiosk attendants.

WEIGHTS & MEASURES

Hong Kong is still making the complicated transition from the Imperial to the metric system of weights and measures. Also, the Chinese have their own methods of weighing and measuring – which are still very much in use today.

WEIGHTS

The following are Chinese-Asian weighing and measuring terms you may encounter while in Hong Kong.

Daam	= 100 catties
Catty (pronounced "gun")	= 16 taels
Tael (pronounced "leung")	= 10 chins
Chin	= 10 guns

The terms "catty" and "tael" are quite commonly used in market places. They are equivalent to 1⅓ lbs and 1⅓ oz respectively. The latter term is also used in gold and silver markets instead of ounce.

MEASURES

Fortunately, Chinese terms are rarely used here; residents prefer mile, foot and inch, and are gradually accepting kilometre, metre, etc. For the record, the Chinese version of a mile or kilometre is lay (equivalent to 0.3107 mile); a foot is tchek (1.0936 feet); and an inch is tchuen (1.312 inches).

BUSINESS HOURS

Local banking hours are now in the process of gradual extension, but 9 a.m. to 4.30 p.m. on weekdays, and 9 a.m. to noon Saturdays (closed Sundays) are normal business hours for foreign exchange services.

HOLIDAYS

On public holidays (indicated by asterisk *), banks and offices close. The quiet Chinese New Year, however, usually does not affect tourist-area restaurants and shops.

Undated listings below are normally set at least 6 months in advance: contact the Hong Kong Tourist Association (HKTA) for precise information.

January 1: New Year's Day*
January–February: Chinese New Year*
February–March: Hong Kong Arts Festival; Yuen Siu (Lantern Festival)
March–April: Ching Ming*; Easter (Good Friday, Easter Sunday and Monday)
May: Birthday of Tin Hau; Buddha's Birthday; Tam King's Birthday; Horse Racing Season ends
June: Tuen Ng* (Dragon Boat Festival); Queen's Birthday
July: Birthday of Lu Pan
August 25: Liberation Day*
September: Mid-Autumn Festival; Horse Racing Season begins

October: Birthday of Confucius; Chung Yueng*
October–November: Asian Arts Festival
December 25: Christmas*
December 26: Boxing Day*

RELIGIOUS SERVICES

There are numerous houses of worship besides Buddhist temples. Although many are mission-oriented and Chinese-speaking, these conduct all or most of their services in English. With the possible exceptions of St John's and the Shelley Street Mosque (both built in the 1840s), none are either as old or notable as those in Macau.

PROTESTANT (CHURCH OF ENGLAND-EPISCOPALIAN)
St John's Cathedral (Anglican), Garden Road (behind the Hilton Hotel), Central District, Hong Kong.
St Andrew's (Anglican), 138 Nathan Road, Tsimshatsui, Kowloon.
English Methodist Church (Methodist), Queen's Road East, Hong Kong.
Church of All Nations (Lutheran), 8 South Bay Close, Repulse Bay Road, Hong Kong.
Truth Luthern Church, 50 Waterloo Road, Kowloon.
Union Church (Interdenominational), Kennedy Road, above Mid-Levels, Hong Kong; and 4 Jordan Road, Yaumatei, Kowloon.

HINDU & SIKH
Temple, Queen's Road East at Stubbs Road, Happy Valley, Hong Kong.

ZOROASTRIAN
Zoroastrian Church, Leighton Road at Caroline Hill Road (near Lee Gardens Hotel), Happy Valley, Hong Kong.

ROMAN CATHOLIC
Cathedral, 16 Caine Road (up Glenealy Path), above Central District, Hong Kong.
St Joseph's, 7 Garden Road, Mid-levels, Central District, Hong Kong.
St Theresa's, 258 Prince Edward Road, Kowloon Tsai, Kowloon.
Rosary Church, 125 Chatham Road, Tsimshatsui, Kowloon.

ISLAMIC
Mohammedan Mosque, Shelly and Mosque streets (off Robinson Road), Mid-Levels, Hong Kong.
Kowloon Mosque, Nathan Road at Cameron Road (in Kowloon Park), Tsimshatsui, Kowloon.

JEWISH
Ohel Leah Synagogue (Orthodox), 70 Robinson Road, Mid-Levels, Hong Kong.
United Jewish Congregation (Reform), GPO Box 6083. Call 463-8156 for details of services.

COMMUNICATIONS

MEDIA

RADIO

There are four radio stations: the government-operated Radio-Television Hong Kong (RTHK) which carries BBC world service feeds, Commercial Radio, Metro Radio and the British Forces Broadcasting Services (BFBS). Hong Kong's radio channels broadcast everything from contemporary pop to magnificent interludes of classical music. RTHK has five channels – two in English, two in Chinese and one bilingual. Commercial Radio has three AM/FM channels – two in Chinese and one in English. BFBS has two channels; it broadcasts two-thirds of its programmes in Nepali, one-third in English. Metro Radio has an English-language, 24-hour all news network on AM and two music channels on FM.

TELEVISION

There are two television stations – **Asia Television Ltd. (ATV)** and **Hong Kong Television Broadcasts Ltd. (TVB)** – broadcasting on four channels. Each has an English-language and a Cantonese-language channel. Overseas news – including daily satellite feeds – is commonly included in their news programmes. CNN is available overnight on ATV while TVB carries the CBS evening news at 7.30 a.m. There is a weekly guide to events and TV in Hong Kong called *Television & Entertainment Times* (HK$12). The recently launched Star Television satellite service includes four English channels: Star Plus, Prime Sports, MTV and BBC World Service.

PRESS

Newspapers: There are 61 Chinese newspapers – though most are referred to as the "mosquito press" and concentrate on either horse racing or sex – and two English local dailies – *The South China Morning Post* and *Hong Kong Standard*. Two international English-language dailies – The *Asian Wall Street Journal* and The *International Herald Tribune* – are also printed here.

The *South China Morning Post* and *The Standard* publish a great deal of international news, more than you would expect for a daily in Hong Kong, and the two international dailies contain almost all the worldwide news.

Magazines: Hong Kong is one of Asia's major printing and publishing centres, so you will find a plethora of magazines – 495 to be exact; 322 in Chinese, 126 in English and 47 bilingual. Asia editions of Time and Newsweek are printed here, as is the Reader's Digest. Regional news magazines such as Far Eastern Economic Review and Asiaweek also originate here.

Foreign Media: If that is not enough to keep you informed, overseas editions of many foreign papers and magazines are flown in daily. Unfortunately, they are quite expensive. The best way to beat exorbitant print media prices is to go to the Star Ferry Concourse, Kowloon-side. As you face the entrance, turn left and walk along the row of news vendors there. You will soon find a woman who has an excellent selection of used foreign newspapers in all languages – most only slightly crumpled, perhaps only a day old and available by late evening on the same day they arrive. This lady, according to local rumor, has a contact with the cleaners at Kai Tak Airport. Her cleaners remove already-read foreign papers from the planes, iron them and pass them on – freshly re-pressed – for re-sale.

LIBRARIES

Borrowing books is normally impossible for short-term visitors, but most libraries here have reading rooms where you can relax or do scholarly research. The best libraries are:

Urban Council Public Library, City Hall, Edinburgh Place (off Star Ferry Concourse), Hong Kong. Large, and usually crowded. Hours: 10 a.m.–7 p.m. Monday to Wednesday; till 9 p.m. Friday; 5 p.m. Saturday; and 1 p.m. Sunday. Closed Thursday.
British Council Library, 255 Hennessy Road, Wanchai, Hong Kong, tel: 831-5138. British books, magazines and newspapers. Hours: 9.30 a.m.–8.30 p.m. weekdays; till 6.30 p.m. Saturday.
American Library, United Centre, 1/f, 95 Queensway, Hong Kong, tel: 529-9661. US books, magazines, newspapers, telephone directories and college catalogues. Hours: 10 a.m.–6 p.m. weekdays.

Note: The four major universities – the University of Hong Kong, the Chinese University, the Hong Kong University of Science and Technology and Hong Kong Polytechnic – all have comprehensive and large libraries, but special permission is required before outsiders can use these facilities.

TELEPHONE

Communications to, from and within the colony work with commendable efficiency. Geared to the needs of an internationally oriented business community, the completely – if at times somewhat halting – bilingual systems are operated by Hong Kong Telecom International.

LOCAL CALLS

There are no area codes. Except for special numbers, the vast majority are seven-digit.

For directory listing, the English-language phonebooks – three residential (for Hong Kong, Kowloon and the New Territories), a Business Directory, plus the "Yellow Pages" which come in four volumes – are often a better bet than wrangling with the information operators (dial 1081). In a pinch, the Hong Kong Tourist Association's enquiries service, tel: 801-7177, can handle many local problems. For collect and operator assisted calls (plus direct dialling to China) dial 010; conference or ship to shore, 011; operator-assistance calls to China, 012; and direct dialling enquiries, 013. Cheaper off-peak charges are in effect midnight to 7 a.m. daily, plus from 1 p.m. Saturday through Sunday.

Because there is no long-distance within the colony and subscribers get unlimited free calls, most restaurants and shops allow use of their phones without charge.

Pay phones take one HK$1 coin (no time limit). The emergency police/fire/ambulance emergency number is 999 – no coin needed from public phones. For time and temperature dial 18501. An ear-rattling wai is the standard Cantonese telephone greeting. Though seemingly rude to most Western ears, the nearest translation is simply "Hello?"

OVERSEAS CALLS

International calls can be placed through hotel switchboards (which add a 10 percent service fee unless they are direct dialled) or directly with Hong Kong Telecom at one of its several public offices:

Central District: Exchange Square, Connaught Place (near the Furama Hotel), tel: 845-1281. Open 24 hours.

Tsimshatsui: Hermes House, 10 Middle Road, tel: 732-4243. Open 24 hours daily.

Causeway Bay: Lee Gardens Hotel, Hysan Avenue, tel: 577-0577. Open 10 a.m.–1 p.m., 2–6 p.m. Monday through Friday; 10 a.m.–3 p.m. Saturday.

Kai Tak Airport: Passenger Terminal Bldg, tel: 362-9676. Open 8 a.m.–11 p.m. daily; noon–7 p.m. Sunday.

Minimum 3-minute operator-assisted calls to the United States, Canada, and Australia cost HK$63, France and Germany HK$72, and the United Kingdom HK$60.

CABLE & TELEX

As with overseas phone calls, these may be placed either through hotels or at any of the Hong Kong Telecom offices listed above.

POSTAL SERVICES

Hong Kong's post offices feature portraits of the Queen and reliable, usually efficient service. Air letters normally take four or five days to Europe or Australia, six to eight to most destinations in the United States and Canada. Surface packages can vary anywhere from three weeks to three months.

The most complete and convenient facility is Hong Kong-side's General Post Office. Located just off the Star Ferry Concourse, the gleaming white GPO has a full range of package and letter services, including a philatelic window and a ground-floor "General Delivery" counter (Poste Restante, GPO, Hong Kong). Outside working hours (8 a.m.–6 p.m. weekdays, till 12.30 pm on Saturdays, closed Sundays and public holidays), the GPO's stamp machines and letter slots are open round-the-clock. For large and delicate items, there are reliable commercial packing and shipping firms. For those doing things themselves, the GPO information number (523-1071) can detail the various regulations on packaging, contents and size.

EMERGENCIES

SECURITY & CRIME

The local legal system is very British, but different from Britain's. Its most notable anachronism is punishment by caning for minor offenders. Also, capital punishment is still permissible.

Lawyers here are called barristers and solicitors, due process works as well as in most places and, despite historical precedent by Hong Kong's founding fathers, drug smugglers should not expect kind treatment. The legal languages are English and Cantonese.

1st class airmail (letter & postcards)

	First 10 grams	Each Additional 10 grams
Asia west through Afghanistan	HK$1.80	HK$1.00
Rest of the world	HK$2.30	HK$1.10

2nd class airmail (unsealed letters & printed matter)

	First 10 grams	Each additional 10 grams
Asia west through Afghanistan	HK$1.20	60¢
Rest of the world	HK$1.70	80¢

Airletters (Aerogrammes)

Anywhere	HK$1.80

Air Parcels (excluding insurance, registration etc.)

	First 500 grams	Each additional 500 grams
USA (excluding Hawaii)	HK$68	HK$43
Australia (excluding W.A.)	HK$85	HK$23
United Kingdom	HK$124	HK$31

Registration: HK$9, Express (Special Delivery): HK$5, Speedpost (guaranteed 24 hours delivery): On demand to certain countries at varying proces. Check at the general Post Office or the Kowloon Central POst Office.

Surface Parcels (excluding insurance, registration etc.)

	1 kilo	3 kilo	5 kilo	10 kilo
USA	HK$60	HK$115	HK$185	HK$320
Australia	HK$85	HK$100	HK$130	HK$170
United Kingdom	HK$110	HK$140	HK$185	HK$230

The British-administered Royal Hong Kong Police wear light green uniforms in summer, blue ones in winter, and carry handguns. English speaking officers have a small red tab below their serial numbers. In emergencies phone 999 and ask for the police, fire department, or ambulance, as required.

Money Thefts: This is a complaint most consulates don't like to hear, but they are usually quite helpful and sympathetic to theft victims. The Royal Hong Kong Police Force is also efficient and helpful. If your hotel is reluctant to assist because of the bad publicity, go to the police directly. Also, the Hong Kong Tourist Association will gladly assist travellers who have been robbed or swindled.

Fraud: To complain about out and out fraud, contact the RHKPF "Fraud Squad," Commercial Crimes, tel: 823-5512. If you find out about a fraudulent sale after you have departed, write to the HKTA or the Consumer Council.

Copyright Infringements: For copyright violations – if you happen to be Messrs. Cartier, Gucci, Lanvin or the like, address your complaints to the Trade Department, 700 Nathan Road, Mongkok, Kowloon, tel: 737-2333.

MEDICAL SERVICES

CHEMISTS

Don't panic if you suddenly discover that you've run out of your urgently needed prescribed medicine. Hong Kong has modern chemists or dispensaries (as they are called here) and you will not have to make do with ground seahorse or some other traditional remedy. The main pharmacies are Watson's The Chemists, Mannings, Colonial Dispensary and the Victoria Dispensary.

There are also hundreds of Chinese medicine companies which accept prescriptions and usually stock both Western and Asian medicines. These, however, should not be confused with traditional herbalists (with whom they sometimes share premises). Herbalists will happily sell you a dried seahorse, a bit of rhinoceros horn, deer's antler, tiger's penis and a selection of special herbs – all prepared while you wait.

HOSPITALS

In descending order of price, the most notable private hospitals are Matilda (on Mt Kellett Road, The Peak, Hong Kong), Canossa (1 Old Peak Road, above Central District, Hong Kong), The Baptist Hospital (222 Waterloo Road, Kowloon, tel: 337-4141), and the Adventist. None are cheap, but all are comfortable and offer highest quality specialists and facilities.

For serious accidents or emergencies, 24-hour casualty wards are operated by Queen Mary (Pokfulam Road, Pokfulam, Hong Kong, tel: 819-2111), Queen Elizabeth (Wylie Road off Gascoigne Road, Kowloon, tel: 710-2111), Princess Margaret (Lai King Shan Road, Laichikok, tel: 742-7111) and Prince of Wales (Shatin, New Territories, tel: 636-2211) hospitals, the four leading government-run institutions. Stays are again in the bargain class.

CLINICS

For the walking wounded, clinics are a practical and economical alternative, most offering the basic range of specialists in-house. The Hong Kong Adventist Hospital (40 Stubbs Road at Wongneichung Road, above Happy Valley, Hong Kong, tel: 574-6211) operates an expat-staff out-patient department Sunday through Friday noon, and also has a good dental clinic with 24-hour emergency service. Anderson & Partners, Vio & Partners and Drs. Oram & Howard, all have clinics on both sides of the harbour.

The undoubted bargain (HK$18 for consultation and medicine, plus a few hours' waiting in line) are the more than 66 government clinics (also called Jockey Club Clinics) scattered around town (look up Medical & Health Department under official government listings at the start of the telephone directory).

PRIVATE PHYSICIANS

Though many people still prefer traditional cures for minor ills, modern Western practices dominate the field. Most doctors took all or part of their training overseas (usually in Britain, north America, Australia or New Zealand), and the medical and dental professions together include several score expatriates. Private physician's fees as well tend to be internationally scaled, particularly room visits by hotel doctors (either resident or on-call at most), which can run to $100 or more. Office consultations are generally less than half of that, specialist treatment (normally by referral only) sometimes more.

ACUPUNCTURISTS

Not every one accepts this traditional type of Chinese medicine so you will have to decide whether the needle treatment is for you. There are many clinics in Hong Kong, but few practitioners speak English or take the time to explain the treatment to a visitor.

LEFT LUGGAGE

Airline passengers should check with the Left Luggage counter at Kai Tak Airport (on the far left side as you enter the departure area).

GETTING AROUND

ORIENTATION

Getting around Hong Kong is much easier than it seems. Though Cantonese is the language spoken by 98 percent of the population, English is also widely used (if only for English place names which differ from their Cantonese counterparts). It helps, however, to have an address or item written out in Chinese characters by a friend or hotel employee.

For tourists heading to Shenzhen (also called Shum Chun), China's first and largest and wealthiest Special Economic Zone (SEZ), and the adjacent oil port of Shekou, it is dead easy because the travel agency does all the work. However, if you prefer to go on your own, whether as a tourist or a businessperson, it can be done. See "Tourist Information" for assistance and information on getting around in Hong Kong.

FROM THE AIRPORT

There is a special airport bus service – both to and from the airport – to and from Tsimshatsui and Hong Kong Island. Route A1 to Tsimshatsui costs HK$8 and Routes A2, A3 and A5 to Hong Kong cost HK$12 (exact fare change only). The routes stop at all major hotels.

Route A1 starts service at 7 a.m., with the last bus from the airport departing at midnight. Route A2 begins at 6.50 a.m. and ends at midnight. Route A3 begins at 6.55 a.m. and ends at midnight. Frequency for all routes is every 20 minutes. Call 745-4466 for details.

Metered taxis are available. Flag fare is HK$9 for the first 2 km, and thereafter, HK$0.90 for every 0.25 km. There is a HK$20 surcharge on any trip through the Cross-Harbour or Eastern Harbour Tunnels, and HK$5 for the Aberdeen and Tate's Cairn Tunnels and HK$6 for the Lion Rock Tunnel, plus a HK$4 charge on each piece of baggage. Taxi drivers are usually honest, but some try to overcharge on the short trip into Tsimshatsui, so just pay whatever is on the meter (which is obviously ticking over in HK$, not the US ones that some wily taxi drivers would have you believe). Avis self-drive cars are also available. Call 890-6988 for information.

DOMESTIC TRAVEL

THE KOWLOON-CANTON RAILWAY

The old Kowloon-Canton Railway is now a modern electrified commuter train because the three through trains to Canton are now Chinese-operated. There are ten stops on this 32-mile segment through Kowloon and the NT. Single, ordinary, one-way fares for the full run begin at HK$6.50. Don't worry about inadvertently chug-chugging into China. Note: There are no toilets on the Hong Kong trains, but there are such facilities on Chinese trains. The main railway station is in Hung Hom, Kowloon, and there is a passenger ferry service near that station from the Star Ferry in Central District. Call 606-9606 for details.

LIGHT RAIL TRANSPORT

This above ground railway runs between Tuen Muen and Yuen Long in the New Territories. Fares range from HK$2.70 to HK$3.90 (adults) and $1.40 to $2 (children). For enquiries, 468-7788.

THE STAR FERRY

You can always tell the tourists from the residents on Hong Kong's most famous mode of transportation, the Star Ferry. The tourists are agog at the magnificent site of the world's third busiest harbour – and one of the best natural harbours in the world – as the double-bowed, green and white, two-decker ferries weave their way through the 0.8 nautical mile course between Hong Kong and Tsimshatsui (Kowloon).

The residents, on the other hand, are quite content to spend the 7-minute sea voyage with their noses tucked into their newspapers or racing sheets. Upper deck, first class seats cost the princely sum of HK$1.50 and the view of the harbour from there will delight any shutterbug. A more exciting ride (closer to the water-racing past) is in second class seats on the lower deck; a ride there costs only HK$1.20. There is also a Kowloon-Wanchai service for HK$1.50 and HK$1.20 a Central-Hung Hom (in Kowloon) service at HK$1.80 upper deck, HK$1.50 lower deck.

WALLA-WALLAS

After the MTR closes at 1 a.m. and the Star Ferry at 11.30 p.m., you can still ride across the harbour in a small motorboat called a walla-walla (supposedly named for the hometown – Walla-Walla, Washington, USA – of this craft's original owner). You can also take a taxi or bus through the cross-harbour tunnel, but if you are staying in Tsimshatsui and end up in Central – or vice versa – the direct cross-harbour water route by Star Ferry, MTR or walla-walla is the fastest and cheapest means of transportation. On Hong Kong Island, walla-wallas are located at Queen's Pier to the East of the Star Ferry concourse (to the right as you face the harbour, facing City Hall) while in Kowloon, they are located at Kowloon Public Pier (to the left of the Star Ferry as you face the water, opposite the Ocean Terminal). The cost starts from about HK$50 per hour.

LOCAL FERRIES

There are other ferry services from the Star Ferry, Wanchai and North Point Piers (on Hong Kong) to various destinations in Kowloon, but these are primarily commuter ferries, rarely taken by visitors.

Inter-Island Ferries: There are 236 islands in the colony (Hong Kong Island of course is just one of them). A convenient inter-island ferries transportation system is in operation here to service many of them. At the **Outlying Districts Ferry Pier**, Connaught Road, Central, Hong Kong, you'll find double and triple-decker ferries – some with air-conditioning – that regularly travel to the outlying islands. The routes and times are too numerous to mention here, but there is regular service – quite crowded during weekends and holidays – to Lantau, Cheung Chau and Lamma islands (the big three) and many of the colony's smaller isles. Fares range from HK$3.50–$23, fare charges vary from children prices to adult ordinary and deluxe.

The Hong Kong Tourist Association has a complete schedule of all ferry services and will answer telephone queries at 801-7177. The **Hong Kong Ferry Company**'s enquiry number is 542-3082.

The **Polly Ferry Company** operates daily services to stops (including Grass Island) along Tolo Harbour and – at weekends and on public holidays – a ferry to Ping Chau. These depart from Ma Liu Shui, near the University KCR station. Call 771-1630 for information.

The ferry to Tung Lung departs from the southern edge of the harbour at Sai Wan Ho (near Hing Man Street), on Hong Kong Island. It operates at weekends and on public holidays, departing Sai Wan Ho at 8am, and Tung Lung at 4pm. Call 560-9929 for information (may be Cantonese only; ask hotel staff to help you). Alternatively, hire a *kaito* (small boat) from Sai Wan Ho, agreeing on a price and time to leave Tung Lung, and paying on the return trip.

PUBLIC TRANSPORT

BUSES

Hong Kong has numerous scheduled buses and bus routes to just about every corner of the colony. China Motor Buses are blue while Kowloon Motor Buses are red. With the advent of the cross-harbour tunnel routes, however, they commute on each other's turf. Bus fares range from HK$1.40 to HK$15. There are too many routes to list here, but those used frequently by tourists are the three airport buses (see "From the Airport" notes) and buses to Repulse Bay Beach and other places on the south side of the island. The deluxe (no standing) buses to Repulse Bay Beach are numbers 260 and 262 and cost HK$7–$10. (There is a convenient bus stop in front of the Hong Kong side Star Ferry Terminal.) The No. 6 bus plies the same route for HK$5.30, but they are regular buses, usually packed like sardine cans during the summer. For either bus, sit on the top deck and enjoy the scenic and swaying ride. Exact change only.

For buses to Shenzhen, the Chinese Special Economic Zone on the border, contact Citybus (China) Ltd. (tel: 745-8888). They run double-decker buses and air-conditioned coaches daily from China Hong Kong City (33 Canton Road, Kowloon) between 7.30 a.m. and 9.30 a.m. on the half hour. Tickets at HK$65 can be purchased from any Ticketmate outlet located in various MTR stations, Exchange Square, Central, and Sun Hung Kai Centre, 30 Harbour Road, both in Hong Kong. (Cash only, no credit cards.)

Hong Kong's Kowloon Canton Railway runs to the border (Lo Wu) many times daily. Call 606-9606 for details. Here, you cross the border on foot. Be prepared for crowds whose pushing and shoving is so renowned they may make it an Olympic sport. The border is at Shenzhen and you take a bus or taxi to Shekou, about 19 miles (30 km) away.

The Miramar Hotel has a fleet of chauffeur-driven cars which run between Hong Kong and Shenzhen (2 hours)/Shekou (3 hours). Hire car rates for Shenzhen are HK$916 one way; HK$1,466 same day return; and HK$2,466 overnight return. To Shekou, add HK$100 to each fare. The service is not restricted to hotel guests and you have to make your own visa arrangements. Call 733-6603 for information.

The resorts in the Special Economic Zone (SEZ), well off the beaten track, often have their own buses direct from Hong Kong or which meet the public transport in the SEZ.

There is also a hovercraft service from Hong Kong departing from Kowloon's China Hong Kong City.

"JETCAT" SERVICE TO SEZ

The Special Economic Zone (SEZ) of Zuhai is another oil exploration port, like the aforementioned Shekou, only this one is near Macau. There is a three-time "jetcat" service leaving from Kowloon's China Hong Kong City. Call 523-2136. It is only a 30-minute ride from Zhuhai to Macau.

MINIBUSES & MAXICABS

Yellow 16-seater vans with a red stripe – called minibuses here – ply all the main routes and make unscheduled stops and charge variable fares. There is a sign in the front indicating their destinations and fare charges. To complicate matters, other yellow 16-

seater vans with a green stripe and roof – called maxicabs – run on fixed routes at fixed prices. There is a special maxicab to The Peak (HK$4.50) and another to Ocean Park (HK$5). The maxi-bus terminal in Central is on the eastern side of the Star Ferry carpark.

TRAMS

On Hong Kong island there are trams running along the north shore from west to east (and vice versa) which pass through the main tourist areas of Central, Wanchai, Causeway Bay and Taikoo Shing Quarry Bay. The cost is HK$1 (exact change). Sit on the upper deck and watch the real Hong Kong bump and grind by. Looking for an interesting way to entertain? Try a Tram Party. Call 801-7427 for details.

THE PEAK TRAM

Hong Kong's other "tram" is the century-old Peak Tram, which is not a tram at all but a funicular railway up to The Peak. It is a form of regular local commuter transport and a favourite "tourist attraction." The funicular rises 1,305 feet (397 metres) above sea level in about 10 minutes on a steep journey over 4,500 feet (1,364 metres) of track. The fare is adults HK$10 (HK$16 return); children HK$4 (HK$6 return), and operates from 7 a.m. to midnight. The Lower Peak Tram Station in Central District is on Garden Road, up the Hilton Hotel and across the US Consulate. A free shuttle bus service operates between the Lower Station and the Star Ferry from 9 a.m.–7 p.m. daily at 20-minute intervals. There are four intermediate stations before the Upper Peak Tram Station nestled underneath the Peak Tower, a futuristic building on stilts that houses a European restaurant, shops, a bank and a supermarket.

MASS TRANSIT RAILWAY (MTR)

The most dramatic change in Hong Kong's public transportation scene is the fully air-conditioned Mass Transit Railway, commonly called the MTR, which in other countries might be called Underground, Tube, Metro or Subway. The 43.2-km system has three lines with 38 stations, stretching from industrial Kwun Tong (Kowloon) and Tsuen Wan (New Territories) through some of Kowloon's most populated areas, underneath Nathan Road to the Tsimshatsui tourist and entertainment district, and under the harbour to Central, the governmental and financial centre of the colony and along the north shore of Hong Kong Island. (With the MTR, it is easy to reach many of the favourite tourist areas on the island, particularly Wanchai, Causeway Bay and Taikoo Shing.)

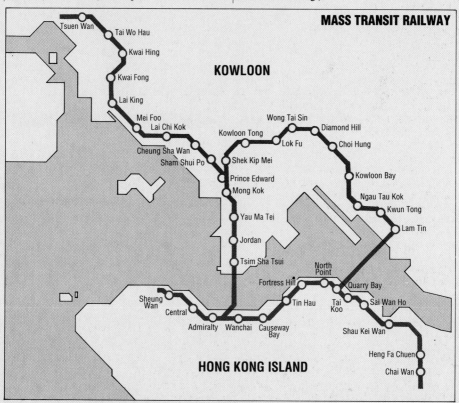

MASS TRANSIT RAILWAY

KOWLOON

HONG KONG ISLAND

The longest trip takes less than 60 minutes and fares range from HK$3–$9. The cross-harbour trip is HK$6–9. You can use the MTR for shopping or sightseeing trips. The MTR is open 6 a.m.–1 a.m. daily. See the MTR Guide for subway directions. For those really on the go, buy a Stored Value Ticket which also allows travel on the KCR (Kowloon Canton Railway). The interchange between the two systems is Kowloon Tong.

A few points before you go charging underground. First, there are no toilets down there, and smoking, drinking and eating are prohibited. The ticket machines take exact change, but there are change booths where you can break notes. After placing money in a ticket machine, you receive a magnetic plastic card about the size of a credit card. This is placed in a slot by the turnstile for entry. Upon departure, the card is again placed in a turnstile. The amount you pay is electronically calculated, and if you've paid enough, you may pass through the exit turnstile.

You will see signs warning about HK$1,000 fines for "ticket flickers" caught in the act. Ticket flickers are people who flick the plastic cards on their nails. In case you thought that Hong Kong has been forced to do something about noise pollution (imagine thousands of commuters ticket-flicking during rush hour), you are wrong. "Ticket-flicking" is banned because the MTR found it damaged the fare cards. A warning: the MTR's shiny metal seats are slippery so be prepared to slide when the train starts up. For further information, call 750-0170.

TAXIS

Have you been introduced to Hong Kong's "national flag" yet? Facetious local wags, tired of fighting for taxis – and being extorted by them during rush hours, holiday periods or late at night – have nicknamed the dirty "vacant" ragflag (supposedly signifying the driver is off duty) as Hong Kong's national standard because of its pesky ubiquitousness. Metered taxis in urban areas are red with silver roofs and the dome atop the roof is lit at night when the taxi is unoccupied. (There are also green and white taxis restricted to the New Territories (NT) and these run on a different – and cheaper – fare system.)

The taxi flagfall costs HK$9 for the first 1.24 miles (2 km) and HK$0.90 for each subsequent 720 feet (250 metres). The charge rate for waiting is HK$0.90 for every minute. The green and white NT taxis have a HK$8 flagfall with a subsequent rate of HK$0.90 for each 720 feet (250 metres). Urban taxis are allowed to charge a HK$20 surcharge for passage through the cross-harbour tunnel, plus HK$4 for each piece of luggage or large package. Also, note that there is a HK$5 surcharge for the Aberdeen Tunnel.

Some taxis are equipped with mobile telephones to phone anywhere in the colony. Charges are HK$2 per minute in addition to the fare.

COMPLAINTS

If you have any trouble with a taxi – say you are victimized, overcharged or you have left your wallet in the back seat – contact the Royal Hong Kong Police special "taxi hotline" at 527-7177. (Don't forget to record the taxi number!)

If a complaint is not resolved, you must be prepared to appear as a witness to the police prosecution. In most cases, the courts will push a tourist's case to the front of its judicial queues to make an example of the offender.

If a constable is nearby, take your complaint directly to him (or threaten to). Such tactics are a marvellous cure for obdurate drivers.

RICKSHAWS

Hong Kong still has a small number of rickshaws that congregate around Star Ferry concourse on Hong Kong Island. Tourists hire the rickshaws more to pose for pictures than as transportation but the unofficial "official" rate is HK$50–$100 for a 5 minute trip around the block. However, because rickshaw-pullers refuse to budge without a round of bartering, the price extracted from visitors is usually more. In one recent incident, a wily puller dashed off with someone who only wanted to have a picture taken. He ran once around the Star Ferry car park, demanded HK$160, and was supported by loud shouting and intimidation by other rickshaw lads. Such intimidation usually happens to elderly tourists. If such problems occur in Kowloon, go to the Police Reporting Centre in the Star Ferry Concourse on either side of the harbour. The price for posing for a picture is between HK$20–$50, depending on how hard you bargain.

PRIVATE TRANSPORT

Self-drive & Chauffeured Cars: Rental cars, with or without drivers, are also available. **Avis** and **Hertz** are here, along with a couple of dozen local firms. Those under 18 cannot hire any motor vehicles (including cycles and scooters). All visitors with a valid overseas driving licence, however, can drive here for a year. Hotels, through their own transportation services, can usually handle requests for chauffeur-driven cars.

WHERE TO STAY

Whether to stay in Hong Kong or Kowloon is a long-standing debate with die-hard aficionados of both harbour sides. Money is not a factor. The best-heeled (at The Peninsula and the Regent) and shoestring travellers (in the YMCA or Chungking Mansions) are next-door neighbours in Kowloon, though these digs are decidedly, well, different.

Access to shops and restaurants is also not a consideration. Both sides of the harbour are commercially endowed. The MTR connects various parts of Kowloon and Hong Kong Island in minutes, as does the Star Ferry.

HOTELS

Despite certain Hong Kong advantages, most people end up in Kowloon's Tsimshatsui District — probably because it has most of the colony's hotels. Hong Kong's Central District is considerably more restrained, because it is the business, financial and government centre. Though there is good shopping in Central, it closes at dusk. Hong Kong's Causeway Bay, however, features a wide range of accommodations, late-night shopping and eating. And between Central and Causeway Bay is the "Suzie Wong" bar district of Wanchai, rife with honky-tonk local colour and just down the tram-line from either Central or Causeway Bay.

Note to listing: All hotels add a 10 percent service charge and 5 percent room tax to room tariffs. The guide-list below categorizes hotels first by region, then by ranking.

KOWLOON & NEW TERRITORIES

LUXURY

Holiday Inn-Harbour View, 70 Mody Road, Tsimshatsui East, Kowloon, tel: 721-5161, fax: 369-5672.
Hyatt Regency, 67 Nathan Road, Tsimshatsui, Kowloon, tel: 311-1234, fax: 739-8701.
Kowloon Shangri-La, 64 Mody Road, Tsimshatsui East, Kowloon, tel: 721-2111, fax: 723-8686.
New World, 22 Salisbury Road, Tsimshatsui, Kowloon, tel: 369-4111, fax: 369-9387.
Nikko, 72 Mody Road, Tsimshatsui East, Kowloon, tel: 739-1111, fax: 311-3122.
Omni Hongkong, 3 Canton Road, Tsimshatsui, Kowloon, tel: 736-0088, fax: 736-0011.

Omni Marco Polo, Harbour City, Canton Road, Tsimshatsui, Kowloon, tel: 736-0888, fax: 736-0022.
Omni Prince, Harbour City, Canton Road, Tsimshatsui, Kowloon, tel: 736-1888, fax: 736-0066.
Peninsula, Salisbury Road, Tsimshatsui, Kowloon, tel: 366-6251, fax: 722-4170.
Ramada Renaissance, 8 Peking Road, Tsimshatsui, Kowloon, tel: 375-1133, fax: 375-1066.
Regal Kowloon, Mody Road, Tsimshatsui East, Kowloon, tel: 722-1818, fax: 369-6950.
Regent, 22 Salisbury Road, Tsimshatsui, Kowloon, tel: 721-1211, fax: 739-4546.
Royal Garden, 69 Mody Road, Tsimshatsui East, Kowloon, tel: 721-5215, fax: 369-9976.
Sheraton, 20 Nathan Road, Tsimshatsui, Kowloon, tel: 369-1111, fax: 739-8707.

FIRST CLASS

Ambassador, 4 Middle Road, Tsimshatsui, Kowloon, tel: 366-6321, fax: 369-0663.
Eaton, 380 Nathan Road, Kowloon, tel: 782-1818, fax: 782-5563.
Holiday Inn-Golden Mile, 50 Nathan Road, Tsimshatsui East, Kowloon, tel: 369-3111, fax: 369-8016.
Kowloon, 19–21 Nathan Road, Tsimshatsui, Kowloon, tel: 369-8698, fax: 739-9811.
Kowloon Panda, Tsuen Wah Street, Tsuen Wan, Kowloon, tel: 409-1111, fax: 409-1818.
Majestic, 348 Nathan Road, Yaumatei, Kowloon, tel: 781-1333, fax: 781-1773.
Miramar, 134 Nathan Road, Tsimshatsui, Kowloon, tel: 368-1111, fax: 369-1788.
New Astor, 11 Carnarvan Road, Tsimshatsui, Kowloon, tel: 366-7261, fax: 722-7122.
Park, 61–65 Chatham Road, Tsimshatsui, Kowloon, tel: 366-1371, fax: 739-7259.
Prudential, 222 Nathan Road, Kowloon, tel: 311-8222, fax: 311-4760.
Ramada, 73 Chatham Road South, Kowloon, tel: 311-1100, fax: 311-6000.
Regal Airport, 30 Sa Po Road, Kowloon, tel: 718-0333, fax: 718-4111.
Regal Riverside, Tai Chung Kiu Road, Shatin, New Territories, tel: 649-7878, fax: 637-4748.
Royal Pacific, China Hong Kong City, 33 Canton Road, Tsimshatsui, Kowloon, tel: 736-1188, fax: 736-1212.
Royal Park, 8 Pak Hok Ting Street, Shatin, New Territories, tel: 601-2111, fax: 601-3666.
Stanford, 118 Soy Street, Kowloon, tel: 781-1881, fax: 388-3733.
Stanford Hillview, 13-17 Observatory Road, Tsimshatsui, Kowloon, tel: 722-7822, fax: 723-3718.
Windsor, 39–43A Kimberley Road, Tsimshatsui, Kowloon, tel: 739-5665, fax: 311-5101.

MODERATE

Bangkok Royal, 2–12 Pilkem Street, Yaumatei, Kowloon, tel: 735-9181, fax: 730-2209.

Concourse, 20 Laichikok Road, Kowloon, tel: 397-6683, fax: 381-3768.

Fortuna, 355 Nathan Road, Yaumatei, Kowloon, tel: 385-1011, fax: 780-0011.

Grand Tower, 627–641 Nathan Road, Mongkok, Kowloon, tel: 789-0011, fax: 789-0945.

Guangdong, 18 Prat Avenue, Tsimshatsui, Kowloon, tel: 739-3311, fax: 721-1137.

Imperial, 30–34 Nathan Road, Tsimshatsui, Kowloon, tel: 366-2201, fax: 311-2360.

International, 33 Cameron Road, Tsimshatsui, Kowloon, tel: 366-3381, fax: 369-5381.

Kimberley, 28 Kimberley Road, Kowloon, tel: 723-3888, fax: 723-1318.

King's, 473 Nathan Road, Yaumatei, Kowloon, tel: 780-1281, fax: 782-1833.

Metropole, 75 Waterloo Road, Kowloon, tel: 761-1711, fax: 761-0769.

Nathan, 378 Nathan Road, Yaumatei, Kowloon, tel: 388-5141, fax: 770-4262.

Newton Kowloon, 58-66 Boundary Street, Mongkok, Kowloon, tel: 787-2338, fax: 789-0688.

Shamrock, 223 Nathan Road, Yaumatei, Kowloon, tel: 735-2271, fax: 736-7354.

The Salisbury – YMCA, 41 Salisbury Road, Kowloon, Hong Kong, tel: 369-2211, fax: 739-9315.

HONG KONG

LUXURY

Conrad, Pacific Place, 88 Queensway, Hong Kong, tel: 521-3838, fax: 521-3888.

Furama Kempinski, 1 Connaught Road, Central, Hong Kong, tel: 525-1111, fax: 849-9339.

Grand Hyatt, 1 Harbour Road, Hong Kong, tel: 588-1234, fax: 802-0677.

Hilton, 2 Queen's Road, Central, Hong Kong, tel: 523-3111, fax: 845-2590.

J.W. Marriott, Pacific Place, 88 Queensway, Central, Hong Kong, tel: 810-8366, fax: 845-0737.

Mandarin Oriental, 5 Connaught Road, Central, Hong Kong, tel: 522-0111, fax: 810-6190.

New World Harbour View, 1 Harbour Road, Hong Kong, tel: 802-8888, fax: 802-8833.

Regal Hong Kong Hotel, 88 Yee Wo Street, Causeway Bay, Hong Kong, tel: 890-6633, fax: 881-5577.

Richmond, 1A Wang Tak Street, Hong Kong, tel: 574-9922, fax: 838-1622.

Shangri-La (Island), Pacific Place, 88 Queensway, Hong Kong, tel: 877-3838, fax: 521-8742.

Victoria, Shun Tak Centre, 200 Connaught Road, Central, Hong Kong, tel: 540-7228, fax: 858-3398.

FIRST CLASS

Century Hong Kong, 238 Jaffe Road, Wanchai, Hong Kong, tel 598-8888, fax: 598-8866.

Charterhouse, 209-219 Wanchai Road, Wanchai, Hong Kong, tel: 833-5566, fax: 833-5888.

Excelsior, Gloucester Road, Causeway Bay, Hong Kong, tel: 894-8888, fax: 895-6459.

Luk Kwok, 72 Gloucester Road, Hong Kong, tel: 866-2166, fax: 866-2622.

Park Lane, 310 Gloucester Road, Causeway Bay, Hong Kong, tel: 890-3355, fax: 576-7853.

MODERATE

China Harbour View, 189–193 Gloucester Road, Wanchai, Hong Kong, tel: 838-2222, fax: 838-0136.

China Merchants, 160–161 Connaught Road West, Hong Kong, tel: 559-6888, fax: 559-0038.

City Garden, 231 Electric Road, Hong Kong, tel: 887-2888, fax: 887-1111.

Emerald, 152 Connaught Road West, Hong Kong, tel: 546-8111, fax: 559-0255.

Evergreen Plaza, 33 Hennessy Road, Hong Kong, tel: 866-9111, fax: 861-3121.

Grand Plaza, 2 Kornhill Road, Quarry Bay, Hong Kong, tel: 886-0011, fax: 886-1738.

Harbour, 116-122 Gloucester Road, Wanchai, Hong Kong, tel; 511-8211, fax: 507-2185.

Harbour View International House, 4 Harbour Road, Hong Kong, tel: 802-0111, fax: 802-9063.

New Cathay, 17 Tung Lo Wan Road, Causeway Bay, Hong Kong, tel: 577-8211, fax: 567-9365.

New Harbour, 41 Hennessy Road, Hong Kong, tel: 861-1166, fax: 865-6111.

Newton Hong Kong, 200-218 Electric Road, North Point, Hong Kong, tel: 807-2333, fax: 807-1221.

South Pacific, 23 Morrison Hill Road, Wanchai, Hong Kong, tel; 572-3838, fax: 893-7773.

Wesley, 22 Hennessy Road, Wanchai, Hong Kong, tel; 866-6688, fax: 866-6613.

Wharney, 61–73 Lockhart Road, Wanchai, Hong Kong, tel: 861-1000, fax: 865-8023.

SERVICED APARTMENTS

Convention Plaza, 1 Harbour Road, Hong Kong, tel: 824-2828, fax: 824-3200.

Parkview, 88 Tai Tam Reservoir Road, Hong Kong, tel: 812-3888, fax: 812-1488.

Sheraton Towers, 20 Nathan Road, Kowloon, tel: 369-1111, fax: 739-8707.

Victoria Apartments, Shun Tak Centre, 200 Connaught Road, Hong Kong, tel: 540-7228, fax: 858-3398.

HOSTELS

In addition to discount air tickets, the **Hong Kong Student Travel Bureau** offers limited accommodation services. Holders of official international student, teacher or youth identity cards can get advice, assistance in booking, access to local university facilities and, occasionally, preferential hotel rates by visiting the bureau's office at 1021 Star House, 10th floor, just off the Star Ferry Concourse in Kowloon (tel: 730-3269). If you have an **International Youth Hostel** card, you will be eligible for their accommodations and activities. There are six youth hostels, four in the New Territories, one each on Lantau and Hong Kong Island. Rates range HK$12–$25 for members. Contact the **Hong Kong Youth Hostel Association**, Room 225, Block 19, Shek Kip Mei Estate, Kowloon, tel: 788-1638. (Note: The summer school holidays is peak season. Occupants must be members of the International Federation of Youth Hostels.)

Garden View International House, 1 MacDonnell Road, Hong Kong, tel: 877-3737, fax: 845-6263.
Holy Carpenter Guest House, 1 Dyer Road, Kowloon, tel: 362-0301, fax: 362-2193.
STB Hostel, Great Eastern Mansion, 2/f 255–261 Reclamation Street, Yaumatei, Kowloon, tel: 332-1073, fax: 385-0153.
YMCA, 23 Waterloo Road, Yaumatei, Kowloon, tel: 771-9111, fax: 388-5926.
YWCA, 5 Man Fuk Road, Waterloo Road Hill, Kowloon, tel: 713-9211, fax: 761-1269.

GUEST HOUSES

Like the Amir Kabir in Tehran or Bangkok's Malaysia Hotel, Hong Kong has its place, that is the place, for impecunious travellers: the **Chungking Mansions** in Kowloon, in the shadow of the lordly Peninsula. The CM rabbit warren offers a huge "high"-rise collection of hostels, dormitories, "guest houses" and mini-hotels. Fierce intramural competition for guests gives the footloose considerable bargaining power.

The cream of the Mansions' crop are in "A" block, the first of four crash complexes encountered past the dingy, arcaded front entrance. **Chungking House** is quite respectable, offering optional air-con, TV, room service and laundry. Doubles at either start around HK$200, with lower rates for longer terms. Prices tend to drop moving farther back along the line of lifts. "B" and "D" blocks have dozens of small places. Although many of the places offer cooking facilities (including refrigerators), throughout the Mansions there are numerous small, cheap eating places, including some quite authentic Indian "messes."

Booth Lodge (Salvation Army), 11 Wing Sing Lane, Yaumatei, Kowloon, tel: 771-9266, fax: 385-1140.
Caritas Bianchi Lodge, 4 Cliff Road, Yaumatei, Kowloon, tel: 388-1111, fax: 770-6669.
Caritas Lodge, 134 Boundary Street, Kowloon, tel: 339-3777, fax: 338-2864.
Chungking House, Chungking Mansions, A Block 4th and 5th floors, 34–40 Nathan Road, Tsimshatsui, Kowloon, tel: 366-5362.

ISLAND LODGINGS

LANTAU ISLAND

Lantau Island is a favourite place for the Hong Kong people to get away from it all. Visitors, if they visit the island at all, usually do it in one day. However, there are a variety of places to stay on the island, two in monasteries. Some of these "sleeps" are quite cheap – around HK$100 – and some are hotels offering cottages or full "units" (suites sleeping 4 or 6 with kitchen facilities). Note: Reserve well in advance.

Lantau Tea Gardens, Lantau Island, Hong Kong, tel: 985-5161. Units sleeping 2–6 cost HK$150+.
Po Lin Monastery, Nong Ping, Lantau Island, Hong Kong, tel: 985-6854. Dormitory accommodation HK$100, including three vegetarian meals.
Silvermine Beach Hotel, Silvermine Bay, Mui Wo, Lantau Island, Hong Kong, tel: 984-8295, fax: 981-907. About HK$480+.

CHEUNG CHAU ISLAND

Cheung Chau Warwick, East Bay, Cheung Chau Island, Hong Kong, tel: 981-0081, fax: 981-9174. For those who really want to get away from it all in first-class style. About HK$700+.
Cheung Sha Resort, c/o Wah Nam Travel Service, 3rd floor, Eastern Commercial Centre, 397 Hennessy Road, Hong Kong, tel: 891-1161. Units sleeping 6 each cost HK$220–$360.

Food Digest

WHAT TO EAT

No one has ever contradicted the guesstimate that there are more than 5,000 restaurants listed in the colony's telephone directories. The exactitude of that figure is debatable, but a hungry fact remains: anywhere you turn in the colony, there is a restaurant.

Hong Kong, like Paris, is a place where conversation invariably involves the current merits and demerits of restaurants. A new restaurant discovery by an old Hong Kong hand is such important intelligence that the "discoverer" often is rewarded with extra rounds of pink gin. Restaurants in Hong Kong, like those in France, tend to be

Our history could fill this book, but we prefer to fill glasses.

When you make a great beer, you don't have to make a great fuss.

extensions of one's living room, places where friends and families gather for celebrations and anniversary feasts.

The listings which follow are an abbreviated sampler of renowned local restaurants. One would require a separate book to list every restaurant in a particular category, but those listed are generally considered to be good representative places. Most Chinese restaurants in hotels have been omitted. They are usually better than average Chinese eating places, but they tend to tailor their food for outsiders who know little about Chinese cuisine. Their dishes – with the exception of those prepared for pre-arranged banquets – are hence rather ordinary, even though they are elegantly served and quite expensive.

However, if you prefer a secure hotel ambience, some of the best Chinese restaurants are located in hotels: the **Man Wah** (Mandarin), **Lai Ching Heen** (Regent), **Spring Moon** (Peninsula) and **Dynasty** (New World).

Hong Kong's first eating rule is to be adventurous; get out of your hotel and sample some of the best Chinese, Japanese, Korean, Singaporean, Malayan, Indonesian, Filipino, Thai, Indian and Vietnamese foods in the world. But don't be too surprised if the local Cantonese cuisine (or any other Chinese food served here) looks and tastes different from hometown "Chinese food". It is the real thing here! It is your favourite Chinese restaurant dishes back home that are, well, different.

CANTONESE

The **Yung Kee** in Central is one of the colony's famous Cantonese eateries because once – many years ago – it was named one of the 10 best restaurants in the world by Fortune magazine.

Regardless of its place in the dining Olympics, this Cantonese restaurant is justifiably famous for its goose dishes. It is also one of the few restaurants that uphold local tradition and still serve pay daan (100-year-old eggs) as an appetizer. Other reputable Cantonese food palaces are the Tin Tin Seafood, North Sea Fish Village, North Park, Unicorn, Sung Tung Lok (for shark's fin), Fook Lam Moon and Tao Yuan.

SPECIAL DISHES

For vegetarian Cantonese food, try the **Wishful Cottage**, **Bodhi** or the **Vegi Food Kitchen**. If you are here at any time but winter, dine out on a floating sampan restaurant on Causeway Bay for freshwater Cantonese seafood.

And finally, a mention of the superb seafood restaurants (Cantonese) along the waterfront of Lamma Island: succulent and fresh. Just about any one will do but the **Shum Kee** (Lamma Hilton), **Chow Kee**, **Peach Garden**, **Lamma Regent** and the **Lamma Fortune** are the most popular. The floating sampan restaurants in the Causeway Bay Typhoon

Shelter opposite Excelsior Hotel, Hong Kong provide another Cantonese seafood taste treat. (October–April only.)

RESTAURANTS

Floating **sampan restaurants**, Causeway Bay Typhoon Shelter opposite Excelsior Hotel, Hong Kong.

Lamma Island seafood restaurants, located at various places.

Big Yen, Hang Seng Bank Bldg, 9-11A Cameron Road, Tsimshatsui, Kowloon, tel: 368-6544.

Bodhi, 388 Lockhart Road, Causeway Bay, Hong Kong; 60 Leighton Road, Causeway Bay, Hong Kong, tel: 890-5565; 56 Cameron Road, Tsimshatsui, Kowloon, tel: 739-2222.

Broadway, Hay Wah Building, 73-85B Hennessy Road, Wanchai, Hong Kong, tel: 529-9233.

Can Do, 37 Cameron Road, Tsimshatsui, Kowloon, tel: 721-8183.

Chinese (The), Hyatt-Regency Hotel, 67 Nathan Road, Tsimshatsui, Kowloon, tel: 311-1234.

East Lake, 68 Hing Fat Street, Causeway Bay, Hong Kong, tel: 807-3328.

East Ocean, Harbour Centre, 25 Harbour Road, Wanchai, Hong Kong, tel: 827-8887.

Flourishing Kitchen, New World Centre, Shopping Mall, 18-24 Salisbury Road, Tsimshatsui, Kowloon, tel: 369-5787.

Flower Lounge, World Commercial Centre, Harbour City, 11 Canton Road, Tsimshatsui, Kowloon, tel: 730-2200; 3 Peace Avenue, Ho Man Tin, Kowloon, tel: 715-6557.

Fontana, Fung Lee Commercial Building, 6-8A Prat Avenue, Tsimshatsui, Kowloon, tel: 369-9898.

Fook Lam Moon, 35-45 Johnston Road, Wanchai, Hong Kong, tel: 866-0663, and 53-59 Kimberley Road, Tsimshatsui, Kowloon, tel: 366-0286.

Full Moon, Barnton Court, Harbour City, 9 Canton Road, Tsimshatsui, Kowloon, tel: 730-9131.

Full Moon Lounge, Empire Centre, 68 Mody Road, Tsimshatsui East, Kowloon, tel: 739-2868.

Guangzhou Garden, Two Exchange Square, 8 Connaught Place, Central, Hong Kong, tel: 525-1163.

Harbour View, Tsimshatsui Centre, West Wing, 66 Mody Road, Tsimshatsui East, Kowloon, tel: 722-5888.

Harbour View Tsui Hang Village, Great Eagle Centre, 23 Harbour Road, Wanchai, Hong Kong, tel: 827-5755.

Heichinrou, Lippo Sun Plaza, 28 Canton Road, Tsimshatsui, Kowloon, tel: 375-7123.

Hei Fung Terrace, The Repulse Bay Shopping Arcade, 109 Repulse Bay Road, Repulse Bay, Hong Kong, tel: 812-2622.

House of Canton, Century Square, 1 D'Anguilar Street, Central, Hong Kong, tel: 868-2988.

Lai Ching Heen, Regent Hotel, 18 Salisbury Road, Kowloon, tel: 721-1211.

Luk Yu, 26 Stanley Street, Central, Hong Kong, tel: 523-5464.

Man Wah, Mandarin Oriental Hotel, 5 Connaught Road, Central, Hong Kong, tel: 522-0111.

Noble House, 71-77 Peking Road, Tsimshatsui, Kowloon, tel: 311-2888.

North Sea Fishing Village, Auto Plaza, 65 Mody Road, Tsimshatsui East, Kowloon, tel: 723-6843.

Orchard Court, Ma's Mansion, 37 Hankow Road, Tsimshatsui, Kowloon, tel: 317-5111.

Pearl Court, Shui On Centre, 8 Harbour Road, Wanchai, Hong Kong, tel: 527-1222.

Round Dragon, Hopewell Centre, 183 Queen's Road East, Wanchai, tel: 861-1668.

Sai Kung Fung Lum, Siu Yat Building, Sai Kung, New Territories, tel: 792-6623.

Seasons, Whampoa Garden, Phase II, Hung Hom, Kowloon, tel: 764-3382, and 23 Playing Field Road, Mongkok, Kowloon, tel: 381-2393.

Siu Lam Kung, 17-21 Minden Avenue, Tsimshatsui, Kowloon, tel: 721-6168.

Spring Moon, Peninsula Hotel, Salisbury Road, Tsimshatsui, Kowloon, tel: 366-6251; Ocean Galleries, Harbour City, 17-19 Canton Road, Tsimshatsui, Kowloon, tel: 730-0288.

Sunning Unicorn, Sunning Place, 1 Sunning Road, Causeway Bay, Hong Kong, tel: 577-6620.

Sun Tung Lok Shark's Fin, 376-382 Lockhart Road, Wanchai, Hong Kong, tel: 574-8261.

Super Star, Tsimshatsui Mansion, 83-97 Nathan Road, Tsimshatsui, Kowloon, tel: 366-0878.

Tai Woo, 15-19 Wellington Street, Central, Hong Kong, tel: 524-5618, and 14-16 Hillwood Road, Tsimshatsui, Kowloon tel: 369-9773.

Tao Yuan, 3rd floor, Great Eagle Centre, 23 Harbour Road, Wanchai, Hong Kong, tel: 827-8088, and Departure Level, China Hong Kong City, 33 Canton Road, Tsimshatsui, tel: 736-1688.

Tin Tin Seafood Harbour, Elizabeth House, 250 Gloucester Road, Causeway Bay, Hong Kong, tel: 833-6683, and Allied Plaza, 760 Nathan Road, Mongkok, Kowloon, tel: 397-2332.

Tsui Hang Village, New World Tower, 16-18 Queen's Road, Central, Hong Kong, tel: 524-2012, and Keewan Tower, Park Lane Square, 132-134 Nathan Road, Tsimshatsui, Kowloon, tel: 368-6363.

Vegi Food Kitchen, Highland Mansion, 8 Cleveland Street, Causeway Bay, tel: 890-6660.

Victoria City, Sun Hung Kai Centre, 30 Harbour Road, Wanchai, Hong Kong, tel: 827-9938.

Wishful Cottage, 336 Lockhart Road, Causeway Bay, Hong Kong, tel: 5735645.

Yucca De Lac, Ma Liu Shui, Shatin, New Territories, tel: 692-1835.

Yung Kee, 32 Wellington Street, Central, tel: 522-1624.

Zen, Pacific Place, Phase 1, 88 Queensway, Hong Kong, tel: 845-4555.

NORTH & WESTERN CHINESE

When one sees a sign advertising "Northern Chinese Food," one's mind usually conjures up images of crisp Beijing Duck. Which is quite right, but remember that there are other types of northern prepared duck quite different from the usual barbecued Beijing Duck. The **Pine & Bamboo**, the **American Restaurant, Peking, Spring Deer, Kowloon Peking** and **North China** and the several **Peking Gardens** should satiate any duck-craving palate. These northern-style places also feature Mongolian hotpots and barbecues. Some of the above, like the **Kowloon Peking**, feature both; others, like The **Mongolian Barbecue** and the **Genghis Khan** serve only that specialty.

Spicy Szechuanese food, usually only popular with serious Chinese food gourmets, has an ardent cult following of fire-breathing aficionados. The **Red Pepper** in the Causeway Bay area is a particularly popular Szechuanese restaurant, especially with expatriates, but purists contend that the Red Pepper's food is not as hot as it should be, or used to be. Therefore, you might want to patronize the **Kam Chuen Lau** which has a no spices barred reputation. The **Cleveland Szechuan, Sichuan Pep 'N Chilli**, and **Sze Chuen Lau** are also guaranteed to keep you crying for more.

Shanghainese food is not nearly as spicy as Szechuanese cuisine, but it is not very well known either. The **Four Five Six, Wu Kong, Grand Shanghai** and **Yick Heung** are recommended. A note about Four Five Six: Shanghainese restaurants all over the world have that same numerical name because that was the name and address of the most famous restaurant in Shanghai before 1949.

CHOP SUEY

A word about the colony's big restaurant chain called **Jade Garden** or **Maxim's**, **Peking** or **Princess** or **Szechuan** or **Shanghai Garden**. They are at various locations throughout the colony and most of them serve you anything from a Beijing Duck or Szechuan Duck or Cantonese Duck to a Beggar's Chicken. It takes a bit of work to get past the usually polite waiters who try to make things easy by having you order what he thinks all foreigners like – sweet 'n' sour pork, fried rice, and the like. But persevere. The food is worth any diplomatic hassling involved.

RESTAURANTS

Beijing (Pekingese)/ Mongolian

American, 20 Lockhart Road, Hong Kong, tel: 527-7277.

Beijing, 34-36 Granville Road, Tsimshatsui, Kowloon, tel: 366-9968.

China Garden, 45-47 Carnarvon Road, Tsimshatsui, Kowloon, tel: 366-0408.

Genghis Khan, 20 Luard Road, Hong Kong, tel: 861-2363.

Hong Kong Chung Chuk Lau, 30 Leighton Road, Causeway Bay, Hong Kong, tel: 577-4914.

King Heung, Riviera Mansion, 59-65 Paterson Street, Causeway Bay, Hong Kong, tel: 577-1035.

Kowloon Peking, 65 Kimberley Road, Kowloon, tel: 367-7933.

Kublai's, 151 Lockhart Road, Hong Kong, tel: 573-2287.

New American, 177-179 Wanchai Road, Wanchai, Hong Kong, tel: 575-0458.

North China, Polly Commercial Building, 21-23 Prat Avenue, Tsimshatsui, Kowloon, tel: 311-6689.

Peking, 227 Nathan Road, Yaumatei, Kowloon, tel: 730-1315.

Pine & Bamboo, 30 Leighton Road, Hong Kong, tel: 577-4914.

Spring Deer, 42 Mody Road, Tsimshatsui, Kowloon, tel: 723-3673.

Sung Hung Cheung Hing, Kimberley Plaza, 45-47 Kimberley Road, Tsimshatsui, tel: 367-7933.

Szechuanese

Cleveland, New Town Mansion, 6 Cleveland Street, Causeway Bay, tel: 567-3876.

Fung Lum, Polly Commercial Building, 21-23 Prat Avenue, Tismshatshui, Kowloon, tel: 367-8686.

Kam Chuen Lau, 4 Observatory Road, Kowloon, tel: 367-5629.

Lotus Pond, 006-007 Ocean Galleries, Phase IV, **Harbour City**, 15 Canton Road, Tsimshatsui, Kowloon, tel: 730-8688.

Pep 'N Chilli, 12 Blue Pool Road, Happy Valley, Hong Kong, tel: 573-8251.

Prince Court, Sutton Court, Harbour City, 9 Canton Road, Tsimshatsui, Kowloon, tel: 730-3100.

Red Pepper, 7 Lan Fong Road, Causeway Bay, Hong Kong, tel: 577-3811.

Szechuan Garden, Gloucester Tower, The Landmark, 11 Pedder Street, Hong Kong, tel: 521-4433.; The Mall, Pacific Place, 88 Queensway, Central, Hong Kong, tel: 845-8433.

Snow Garden, 233 Electric Road, Hong Kong.

Wishful Cottage, 336 Lockhart Road, Hong Kong, tel: 573-5645.

Sze Chuan Lau, 466 Lockhart Road, Causeway Bay, Hong Kong, tel: 891-9027.

Shanghainese

Dim Sum Burger, Miami Mansion, 13-15 Cleveland Street, Causeway Bay, Kowloon, tel: 577-7199.

Grand Shanghai, 4th floor, Island Shopping Centre, Great George Street, Causeway Bay, Hong Kong, tel: 890-6828.

Great Shanghai, 26 Prat Avenue, Tsimshatsui, Kowloon, tel: 366-8158.

Shanghai, 24 Prat Avenue, Tsimshatsui, Kowloon,

tel: 739-7083.

Snow Garden, London Plaza, 219 Nathan Road, Yaumatei, tel: 736-4341.

Tien Heung Lau, 18C Austin Avenue, Tshimshatshui, Kowloon, tel: 368-9660.

Wu Kong, 27 Nathan Road, Tsimshatsui, Kowloon, tel: 366-7244.

OTHER CHINESE

Chiu Chow food is primarily known for its "Iron Maiden" tea, which precedes the meal and is so strong it is served in thimble-like cups. The **Carrianana Chiu Chow** and **Siam Bird's Nest** are the two most popular Chiu Chow restaurants here but you might also try the **Golden Red Chiu Chow**, **Tsui Hung** or **Pak Lok**.

For Hakka food, drop by **Franho**, **Tsiu King Lau**, **Home** or **Fu Dao**. Hakka Chinese are people indigenous to Hong Kong's rural New Territories. Hangchow food is probably the rarest in Hong Kong and its entreé de resistance is Beggar's Chicken. Try the **Tien Hung Lau**.

RESTAURANTS
Chiu Chow

Carrianna Chiu Chow, 151 Gloucester Road, Hong Kong, tel: 574-1282.

Chiu Chau, 63 Peking Road, Kowloon, tel: 368-9052.

Chiuchow Garden, Jardine House, 1 Connaught Place, Central, Hong Kong, tel: 525-8246; Vicwood Plaza, 199 Des Voeux Road, Central, Hong Kong, tel: 545-7778; Hennessy Centre, 500 Hennessy Road, Causeway Bay, tel: 577-3391; Lippo Centre, Queensway, Central, Hong Kong, tel: 845-1323; and Tsimshatsui Centre, 66 Mody Road, Tsimshatsui East, Kowloon, tel: 368-7266.

City Chiu Chow, East Ocean Centre, 98 Granville Road, Tsimshatsui, Kowloon, tel: 723-6226.

Golden Island, BCC Building, 25-31 Carnarvon Road, Tsimshatsui, Kowloon, tel: 369-5211; East Half, Star House, 3 Salisbury Road, Tsimshatsui, Kowloon, tel: 736-6228.

Harbour City, Elizabeth House, 250 Gloucester Road, Hong Kong, tel: 833-6678.

Jackie Shark's Fin, Carnarvon Plaza, 20-20C Carnarvon Road, Tsimshatsui, Kowloon, tel: 311-9898.

Pak Lok, 24 Hysan Avenue, Hong Kong, tel: 576-8886.

Siam Bird's Nest, 55 Paterson Street, Hong Kong, tel: 577-3362.

Hakka

Franho, 24 Percivel Street, Hong Kong.

Fu Dao, 3 Saigon Street, Kowloon.

New Home, 19 Hanoi Road, Tsimshatsui, Kowloon, tel: 366-5876.

Tsui King Lau, various locations.

Hunanese

Hunan Garden, The Forum, Exchange Square, Hong Kong, tel: 868-2880.

Taiwanese

Forever Green, 93-95A Leighton Road, Causeway Bay, tel: 890-3448.

VIETNAMESE

Vietnamese refugees have encouraged the growth of small establishments specializing in the delectable mint-flavoured food of their country.

The distinctive fish sauce called *nuoc mam* is an important flavouring element in Vietnamese food. This pungent sauce is made from the juices of rice fish that have been salted and fermented in the sun; it's the main source of protein for poor Vietnamese. You need not ask for it in restaurants – it's always on the table, mixed with chillies and grated vegetables.

Most Vietnamese food portions are small and spicy and always accompanied by a colander of lettuce and mint. Vietnamese spring rolls are eaten wrapped in lettuce leaves and dunked in *nuoc mam*. *Chao-tom*, a shrimp delicacy moulded round a stick of sugar cane is eaten in a sheet of rice paper with mint. Also good is sliced beef in vinegar, a do-it-yourself hotpot.

An essential course during a Vietnamese meal is *pho tai*, a soup of noodles and rare beef slices with *nuoc nam* stirred into it. Seven-style Beef is a specialty, and *nem chua* is a raw pork delicacy marinated in wine. It's excellent as a starter. If you want to drink beer ask for "33," a French lager brewed in Ho Chi Minh City. Vietnamese restaurants also serve good filtered coffee and a refreshing iced drink, *che dau sanh*, made with yellow beans and sago.

Hong Kong probably has the best Vietnamese restaurants outside of Vietnam because all the above ingredients are easily obtainable.

RESTAURANTS

Golden Bull, 101 Ocean Centre, Harbour City, 5 Canton Road, Tsimshatsui, Kowloon, tel: 730-4866; New World Centre, 18 Salisbury Road, Tsimshatsui, Kowloon, tel: 369-4617.
Mekong Vietnamese, Miramar Hotel, 130 Nathan Road, Tsimshatsui, tel: 311-3303.
Paterson, Marco Polo Mansion, 10 Cleveland Street, Causeway Bay, Hong Kong, tel: 890-6146.
Saigon, 66 Lockhart Road, Hong Kong.
Vietnam, Grand Building, 18 Connaught Road, Central, tel: 522-5523.
Vietnam City, Energy City, 92 Granville Road, Tsimshatsui East, Kowloon, tel: 366-7880.
Yin Ping, 24 Cannon Street, Hong Kong, tel: 832-9038.

FILIPINO

Only a few restaurants specialize in Filipino food, but here you can sample the much-loved *sinigang*, sour soup seasoned with tarmarinds, mangoes and limes. Filipinos are also fond of *dinuguan*, a rich casserole of pork stewed in blood, and the national beverage is *halo halo*, a lush concoction of cooked fruit in milk and sugar topped with crushed ice. You can also find the Filipino aphrodisiac, *balut*, which is a crunchy and unhatched duck embryo eaten straight from the shell.

RESTAURANTS

Little Manila, 9 Minden Avenue, Kowloon.
Mabubay, 11 Minden Avenue, Kowloon, tel: 367-3762.

INDIAN

Most of Hong Kong's Indian restaurants specialise in North Indian dishes, and sometimes the meal is served in the traditional way in small bowls assembled on a brass tray called a *thali*. This is a good way to experience many flavours.

Several of these dishes are named after Shah Jehan, who built the Taj Mahal at Agra. Rice dishes are often flavoured with saffron, the most expensive spice in the world. One ounce of pure saffron is said to be made from 75,000 flowers. You might like to try Bombay Duck, which is not a bird at all, but a small curried fish delicacy. Try all the above Indian food and more at these restaurants.

RESTAURANTS

Ashoka, 57 Wyndham Street, Hong Kong, tel: 524-9623; Connaught Commercial Building, 185 Wanchai Road, Wanchai, Hong Kong, tel: 891-8981.
Bombay Palace, Far East Finance Centre, 16 Harcourt Road, Central, Hong Kong, tel: 527-0115.
Bukhara, Sheraton Hotel, 20 Nathan Road, Tsimshatsui, Kowloon, tel: 369-1111.
Gaylord, 23-25 Ashley Road, Tsimshatsui, Kowloon, tel: 376-1001.
Gunga Din's, 59 Wyndham Street, Hong Kong.
Koh-I-Noor, 103 California Entertainment Building, 34 D'Aguilar Street, Central, Hong Kong, tel: 877-9706; Peninsula Apartments, 16C Mody Road, Tsimshatsui, Kowloon, tel: 368-3065
Maharaja I, 222 Wanchai Road, Hong Kong, tel: 574-9838.
Maharajah II, 1-3A Granville Circuit, Tsimshatsui, Kowloon, tel: 366-6671.
Surya, Lyton Building, 34-48 Mody Road, Tsimshatsui, Kowloon, tel: 366-9902.
Viceroy of India, Sun Hung Kai Centre, 30 Harbour Road, Hong Kong, tel: 827-7777.
Woodlands, 8 Minden Avenue, Tsimshatsui, Kowloon, tel: 369 3718.

BURMESE

Non-aficionados will classify the cuisine as some form of "Indian." There are of course many similarities due to proximity of the two countries, but there are also many differences in the cuisines. Try the *Khaukswe*, a chicken and noodles dish prepared with coconut milk, or mohinga, a fish soup with rice noodles served traditionally at lunch at the **Rangoon**, 265 Gloucester Road, Hong Kong, tel: 892-1182.

SRI LANKAN

Another country whose cuisine is dismissed as "Indian." Lots of hot curries of course, but also such favourites as hoppers (thin cup-shaped pancakes made from a fermented batter of rice flour, coconut milk and a dash of palm toddy), the ancient Cutch dish of lumprais, curry steamed in a banana leaf and sambol, which is very different from the South Indian variety, at the **Club Sri Lanka**, 17 Hollywood Road, Hong Kong.

INDONESIAN

Several restaurants feature highly-seasoned food from the Spice Islands of Indonesia. One of the most popular dishes is satay, skewered meats marinated and basted with pungent sauces, grilled on a charcoal burner at your table, and then dipped into a peanut sauce spiked with hot peppers. They also serve rijsttafel, a "rice table" buffet of 16 dishes or more said to have been invented because Dutch settlers couldn't decide which local dishes they liked best. For the most *bagus* (good) local Indonesian *makan* (food), try the following restaurants.

RESTAURANTS

Cinta, Hotel New Harbour, 6 Fenwick Street, Wanchai, Hong Kong, tel: 527-1199.
Java Rijstaffel, Han Hing Mansion, 38 Hankow Road, Tsimshatsui, Kowloon, tel: 367-1230.
SMI Curry Centre, 81–85 Lockhart Road, Wanchai, Hong Kong, tel: 527-3107.
Stanley's Oriental, 90B Stanley Main Street, Stanley, Hong Kong, tel: 813-9988.

STRAITS MALAY/NONYA

For a non-stop Straits-style eating binge, try the **SMI Curry Centre**.

RESTAURANTS
Malaysian

SMI Curry Centre, see Indonesian above.
Asian Gourmet, Grand Tower Hotel, 627-641 Nathan Road, Mongkok, Kowloon, tel: 789-0011.

Spice Market, Omni Prince Hotel, Harbour City, Canton Road, Tsimshatsui, Kowloon, tel: 736-1888.

Singaporean

SMI Curry Centre, see Indonesian above.
Spices, The Mall, One Pacific Place, 88 Queensway, Central, Hong Kong, tel: 845-4798. Repulse Bay Road, Repulse Bay, Hong Kong, tel: 812-2711.

JAPANESE

Japanese restaurants here are more expensive than Chinese restaurants – or any other Asian restaurant for that matter – but they are still half the price of counterparts in Tokyo.

RESTAURANTS

Ah-So, 159 Craigie Court, World Finance Centre, **Harbour City**, Canton Road, Tsimshatsui, Kowloon, tel: 730-3392.
Banka, Grand Tower Hotel, 627-641 Nathan Road, Mongkok, Kowloon, tel: 789-0011.
Benkay, Gloucester Tower, The Landmark, 11 Pedder Street, Central, Hong Kong, tel: 521-3344.
Fukui, Hotel Fortuna, 351-361 Nathan Road, Yaumatei, Hong Kong, tel: 385-1011.
Genji, Hong Kong Hilton, 2 Queen's Road, Central, Hong Kong, tel: 523-3111.
Hanagushi, California Entertainment Bldg, 34-36 D'Aguilar Street, Central, Hong Kong, tel: 521-0868.
Kanetanaka, East Point Centre, 545-563 Hennessy Road, Causeway Bay, tel: 833-6018.
Kotobuki, Good Result Building, 176 Nathan Road, Tsimshatsui, Kowloon, tel: 368-2711.
Matsuzaka, South Seas Centre, 75 Mody Road, Tsimshatsui East, Kowloon, tel: 724-3057.
Momoyama, Jardine House, 1 Connaught Place, Central, Hong Kong, tel: 845 8773.
Nadaman, Island Shangri-La Pacific Place, Supreme Court Road, Central, Hong Kong, tel: 820 8570; Kowloon Shangri-La Hotel, 64 Mody Road, Tsimshatsui, Kowloon, tel: 721-2111.
Nanbantei, 52-54 D'Aguilar Street, Central, Hong Kong, tel: 526-7678.
Nagoya, 21A Lock Road, Tsimshatsui, Kowloon, tel: 739-5566.
Nishimura, Regal Kowloon Hotel, 71 Mody Road Tsimshatsui East, Kowloon, tel: 367-1700; Omni The Hongkong Hotel, Harbour City, Canton Road, Tsimshatsui, tel: 735-6899; The Mall, Pacific Place One, 88 Queensway, Central, Hong Kong, tel: 845-4228.
Sagano, Nikko Hotel, 72 Mody Road, Tsimshatsui East, Kowloon, tel: 739-1111.
Sakurada, Royal Park Hotel, 8 Pak Hok Ting Street, Shatin, New Territories, tel: 601-2111.

Sui Sha Ya, Lockhart House, 440 Jaffe Road, Causeway Bay, Hong Kong, tel: 838-1808; 9 Chatham Road, Tsimshatsui, tel: 722-5001.
Unkai, Sheraton Hotel & Towers, 20 Nathan Road, Tsimshatsui, Kowloon, tel: 369-1111.
Yorohachi, 5-6 Lan Kwai Fong, Central, Hong Kong, tel: 524-1251.

THAI

Meals in ancient Siam were eaten lounging on floor cushions. Some restaurants in Thailand still honour that comfortable custom, but Hong Kong's Thai eating places have standard tables, chairs, spoons and forks. The central flavour of this chilli-based cuisine is packed in a powerful shrimp soup called *tom yam kung*. Watch out for the tiny red chillies. Some gourmets consider Thai cuisine to be the hottest in the world. For dessert try *songaya*, an ambrosia baked inside a coconut husk.

RESTAURANTS

Asian Delights, Regal Riverside Hotel, Tai Chung Kiu Road, Shatin, New Territories, tel: 649-7878.
Chili Club, 88 Lockhart Road, Hong Kong
Golden Elephant, Barnton Court, Phase I, Harbour City, Kowloon, tel: 735-0733.
Golden Poppy, Henan Bldg, 90-92 Jaffe Road, Wanchai, tel: 528-3128.
Her Thai, China Hong Kong City, 33 Canton Road, Kowloon, tel: 735-8898.
Rangoon, 265 Gloucester Road, Causeway Bay, tel: 892-1182.
Siam Palace, Bowa House, 180 Nathan Road, Tsimshatsui, Kowloon, tel: 368-3983.
Supatra's, 50 D'Aguilar Street, Lan Kwai Fong, Central, Hong Kong, tel: 522-5073.
Thai, Bangkok Royal Hotel, 2-12 Pilkem Street, Yaumatei, Kowloon, tel: 735-9181.
Thai Food, City Garden Plaza, Electric Road, North Point, Hong Kong, tel: 807-1962.

KOREAN

The spicy and pungent cuisine of Korea is characterized by a much-loved condiment called *kimchi*. Various vegetables, but usually cabbage, are preserved in a brine of salt, ginger root, garlic and hot peppers. It's as essential a part of a Korean meal as salt and pepper are in the West. Most Korean restaurants serve meat barbecues (*bulgogi*) as a set meal, and *kimchi* is always included. *Bulgogi* dishes include a variety of meats and fishes which arrive at your table finely-sliced, marinated and ready for cooking.

Korean ginseng has legendary pepper-upper and aphrodisiacal qualities and some restaurants offer ginseng specialties for those seeking such sensations. Ginseng soup is made of a whole chicken stuffed with glutinous rice, red dates and that magic root. It's boiled for 6 hours until it becomes an "invigorating" broth. It must be ordered in advance. If you forget, take your ginseng in a vodka cocktail.

RESTAURANTS

Arirang, 76 Morrison Hill Road, Happy Valley, Hong Kong, tel: 572-3027; Sutton Court, Harbour City, 19 Canton Road, Tsimshatsui, Kowloon, tel: 735-2281.
Daewongak, Hotel Concourse, 20-46 Lai Chi Kok Road, Mongkok, Kowloon, tel: 397-6683.
Koreana, Vienna Mansion, 55 Paterson Street, Hong Kong, tel: 577-5145.
Korea House, 101-105 Blissful Bldg, 247 Des Voeux Road, Western District, tel: 541-6930.
Silla Wan, 47 Connaught Road Central, Hong Kong.

CONTINENTAL/WESTERN

Continental cuisine is the most popular form of European cuisine served here. **Gaddi's** is certainly top of the list, but don't discount such restaurants as **Napoleon**, **Margaux**, **Belvedere**, **Park Inn**, **La Ronde** and **Lalique**. Also recommended in hotels are the **Sheraton Grill**, **Mandarin Grill**, **Hilton Grill**, **Rotiserrie** (Furama-Kempinski), **Banyan Grill** (Conrad), **JW's Marriott** and **Bocarinos** (Victoria). Outside the hotels, one of the most famous, venerable and oldest eateries is **Jimmy's Kitchen**, a pleasant place (with branch restaurants) that features reasonable prices. Another good spot, **Landau's**, is part of the Jimmy's group.

For steaks, try the **San Francisco Steak House**, **Louis' Steak House**, the **Texas Rib House** and the **Steak House** (Regent).

Top of the line for pure and opulent French cuisine are **Le Pierrot** (Mandarin), **Plume** (Regent), **Amigo**, **Le Restaurant de France** (Regal Meridien), **Cafe de Paris** and **Petrus** (Island Shangri-La). They are expensive, but superb. The favourite local provencale French restaurant is **Au Trou Normand**, complete with proper shots of Calvados to fill the trou (the between courses "hole") Normandy-style. A lesser known provencale-style restaurant is **Stanley's**. And for French seafood, **The Mistral** and **La Brasseries** (there are two) are also good choices.

German cuisine, including game, is the specialty of **Hugo's** and the **Baron's Table**, but the latter also has the best smoked food in the colony, direct from its own smokehouse.

For Austrian food, try **Mozart Stub'n**.

For Swiss fare, the **Chesa** (Peninsula) and **The Chalet** (Royal Pacific).

For a one-of-a-kind seafood splash try **The Bostonian** (Ramada Renaissance) – they have fresh Maine lobsters among many other types of seafood. Also in the western seafood category is **Bentley's**, which sports an oyster bar as does **The Lobster Bar** (Island Shangri-La).

There is a large selection of Italian food available, both in and out of the hotels. **Grissini** (Grand Hyatt), **Nicholini's** (Conrad) and **Scala** (New World Harbour View) lead the hotel selections. **Il Mercato, Rigoletto, Bella Donna Grappa** and **The Pizzeria** (Kowloon Hotel) round out the medium-priced list. **Pizza Hut** and **Spaghetti House** offer the most inexpensive Italian nosh.

For those hankering for some Spanish tapas to accompany their vino tinto and vino blanco, **La Bodega Tapas Bar** is the answer.

And for the Scots who miss their haggis, **Mad Dogs** will ease the pangs of hunger.

Good old American food is served at **California**, **Al's Diner** and **Dan Ryan's**, while for Mexican or Tex-Mex fare, try **Casa Mexicana** or **Someplace**. **The Beverly Hills Deli** will guarantee you an instant food trip back to New York with your first chomp into a corned beef 'n' rye or hot pastrami. The **Delicatessen Corner** is more European-style and features excellent smoked meats.

Those from Down Under who are experiencing Vegemite withdrawals and craving a meat pie with a tube of Fosters should try the **Stoned Crow** and **Ned Kelly's Last Stand**. Both serve Australian plonk (wine), and the former has a pretty decent menu once you get past the pies. And speaking of meat pies, all the pubs and taverns listed in the nightlife listing feature traditional pub meals.

For the best cheap eats, excluding fast food outlets and street stalls, you can't beat **Sammy's Kitchen**, well known to those on the road, or the **YMCA** or **China Fleet Club**.

RESTAURANTS

Al's Diner, 39 D'Aguilar Street, Hong Kong, tel: 869-1869.

Amigo, Amigo Mansion, 79A Wong Nei Chong Road, Happy Valley, Hong Kong, 577-2202.

Au Trou Normand, 6 Carnarvon Road, Tsimshatsui, Kowloon, tel: 366-8754.

Barcelona, Prospect Mansion, 68 Paterson Street, Causeway Bay, Hong Kong, tel: 577-8076.

Baron's Table, Holiday Inn Golden Mile, 46-52 Nathan Road, Tsimshatsui, Kowloon, tel: 369-3111.

Belvedere, Holiday Inn Crowne Plaza Harbour View, 70 Mody Road, Tsimshatsui, tel: 721-5161.

Bentley's Seafood & Oyster Bar, Prince's Bldg, 10 Chater Road, Central, Hong Kong, tel: 868-0881.

Beverly Hills Deli, New World Centre, 18 Salisbury Road, Tsimshatsui, Kowloon tel: 369-8695.

Bistro, The Metropole Hotel, 75 Waterloo Road, Ho Man Tin, Kowloon, tel: 761-1711.

Bocarinos Grill, Hotel Victoria, 200 Connaught Road Central, Sheung Wan, Hong Kong, tel: 540-7228.

Bologna Ristorante Italiano, Elizabeth House, 250 Gloucester Road, Causeway Bay, Hong Kong, tel: 574-7282..

Bostonian, Ramada Renaissance, 8 Peking Road, Tsimshatsui, Kowloon, tel: 375-1133.

Boulevard, Ocean Terminal, Harbour City, 3 Canton Road, Tsimshatsui, Kowloon, tel: 730-3377.

Brasserie On The Eighth, Hotel Conrad Hong Kong, Pacific Place, 88 Queensway, Central, Hong Kong, tel: 521-3838.

Cafe de Paris, 30 D'Aguilar Street, Hong Kong, tel: 524-7521.

Capriccio, Ramada Renaissance Hotel, 8 Peking Road, Tsimshatsui, Kowloon, tel: 375-1133.

California, California Tower, 24-26 Lan Kwai Fong, Central, Hong Kong, tel: 521-1345.

Cammino, The Excelsior, 281 Gloucester Road, Causeway Bay, Hong Kong, tel: 894-8888.

Casa Mexicana, Victoria Centre,15 Watson Road, North Point, Hong Kong, tel: 566-5560.

Chalet, Royal Pacific Hotel & Towers, 33 Canton Road, Tsimshatsui, Kowloon, tel: 736-1188.

Charlotte's, Ambassador Hotel, 26 Nathan Road, Tsimshatsui, Kowloon, tel: 366-6321.

Chesa, Peninsula, Salisbury Road, Tsimshatsui, Kowloon, tel: 366-6251.

Chinnery, Mandarin Oriental, Hong Kong, 5 Connaught Road, Central, Hong Kong, tel: 522-0111.

Club Maxim's, One Exchange Square, 8 Connaught Road, Central, Hong Kong, tel: 521-0565.

Dan Ryan's, The Mall, Pacific Place, 88 Queensway, Hong Kong, tel: 845-4600; Ocean Terminal, Harbour City, Canton Road, Tsimshatsui, Kowloon, tel: 735-6111.

Delicatessen Corner, Holiday Inn Golden Mile, 46-52 Nathan Road, Tsimshatsui, Kowloon, tel: 369-3111.

Excelsior Grill, The Excelsior, 281 Gloucester Road, Causeway Bay, Hong Kong, tel: 894-8888.

Fountainside, The Landmark, 16 Des Voeux Road, Central, Hong Kong, tel: 526-4018.

Gaddi's, Peninsula Hotel, Salisbury Road, Tsimshatsui, Kowloon, tel: 366-6251.

Galley & Pier One, Jardine House, 1 Connaught Place, Central, Hong Kong, tel: 526-3061.

Gigi, Swire House, 11 Chater Road, Central, Hong Kong, tel: 526-1830.

Godown, Admiralty Centre, Tower II, 18 Harcourt Road, Central, Hong Kong, tel: 866-1166.

Grill, Hongkong Hilton, 2 Queen's Road, Central, tel: 523-3111.

Grissini, Grand Hyatt, 1 Harbour Road, Wanchai, Hong Kong, tel: 588-1234.

Grandstand Grill, Sheraton Hotel & Towers, 20 Nathan Road, Tsimshatsui, Kowloon, tel: 369-1111.

Grappa, Pacific Place, 88 Queensway, Hong Kong.

Gripps, Omni Hongkong Hotel, 3 Canton Road, Tsimshatsui, Kowloon, tel: 736-0088.

Harbour View, China Harbour View Hotel, 189 Gloucester Road, Wanchai, Hong Kong, tel: 838 2222.

Harry Ramsden's, 213 Queen's Road East, Hong Kong, tel: 832-9626.

Hilton Grill, Hilton Hotel, Hong Kong.

Hugo's, Hyatt-Regency Hotel, 67 Nathan Road, Tsimshatsui, Kowloon, tel: 311-1234.

Il Fantino, Eastin Valley Hotel, 1A Wang Tak Street, Happy Valley, Hong Kong, tel: 574-9922.

Il Mercato, 34 D'Aguilar Street, Central, Hong Kong, tel: 868-3068; 126 Stanley Main Street, Stanley, tel: 813-9090.

Italian Garden, Swimming Pool Complex, Kowloon Park, 22 Austin Road, Tsimshatsui, Kowloon, tel: 722-4412.

Jaffe's, Century Hong Kong Hotel, 238 Jaffe Road, Wanchai, Hong Kong, tel: 598-8888.

JW's California, J.W. Mariott Hotel, Pacific Place, 88 Queensway, Central, Hong Kong, tel: 810-8366.

Jimmy's Kitchen, South China Bldg., 1 Wyndham Street, Central, Hong Kong, tel: 526-5293; Kowloon Centre, 29 Ashley Road, Tsimshatsui, Kowloon, tel: 376-0327.

Kangaroo Pub & Windjammer, 35 Haiphong Road, Tsimshatsui, Kowloon, tel: 312-0083.

La Bella Donna, Shui On Centre, 6-8 Harbour Road, Wanchai, Hong Kong, tel: 802-9907.

La Bodega, 31 Wyndham Street, Hong Kong, tel: 877-5472.

La Boheme, 151 Lockhart Road, Wanchai, Hong Kong, tel: 511-7717.

La Brasserie, Regal Kowloon Hotel, 71 Mody Road, Tsimshatsui, Kowloon, tel: 722-1818.

La Brasserie, Omni Marco Polo Hotel, Harbour City, Canton Road, Tsimshatsui, Kowloon, tel; 736-0888.

La Ronda, Furama Kempinski, 1 Connaught Road, Central, Hong Kong, tel: 525-5111.

La Rose Noire, 8 Wo On Lane, Hong Kong.

La Taverna, Shun Ho Tower, 24-30 Ice House Street, Central, Hong Kong, tel: 523-8624; Astoria Building, 34-38 Ashley Road, Tsimshatsui, Kowloon, tel: 376-1945.

La Terrazza, The Landmark, 16 Des Voeux Road, Central, Hong Kong, tel: 526-4200.

Lalique, Royal Garden Hotel, Kowloon.

Landau's, Sung Hung Kai Centre, 30 Harbour Road, Wanchai, Hong Kong, tel: 827-7901.

Le Provencal Seaview, China Merchants Hotel, 160-161 Connaught Road West, Western, Hong Kong, tel: 559-6888.

Le Restaurant de France, Regal Kowloon Hotel, 71 Mody Road, Tsimshatsui, Kowloon, tel: 722-1818.

Les Celebrites, Hotel Nikko, 72 Mody Road, Tsimshatsui, Kowloon, tel: 739-1111.

Le Tire Bouchon, 9 Old Bailey Street, Hong Kong, tel: 523-5459.

Lobster Bar, Island Shangri-La Hotel, Pacific Place, Supreme Court Road, Central, Hong Kong, tel: 877-3838.

Lord Stanley's, 92A Stanley Main Street, Stanley, Hong Kong, tel: 813-8562.

Louis Steak House, 61 Connaught Road Central, Hong Kong, tel: 529-8933.

Mad Dogs, 32 Nathan Road, Kowloon, tel: 301-2222.

Mandarin Grill, Mandarin Oriental, 5 Connaught Road, Central, tel: 522-0111.

Margaux, Kowloon Shangri-La, 64 Mody Road, Tsimshatsui East, Kowloon, tel; 721-2111.

Martino, Prospect Mansion, 68 Paterson Street, Causeway Bay, Hong Kong, tel: 576-4680.

Mecca 97, Cosmos Building, 8-11 Lan Kwai Fong, Central, Hong Kong, tel: 810-9333.

Mistral, Holiday Inn Crowne Plaza Harbour View, 70 Mody Road, Tsimshatsui East, Kowloon, tel: 721-5161.

Mozart Stub'n, 8 Glenealy Road, Central, Hong Kong, tel: 522-1763.

Napoleon Grill, Miramar Hotel, 130 Nathan Road, Tsimshatsui, Kowloon, tel: 368-6861.

Ned Kelly's Last Stand, 11A Ashley Road, Kowloon.

Nicholini's, Conrad Hotel, Pacific Place, 88 Queensway, Central, Hong Kong, tel; 521-3838.

Palm, 38 Lock Road, Tsimshatsui, Kowloon, tel: 721-1271.

Panorama, New World Hotel, 22 Salisbury Road, Tsimshatsui, Kowloon, tel: 369-4111.

Parc 27, Park Lane Hotel, 310 Gloucester Road, Causeway Bay, Hong Kong, tel: 890-3355.

Park Inn, Hong Kong Park, Cotton Tree Drive, Central, Hong Kong, tel: 522-6333.

Pavilion, Lee Gardens Hotel, 33 Hysan Avenue, Causeway Bay, Hong Kong, tel: 895-3311.

Peak Cafe, 121 Peak Road, The Peak, Hong Kong, tel: 849-7868.

Peak Tower, The Peak Tower, The Peak, Hong Kong, tel: 849-7381.

Petrus, Island Shangri-La, Pacific Place, Supreme Court Road, Central, Hong Kong, tel: 820-8590.

Pierrot, Mandarin Oriental, 5 Connaught Road, Central, Hong Kong, tel: 522-0111.

Pizza Hut, The Landmark, 11-19A Queen's Road, Central, Hong Kong, tel: 523-8689; Jardine's Bazaar, Causeway Bay, Hong Kong, tel: 577-9172; Ocean Terminal, Harbour City, Canton Road, Tsimshatsui, Kowloon, tel: 736-2715; Autoplaza, 65 Mody Road, Tsimshatsui East, Kowloon, tel: 369-2575.

Pizzeria, The Kowloon Hotel, 19-21 Nathan Road, Tsimshatsui, Kowloon, tel: 369-8698.

Pizzeria Giovanni, 7-9 On Lok Road (Main Road), Yuen Long, New Territories, tel: 477-8935.

Plume, Regent Hotel, 18 Salisbury Road, Tsimshatsui, Kowloon, tel: 721-1211.

Poinsettia, Park Hotel, 61-65 Chatham Road South, Tsimshatsui, Kowloon, tel: 366-1371.

Pomeroy's, The Mall, Pacific Place Two, 88 Queensway, Central, Hong Kong, tel: 523-4772.

Prince's Tavern, Prince's Building, 10 Chater Road, Central, Hong Kong, tel: 523-9352.

Revolving 66, Hopewell Centre, 183 Queen's Road East, Wanchai, tel: 862-6166.

Rotiserrie, Furama Kempinski, 1 Connaught Road, Central, Hong Kong, tel: 525-5111.

Rigoletto, 14 Fenwick Street, Hong Kong, tel: 527-7144.

Sammy's Kitchen, 204 Queen's Road West, Western, Hong Kong, tel: 548-8400.

San Francisco Steak House, 101 Barnton Court, Harbour City, 7 Canton Road, Tsimshatsui, Kowloon, tel: 735-7576.

Scala, New World Harbour View Hotel, 1 Harbour Road, Wanchai, Hong Kong, tel: 802-8888.

Skettis, Hongkong Hilton, 2 Queen's Road Central, Central, Hong Kong, tel: 523-3111.

Spaghetti House, 10 Stanley Street, Central, Hong Kong, tel: 523-1372; 85B Hennessy Road, Wanchai, Hong Kong, tel: 529-0901; 3B Cameron Road, Tsimshatsui, Kowloon, tel: 368-8635; 6-6A Hart Avenue, Tsimshatsui, Kowloon, tel: 739-2111.

Stanley's, 86 Stanley Main Street, Stanley, Hong Kong, tel: 813-8873.

Steak House, Regent Hotel, 18 Salisbury Road, Tsimshatsui, Kowloon, tel: 721-1211.

Steak Place, Kowloon Shangri-La Hotel, 64 Mody Road, Tsimshatsui East, Kowloon, tel: 721-2111.

Stoned Crow, 12 Minden Avenue, Kowloon.

Someplace Else, Sheraton Hong Kong Hotel & Towers, 20 Nathan Road, Tsimshatsui, tel: 369-1111.

Tai Pan Grill, Omni The Hongkong Hotel, Harbour City, 3 Canton Road, Tsimshatsui, tel: 736-0088.

Texas Rib House, Victoria Centre, 15 Watson Road, North Point, Hong Kong, tel: 566-5560.

Tong Fuk Store, 13-14 Law Uk Village, Pui O, Lantau Island, tel: 984-8329.

Uptown, Wing On Centre, 111 Connaught Road, Central, Hong Kong, tel: 545-1199.

Valentino, 16 Hanoi Road, Tsimshatsui, Kowloon, tel: 721-6449; 115 Chatham Road South, Tsimshatsui, Kowloon, tel: 721-6653.

Venezia, Ocean Terminal, Harbour City, Canton Road, Tsimshatsui, Kowloon, tel: 735-3595.

Verandah, The Repulse Bay, 109 Repulse Bay Road, Hong Kong, tel: 812-2722.

Verandah Grill, The Peninsula, Salisbury Road, Tsimshatsui, Kowloon, tel: 366-6251.

FAST FOOD

How can Hong Kong be "Chinese" with more than a dozen **MacDonald's**, plus **Burger King**, **Orange Julius**, **Shakey's**, **Mr Donut**, **Pizza Hut**, **Hardee's**, **Wendy's** and other quickie eateries.

What Westerners do not realise, and rarely partake of, is the traditional Chinese version of a fast food outlet, the *dai pai dong* (street stall). Street stalls are everywhere and it is at these little venues that a good percentage of the population eats.

These are not to be confused with Chinese Western-style takeaways – aptly named **Wong's Fast Foods** or **Whispering Brook** which specialise in inexpensive Chinese dishes which are extremely popular and served fast. They also carry Western items. All of the foods at these places are served as "lunch-boxes," regardless of the time of day.

ICE CREAM

Despite a very suitable climate, this deep Western mystery remains only partly slurped. Pushcart men and grocers do a fair business in mass-produced, on-the-stick varieties, most at least okay – but beware the red-bean popsicle! For serious students, though, the only recourse is a specialist: **Colorado Meat Co.**, 14 Wellington Street, Central, Hong Kong. Solid, made-in-USA takeaways; **Dairy Farm Creameries** which are scattered around the colony; and **Swensen's**.

Also try cooling ice cream fantasies served at hotel coffee shops among which the Hilton's **Cat Street** and the Excelsior's **Windmill** stand out. More elegant will certainly be an afternoon cooler at the Peninsula's **Lobby**, the Mandarin's **Clipper Lounge** or The Regent's **Lobby Lounge**.

HIGH TEA

Hong Kong's most well-known place for high tea during the past half century has been the colonnaded lobby of the **Peninsula Hotel**. Anyone who is anyone passes through the Pen's gilded lobby. High tea there is a good place to watch the world go by: "What ho! I say old chappie," and colonial et al. Unfortunately, these days Asian and American tourists seem to outnumber the faithful old Brits at tea time; but it is still the place for this British ritual.

One of the "newer" places for high tea is the lobby of the **Regent**. Opened in late 1980, this hotel is still "new," but while sipping a traditional cuppa in its 40-foot (12-metre) high glass-walled lobby you can marvel at life sailing by in Hong Kong harbour.

RELICS & VESTIGES

Confucius and the British Empire are paid their respects in institutions such as the **Luk Yu Tea House** – 26–42 Stanley Street, Central, Hong Kong, tel: 523-1970 – in Chinese, please. Three thousand years of civilization haven't quite ended yet. No fluorescent formica flashes here; black-wood tables, marble-backed benches and brass spittoons do graceful justice to classic Cantonese food and 30-year-old teas. Un-foreign tongues are almost insistently not spoken, and the English menu is pointedly brief. Centrally located, open 7.30 a.m.–10 p.m. Less expensive than it looks.

THINGS TO DO

Your first stop should be at one of the Hong Kong Tourist Association's excellent Information & Gift Centres (Star Ferry Concourse, Kowloon or in the basement of Jardine House, Hong Kong) to collect some of their excellent literature on what-to-do in Hong Kong and how-to-do-it. There are dozens of booklets and pamphlets – everything from the obligatory eating out and shopping to walking tours on the Outlying Islands. The HKTA also runs a variety of tours, including a Housing Tour & Home Visit (see what life in Hong Kong is like outside the tourist and shopping areas), sports (including horse-racing) tours and a New Territories tour. Call 801-7177. And you can get an early start in planning your trip by visiting one of their overseas offices.

ATTRACTIONS

Hong Kong's four most unique tour attractions – **Ocean Park/Water World**, **Sung Dynasty Village**, **Museum of Science & Technology** and the **Space Museum** are great attractions for children. On the contrary, more adult visitors go to Ocean Park and the Sung Dynasty Village than children.

OCEAN PARK

The Ocean Park is divided between two levels and it is on the headland – connected to the lowland by 0.93-miles (1.5-km) cable-car system – where you will find the **Ocean Theatre**, a 3,500-seat aquatic theatre for performing dolphins and a killer whale. (There is also an occasional high dive act to enliven things.) The **Wave Cove** with its rocky shoreline is home to a variety of seals and penguins and birds. Viewing is above and below the waterline. The **Atoll Reef** is the three-level aquarium housing some 30,000 fish, including sharks which are hand fed. Perhaps the most exciting attraction is **Shark Tunnel** – a la Jaws 3 – which takes you through a Shark Aquarium with more than 50 varieties of shark swimming just above you.

On the same level is the amusement section featuring, among other rides, **The Dragon**, one of the longest (2,772 feet/840 metres) and most spectacular roller coasters in the world. There is also an escalator leading to yet another section which, according to the Guinness Book of Records is the longest in the world.

On the lower level are the children's play area and petting zoo, dolphin feeding pools, trained bird and sea shows, plus delightful gardens.

THE MIDDLE KINGDOM

The **Middle Kingdom** may seem like a strange attraction near Ocean Park, but it is a popular one nevertheless – and one you can partake of, like everything else except Water World, for the price of admission. Middle Kingdom is a living museum encompassing 5,000 years – that's 13 dynasties – of Chinese history. There are full-sized replicas of temples, shrines, houses and public squares while craftsmen dressed in period costume perform their specialities – whether that be calligraphy or jade carving.

Other non-aquatic attractions are the **Greenhouse** (there are actually three), a walk-in **Butterfly House** and an **Aviary** (in four sections).

WATER WORLD

Adjacent to the Ocean Park, yet distinctly separate, is **Water World**, which, as the name implies, is a water play park, complete with five slides, a beach, and a variety of other aquatic attractions.

Ocean Park, Middle Kingdom and Water World are easily accessible, even though they are on the south side of Hong Kong Island, near Aberdeen and you are staying in a hotel in Kowloon. (It is a good opportunity to combine a trip to Aberdeen or the floating restaurants or Stanley Market with a stop at these two attractions). All three venues are served by special Citybus transport from Admiralty (it is an MTR stop too) and tickets can be purchased in the MTR stations which include the round trip bus fare.

Tickets to Ocean Park and Middle Kingdom cost HK$135 for adults and HK$65 for children of age 6–16 (free for those below 6), including bus fare (it is HK$60 and HK$40 without). Senior citizens (60+) are also free. The park is open all year. For information and show times, call 555-3554.

Water World is only open from May through October. The cost is HK$60 adults and HK$30 for children. (If you take the bus, add HK$10 and HK$8.) Call 555-3554 for information and to check the weather.

AW BOON HAW GARDENS

Another great place for kids is the **Aw Boon Haw Gardens** on Tai Hang Road, also on Hong Kong Island. This is a Chinese version of Disneyland with weird sculptured and painted monsters and demons from Chinese mythology.

SPACE MUSEUM

Besides these, the **Space Museum** (which is actually a Planetarium and Museum) is another good place for children (over 6). Sitting in the **Space Theatre** watching skies whiz by makes one feel like he's on a hyper-speed space journey in Star Wars. There are scheduled "trips" a day, each lasting for about an hour, but only four in English per week (call 734-2722 for opening times.) In the **Exhibition Hall** there is a piece of the moon and other space exhibits brought back to Earth by American astronauts.

Book your tickets early (up to 4 days in advance is allowed) at the Space Museum itself in Kowloon, just across from the Peninsula Hotel.

SUNG DYNASTY VILLAGE

In the Laichikok area of Kowloon is the **Sung Dynasty Village**. China's Sung dynasty began 1,000 years ago, and this village is a "living" replica of a small Sung community. Passing through the village gates is like stepping out of a capsule after a trip through time. One second you're in modern Hong Kong – and the next you're 1,000 years back in time on the main street of a Chinese village, surrounded by acrobats, kung fu artists and shops selling traditional Chinese goods.

When you buy tickets you are given a packet of Sung dynasty paper money, invented during this era, which you use to buy things. At the village's wax museum – which of course would not have existed 1,000 years ago – there are life-like figures from Chinese history; one of the two guards at the entrance is real, the other is wax – guess which is which?

Phone 741-5111 for opening hours and show times. Travel agencies arrange tours, which include lunch or a snack, for HK$190–$250.

The local entrance fee is HK$75–$110 for adults, HK$30–$60 for children, but doesn't include transportation or food.

LAICHIKOK AMUSEMENT PARK

This park, adjacent to the Sung Dynasty Village, is not as glamourous as those in the United States, but it's still fun, especially for children. Laichikok has an ice-skating rink, a small zoo and numerous carnival-style rides.

TRAVEL PACKAGES

1) The best trips are usually the simplest, notably **half-day circular tours** of Hong Kong or Kowloon and the New Territories.

2) Particularly with three or four people, the higher priced **limousine tours** are well worth the extra flexibility and speed. Most will happily alter itineraries to suit particular tastes.

3) **Outlying island excursions** are just as easily and comfortably done by ordinary ferry – at as little as one quarter the cost, even including a gourmet-shop picnic lunch.

4) **Tour-group dinners and nightclub shows** are invariably awful, doubly so at Aberdeen's infamous floating restaurants. Save the often considerable sums and have a first-class meal at a real restaurant. But by all means take the pleasant **sunset cruise** which ends up in Aberdeen Harbour. Just refuse to be pressured into dinner on those floating restaurants and return to shore.

5) Avoid Saturdays and Sundays, when time spent sitting in traffic is subtracted from already too-short stopovers.

CHINA TOURS

Hong Kong is the place to book one of those "fully booked" China tours which have recently been heavily advertised in your home country. Time and again, visitors who wanted to visit the Middle Kingdom and were turned down in London, New York or Paris because those city's China tour quotas were used up, arrive here and find out – after their travel plans have been made – that had they booked in Hong Kong, they would have found space on a China-bound excursion.

If you want to tour China write ahead. **Swire Travel** (c/o Swire House, 2nd floor, Hong Kong, tel: 844-8448) is one of the largest and most reputable agencies dealing in China tours, but there are many others available. You will need to send a deposit – a minimum of US$60 for the cheapest Canton tours – which is non-refundable if you cancel. The deposit, however, is applied to the full tour cost when you finally book and pay. Also send a photocopy of every page in your passport – not just the page with identity data.

If you are in Hong Kong shopping for a China tour (dozens advertised in the papers daily) and you find that the particular time you want to go is fully-booked, or if it is a public holiday in Hong Kong (especially the Chinese New Year period, or during a Canton Trade Fair held in April or October), you will probably not make it. But at other times, there often is space available on China tours. After trying a couple of agents with no success, trot along to the **China Travel Service** (tel: 853-3888) before giving up hope. It is better to go in person, but you can also inquire by phone (tel: 853-3533).

Persons with limited time here can peek at China from the **Lok Ma Chau Lookout point** (in Hong Kong's New Territories) or take a day trip just across the border into **Shenzhen** (which you will also see advertised as Shum Chun). This industrial area has vastly expanded from a little border village into a new joint venture economic zone. The Shenzhen trip is not an exciting China sojourn, but if you only have a day, it is the best available. The itinerary includes a visit to **Splendid China**, **China Ethnic Culture Demonstration Village**, **Shenzhen Reservoir** (adjacent parklands), a **kindergarten** and an **Arts & Crafts Centre**. Lunch is served at the reservoir. These tours leave from the **Hung Hom Railway Station** (Kowloon) for the 75-minute ride to **Lowu**, the border crossing with the famous-covered wooden railway bridge. You walk over this bridge into busy Shenzhen "on the other side."

Note: Many of mainland China's goods are available in Hong Kong – at better prices too. Hong Kong steers pragmatically clear of the two-China problem: neither the People's Republic nor Taiwan has official diplomatic representatives in the colony. Nevertheless, barring major shifts in policy, travel hitches can be resolved at the these Chinese offices:

China Travel Service (People's Republic of China) 77 Queen's Road Central, Hong Kong, tel: 525-2284. Hours: 9 a.m.–1 p.m. and 2–5 p.m. Monday through Friday, 9 a.m.–1 p.m. Saturday.

Chung Hwa Travel (Taiwan) Bond Centre, East Tower, Queensway, Hong Kong, tel: 525-8315. Hours: 9 a.m.–12.30 p.m. and 2–5 p.m. Monday through Friday, and until noon Saturday.

CULTURE PLUS

Hong Kong does not have a reputation for the arts, performing or otherwise. To tourists, Hong Kong is an interesting venue which can be taken by itself or can serve as a gateway to or exit from China. Its key attractions are shopping and eating. To the business visitor, all the aforementioned is true. Hong Kong is an excellent place to conduct business – the laws, the infrastructure, the geography, and most of all the people, are all present in the right mix. Visitors do not come to Hong Kong for the arts – they do not come to this colony to visit museums and see plays or musicals.

Yet Hong Kong is by no means a cultural desert. Broadway and West End shows pass through, to say nothing of renown symphony orchestras and opera troupes.

The action takes place at the **Hong Kong Arts Centre**, where, in addition to plays and shows being performed in its theatres, small film festivals are almost a monthly occurrence. Just across the street is the **Hong Kong Academy for Performing Arts** – both buildings are on Harbour Road in Wanchai on Hong Kong Island. Again, it is a superb venue, complete with an outdoor amphitheatre, for all kinds of performances. But more important it is a training ground for budding members, both on stage and behind, of the performing arts. Across the harbour in Kowloon, just adjacent to the Star Ferry, is the Hong Kong Cultural Centre. Wing-shaped, it has three first class venues that can stage anything

from grand opera to intimate performances. Rarely visited by tourists is the Ko Shan Theatre in Kowloon, an outdoor venue used for pop concerts, operas and variety shows.

Hong Kong Island's City Hall also has hosted thousands of international performances. A new cultural centre for Tsimshatsui (near the Star Ferry) is planned for the near future.

There are also local symphonic orchestras, such as the **Hong Kong Philharmonic** and the **Hong Kong Chinese Music Orchestra**, plus several amateur and professional theatres which employ full-time professional musicians and actors. These arts organizations reflect Hong Kong's cosmopolitan and international cultural life.

Hong Kong indulges in not one but two annual international arts festivals.

The **Hong Kong Arts Festival**, in January and February, features an intriguing program of Western and Eastern art. Renowned orchestras, dance companies, drama groups, opera companies and jazz ensembles are invited to perform here alongside talented local artists. Traditional Chinese herbs blend with Western cultural fare to create a uniquely Hong Kong arts extravaganza.

Another annual arts affair, the **Festival of Asian Arts**, is sponsored by the Urban Council and invites artists and performers from various cultural regions in Asia to introduce to Hong Kong audiences their indigenous art forms. During the cultural orgy, Hong Kong is represented by groups that perform traditional Cantonese and Peking opera, Cantonese drama, multi-regional Chinese folk dance and music. Also included are performances by the Hong Kong Philharmonic Orchestra and the Hong Kong Chinese Music Orchestra. This festival is held during October and November.

Chinese operas, puppet shows, dancing and other "local" cultural fare occur regularly throughout the year, especially during traditional festivals. There are **free weekly Chinese cultural performances** at Cityplaza sponsored by the Hong Kong Tourist Association. See "Festivals" for details about Hong Kong's major annual religious festivals.

MUSEUMS

Museums are rarely considered a tourist attraction in a frantic shopping bazaar like Hong Kong. **The Hong Kong Museum of Art** has a diversified collection, including contemporary and classical paintings, calligraphic scrolls, ceramics, sculpture, lacquerware, jade and cloisonne. Its most distinctive holdings are an extensive collection of oil paintings, drawings, prints, lithographs and engravings of historical Hong Kong. They provide a vivid pictorial record of Sino-British contacts in the 18th and 19th centuries. Contemporary works by Hong Kong artists are also regularly exhibited in this museum. The Museum of Art is located on Salisbury Road, just next to the Hong Kong Cultural Centre, adjacent to the Star Ferry Concourse in Kowloon. Admission is free. Hours: 10 a.m.–6 p.m. Monday through Saturday (except Thursday) and 1–6 p.m. Sunday. Admission HK$10 adult, HK$5 student/senior.

The Hong Kong Museum of History has in its permanent collection fine model junks that illustrate the colony's traditional fishing industry and one of the most comprehensive collections of late 19th and early 20th-century photographs of Hong Kong that document Fragrant Harbour's historic realities. Also significant is a collection of Hong Kong's coinage and the currencies of nearby Kwangtung Province. With the co-operation of the Hong Kong Archaeological Society, excavated objects, representative of the colony's earliest prehistoric periods, are on display in the museum's archaeological section. Disappearing local arts and crafts, traditional agricultural and fishing implements and rural architectural displays reminiscent of the old New Territories are an important part of the museum's ethnographic collection.

The Museum of History is at 58 Haiphong Road in Kowloon park. Hours: 10 a.m.–6 p.m. Monday through Saturday (except Friday) and 1–6 p.m. Sunday. Admission HK$10 adult, HK$5 student/senior.

The Lei Cheng UK Branch Museum is at the site of a Later Han dynasty (AD 25–220) tomb. In its display halls are funerary wares and models of clay houses typical of that period. This museum-tomb is located at 41 Tonkin Street, Kowloon. Admission is free. Hours: 10 a.m.–1 p.m. and 2–6 p.m. daily (except Thursday), and 1–6 p.m. Sunday and public holidays.

The Fung Ping Shang Museum at Hong Kong University is the oldest museum in Hong Kong, founded in 1953. Its excellent bronze collection is divided into three groups: Shang and Chou era (15th–3rd centuries BC) ritual vessels which testify to the superb achievement of early Chinese metallurgy; decorative mirrors from the Warring States period (480–221 BC) to the T'ang dynasty (AD 618–906); and 966 Nestorian crosses of the Yuan dynasty (AD 1260–1368), the largest collection of its kind in the world. Ceramics including simple pottery of the Third Millenium BC, a number of Ming (AD 1368–1644), and Ch'ing (AD 1644–1900) dynasty paintings and specimens of Buddhist sculptural art from India are also on permanent display.

This museum is located at 94 Bonham Street, Pokfulam, Hong Kong. Hours: 10 a.m.–6 p.m. daily (except Sunday). Free admission.

Museum of Tea Ware, Flagstaff House, Hong Kong Park, Hong Kong. A branch of Museum of Art, it contains more than 500 pieces of tea ware. Hours: 10 a.m.–5 p.m. daily. Closed Wednesdays and public holidays.

Museum of Chinese Historical Relics serves as a permanent exhibition site for cultural treasures from China. Twice yearly exhibits. Causeway Centre, 1st floor, 28 Harbour Road, Wanchai, Hong Kong. Open Monday-Saturday 10 a.m.–6 p.m., Sundays & public holidays 1 p.m.–6 p.m.

Hong Kong Space Museum – not really a museum. The Space Theatre, known as a planetarium in other lands, offers between 7 and 10 shows daily, depending on the day. Most shows are in Cantonese, only some in English (call to find out which), however, a simultaneous translation service is available in English, Japanese and Mandarin, should you find yourself at a Cantonese show. Arrive 30 minutes ahead to make arrangements. There are also an Exhibition Hall and Hall of Solar Sciences with excellent exhibitions. Open daily except Tuesday 2–9.30 p.m. Space Theatre tickets are at HK$20 for adults, and HK$13 for children. Admission to Exhibition Hall and Hall of Solar Sciences HK$10 adult and HK$5 children/senior. Call 734-2722. Open: Weekdays except Tuesday 1–9 p.m. Saturdays, Sundays and public holidays 10 a.m.–9 p.m.

Hong Kong Science Museum, Science Museum Road, Tsimshatsui East, Kowloon. Of the 500 exhibits, more than 60 percent are hands-on which means kids of all ages – including those who paid for an adult ticket to get in – can while away the time watching and experimenting with the mysteries of science. Areas covered include computers, robotics, communications, transportation, electronics and much much more. Open 1–9 p.m., Tuesday–Friday; 10 a.m.–9 p.m. Saturdays, Sundays and public holidays. Admission fees are HK$25 for adults and HK$15 for children, students and senior citizens (60+).

Sam Tung Uk Museum, Kwu Uk Lane, Tsuen Wan, New Territories. This 2,000 sq. metre museum is housed in a two-century old walled village. A wander through the village and the restored homes will give you an idea what Hakka life was like before Hong Kong was ever dreamed of. Open 9 a.m.–4 p.m. daily except Tuesdays and public holidays. Admission free.

Hong Kong Railway Museum, Old Taipo Market Railway Station. The station itself dates back to 1913 and is designed in a Chinese style. Historic railway coaches dating from 1911 are lined up. Open 9 a.m.–4 p.m. except Tuesdays. Admission free.

Sheung Yiu Folk Museum, Pak Tam Chung Nature Trail, Sai Kung, New Territories. This is another example of Hakka life and lifestyles from days of yore. Be prepared to do a bit of hiking, though. Open 9 a.m.–4 p.m. except Tuesdays. Admission free.

Law Uk Folk Museum, 14 Kut Shing Street, Chaiwan, Hong Kong. This is another Hakka home restored to its original state. Open daily (except Monday) 10 a.m.–1 p.m., 2–6 p.m. Sundays and public holidays 1–6 p.m. Admission free.

Tsui Museum of Art, 10th floor, Rediffusion House, 822 Laichikok Road, Kowloon. A private museum with over 2,000 pieces of Chinese pottery, bronzes, carvings, glassware and furniture. Open 10 a.m.–4.30 p.m. daily except Sunday. Admission HK$20 adult, HK$10 child/student.

There are also two living museums, the **Sung Dynasty Village** (tel: 741-5111) in Kowloon and the **Middle Kingdom** (tel: 552-0291) at the Ocean Park, Hong Kong. The former depicts life between 912–1279 and is included on various tours and also sells self-tour visits. The latter, covering 5,000 years of history, may be visited as part of a trip to the Ocean Park, either on a tour or individually.

ART GALLERIES

The **Art Gallery of the Chinese University** is relatively new, but houses an important collection of paintings and calligraphy by Kwantung artists from the Ming period to modern times. Other impressive displays are a collection of 300 bronze seals of Han and pre-Han provenance, and stone rubbings from monuments of the Han and Sung dynasties. The Art Gallery is located on the campus of the Chinese University in the New Territories. Admission is free. Hours: from 10 a.m.–4.30 p.m. daily, 12.30–4.30 p.m. Sundays and public holidays.

Pao Sui Loong Galleries of the Hong Kong Arts Centre holds exhibitions from 10 a.m.–8 p.m. daily. Admission is free.

CINEMAS

Hong Kong movie houses also offer a spectrum of foreign language films besides those in Mandarin and the few in Cantonese.

The biggest deterrents to good commercial films here are the government censors and distributors, the latter being the worst culprits. The distributors arbitrarily cut (not edit) films to fit neatly into a convenient time frame (usually 2 hours) so they can cram in five or six showings a day. *A Bridge Too Far* is a classic example. Sir Laurence Olivier's visage and name were posted over the marquee (along with the other stars) but his one cameo appearance in the film was completely cut out.

To combat this clip-clip mentality, theatres now have to advertise the time length of a flick. Therefore, if *The Longest Day* is shown in 120

minutes, you know that 60 minutes have been chopped.

Nearly a hundred theatres here screen everything from demure Chinese costume dramas to gory "spaghetti" Westerns. Most screen four shows daily – usually at 2.30 p.m., 5.30 p.m., 7.30 p.m. and 9.30 p.m. Some add morning, noon or midnight showings during holidays or weekends, and all include 20 to 30 minutes of often amusing pre-film advertisements. Though programs can change without warning virtually overnight, the *Hong Kong Standard*'s day-to-day listings are generally accurate and complete.

Because of frequent crowds, most theatres sell reserved seats only. During the week, or in the case of more obscure offerings, show up at screen time and you should be able to secure a seat. You can also make a reservation over the phone but remember that tickets are held only until 15 minutes before the start of the show. Ticket prices are HK$25–$40.

HONG KONG

Cathay, 125 Wanchai Road, Wanchai.
Cine Art, Sun Hung Kai Bldg, 30 Harbour Road, Hong Kong.
Columbia Classics, Great Eagle Centre, 23 Harbour Road, Wanchai.
Imperial, Wood Road (off Wanchai Road), Wanchai.
Isis, 7 Moreton Terrace (opposite Victoria Park).
Jade, Paterson Street, Causeway Bay.
Palace, World Trade Centre, 20 Gloucester Road, Causeway Bay.
Park, Tung Lo Wan Road (opposite Victoria Park), Causeway Bay.
Pearl, Paterson Street, Causeway Bay.
President, Jaffe Road at Cannon Street, Causeway Bay.
UA Queensway, Pacific Place, 88 Queensway, Hong Kong.

KOWLOON

Broadway, 6–12 Sai Yeung Choi Street, Kowloon.
Chinachem, Chinachem Golden Plaza, Kowloon.
Empress, Sai Yung Choi Street, Mongkok.
Golden Harvest, 23 Jordan Road, Yaumatei.
Harbour City, Harbour City, Kowloon.
Liberty, 26 Jordan Road, Yaumatei.
Majestic, 334 Nathan Road, Yaumatei.
M2, 6–22 Saigon Street
Ocean, Canton Road, Tsimshatsui.
Rex, Portland Street (off Argyle Street), Mongkok.
Washington, 92 Parkes Street (off Jordan Road),
Yaumatei, tel: 3-310-405.

NEW TERRITORIES

UA, Shatin, New Territories.
UA Whampoa, Hung Hom, Kowloon.

NIGHTLIFE

NIGHTSPOTS

The following are some of the colony's most well-known night spots:

Blacksmiths Arms, 16 Minden Avenue, Kowloon.
Bottom's Up, 14 Hankow Road, Kowloon.
Brown's Wine Bar, Exchange Square, Hong Kong.
Bull & Bear, Hutchison House, Hong Kong.
California, 30–32 D'Aguilar Street/Lan Kwai Fong, Hong Kong.
Caesar Night Club, Miramar Hotel, Kowloon.
Captain's Bar, Mandarin, Hong Kong.
Catwalk, New World Hotel, Kowloon.
Champagne Bar, Grand Hyatt, Hong Kong.
Chin Chin, Hyatt Regency Hotel, Kowloon.
China City Night Club, Peninsula Centre, Tsimshatsui East, Kowloon.
China Coast Pub, Regal Airport Hotel, Kowloon.
Club B Boss, Mandarin Plaza, Tsimshatsui East, Kowloon.
Club De Luxe, New World Centre, Kowloon.
Club Karaoke, China Merchants Hotel, Hong Kong.
Club Metropolitan, Chinachem Bldg, Tsimshatsui East, Kowloon.
Cosmo Disco, Regal Riverside, Shatin, New Territories.
Crossroads, 42 Lockhart Road, Hong Kong.
Cyrano, Island Shangri-La Hotel, Hong Kong.
Dai-Ichi, 257 Gloucester Road, Hong Kong.
Dickens Bar, Excelsior Hotel, Hong Kong.
Dragon Boat Bar, Hilton Hotel, Hong Kong.
Duddell's, 1 Duddell Street, Hong Kong.
Flagstaff Inn, Mui Wo, Lantau Island.
Flying Machine, Regal Airport Hotel, Kowloon.
Ginza, 18 Hankow Road, Kowloon.
Goldstar, Fenwick Street, Hongkong.
Graffiti, 17 Lan Kwai Fong, Central, Hong Kong.
Godown, Admiralty Centre, Tower 2, Queensway, Hong Kong.
Great Wall, Sheraton Hotel, Kowloon.
Hardy's, 35 D'Aguilar Street, Hong Kong.
Hollywood East, Regal Meridien Hotel, Kowloon.
Horse & Carriage, 117 Lockhart Road, Hong Kong.
Inn Bar, Holiday Golden Mile, Kowloon.
Jazz Club, 34 D'Aguilar Street, Hong Kong.
JJ's, Grand Hyatt, Hong Kong.
Jockey, Swire House, Hong Kong.
Joe Bananas, 23 Luard Road, Hong Kong.

Kangeroo Pub, Haiphong Road, Kowloon.
Kara Karaoke, New World Harbour View Hotel, Hong Kong.
Kismet, 71 Peking Road, Kowloon.
Kokusai, 81 Nathan Road, Kowloon.
La Bodega, 31 Wyndham Street, Hong Kong.
La Rose Noire, 8–13 Wo On Lane, Hong Kong.
Latin Quarter, 40 Nathan Road, Kowloon.
Lau Ling Bar, Furama, Hong Kong.
Le Tire Bouchon, 9 Old Bailey Street, Hong Kong.
Mad Dogs, 32 Nathan Road, Kowloon.
Manhattan, New World Harbour View Hotel, Hong Kong.
Mandarin Palace Night Club, 24 Marsh Road, Hong Kong.
Nation 97, 9 Lan Kwai Fong, Hong Kong.
Ned Kelly's Last Stand, 11A Ashley Road, Tsimshatsui, Kowloon.
Neptune, Lockhart Road, Hong Kong.
New Lido, 36 Hankow Road, Kowloon.
New Makati, 100 Lockhart Road, Hong Kong.
New Playboy, 69 Peking Road, Kowloon.
New Tonnochy, 1 Tonnochy Road, hong Kong.
Nineteen 97, 9 Lan Kwai Fong, Hong Kong.
Oasis, New World Harbour View Hotel, Hong Kong.
Old China Hand, 104 Lockhart Road, Central, Hong Kong.
Panda, 123 Lockhart Road, Hong Kong.
Pink Giraffe, Sheraton, Kowloon.
Pussycat, Fenwick Street, Hong Kong.
R.J. Cass, Aberdeen Marina Club Bldg, Shum Wan Road, Aberdeen.
Red Lion, 15 Ashley Road, Kowloon.
Red Lips, 1A Locke Road, Hong Kong.
Rick's Cafe, 4 Hart Avenue, Kowloon.
Royal Falcon, Royal Garden Hotel, Kowloon.
Safari, Bar City, New World Centre, Kowloon.
San Francisco, 129 Lockhart Road, Hong Kong.
Scotties, 58 Lan Kwai Fong, Hong Kong.
Shakespeare, 30 Cannon Street, Hong Kong.
Ship Inn, 4 Cornwall Avenue, Kowloon.
Stoned Crow, 12 Minden Road, Kowloon.
Suzie Wong, 21 Fenwick Street, Hong Kong.
Talk of The Town, Excelsior Hotel, Hong Kong.
Waltzing Matilda Inn, 9 Cornwall Avenue, Tsimshatsui, Kowloon.
Wanch (The) Folk Club, 54 Jaffe Road, Hong Kong.
White Stag, 72 Canton Road, Kowloon.
Yum Sing, Lee Gardens Hotel, Hong Kong.

SHOPPING

WHAT TO BUY

Be prepared to be walked off your feet in this shopping bazaar. Two of the best guides to shopping are free and available through the Hong Kong Tourist Association – *Shopping and Factory Outlets*.

Others include *Hong Kong Factory Bargains* and *The Book of Yang – A Shopping Guide* (attached to *A Book of Ying – A City Guide*) and Drummond's *Hong Kong Guide to Art & Antique Dealers and Born to Shop – Hong Kong*. The big international names are in the shopping centres and hotel arcades. But the factory clothing outlets, some with retail shops, are more difficult to find.

ANTIQUES/HANDICRAFTS

Amazing Grace, Excelsior Hotel and Cityplaza, Hong Kong; Harbour City, Kowloon.

Banyan Tree, Prince's Bldg, Hong Kong; and Harbour City, Kowloon.

Charlotte Horstmann, Ocean Terminal, Kowloon.

China Arts, G/F 25 Kimberley Road, Tsimshatsui, Kowloon.

Chinese Arts & Crafts (HK) Ltd., Shell House, 24-28 Queens's Road, Hong Kong; 230 The Mall, Pacific Place, 88 Queensway, Hong Kong.

Eileen Kershaw, Peninsula Hotel, Kowloon.

Hai Feng Wood Arts, 19th floor, Canny Industrial Bldg, 33 Tai Yau Street, San Po Kong, Kowloon.

Hanart Gallery, 50 Hollywood Road, Hong Kong.

Hobbs & Bishops Fine Art Limited, G/F., 152 Hollywood Road, Hong Kong; G/F., 81 Hollywood Road, Hong Kong.

Honeychurch Antiques, 29 Hollywood Road, Hong Kong.

Plum Blossoms (International) Ltd., 305-307 Exchange Square One, 8 Connaught Place, Hong Kong.

Regalia Art Treasures, New World Shopping Centre, Tsimshatsui, Kowloon.

Schoeni, 27 Hollywood Road, Hong Kong.

Welfare Handicrafts, Jardine House, Hong Kong; and Salisbury Road, Kowloon.

BOOKS

Bookshops: Hong Kong patronizes some of Asia's best overseas book-sellers, even though their price marks are high. Among the principal ones are:

Bookazine, Alexandra House, Central.

Hong Kong Book Centre, basement, 25 Des Voeux Road Central, Hong Kong.

Jumbo Grade, Pacific Place, Queensway.

Kelly & Walsh at Pacific Place, Hong Kong.

SCM Post Family Bookshops at Star Ferry (Hong Kong), Ocean Centre (Kowloon) and at various Mass Transit Railway stations.

Swindon Book Company, Ocean Terminal, 2nd floor (near Star Ferry, Kowloon), Ocean Centre, next to Ocean Terminal, and at 13–15 Lock Road, Kowloon.

Times Book Centre, Shop LG 31A, Man Yee Building, Pottinger Street, Central; and Shops C&E, Milton Mansion, 96 Nathan Road, Kowloon.

Wanderlust, 30 Hollywood Road, Central.

COMPUTERS

A-1 Electronics Co., Shop 117A, Holiday Inn, Golden Mile, 50 Nathan Road, Tsimshatsui, Kowloon.

Continental Computer Systems, Shop 214, 2/F., Vicwood Plaza, 199 Des Voeux Road, Hong Kong.

East Asia Company, 12/F., Tung Ying Bldg, 100 Nathan Road, Tsimshatsui, Kowloon.

Mastertech Office Automation Co., LG48 Asia Computer Plaza, Silvercord, 30 Canton Road, Tsimshatsui, Kowloon.

Mastor Technology, Shop 304, Cityplaza I, Taikoo Shing, 1111 King's Road, Quarry Bay, Hong Kong.

CLOTHING

Alfred Dunhill (H.K.) Ltd., Prince's Bldg, Chater Road, Hong Kong; Sogo Department Store, 555 Hennessy Road, Causeway Bay, Hong Kong.

Anne Klein II (Takpac), 301 Pedder Bldg, Pedder Street, Hong Kong; Harbour City and Kowloon Hotel, Kowloon. (Ladies' Fashions)

Baleno, Shun Tak Centre, 200 Connaught Road Central, Hong Kong.

Ballantyne Boutique, Gloucester Tower, The Landmark, Des Voeux Road, Hong Kong; Regent Hotel Shopping Arcade, Salisbury Road, Kowloon.

Basile, Lobby Level, Regent Hotel Shopping Arcade, 18 Salisbury Road, Tsimshatsui, Kowloon.

Benetton, Daimaru Department Store, Paterson Street, Hong Kong; The Sincere Department Store, Des Voeux, Hong Kong; Sun Plaza, 30 Canton Road, Tsimshatsui, Kowloon; New World Centre, Salisbury Road, Tsimshatsui, Kowloon.

Boutique Christian Dior, Peninsula Hotel, Salisbury Road, Tsimshatsui, Kowloon.

Boutique Lacoste, 50 Connaught Road, Hong Kong; Cityplaza II Taikoo Shing, 1111 King's Road, Quarry Bay, Hong Kong.

Buttons & Bows Ltd., Omni The Hong Kong Hotel Arcade, Canton Road, Kowloon. (Accessories)

Byblos, Ocean Terminal, Harbour City, Canton Road, Tsimshatsui, Kowloon.

Camberley, Block B, 8th floor, Eldex Industrial Bldg, 21 Ma Tau Wai Road, Tokwawan, Kowloon. (Ladies' Fashions)

Camberley Enterprises Ltd., Hong Kong Spinners Bldg, 800 Cheung Sha Wan Road, Kowloon. (Factory Outlet)

Chanel Boutique, Prince's Bldg, 3 Des Voeux Road, Hong Kong; Peninsula Hotel Shopping Arcade, Salisbury Road, Tsimshatsui, Kowloon. (Ladies' Fashions)

Caratiga, Ocean Terminal, Harbour City, Canton Road, Tsimshatsui, Kowloon. (Ladies' Fashions)

Ca Va, 1726 Star House, Salisbury Road, Kowloon. (Ladies' Fashions)

Cheetah Management, 13th floor, Tung Fai Bldg, 27 Cameron Road, Tsimshatsui, Kowloon. (Ladies' Fashions)

Celine, Repluse Bay Hotel, Hong Kong.

Collections, The Mall, Pacific Place Two, 88 Queensway; Prince's Bldg, Des Voeux Road; Sogo Department Store, Hong Kong.

Comey Ltd. (Trading as Jennie), Well On Commercial Bldg 60 Wellington Street, Hong Kong. (Ladies' Fashions)

Courreges Boutique, Gloucester Tower, The Landmark, 11 Pedder Street, Hong Kong; Ocean Centre, Harbour City, Canton Road, Tsimshatsui, Kowloon.

Crocodile Garments Ltd., 50 Connaught Road; Cityplaza, Taikoo Shing, 1111 King's Road, Quarry; Capitol Centre, Jardine's Bazaar, Hong Kong; Nathan Road, Yaumatei; Ocean Terminal, Harbour City, 3 Canton Road, Tsimshatsui, Kowloon.

Daks, Prince's Bldg, 5 Ice House Street; Sogo Department Store, Hong Kong.

Diane Freis, Prince's Bldg and Pacific Place, Hong Kong; Regent Hotel, Harbour City and Ocean Terminal, Kowloon. (Ladies' Fashions)

DKNG, Edinburgh Tower, The Landmark, Hong Kong. (Ladies' Fashions)

Dolce & Gabbana, Ocean Centre, Harbour City, Tsimshatsui, Kowloon. (Ladies' Fashions)

Donna Karan, The Regent Hotel, Salisbury Road, Tsimshatsui, Kowloon. (Ladies' Fashions)

Dorfit, 1101 Sands Bldg, 17 Hankow Road, Harbour City and Tsimshatsui Centre, all in Kowloon; Admiralty in Hong Kong. (Wool and silk)

Dynasty Salons Limited, Hilton Hotel Arcade, Queen's Road, Hong Kong. (Ladies' Fashions)
Elegance, Peking Road, Tsimshatsui, Kowloon.

Emporio Armani, New World Tower, 16 Queen's Road, Hong Kong.

Ermenegildo Zegna, The Mall, One Pacific Place, 88 Queensway, Hong Kong; The Regent Hotel Shopping Arcade, Salisbury Road, Tsimshatsui, Kowloon. (Men's Fashions)

Esprit, Prince's Bldg, Ice House Street; Excelsior Hotel Shopping Arcade; The Landmark, 12-16 Des Voeux Road, Hong Kong.

Esti Tahina, Star House, 3 Salisbury Road, Tsimshatsui, Kowloon. (Ladies' Fashions)

Etienne Aigner, Alexandra House, 16A Chater Road; Matsuzakaya Department Store, Paterson Street, Hong Kong; Hyatt Regency Hotel Shopping Arcade, 67 Nathan Road, Tsimshatsui, Kowloon.

Eurotex Fashion Ltd., Pedder Bldg, 12 Pedder Street, Hong Kong. (Ladies' Fashions)

Fame, 36 Queen's Road East, Hong Kong. (Leotards, tights etc.)

Fashions of Seventh Avenue, Unit M, 9th floor, Kaiser Estate Phase III, 9 Hok Yuen Street Hung Hom and Mirror Tower, 61 Mody Road, Tsimshatsui East, Kowloon; Convention Plaza, 1 Harbour Road and Sing Pao Centre, 8 Queen's Road Central, Hong Kong. (Ladies' fashions)

First Concept, Cityplaza Phase II, Taikoo Shing, 1111 King's Road, Quarry Bay; 384 Hennessy Road, Wan Chai, Hong Kong; 38 Sai Yeung Choi street, Mong Kok, Kowloon; 38 Grandville Road, Tsimshatsui, Kowloon.

Four Seasons, Room B, 10th floor, South China Bldg, 1 Wyndham Street, Hong Kong; and 1st floor, G1, Kaiser Estate, Phase II, 51 Man Yue Street, Hung Hom, Kowloon. (Ladies' Fashions)

Francescatti, 545 Hennessy Road, Causeway Bay, Hong Kong; Luk Hoi Tung Bldg, 31 Queen's Road, Hong Kong. (Men's Fashions)

Fringe, Tower A, Hunghom Commercial Centre, Ma Tau Wai Road, Hung Hom, Kowloon. (Ladies' Fashions)

G2000, Manning House, 38 Queen's Road; Cityplaza, Taikoo Shing, 1111 King's Road, Quarry Bay, Hong Kong.

Gat Design, 10th floor, Cosmos Bldg, 8 Lan Kwai Fong, Hong Kong. (Ladies' Fashions)

Genny, Edinburgh Tower, The Landmark, 16 Des Voeux Road, Hong Kong.

Gianfranco Ferre, Edinburgh Tower, The Landmark, 15 Queen's Road, Hong Kong. (Ladies' Fashions)

Giorgio Armani, Gloucester Tower, The Landmark, Pedder street, Hong Kong.

Givenchy Gentleman, Shop 102A, Gloucester Tower, The Landmark, 11 Pedder Street, Hong Kong. (Men's Fashions)

Henry Cotton's, Hong Kong Daimaru Department Store, Paterson Street, Causeway Bay, Hong Kong.

Hermes Boutique, Gloucester Tower, 16 Des Voeux, Hong Kong. (Ladies' Fashions)

Hugo, Ocean Terminal, Harbour City, Canton Road, Tsimshatsui, Kowloon. (Men's Fashions)

Inscription Rykiel, The Landmark, 12-16 Des Voeux Road, Hong Kong. (Ladies' Fashions)

Issey Miyake, Swire House, 11 Chater Road, Hong Kong; The Kowloon Hotel, Nathan Road, Tsimshatsui, Kowloon.

Jaeger, The Landmark, Pedder Street, Hong Kong; Lobby Level, Regent Hotel, Salisbury Road,

Tsimshatsui, Kowloon.

Jenny Fashion, Holiday Inn Harbour View, 70 Mody Road, Tsimshatsui East, Kowloon. (Ladies' Fashions)

Jil Sander, The Regent Hotel, Salisbury Road, Tsimshatsui, Kowloon. (Ladies' Fashions)

Joyce Boutique Ltd., Gloucester Tower, The Landmark, Des Voeux Road, Hong Kong (Ladies' Fashions); Level 3 Pacific Place, Phase II, 88 Queensway, Hong Kong.

Joyce Man, Mandarin Oriental Hotel, 5 Connaught Road, Hong Kong. (Men's Fashions)

Jumbo Knitwear, 4th floor, Kai It Bldg, 58 Pak Tai Street, Tokwawan, Kowloon. (Knitwear)

K International, 12th floor, Unit J, Kaiser Estate Phase II, 47 Man Yue Street, Hung Hom, Kowloon. (Ladies' Fashions)

Lanvin, The Landmark, 11 Pedder Steet; Mitsukoshi Department Store, 500 Hennessy Road, Causeway Bay, Hong Kong; Lobby Level, Regent Hotel, 18 Salisbury Road, Tsimshatsui, Kowloon.

Laura Ashley, Prince's Bldg, Des Voeux Road, Hong Kong. (Ladies' Fashions)

Leslie Fay, Wing On Plaza, Mody Road Tsimshatsui East, Kowloon; and Baskerville House, 22 Ice House Street, Hong Kong. (Ladies' Fashions)

Lily Chau, New World Centre and Tsimshatsui Centre, Kowloon. (Ladies' Fashions)

Lim Ying Ying, 2G 1st floor, Hok Yuen Street, Hang Fung Industrial Bldg, Phase II, Hung Hom, Kowloon. (Lingerie)

Loewe, Shop G-7, G/F., Hyatt Regency Hotel Shopping Arcade, 67 Nathan Road, Tsimshatsui, Kowloon. (Men's Fashions)

Luciano Soprani, Deck 2, Ocean Terminal, Harbour City, Canton Road, Tsimshatsui, Kowloon.

Marguerite Lee, Landmark and Pacific Place, Hong Kong; Peninsula Hotel and Harbour City, Kowloon. (Lingerie)

Mayleelok, Silvercord and Sun Plaza, both on Canton Road, Hyatt Hotel, all in Tsimshatsui, Kowloon. (Ladies' Fashions)

Missoni, 216B The Landmark, Pedder Street, Hong Kong; The Peninsula, Salisbury Road, Tsimshatsui, Kowloon.

Mon Chapeau By Ellas, The Repluse Bay Shopping Arcade, 109 Repluse Bay Road, Hong Kong. (Accessories)

Mosaic Designs, Silvercord Kowloon and 24, 2nd floor, Sino-Industrial Plaza Kai Cheung Road, Kowloon Bay, Kowloon; Star Ferry Pier Lobby, Hong Kong. (Ladies' Fashions)

Mitsumine, One Pacific Place, 88 Queensway, Hong Kong (Men's Fashions); Uny Department Store, Cityplaza 2, Taikoo Shing, 1111 King's Road, Quarry Bay, Hong Kong (Ladies' Fashions).

Moschino, Swire House, 10 Chater Road, Hong Kong; The Regent Hotel Shopping Arcade, Salisbury Road, Tsimshatsui, Kowloon.

Naf Naf Boutique, Peninsula Hotel, Salisbury Road, Tsimshatsui; Mitsukoshi Department Store, Sun

Plaza, Canton Road, Tsimshatsui, Kowloon.

Nina Ricci Boutique, Ladies Department, Matsuzakaya Department Store, Paterson Street, Causeway Bay; Mandarin Oriental Hotel, 5 Connaught Road, Hong Kong; The Regent Shopping Arcade, 18 Salisbury Road, Tsimshatsui; China Hong Kong City, Canton Road, Tsimshatsui, Kowloon.

Pearls & Cashmere, Sheraton Hotel, 20 Nathan Road, Tsimshatsui, Kowloon.

Peggy Boyd (Sheila Fashions Ltd.), Prince Bldg, Chater Road, Hong Kong. (Ladies' Fashions)

Rileys, Cosmo Bldg, 8 Lan Kwai Fong, Hong Kong. (Factory Outlet)

Romeo Gigli, The Regent Hotel, Salisbury Road, Tsimshatsui, Kowloon. (Ladies' Fashions)

Rosalie, 28 Mody Road, Tsimshatsui, Kowloon.

Rudolph, B8 The Landmark, 12-16 Des Voeux Road, Hong Kong. (Men's Fashions)

Salvatore Ferragamo, 20 Queen's Road; Mandarin Oriental Hotel, 5 Connaught, Hong Kong.

Sang Woo, 5A & B, Phases I & II, Hong Kong Spinners Industrial Bldg, 601 Tai Nan West Street, Cheung Sha Wan, Kowloon. (Leather)

Shirt Stop, 5th floor, Pedder Bldg, Pedder Street, Hong Kong; and Towning Mansion, 50 Paterson Street, Hong Kong and Hyatt Hotel, Kowloon. (Shirts)

Shoppers' World, 708 Sands Bldg, 17 Hankow Road, Tsimshatsui, Kowloon. (Ladies' Fashions)

Silkwear House, 207 Pedder Bldg, 12 Pedder Street and Paterson Plaza, Paterson Street, Hong Kong. (Silk)

Sonia Rykiel, Edinburgh Tower, The Landmark, Pedder Street, Hong Kong. (Ladies' Fashions)

S.T. Dupont Boutique, Central Bldg, Pedder Street, Hong Kong. (Accessories)

Swank Shop Ltd., Gloucester Tower, The Landmark, 11 Pedder Street, Hong Kong; W-1 The Peninsula Hotel, Salisbury Road, Tsimshatsui, Kowloon; Regent Hotel Shopping Arcade, Salisbury Road, Tsimshatsui, Kowloon.

Takpac Retail, Pedder Bldg, 12 Pedder Street, Hong Kong; The Kowloon Hotel, 19 Nathan Road, Tsimshatsui, Kowloon. (Ladies' Fashions)

Thierry Mugler, 242 The Landmark, Des Voeux Road, Hong Kong. (Ladies' Fashions)

Tonino Lamborghini Men's Boutique, Ocean Centre, Harbour City, Canton Road, Tsimshatsui, Kowloon. (Men's Fashions)

Top Knitters, 1006, 10th floor, Sand Bldg, 17 Hankow Road, Tsimshatsui, Kowloon. (Knitwear)

Tuxe Top, 1st floor, 18 Hennessy Road, Hong Kong; and 3rd floor, 16 Peking Road, Tsimshatsui, Kowloon. (Tuxedos for rental)

Ungaro Boutique, Edinburgh Tower, The Landmark, 15 Queen's Road, Hong Kong. (Ladies' Fashions)

Valentino Garavani Boutique, Gloucester Tower, The Landmark, Des Voeux Road, Hong Kong; The Regent Shopping Arcade, 18 Salisbury Road,

Tsimshatsui, Kowloon.

Vica Moda, Winner Bldg, 40 Man Yue Street and G2, 1st floor, Kaiser Estate, Phase II, 47 Man Yue Street, Hung Hom and Omni Hong Kong Hotel, both in Kowloon; Landmark, Hong Kong. (Ladies' Fashions)

Washed Silk, 1308 Central Bldg, 1 Pedder Street, Hong Kong. (Silk)

Wintex, 401 Pedder Bldg, 12 Pedder Street, Hong Kong. (Silk)

Yves Saint Laurent Men's Boutique, China Bldg, 29 Queen's, Hong Kong; Prince's Bldg, 1A-3A Des Voeux Road, Hong Kong. (Men's Fashions)

Yves Saint Laurent Rive Gauche, Edinburgh Tower, The Landmark, Queen's Road, Hong Kong. (Ladies' Fashions)

CARPETS

Banyan Tree Ltd., Prince's Bldg., Chater Road, Hong Kong.

Carpet House, Level 2 New World Centre, 18-24 Salisbury Road, Tsimshatsui, Kowloon.

Carpet World (HK Oriental Rug Co. Ltd.), 46 Morrison Hill Road, Wanchai, Hong Kong.

Ethnic Rugs, 55 Wyndham Street, Hong Kong.

Karim's Oriental Carpets Limited, 1A Wong Nai Chung Road, Happy Valley, Hong Kong.

Oriental Carpet Palace, Suite D, 52-60 Lyndhurst Terrace, Hong Kong.

Oriental Carpet Trading, 41 Wyndham Street, Hong Kong.

Persian Carpets Ltd., 22 Staunton Street, Hong Kong.

Tai Ping, Hutchinson House, Hong Kong; and Tai Ping Industrial Park, 51 Ting Kok Road, Tai Po, New Territories.

DEPARTMENT STORES

China Products Co. (HK) Ltd., Lok Sing Centre, Yee Wo Street, Causeway Bay, Hong Kong.

Chinese Merchandise Emporium Ltd., Chiao Shang Bldg, Queen's Road, Hong Kong.

Duty Free Shoppers Hong Kong Ltd., Convention Plaza Shopping Arcade, Harbour Road, Hong Kong.

Hong Kong Daimaru Department Store Ltd., Great George Street, Causeway Bay, Hong Kong.

Hong Kong Matsuzakaya Department Store, Hang Lung Centre, Paterson Street; Queensway Plaza, Hong Kong.

Hong Kong Tokyu Department Store Co Ltd, New World Centre, Salisbury Road, Kowloon.

Isetan Of Japan Ltd., Aberdeen Centre, Nam Ning Street, Hong Kong.

Lane Crawford Ltd., Lane Crawford House, Queen's Road; Windsor House, Gloucester, Hong Kong..

Mark & Spencer P.L.C., Cityplaza I, King's Road; Excelsior Plaza, East Point Road, Hong Kong.

Mitsukoshi Enterprises Co. Ltd., Hennessy Centre, Hennesy Road, Hong Kong.

Seibu Department Store, The Mall, Pacific Place, 88 Queensway, Hong Kong.

Sincere Co. Ltd., 173 Des Voeux Road, Hong Kong.

Sogo Hong Kong Co. Ltd., East Point Centre, Hennessy Road, Hong Kong.

Wing On Department Stores, Hopewell Centre, Queen's Road; Cityplaza I, Taikoo Shing, King's Road, Hong Kong.

Yaohan Department Store (H.K.) Ltd., Whampoa Garden, Hung Hom, Kowloon; New Town Plaza, Shatin Centre Road, New Territories.

ELECTRICAL APPLIANCES

Chung Yuen Electrical Co. Ltd. (Sony Service Centre), G/F., 105 Des Voeux Road, Hong Kong.

Fortress Ltd., Yu Sung Boon Bldg, 107-111 Des Voeux Road, Hong Kong; China Bldg, 29 Queen's Road, Hong Kong.

Philips Hong Kong Ltd., Hopewell Centre, 17 Kennedy Road Wan Chai, Hong Kong.

Philips Hong Kong Ltd., 214 Barnton Court, 2/F., Harbour City, Canton Road, Tsimshatsui, Kowloon.

Siemens Limited, Fleet House, 38 Gloucester Road, Wan Chai, Hong Kong.

ELECTRONIC EQUIPMENT

Bushton Ltd., 1001 Kai Tak Commercial Bldg, 66-72 Stanley Street, Hong Kong.

Electronics 2000, China Hong Kong City, 33 Canton Road, Tsimshatsui, Kowloon.

Javys-Casio (Full Casio product line), G/F., New York House, 60 Connaught Road, Hong Kong.

FURNITURE

Luk's, Aberdeen Harbour Mansion, 52 Aberdeen Main Road, Aberdeen, Hong Kong.

Maitland-Smith, 4th floor, Wyler Centre, 210 Tai Lin Pai Road, Kwai Chung, Kowloon.

FURS

Broadway, 407 Pedder Bldg, 12 Pedder Street, Hong Kong; and Houston Centre, 63 Mody Road, Kowloon.

Camay Fur Co., The, Gloucester Tower, The Landmark, 12-16 Des Voeux Road, Hong Kong.

City Fur Co., Chinachem Golden Plaza, 77 Mody Road, Tsimshatsui, Kowloon.

East Asia Fur Co., Tsimshatsui Centre, 66 Mody Road, Tsimshatsui, Kowloon.

Jumbo Fur Co. Ltd., Century House, 3-4 Hanoi Road, Tsimshatsui, Kowloon.

Philip Chin's, Hilton Hotel, Hong Kong; and 1st floor, Tai Tat Bldg, 226 Pilken Street, Kowloon.

Siberian Furs, 29 Des Voeux Road, Central Hong Kong; and 21 Chatham Road, Kowloon.

JADE

Chu's Jade, 1A Kimberley Road, Kowloon.
Hong Kong Jade House, Ocean Terminal, Kowloon.
Jade Creations, Lane Crawford House, Queen's Road Central, Hong Kong.

JEWELLERY

Amerex, 702 Tak Shing House, 20 Des Voeux Road, Hong Kong; and Hankow Centre, 15 Hankow Road, Kowloon.
Anglo-Tex (HK) Ltd., Wing On Life Bldg, 22 Des Voeux Road, Hong Kong.
Anju, Block B2, 1st floor, Kaiser Estate Phase I, 51 Man Yue Street, Hung Hom, Kowloon.
Associated Lapidaries (HK) Ltd., Prince's Bldg, 10 Chater Road, Hong Kong.
Blue Spirit Ltd., Alexandra House, 16 Chater Road, Hong Kong.
Blunco, Flat B, 13th floor, 68 Canton Road, Kowloon.
Chow Sang Sang Jewellery Co. Ltd., 72 Queen's Road, Hong Kong.
Continental, 1st Floor, Kaiser Estate Phase III, 11 Hok Yuen Street, Hung Hom, Kowloon.
Edelweiss, Harbour City and Hankow Centre, 15 Hankow Road, Kowloon.
Enchante, Wilson House, Wyndham Street, Hong Kong.
Eurasia Jewellery, Hilton Hotel Arcade, 2 Queen's Road, Hong Kong.
Everrich Jewellery Manufacturer Ltd., Lane Crawford House, 70 Queen's Road, Hong Kong.
Favourite Jewellers, Prince Bldg, 10 Chater Road, Hong Kong.
George Chen Jewelry & Watch Co., Excelsior Hotel, Gloucester Road, Causeway Bay.
Golay Buchel & Co. (HK) Ltd., Hang Chong Bldg, Queen's Road, Hong Kong.
Fu Hing, 4th floor, Kaiser Estate Phase II, 41 Man Yue Street, Hung Hom, Kowloon.
Henry, Pacific Place and Edinburgh Tower, Landmark, Hong Kong; and 29 Nathan Road, Kowloon.
Hing Fung Jewellery Co. Ltd., Hong Kong Diamond Exchange Bldg, Duddell Street, Hong Kong.
House of Shen, Peninsula Hotel, Kowloon.
Jade Creations Ltd., Lane Crawford House, Queen's Road, Hong Kong.
Kai-Yin Lo, Pacific Place and Mandarin Oriental, Hong Kong; Peninsula Hotel, Kowloon.
Kay Tai Jewllery Co., Furama Kempinski Hotel, Connaught Road, Hong Kong.
K. S. Sze, Mandarin Oriental, Hong Kong.
Larry Jewelry, Pacific Place and Edinburgh Tower, Landmark Hong Kong; Ocean Terminal and 33 Nathan Road, Kowloon.
Les Must De Cartier (FE) Ltd., Prince's Bldg, Chater Road, Hong Kong.

Lloyd's, Unit C, 68 Sung Wong Toi Road, Kowloon.
New Universal Jewelry Co., Hilton Hotel Arcade, Queen's Road, Hong Kong.
Tse Sui Luen Jewellery Co. Ltd., Commercial House, Queen's Road, Hong Kong.
Wing On Jewelry Ltd., Johnston Road, Wanchai, Hong Kong.

LEATHER GOODS

Bally Boutique, The Landmark, Des Voeux Road; Swire House, Chater Road, Hong Kong; Peninsula Hotel, Salisbury Road; Royal Garden Hotel, Mody Road, Kowloon.
Carlos Falchi, Hyatt Regency Hotel, Nathan Road, Kowloon.
Celine, Sogo Hong Kong Co. Ltd., Causeway Bay, Hong Kong.
Chanel Boutique, Matsuzakaya Department Store, Paterson Street, Hong Kong; Peninsula Hotel Shopping Arcade, Salisbury Road, Tsimshatsui, Kowloon.
Companion Reptile, 9A Lock Road, Kowloon.
Dickson & Co. Ltd., Melbourne Plaza, Queen's Road, Hong Kong. (Handbags only)
Etro, Mitsukoshi TST Store, Lippo Sun Plaza, Peking Road, Kowloon.
Fontana Di Trebbia, The Landmark, Des Voeux Road, Hong Kong.
Fratelli Rossetti, Ocean Centre, Harbour City, Canton Road, Kowloon.
Granfranco Lotti, Peninsula Hotel, Salisbury Road, Kowloon.
Great Wall Luggage, 16 Lyndhurst Terrace, Hong Kong.
Gucci Company Ltd., Gloucester Tower, Des Voeux Road; Repluse Bay Shopping Arcade, Hong Kong.
Hermes Boutique, Gloucester Tower, Des Voeux Road, Hong Kong.
Hugo, Excelsior Plaza, Jaffe Road, Causeway Bay, Hong Kong.
I Santi, Edinburgh Tower, Des Voeux Road, Hong Kong.
Lancel Boutique, Prince's Bldg, Chater Road; Sogo Department Store; Damairu Department Store, Hong Kong.
Le Monde Boutique Ltd., Shun Tak Centre, Connaught Road, Hong Kong.
Le Saunda, Island Centre, Great George Street; Prince's Bldg, Chater Road, Hong Kong.
Loewe, Gloucester Tower, Pedder Street, Hong Kong.
Longchamp Co. Ltd., Central Bldg, Pedder Street, Hong Kong.
Louis Vuitton Boutique, The Landmark, Des Voeux Road; Repluse Bay Shopping Arcade, Hong Kong.
Mandarin Duck, The Landmark, Des Voeux Road; Excelsior Plaza, Gloucester Road, Hong Kong.
Maud Frizon, The Landmark, Des Voeux Road, Hong Kong.

Mayer Shoes Co., Mandarin Oriental Hotel, Connaught Road, Hong Kong.

Nazareno Gabrielli, Alexandra House, Des Voeux Road, Hong Kong.

Offenbach Store Ltd., Hong Kong Club Bldg, Chater Road, Hong Kong.

Prada, Peninsula Hotel, Salisbury Road, Kowloon. Tanino Crisci, Prince's Bldg, Chater Road, Hong Kong.

Toyo Leather Ware Co., Carnarvon Road, Tsimshatsui, Kowloon.

Walter Steiger, Ocean Terminal, Harbour City, Canton Road, Kowloon.

OPTICAL GOODS

Asian Optical Co., Carnarvon Road, Tsimshatsui, Kowloon.

Canaan Optical Co. Ltd., Stanley Street, Hong Kong.

Chinese Optical Co. Ltd., World Wide Plaza, Des Voeux Road, Hong Kong.

Cony Optical Co. Ltd., New World Centre, Salisbury Road, Kowloon.

Frames, The Optical Gallery, Ambassador Hotel Arcade, Nathan Road, Kowloon.

Hong Kong Optical, Hongkong Mansion, Great George Street; Central Bldg, Queen's Road, Hong Kong.

Hong Kong Arts Optical Centre, Fuk Lo Tsun Road, Kowloon City, Kowloon.

Iris Optical International Co. Ltd., Manning House, Queen's Road, Hong Kong.

Optical 88 Ltd., Hennessy Road, Causeway Bay; Pacific Place Two, 88 Queensway, Hong Kong.

Optical Shop, The, Hongkong Hotel Shopping Arcade, Canton Road; Ocean Terminal, Canton Road, Kowloon.

Paris Maki Optical International Limited, Princess Shopping Arcade, Nathan Road, Kowloon.

Peninsula Optical Co., Star House Arcade, Salisbury Road; Sheraton Hotel, Nathan Road, Kowloon.

Professional Optical & Contact Lens Centre, China Hong Kong City, Canton Road, Kowloon.

Sunrise Jewellery Optical Co., Carnarvon Road, Tsimshatsui, Kowloon.

University Optical Shop Ltd., Regent Hotel, Salisbury Road, Kowloon.

Victoria Optical Co., Peninsula Hotel, Salisbury Road, Kowloon.

PEWTER

Selangor, Swire House, Hong Kong; and Harbour City, Kowloon.

Selangor Pewter (HK) Ltd., Standard Chartered Bank Building, Des Voeux Road, Hong Kong.

PHOTOGRAPHIC EQUIPMENT

Broadway, 78 Queen's Road Central, Hong Kong.

Crown, 27 Hankow Road, Kowloon.

Esquire, Melbourne Plaza, Hong Kong; and 8 Cameron Road, Kowloon.

Fujimage, China Resources Bldg, 26 Harbour Road, Wanchai, Hong Kong; Jardine House, 1 Connaught Place, Hong Kong; Hennessy Apartments, 1 Lee Garden Road, Causeway Bay, Hong Kong.

Kodak (Far East) Ltd., G/F., Liu Chong Hing Bank Bldg, 24 Des Veoux Road, Hong Kong.

Mark's Photo Supplies, G/F., Tak Shing House, 20 Des Voeux Road, Central, Hong Kong.

Master Photo & Hi-Fi Ltd., G/F., 2 Cannon Street, Causeway Bay, Hong Kong.

Realty Audio & Video Supplies Ltd., G/F., Wing On House, 71 Des Voeux Road, Hong Kong.

Photo Scientific, 6 Stanley Street, Central, Hong Kong

Woods, Rm 1004, 10/F, Silvercut Tower 2, 30 Canton Road, Kowloon.

PORCELAIN

Ah Chow, B1, 7th floor, Block B, Hong Kong Industrial Centre, 489 Castle Peak Road, Cheung Sha Wan, Kowloon.

Craig's, St George's Bldg, Hong Kong; Harbour City, Kowloon and Omni Hong Kong Hotels, Kowloon.

C & T Porcelain, 53A Graham Street, Hong Kong.

Craig's Ltd., St. George Bldg, 2 Ice House Street, Hong Kong.

Genesis Fine Porcelain & Crystal, China Hong Kong City, 33 Canton Road, Tsimshatsui, Kowloon.

Hunter's, Pacific Place and The Repulse Bay, Hong Kong; Harbour City, Peninsula and Kowloon Hotels, Kowloon.

Lladro, Alexandra House, Hong Kong; and Peninsula Hotel, Kowloon.

Mei Ping (Far East) Ltd., Ocean Terminal, 3 canton Road, Tsimshatsui, Kowloon.

Meissen, The Landmark, Des Voeux Road, Hong Kong.

Noritake, Hilton Hotel and 20 Lockhart Road, Hong Kong; Harbour City, Kowloon.

Overjoy, Block B, 1st floor, 10 Chun Pin Street, Kwai Chung, New Territories.

Royal Copenhagen, Prince's Bldg, Hong Kong; and Harbour City, Kowloon.

Royal Doulton, Pacific Place, Hong Kong.

Town House, Ocean Terminal, Kowloon.

Waterford Wedgwood, Gloucester Tower, Landmark, Hong Kong; and Peninsula Hotel, Kowloon.

RATTAN

Elite Rattan, 90A Stanley Main Street, Hong Kong.

Fidelity Mercantile, 19th floor, Gee Chang Hong Centre, 65 Wong Chuk Hang Road, Aberdeen, Hong Kong.

Kowloon Rattan Ware, Chung Hing Industrial Bldg, 19 Fu Uk Road, Kwai Chung, New Territories.

TAILORS

Ascot Chang, Prince's Bldg, Hong Kong; Peninsula and Regent Hotels, Kowloon.
Charley Chang, Hilton Hotel, Hong Kong.
George Chen, Peninsula Hotel, Kowloon.
Jimmy Chen, Omni Hong Kong Hotel, Kowloon; and Edinburgh Tower, Landmark, Hong Kong.
Custom Shop, Landmark and Prince's Bldg, Hong Kong.
David's, Mandarin Oriental Hotel and Shun Tak Centre, Hong Kong.
Regent, Hyatt Hotel, Kowloon.
Robert, Mandarin Oriental, Hong Kong.
Sam's, Burlington Arcade, 94 Nathan Road, Kowloon.
Y. William Yu Co. Ltd., Lyton Bldg, Mody Road, Tsimshatsui, Kowloon.

WATCHES

Budson Watch & Jewellery Co. Ltd., Cat Street Galleries, 38 Lok Ku Road, Hong Kong.
City Chain Co. Ltd., Lockhart Road, Causeway Bay; Edinburgh Tower, Queen's Road; Excelsior Shopping Centre, Gloucester Road, Hong Kong.
East Asia Watch Co., Tsimshatsui Centre, 66 Mody Road, Tsimshatsui, Kowloon.
Eldorado, 60 Queen's Road Central, Hong Kong.
Emperor Watch & Jewellery Co. Ltd., 81 Nathan Road, Tsimshatsui, Kowloon.
Heiwado & Company (HK) Ltd., Tai Sang Bank Bldg, Des Voeux Road, Hong Kong.
King's Watch Co., 49 Queen's Road, Hong Kong.
Kung Brothers, Park Land Shoppers Boulevard, Nathan Road, Kowloon.
Labella, Hyatt Regency and 65 Nathan Road, Kowloon.
La Suisse Watch Co. Ltd., Nathan Road, Mong Kok, Kowloon.
Les Must De Cartier (FE) Ltd., Prince's Bldg, Chater Road, Hong Kong.
Shui Hwa Watch Co. Ltd., 50 Des Voeux Road, Hong Kong.
Swatch, Goldmark, Hennessy Road, Kowloon.
Watches of Switzerland, 21 Mody Road, Kowloon.
Zurich Watch Co., Nathan Road, Tsimshatsui, Kowloon.

MISCELLANEOUS GOODS

Davidoff Cigar Boutique, Gloucester Tower, Pedder Street; Mandarin Oriental Hong Kong, Connaught Road; Hilton Hotel, Queen's Road, Hong Kong; Peninsula Hotel, Salisbury Road; The Regent Hotel, Salisbury Road, Kowloon. (Smokers' needs)
Duty Free Shoppers Hong Kong Ltd., Convention Plaza Shopping Arcade, Harbour Road; Hankow Centre, Hankow Road; Ocean Terminal, Canton Road, Kowloon. (Wines & Spirits)
Friendship Store International, Haiphong Road, Tsimshatsui, Kowloon. (Souvenirs & Gifts)
JL Pedder, Pedder Bldg, Pedder Road, Hong Kong. (Souvenirs & Gifts)
Kalm's, The Landmark, Des Voeux Road; Queensway Plaza; Pacific Place, 88 Queensway, Hong Kong. (Souvenirs & Gifts)
King & Country, Pacific Place Two, 88 Queensway, Hong Kong. (Souvenirs & Gifts)
Paris (H.K.) Co., Lee Gardens Hotel Shopping Arcade, Hysan Avenue, Hong Kong. (Souvenirs & Gifts)
Reason Arts Ltd., Furama Kempinski Hotel, Connaught Road, Hong Kong. (Souvenirs & Gifts)

COMPLAINTS

The Hong Kong Tourist Association (HKTA) has a wide-ranging and reputable membership but they cannot vouch for every member firm; they can, however, exert a certain amount of pressure in a dispute. If you have a legitimate complaint, see them (at Jardine House, 35th floor, Hong Kong, tel: 801-7278), especially if the firm has the HKTA decal (a junk logo) on its door or window. Or you might try the Consumer Council (19th floor, Block 6, China Hong Kong City, 33 Canton Road, Kowloon, tel: 736-3322) to air complaints.

Gold Purchases: Hong Kong's jewellers since 1972 have been legally required to adhere to a gold hallmark (if they sell a gold bracelet at 18K, it must really be 18K and so marked) and since 1981 the parts-per-thousand gold content of a piece is also guaranteed by law, so you should get what you pay for. This is an elementary safeguard, because Hong Kong jewellers have long felt it is "against Chinese tradition" to properly hallmark jewellery. Also, when called on the carpet for dishonesty a jeweller usually blames "language problems" – even if a tourist or resident testifies that a sales clerk spoke English better than he or she did. Let the buyer beware, because occasionally this causes problems when gold purchases are made.

Diamond Purchases: Complaints should be forwarded to Diamond Importers Association (Room 1102, Paker House, 72 Queen's Road Central, Hong Kong, tel: 523-5497). This association polices its members.

Identifying Gems and Metals: If you want your gem's identity and value confirmed, go to Artasia at 10th floor, 57 Peking Road, Tsimshatsui, Kowloon (tel: 368-7331).

Though Hong Kong's laws are fairly strict when compared with those enforced by other Asian countries, there is always somebody in the colony ready to fleece a bewildered visitor.

SPORTS

PARTICIPANT

Fitness fanatics can indulge in a wide range of sports; they can take up kung fu , go scuba diving or explore country trails.

Note: The Hong Kong Tourist Association conducts a Sports & Recreation Tour at the Clearwater Bay Golf & Country Club in Sai Kung. Activities include golf, tennis, squash, badminton and swimming at nominal rates. Ask for the brochure.

MARTIAL ARTS

Several local martial arts institutions welcome interested visitors, whether you are skilled or a novice. Both the **South China Athletic Association** (particularly for tai chi chuan, shiu lam, judo and yoga), and the **YMCA International House** (for judo, tae kwon do, hung kuen and hak kei do) teach regular, inexpensive classes at all proficiency levels. Specialized kung fu schools include **Luk Chi Fu** (446 Hennessy Road, 3rd floor, Causeway Bay, Hong Kong, tel: 891-1044) and **Hong Kong Chinese Martial Arts Association** (687 Nathan Road, ground floor, Blocks A & B, Mongkok, Kowloon, tel: 394-4803). (Chinese speakers may be necessary for effective communication at the latter two associations.)

For the simply curious, parks throughout the colony (notably **Hong Kong Park** in Central, **Chater Garden** in Central, the **Botanical Gardens** above Central, **Victoria Park** in Causeway Bay, and **Kowloon Park** in Tsimshatsui) are alive just after dawn every morning with mass displays of tai chi chuan.

BOATING

So called **"pleasure junks"** can be found and hired through the classified listing in *The South China Morning Post*'s classified section. You might also try **Simpson Marine** (tel: 555-8377). Prices vary, but begin at about HK$400 per hour for a minimum of 2 to 3 hours.

More colourful are motorized sampans, which can accommodate up to a dozen people. Sampans can be rented dockside in **Aberdeen** or at the **Causeway Bay Typhoon Shelter**. The owners tend to view tourists as easy money, so hire sampans at Aberdeen will often demand up to HK$100 for an hour's swing through the anchorage. Barter aggressively.

SWIMMING

Can be quite good, particularly at the colony's more isolated beaches. Many top hotels – and the Tsimshatsui YMCA – have pools.

BEACHES

Hong Kong is not known as a beach resort, but the island does have a number of beautiful beaches which are accessible by public land transport. Additionally, a great number of beaches on the outlying islands are accessible by inter-island ferry and private boats.

On Hong Kong, Kowloon, Lantau, and Cheung Chau islands, there are **42 gazetted beaches**. "Gazetted" means the beaches are under the care and protection of the Urban Council and have lifeguards and changing facilities, barbeque pits, restaurants and other amenities.

WATER-SKIING

Very popular in summer at the more fashionable beaches. Skis and a boat with driver can be rented for HK$390 per hour from several companies in Deep Water Bay, notably the **Deep Water Bay Speedboat Co.** (tel: 812-0391).

SAILING

Members of yacht clubs with reciprocal privileges can find a crew slot or rent dinghies from the Royal Hong Kong Yacht Club, at Kellett Island (opposite Excelsior Hotel), Causeway Bay, Hong Kong, tel: 832-2817.

SCUBA DIVING

There are interesting scuba sites here, but often the water is less than perfectly clear. Unless you have an "in" to one of the many underwater clubs here, your best bet is to contact **Bunn's Diving Shop**, 188 Wanchai Road, Wanchai, Hong Kong, tel: 891-2113. Note: If you are a British Sub-Aqua Club member, there are more than a half dozen club branches here. Check the club list or write to the headquarters in London for specific addresses in Hong Kong.

WINDSURFING

There are four windsurfing centres here which rent surfboards or give lessons. **Stanley Main Beach**, Hong Kong (call the Pro-shop, 723-6816), **Cheung Chau Island** at Tung Wan Beach, at the **Surf Hotel**, Sha Beach, Sai Kung, and at **Silver Mine Beach**, Lantau Island.

GOLF

The **Royal Hong Kong Golf Club** has three 18-hole courses at Fanling, New Territories (about 70 minutes by train from Kowloon); and a nine-hole course at Deep Water Bay, Hong Kong (between Aberdeen and Repulse Bay, about 20 minutes by cab from Central). Visitors may play these courses on Mondays through Fridays only. Green fees are expensive – HK$850 residents, HK$1,100 visitors per day at Fanling; HK$350 per round at Deep Water Bay. (Phone 670-1211 for Fanling or 812-7070 for Deep Water Bay.)

At the **Discovery Bay Golf Club** on Lantau, easily reached by hoverferry from Blake Pier in Central, the green fees for an 18-hole round will cost non-members HK$700 on weekdays (no visitors are allowed on weekends or public holidays). Club rental is HK$150 and an electric cart HK$180. There are no caddies but hand carts are free. Call 987-7273 for information.

At the **Clearwater Bay Golf & Country Club** in Sai Kung, visitors who do not carry a Hong Kong identity card will be charged HK$1,100 to play 18 holes, HK$850 if you have the requisite ID. Clubs can be rented for HK$100, electric carts for HK$200. Call 719-1595. Note: One way to partake of a lovely day out at the club – which includes tennis, squash, swimming etc. plus a discounted (i.e. HK$600) round of golf – is to sign on for the HKTA's **Sports & Recreation Tour**.

SQUASH

Not yet the vogue in hotels (and a fair hassle for those without an acquaintance in one of the several private clubs). **Victoria Park** in Causeway Bay, Hong Kong, has a handful of public courts open from 7 a.m.–9 p.m. daily. Fee: HK$26–$40 per hour. Booking, however, is often difficult (call 570-6186 after 10 a.m.). Courts are also available at the **Hong Kong Squash Centre** (tel: 521-5072) and **Kowloon Tsai Park** (tel: 336-7878).

TENNIS

Like the problem of booking a squash court, reserving a tennis court is easier said than done. Try **Victoria Park** in Causeway Bay (tel: 570-6186), open from 7 a.m.–11 p.m. The newest courts are on Wongneichung Road en route to Repulse Bay (tel: 574-9122), open 7 a.m.–11 p.m., but **Kowloon Tsai Park** in North Kowloon (tel: 336-7878), open 7 a.m.–11 p.m., also has public courts. The cost for courts ranges from HK$32–$44 per hour depending on the time of the day. Courts are also available at the **Hong Kong Sports Institute** in Shatin (tel: 605-1212).

TABLE-TENNIS (PING PONG)

Ping pong isn't quite up to Mainland "diplomatic" standards, but is very good here nonetheless. There are public tables at **Morse Park Indoor Games Hall** in Hong Kong. Fees are a nominal HK$16 per hour.

BOWLING

There are three modern bowling alleys in Kowloon at the **Brunswick Bowling Centre**, Energy Plaza, Mody Road, Kowloon. The best alleys in Hong Kong are at the **South China Athletic Association** on Caroline Hill Road, Happy Valley.

HIKING

Serious and avid trekkers might want to tackle the 62-mile (100-km) **MacLehose Trail** (named for the former governor, an outdoorsman who was the official impetus behind the establishment of many new parks and trails in Hong Kong) in the New Territories. Though it has been navigated in less than 54 hours, the less energetic can opt to hike any of its 10 segments.

Hong Kong has "protected" some 40 percent of its 412 sq. miles (1,070 sq. km) and calls these countryside areas "**country parks**." Trails have been cut out of the rugged countryside, camping places built, and they are guarded by police patrols. There are a total of 21 such country parks, five on the south side of Hong Kong Island, two on Lantau island, one in Kowloon and the rest in the New Territories.

There is a handy collection of brochures distributed by the Government. However, the bible for anyone who wants to really enjoy the Hong Kong countryside is *Selected Walks in Hong Kong* by Ronald Forrest and George Hobbins, which details more than 75 rural walks. (Note: There are snakes in Hong Kong, so a sturdy walking stick can prove handy.)

JOGGING

A better urban bet than cycling, but still a bit awkward. Runners staying in Tsimshatsui or Causeway Bay can try, respectively, **Kowloon** or **Victoria parks**, neither of them terribly exciting. More expansive, flat, scenic and for most of its length carless is **Bowen Road**, a 5-minute cab ride – or serious climb – above **Central District**. Peak jogging experiences can be enjoyed on **The Peak**'s flat, car-free, 2-mile loop along Harlech and Lugard roads. It is well worth the hardcore ascent/descent efforts required. The Hilton Hotel, Central, offers its visitors an early morning jogging programme, as does the Regent of Hong Kong in Tsimshatsui, Kowloon. Also try the Adventist Hospitals **jogging clinic** each Sunday (tel: 574-6211). The Hash House Harriers are also prevalent.

CYCLING

Traffic, narrow roads and hills make this sport a problematic one, but bicycles can be rented at the less harrowing **Silvermine Bay** on Lantau Island.

ICE SKATING

At **Laichikok Amusement Park** (near the Mei Foo Sun Cheun apartment complex), Kowloon, open daily with varying hours. (Call 741-4281). Travel there by the Mass Transit Railway or bus from the Kowloon Star Ferry. Laichikok is a complete amusement park.

At the ice rink at **Cityplaza**, Taikoo Shing Quarry Bay, Hong Kong, it costs HK$25 weekdays, $35 weekends, including the use of skates for every session, tel: 741-4281. The hours are from 7 a.m.–10 p.m. There are also rinks at the **Riviera Ice Chalet** (Riviera Gardens, Tsuen Wan, New Territories, tel: 415-7888) and **Whampoa Super Ice** (Whampoa Gardens, Hung Hom, Kowloon. tel: 774-4899).

ROLLER SKATING

The charges of rinks at **Cityplaza**, Taikoo Shing, Hong Kong (tel: 567-0391), and **Telford Gardens**, Kowloon (tel: 757-2211), vary with time of day.

HORSEBACK RIDING

Try the **Jockey Club** stables in Pokfulam, Hong Kong (tel: 550-1359), or the **Hong Kong Riding Union** in Shatin (tel: 604-5111), at HK$400 per hour.

SPECTATOR

HORSE RACING

Horse races are Hong Kong's Roman Circus, an orgy of betting for everyone from the day-labourer to the taipan (top executive). Annual meeting dates – some 60 in all, and more than 400 actual races – take place on Wednesday nights, and Saturday and Sunday afternoons, September through May. They alternate weekly between two courses – the urban original course in **Happy Valley**, Hong Kong, and a massively modern facility at **Shatin** in the New Territories. Betting, controlled by the **Royal Hong Kong Jockey Club**, follows standard parimutuel rules and includes both on- and off-course wagering.

Tickets to the exalted **Member's Enclosure** are available at the RHKJC Off-Course Betting Centre, at the Star Ferry (Hong Kong) or the Membership Department Office, RHKJC Building, 12th floor, 2 Sports Road, Happy Valley, Hong Kong (the tall building by the grandstands at the Happy Valley track), two days before a race meeting. (Call 1817 for enquiries.) Guest badges are HK$50 and valid for that day only. Bring your passport to prove you are a visitor. If you miss the above two outlets, apply at either track on the day of the races (from noon for day races; 6 p.m. for night meetings) at the Badge Enquiry Office inside the main entrance to the member's enclosure of either track. At Happy Valley, however, the stands fill up early, so be there an hour early. Special buses and trains run to the more distant Shatin course. For racing information, call 1817.

Tip sheets and racing forms are published for each meeting in the English-language newspapers and are also broadcast on the radio. The HKTA operates a Come Horseracing Tour which includes transfers, meals, guides and entrance to the members' enclosure for HK$350. Call 801-7177 for details.

Special Betting Terms
Quinella: 1st and 2nd in one race.
Double Quinella: Pick one of the first two horses in two specific races.
Six Up: Choosing one of the first two horses in each of the day's six races.
Triple: Pick three winners from three specific races.

RUGBY

League play occurs at various locations, generally during the cooler months. Contact the **Hong Kong Rugby Football Union**, GPO Box 1088, Hong Kong, tel: 566-0719.

FOOTBALL (SOCCER)

Professional and semi-professional matches are held at various stadia in the colony. Check the newspapers' sports sections.

CRICKET

Both the **Hong Kong Cricket Club** and the **Kowloon Cricket Club** host league games on weekends during cooler months.

SPECIAL INFORMATION

DOING BUSINESS

Most foreigners who work here are professionals, "expats" who were hired back home. Menial or temporary jobs are invariably filled by locals for pay per month what most from the West would expect per week. The only real exception are girlie bars, escort services and British-style pubs, where foreign females command a distinct premium and may or may not be on a "work visa."

Teaching languages, though, is one good possibility, particularly for native speakers of English. The commercial language schools and occasional private students advertised in *The South China Morning Post* classifieds are okay for a start, but the first can be depressing and the second few. There are official national programmes conducted by the **British Council**, **Alliance Francaise**, and the **Goethe Institute** (see phone book), but they do not hire visitors. Stopping by to chat with the teachers is a good beginning, but a university degree, prior experience and reasonably long-term plans are essential.

Without solid professional qualifications or an inside track, the only other halfway decent chance are the English-language media. Whether from liberal outlook or desperation, the lower-prestige print and broadcast organizations occasionally give a chance to simple energetic enthusiasm. More than one career has started at The Hong Kong Standard, but nevertheless this is strictly hit or miss; the days are long gone when you could arrive on a tourist visa and start working for a paper the next day. Phoning around to ad agencies will sometimes turn up modelling or soundtrack dubbing assignments.

Except for British (UK) passport-holders, official policy on work permits for foreigners is somewhat exclusionary. Those still overseas with a firm commitment on paper from an established local company will have no problems: any British embassy or consulate will clear a residence visa in a few days. But within the colony on a visitor's pass, it is technically illegal to even seek employment. And unless a prospective employer is willing to go through a lot of bureaucratic hassling, this means having to leave for a week or so to apply for the visa at an embassy elsewhere. Short-timers can and do – illegally, of course – work under-the-table by stretching out a visitor's pass. But they tend to get increasingly hostile questions when applying for extensions.

Those with serious imperial aspirations should contact the **Hong Kong Government Office Recruitment Department**, 6, Grafton Street, London W1X3LB. Official jobs for expatriates run the gamut from police officer to film director, and include anachronistic perks and benefits. Everyone, though, pays salaries tax, up to a maximum of only 15 percent.

LEGAL REQUIREMNTS

If you want to do business here, consider the following basic business procedures:

Registering a **limited company** in Hong Kong requires little paper work and very little money. The standard business **Registration Fee** is HK$730 plus HK$6 for each HK$1,000 of nominal capital. A **name filing fee** costs HK$105 per name (which is reserved for 3 months if acceptable). **Sole proprietorships** cost HK$1,000 (annually) to register and are simpler to set up. (Free brochures are available from government departments involved.)

There are solicitors and accountants here who specialize in such things, but the legal procedure is really quite painless. If you wish, you can register your company at your accountants' or solicitors' office and keep your actual "office" in your briefcase and hotel room. For **limited companies**, contact the **Registrar General's Office**, and for **sole proprietorships**, the **Business Registration Office**. **Factory registration** is handled by the **Labour Department** and **work permits/visas** are the concern of the Immigration Department.

IDENTITY CARDS

In 1980, the Hong Kong government passed legislation requiring everyone to carry a Hong Kong identity card. If you are going to remain here for more than 180 days, you must register for a Hong Kong identity card within 30 days of arrival. Such ID cards are issued by the Immigration. By law, everyone, including visitors, must carry some form of identification and an identity card must be presented before any Government service – business or otherwise – is performed.

If you prefer to keep your passport in the hotel's safe deposit box, some other document with a photo (driver's licence or the like) will suffice. This is especially necessary if you are going out to the New Territories or one of the outlying islands.

TAXES

Limited companies pay **basic taxes** of 16.5 percent. **Property tax** – the English term is rates – comes with your rent and is usually excluded from most rental agreements. (The property rates are set by the government and are periodically updated.) There is a simplified **graduated salaries tax**, with few deductions allowed, but a salaries tax cannot exceed 15 percent of one's total salary. There is no capital gains tax (per se), dividend tax or a tax on income or profits earned overseas or offshore.

REMITTANCES & INVESTMENTS

Hong Kong is a free **money market**. Any amount of any currency can be moved in or out of the colony. There are controls on capital or profit remittances.

SPECIAL ECONOMIC ZONE (SEZ)

Lately, an additional trading venue has been established in a Special Economic Zone on the Chinese side of the Sino-British border at **Shenzhen** (also called Shum Chun) where more than 1,000 co-ventures between Hong Kong and Chinese companies were in full operation at the end of 1982. The Chinese usually supply land, which is scarce and expensive in Hong Kong, and labour, which is cheaper than in Hong Kong, in exchange for modern manufacturing and marketing know-how.

CHILDREN

What about kids who accompany their parents on a trip here?

Ocean Park, and its neighbours, Water World and the Middle Kingdom, are natural attractions for kids who are fed up with flying or hotel rooms or shopping in hot humid weather. The Ocean Park, a combination marineland and amusement park, is on quite a large scale while the Water World, though smaller than those giant parks back home, is still spectacular. And, of course, fun. See "Things to Do" for details of these places as well as other recommended attractions such as Aw Boon Haw Gardens, Sung Dynasty, and Laichikok Amusement Park.

OTHER ACTIVITIES

There are **Chinese shadow-boxing**, or tai chi chuan, demonstrations every morning in the parks (7.30–8.30 a.m. Monday through Saturday) at Chater Gardens and Hong Kong Park, Central, and Victoria Park, Causeway Bay, both in Hong Kong. Also from 7–8 a.m. Monday through Friday at Kowloon Park and King George V Park, Kowloon. The Hong Kong Tourist Association sponsors free **kung fu demonstrations**, **puppet shows**, **acrobats**, **jugglers** at Cityplaza on Hong Kong Island and at the Ocean Terminal and New World Centre in Kowloon. Telephone 801-7177 for the times.

Hong Kong's main zoo is the **Botanical Gardens** in Mid-Levels, across the street from the Governor's mansion. There are more than 300 different kinds of birds, many monkeys, a red panda, even a jaguar.

Horse Riding? Ring the Hong Kong Riding Union in Shatin at 604-5111.

The YMCA on Salisbury Road, Tsimshatsui, Kowloon, has **youth activities** scheduled all year, but especially during the summer. Pop in and see what's going on. You might also want to check the **Girl Guides** (Girl Scouts), the **Brownies** (332-5523), the **Boy Scouts** (367-3096) or the **Outward Bound School** (792-4333) to see what is planned for children.

LANGUAGE

Hong Kong is officially bilingual (English & Cantonese), which means more on paper than it does on a street corner in North Kowloon. Many residents, of course, can hold their own in one or several of the other Chinese dialects. There is no such thing as spoken "Chinese," only various Chinese dialects. The written language is the same for all areas, which means if two Chinese cannot speak to each other, they can write each other a note, even though each character has a different dialectical pronunciation for the same meaning. For most of the population though, English is at best a few numbers, the ubiquitous "hello," "bye-bye" and a few street and place names.

Fortunately for visitors, most of the million or so effective English-speakers are concentrated in and around the downtown business and tourist districts. Even fairly far afield shops and restaurants invariably have a resident linguist able enough to get things done. Often this will be a teenage or younger student, who together with red-badged cops and more fashionable dressers are the most dependable targets for on-the-street queries.

Even gestures, though, usually go a lot farther than phrasebook attempts at Cantonese, universally acknowledged as one of the world's most difficult languages for foreigners. The reason is tones – low, middle and high, and rising neutral and falling, used in every combination – which are both absolutely crucial to meaning and next to imperceptible to unpractised Western ears. As one of literally hundreds of examples, the word "ma" varies according to pronunciation from "rope" to "mother" to "horse" (the written characters, of course, would all be different – and intelligible to any literate Chinese, no matter what his dialect). For those who insist on verbal communication, here is a list of useful phrases.

Greetings:

English	Romanization	Chinese
Hello! (only for answering telephone)	Wai!	喂！
How are you?	Néih hou ma?	你好嗎？
What's your name?	Gwai sing a?	貴姓亞？
Good morning	Jóu Sahn	早晨
Good night	Jóu Táu	早抖
Good-bye	Joi Gin	再見
Thank you (for a service)	M̀gòi	唔該
Thank you (for a gift/dinner)	Dò jeh	多謝
You're welcome/Not at all	Hóu Wah	好話
I'm sorry	Deui M̀juh	對唔住
Can you speak English?	Néih wúih m̀wúih góng yìng màhn?	你會唔會講英文
Yes	Haih	係
	or Hou	好
No	Mhaih	唔係
	or Mhou	唔好

Orientation Directions:

English	Romanization	Chinese
Hong Kong	Hèung góng	香港
Kowloon	Gáu lùhng	九龍
The New Territories	Sàn gaai	新界
The Peak	Sàan déng	山頂
How far is A from B?	A lèih B géi yúhn?	距離幾遠？
Where?	Bīn-douh?	邊度？
How long does it take?	Yiu géi nói?	要幾耐？

Commerce:

English	Romanization	Chinese
How many?/How much?	Géi dō?	幾多？
How much is it?	Géi dō chín?	幾多錢
Dollar $	Mān	文
One dollar	Yāt mān	一文
Ten dollars	Sahp mān	十文

Transport:

English	Romanization	Chinese
Bus	Bā-sí	巴士
Peak Tram	Laahm chè	纜車
Tram	Dihn chè	電車
Mini-bus	Síu Bā	小巴
Plane	Fèi gèi	飛機
Taxi	Dīk-sí	的士
Mass Transit Railway (MTR)	Deih hah tit-louh	地下鐵路
Train station	Fó-chè jaahn	火車站
Pier	Máh-tàuh	碼頭
Airport	Fèi gèi chèuhng	飛機場
Cross-harbor tunnel	Hói dái seuih douh	海底隧道

Etceteras:

English	Romanization	Chinese
May I ask	Chéng mahn	請問
Bring me the menu please.	Chāan Páai M̀gòi	菜牌唔該
I'd like to drink "Jasmine" tea.	Ngóh yám hèung pín chàh	我飲香片茶
To drink	Yám	飲
To eat	Sihk	食
Tea	Chàh	茶
Report to the police.	Bou gíng	報警
What time is it?	Géi dím jūng?	幾點鐘
o'clock	Dím jūng	點鐘
3 o'clock	Sàam dím-jūng	三點鐘
Minute	Fàn	分

Numbers: In Cantonese, counting is based on the pattern of numbers from "one" to "ten." The following is a list of basic numbers and their pronunciation in Cantonese. *

1	Yāt	一	20	Yih-sahp	二十
2	Yih	二	30	Sàam-sahp	三十
3	Sàam	三	40	Sei-sahp	四十
4	Sei	四	50	Ńgh-sahp	五十
5	Ńgh	五	60	Luhk-sahp	六十
6	Luhk	六	70	Chát-sahp	七十
7	Chát	七	80	Baat-sahp	八十
8	Baat	八	90	Gáu-sahp	九十
9	Gáu	九	99	Gáu-sahp Gáu	九十九
10	Sahp	十	100	Yāt-baak	一百
11	Sahp-yāt	十一	1,000	Yāt-chihn	一千
			10,000	Yāt-mahn	一萬

* The romanization system used here is the Yale System.

USEFUL ADDRESSES

TOURIST INFORMATION

HONG KONG TOURIST ASSOCIATION (HKTA)

This is a bubbling fount of information – verbally or in the form of numerous brochures advising about everything from eating and shopping to hiking and horseraces. Frontline HKTA (Hong Kong Tourist Association) staff seem genuinely interested in helping visitors.

For brochures, maps or basic questions and answers, as well as souvenirs and gifts, the HKTA has walk-in Information & Gift Centres at Kai Tak Airport (just outside customs) at the Kowloon Star Ferry Concourse (8 a.m.–6 p.m. weekdays; and 9 a.m.–5 p.m weekends), Jardine House basement (9 a.m.–6 p.m; Saturdays till 1 p.m.) on Hong Kong Island. The centre at the airport stays open from 8 a.m.–10.30 p.m. daily.

For elusive addresses, lost directions and train or ferry schedules, there is also a telephone enquiries service: 801-7177 (from 8 a.m.–6 p.m. weekdays; 9 a.m.–5 p.m. weekends.) For serious queries or shopping complaints, the best bet is to contact HKTA Headquarters on the 35th floor of Jardine House.

The HKTA Official Hong Kong Guide (updated monthly) is a good information source. Many hotels also offer this book free with their own name and logo printed on the cover, as does the HKTA.

Overseas, the HKTA maintains offices in Chicago, Frankfurt, London, New York, Osaka, Paris, Rome, Singapore, Sydney, Barcelona, Los Angeles, Toronto, Auckland and Tokyo, and in all Cathay Pacific Airways offices.

EMBASSIES & CONSULAR SERVICES

Aside from complaints regarding lost passports, vanished funds and assorted legal troubles, foreign embassies also provide the only authoritative advice on what you can buy and how much you can take back home. They can advise you about duties, tariffs and how much that "bargain" jade necklace you covet is likely to cost.

These embassies are also the all-important dispensers of visas, a bureaucratic shoal on which more than one unplanned trip has foundered. Those travelling in Asia will do well to utilize efficient and business-like Hong Kong for setting passport matters in order.

Because Hong Kong is a colony, not a country, demanding to speak to the "ambassador" will require a phone call to another country. However, the consulates and, for British Commonwealth countries, commissions can handle most problems raised by travellers.

The only exception to the above is the British. Because this is their colony, there is no Britannic diplomatic mission as such. Holders of United Kingdom passports, or those planning to visit England or any British possession or Commonwealth country not represented here, should refer visa and other travel queries to the **Overseas Visa Section** of the **Hong Kong Immigration Department**.

OTHER INFORMATION SOURCES

Other sources of information on Hong Kong are the **Government Publications Centre** in the General Post Office Building, Hong Kong Island (9 a.m.–6 p.m., Saturdays till 1 p.m.) and the **Urban Council Publication Centre** in Club Lusitano, Ice House Street, Central, Hong Kong (9 a.m.–5.30 p.m., Saturdays till 12.30 p.m.)

Other information lodes are the **Community Advice Bureau** (St John's Cathedral, Garden Road, Central, Hong Kong, tel: 524-5444). This association is normally for residents, but they will assist if they can. Also try the **Trade Development Council** (38th floor, Office Tower, Convention Plaza, 1 Harbour Road, Hong Kong, tel: 584-4333), used mainly by businessmen, but helpful.

For serious problems that may require a friend

No-one appreciates the special needs of business travellers more than Thai. We were, after all, the first Asian airline to offer a business class.

Thai's Royal Executive Class fulfils every wish of the business traveller. From bigger, wider seats to more leg room between your seat and the one in front.

This extra room gives you generous space to wo[...] or relax. And, of course, Thai's fabled inflight servi[...] is always at your beck and call.

Our Royal Executive Class passengers savo[...]

cially selected champagnes and vintage wines from rkling crystal. Meals are served from fine china on p table linen.

Speedy check-ins at special Royal Executive ss counters together with lounge facilities at most airports are yours for just a small premium over the full economy fare.

Where business takes you, Thai probably can too. In fact, for business travel that's smooth as silk, it's really an open and shut case.

TH

as silk

rather than a police officer, call the **Samaritans** at 834-3333. They speak English and answer phone calls 24 hours a day.

The **Alcoholics Anonymous** branch in Hong Kong can be reached at 522-5665. If you are a serviceman, the **Sailors and Soldiers Home** is on the 3rd floor, 22 Hennessy Road, Wanchai, Hong Kong.

For time and temperature dial 18501. The **Consumer Council** (tel: 736-3636) may be of help in altercations with shopkeepers. Assistance also may be sought from the **Legal Aid Department** (tel: 867-3030).

AIRLINES

Aer Lingus, see Jardine Airways.

Aeroflot, see Global.

Aerolineas Argentina, G/F, 34A-37A Hyatt Regency, 20 Lock Road, Kowloon, tel: 369-2288.

Air Canada, 1026 Prince's Bldg, Hong Kong, tel: 522-1001.

Air France, 21st floor, Alexandra House, Hong Kong, tel: 524-8145.

Air India, 42nd Floor, Gloucester Tower, Hong Kong, tel: 522-1176.

Air Lanka, 602 Lippo Centre, Central, tel: 521-0708.

Air Malawi, see Jardine Airways.

Air Mauritius, 1512 Melbourne Plaza, 30 Queen's Road Central, Hong Kong, tel; 523-1114.

Air New Zealand, 902 Exchange Square Tower 3, Central, tel: 524-9041.

Air Niugini, Room 705, Century Square, 1 D'Aguilar Street, Hong Kong, tel: 524-2151.

Air Seychelles, see Union Express.

Air UK, see Union Express.

Alia, 1603 Fleet House, 38 Gloucester Road, Hong Kong, tel: 861-1811.

Alitalia, 2101 Hutchison House, Central, Hong Kong, tel: 523-7047.

All Nippon Airways, Room 2512, Pacific Place, 88 Queensway, Hong Kong, tel: 810-7100.

American, 3701 Edinburgh Tower, 18 Queen's Road, Hong Kong, tel: 826-9269.

Ansett, see Qantas.

Asiana, 34th floor, Gloucester Tower, Pedder Street, Hong Kong, tel: 523-8585.

Australian, see Jardine Airways.

Avianca, Asian Transportation Ltd, 1/f First Pacific Bank Centre, 51-57 Gloucester Road, Wanchai, tel: 529-2208.

Biman Bangladesh, 207 Houston Centre, 63 Mody Road, Kowloon, tel: 721-5393.

British Airways, see Jardine Airways.

China National Aviation Corporation, 34th floor, United Centre, 85 Queensway and 17 Queen's Road, Hong Kong; 4 Ashley Road, Kowloon, tel: 861-0322.

Canadian, 1738 Swire House, Hong Kong, tel: 868-3123.

Cathay Pacific Airways, Grd floor, Swire House,

Hong Kong; Royal Garden Hotel and Ocean Centre, Kowloon, tel:747-1888.

City Check: Pacific Place, 88 Queensway, Hong Kong, tel: 747-1788; and China Hong Kong City, 33 Canton Road, Kowloon, tel: 747-1688. (Complete downtown check-ins, including luggage, 8 a.m.–8 p.m.)

Ceskoslovenske, see Global.

China Airlines, St George's Bldg, Hong Kong; Tsimshatsui Centre, Kowloon, tel: 868-2299.

Cubana de Aviacon, see Jardine Airways.

Cyprus Airways, see Jardine Airways.

Delta, Rm 2915, 2 Pacific Place, Central, tel: 526-5875.

Dragon Air, 12th floor, Tower 6, China Hong Kong City, 33 Canton Road, Kowloon, tel: 590-1188.

Federal Express, 221 Cargo Complex Building, Kai Tak Airport, Kowloon, tel: 730-3333.

Finnair, 8th floor, Pedder Bldg, Pedder Street, Hong Kong, tel: 521-5175.

Garuda, 2/A, Sing Po Centre, 8 Queen's Road Central, Hong Kong, tel: 840-0000.

Gibraltar Airways, see Jardine Airways.

Global, 96 New Henry House, 10 Ice House Street, Hong Kong, tel: 845-4232.

Hawaiian Air, M1 New Henry House, 10 Ice House Street, Central, Hong Kong, tel: 523-3550.

Iberia, 19th floor, Room B, Chung Hing Commercial Bldg, 62–63 Connaught Road, Central, Hong Kong, tel: 542-3228.

Icelandair, see Union Express.

Jardine Airways, 13/f Alexandra House, Hong Kong; 112 Royal Garden Hotel, Kowloon. Flight Information: 868-0768. Reservations: 868-0303. Check-in from 3.30 p.m.

Japan Air Lines/Japan Asia Airways, 20/f Gloucester Tower, Hong Kong; Harbour View Holiday Inn Lobby, Kowloon, tel: 523-0081, 521-8102.

Kenya, see Jardine Airways.

KLM, Room 701, Jardine House, Connaught Place, Hong Kong, tel: 822-8111.

Korean Air, St George's Bldg, Hong Kong; Tsimshatsui Centre, Kowloon, tel: 368-6221.

Lanchile, see Union Express.

Lauda Air, M1, New Henry House, 10 Ice House Street, Hong Kong, tel: 524-6178.

Libyan Arab Airlines, see Jardine Airways.

Lot, see Global.

Lufthansa German Airlines, 6th floor, Landmark East, Hong Kong; Empire Centre, Tsimshatsui East, Kowloon, tel: 868-2313.

Luxavia, see Union Express.

Malaysian Airline System, 1306, Prince's Bldg., Hong Kong, tel: 521-8181.

Mexicana Airlines, see Union Express.

Northwest Airlines, St George's Bldg, Hong Kong, tel: 810-4288.

PIA, 401A Empire Centre, Mody Road Kowloon, tel: 366-4770.

Philippine Airlines, 305 East Ocean Centre,

Tsimshatsui East, and 98 Granville Road, Kowloon, tel: 369-4521.

Qantas Airways, 14/f Swire House, Hong Kong, Kowloon, tel: 524-2101.

Royal Brunei Airlines, see Cathay Pacific.

Royal Nepal, 704 Sun Plaza, 28 Canton Road, Kowloon, tel: 369-9151.

Sabena, see Union Express.

SAS, 20th floor, Wilson House, 19 Wyndham Street, Hong Kong, tel: 526-5978.

Saudi, Rm 2802A, Lippo Tower, Lippo Centre, 89 Queensway, Hong Kong, tel: 522-8439.

Singapore Airlines, 17/F United Centre, Hong Kong; Wing On Plaza, Tsimshatsui East, Kowloon, tel: 520-1313.

South African Airways, see Jardine Airways.

Swissair, Tower 2, 8th floor, Admiralty Centre, Hong Kong, tel: 529-3670.

Thai International, Shop 122, Worldwide Plaza, Hong Kong; Hong Kong Hotel Arcade, Kowloon, tel: 529-5601.

Trans Australia, see Cathay Pacific.

TWA, Mezzanine Floor, Sun House, 90 Cannaught Road, Central, tel: 523-6181.

United, 29th floor, Gloucester Tower, Pedder Street, Hong Kong, tel: 810-4888. (Early check-in. Seating/boarding pass only.)

Varig, 2106 Lippo Centre, West Tower, Queensway, Hong Kong, tel: 526-0213.

Vasp Brazilian Airlines, 902 Tung Ming Bldg, 40 Des Voeux Road, Central, Hong Kong, tel: 525-1365.

Union Express, 16/f Heng Shan Centre, 145 Queen's Road East, Hong Kong, tel: 866-8826.

MAIN BUILDINGS IN HONG KONG

AIA Building, 1 Stubbs Road, Happy Valley.

Admiralty Centre, 18 Harcourt Road, Central.

Alexandra House, 11 Des Voeux Road, Central.

Alliance Building, 130–136 Connaught Road, Central.

Asian House, 1 Hennessy Road, Wanchai.

Bank of America Tower, 12 Harcourt Road, Central.

Bank of Canton Building, 6 Des Voeux Road.

Bank of China Building, Des Voeux Central.

Bank of China Tower, 1 Garden Road.

Baskerville House, 13 Duddell Street, Central.

Beaconsfield House, 4 Queen's Road, Central.

Belgian House, 77–79 Gloucester Road, Wanchai.

Capitol Centre, 5–19 Jardines Bazaar, Causeway Bay.

Causeway Centre, 28 Harbour Road, Wanchai.

Caxton House, 54–56 Queen's Road, Central.

Central Building, 3 Pedder Street, Central.

Central Plaza, 18 Harbour Road.

Centrepoint Building, 181–185 Gloucester Road, Wanchai.

Century Square, 1 D'Aguilar Street.

Chartered Bank Building, 3 Queen's Road, Central.

China Building, 29 Queen's Road, Central.

China Resources Building, 26 Harbour Road, Wanchai.

Chinese General Chamber of Commerce Building, 24–26 Connaught Road, Central.

City Hall, Edinburgh Place, Central.

Cityplaza, Taikoo Shing, King's Road, North Point.

Citibank Plaza, Garden Road.

Club Lusitano Building, 16 Ice House Street, Central.

Dina House SA, Duddell Street, Central.

East Point Building, 92 Gloucester Road, Wanchai.

Edinburgh Tower, 18 Queen's Road.

Elizabeth House, 250 Gloucester Road.

Exchange Square, 8 Connaught Place.

Eurotrade Centre, Des Voeux Road.

Fairmount House, Murray Road, Central.

Far East Finance Building, Harcourt Road, Central.

Fleet House, 6 Arsenal Street, Hong Kong.

Fu House, 7 Ice House Street.

Fung House, 19–21 Connaught Road.

General Post Office, Connaught Place.

Gloucester Tower, 11 Pedder Street.

Great Eagle Centre, 23 Harbour Road.

Hang Lung Bank Building, 8 Hysan Avenue, Causeway Bay.

Hang Lung Centre, 2-20 Paterson Street, Causeway Bay.

Hang Seng Bank Building, Des Voeux Road, Causeway Bay.

Harbour Centre, 25 Harbour Road.

Harbour View Mansions, 257 Gloucester Road, Causeway Bay.

Harcourt House, 39 Gloucester Road.

Hennessy Centre, 500 Hennessy Road.

Hongkong and Shanghai Bank Building, 1 Queen's Road, Central.

Hong Kong Convention and Exhibition Centre, 1 Harbour Road.

Hong Kong Diamond Exchange Centre, Ice House Street, Central.

Hong Kong Exhibition Centre, 26 Harbour Road, Wanchai.

Hopewell Centre, 183 Queen's Road, East.

Hutchison House, 10 Harcourt Road, Central.

International Building, 139–141 Des Voeux Road, Central.

Jardine House, 1 Connaught Place.

Korea Centre, 119 Connaught Road, Central.

Landmark, 11 Pedder Street, Central.

Lane Crawford House, 70 Queen's Road, Central.

Lippo Centre, 89 Queensway.

Liu Chong Hing Building, 24 Des Voeux Road, Central.

Luk Kwok Centre, 72 Gloucester Road.

Melbourne Plaza, 33 Queen's Road, Central.

Mercantile Bank Building, 7 Queen's Road, Central.

New World Tower, Queen's Road, Central.

Overseas Trust Bank Building, 160 Gloucester Road, Wanchai.

Pacific House, 16 Queen's Road, Central.

Pacific Place, 88 Queensway.
Paterson Plaza, 22–36 Paterson Street, Causeway Bay.
Pedder Building, 12 Pedder Street.
Peter Building, 58 Queen's Road, Central.
Prince's Building, 5 Ice House Street, Central.
Printing House, 6 Duddell Street, Central.
Queen's Building, 74 Queen's Road, Central.
Realty Building, 67–73 Des Voeux Road, Central.
Royal Hong Kong Jockey Club, 2 Sports Road, Happy Valley.
St George's Building, 2 Ice House Street, Central.
Shell House, 24 Queen's Road, Central.
Seaview Estate, Watson's Road, North Point.
Shui On Building, 6 Harbour Road.
Solar House, 28 Des Voeux Road, Central.
Sun Hung Kai Centre, 30 Harbour Road, Wanchai.
Swire House, 9 Connaught Road, Central.
Tak Shing House, 20 Des Voeux Road, Central.
Telecom House, 3 Gloucester Road.
United Centre, 95 Queensway, Central.
Wheelock House, Pedder Street, Central.
Wilson House, 19 Wyndham Street.
Windsor House, 311 Gloucester Road, Causeway Bay.
Wing On Centre, 122 Connaught Road, Central.
World-Wide Plaza, Des Voeux Road, Central.
Yu Yuet Lai Building, 53 Wyndham Street.

MAIN BUILDINGS IN KOWLOON

Bank of America Building, 1 Kowloon Park Drive, Tsimshatsui.
China Hong Kong City, 38 Canton Road.
Chungking Mansions, 36–44 Nathan Road, Tsimshatsui.
Eldex Industrial Building, 21 Matauwei Road, Tokwawan.
Empire Centre, Mody Road, Tsimshatsui East.
Hankow Centre, 5–15 Hankow Road, Tsimshatsui.
Harbour City, 11 Canton Road, Tsimshatsui.
Houston Centre, Mody Road, Tsimshatsui East.
Jordan House, 6–8 Jordan Road.
Kowloon Centre, 29 Ashley Road.
Mirror Tower, Mody Road, Tsimshatsui East.
New World Centre, Salisbury Road, Tsimshatsui.
Ocean Centre, 5 Canton Road, Tsimshatsui.
Ocean Terminal, Tsimshatsui.
Silvercord, Canton Road, Tsimshatsui.
South Seas Centre, Mody Road, Tsimshatsui.
Star House, 3 Salisbury Road, Tsimshatsui.
Tsimshatsui Centre, Mody Road, Tsimshatsui East.
Wing On Plaza, Mody Road, Tsimshatsui East.

BUREAUCRACIES

American Chamber of Commerce, 1030 Swire House, Central District, Hong Kong, tel: 526-0165. Hours: 9 a.m.–12.30 p.m. and 2–5 p.m. weekdays, and until 12.30 p.m. Saturday.
Companies Registry, 13–14th floors, Queensway

Government Office Bldg, 66 Queensway, Hong Kong, tel: 867-2604. Hours: 9 a.m.–1 p.m. and 2–5 p.m. weekdays, and until 1 p.m. Saturday.
General Chamber of Commerce, 22nd floor, 95 Queensway, Hong Kong, tel: 529-9229. Hours: 9 a.m.–1 p.m. and 2–5 p.m. weekdays, and until 1 p.m. Saturday.
Immigration Department, Immigration Tower, 7 Gloucester Road, Hong Kong, tel: 824-6111. Hours: 9 a.m.–5 p.m. weekdays, and until 12.30 p.m. Saturday.
Inland Revenue Department, Windsor House, 311 Gloucester Road, Causeway Bay, Hong Kong, tel: 894-5098. Hours: 8.30 a.m.–12.30 p.m. and 1.30–5 p.m. weekdays, and 9 a.m.–noon Saturday.
H.K. Trade Development Council, 38th floor, Office Tower, 1 Harbour Road, Hong Kong, tel: 833-4333. Hours: 8.30 a.m.–5 p.m. weekdays, and till 12.30 p.m. Saturday.

SPECIAL CLUBS

Hong Kong has a full complement of societies and clubs that specialize in everything from birdwatching to archaeology. Not many unofficial visitors drop in on these special interest groups, but they are very hospitable to those who do. (For information regarding service clubs such as Rotary, Lions, Kiwanis, etc., check with your hotel for the nearest chapter's address.) Among local clubs and societies are:

Aviation Club, Sung Wong Toi Road, Kai Tak Airport, Kowloon, tel: 713-5171.
Archaeological Society, c/o Museum of History, 58 Haiphong Road, Tsimshatsui, Kowloon, tel: 723-5765.
Royal Asiatic Society, GPO Box 3864, Hong Kong, tel: 551-0300.
Bird Watching Society, c/o GPO Box 12460, Hong Kong, tel: 524-9938.
Ceramic Society, GPO Box 6202, Hong Kong, tel: 528-5483.
Chess Federation, 1202 Luk Hoi Tung Bldg, Hong Kong, tel: 522-6081.
Contract Bridge Association, GPO Box 1445, Hong Kong, tel: 641-3666.
Foreign Correspondents Club, 2 Lower Albert Road, Hong Kong, tel: 521-1511.
Darts Association, GPO Box 11501, Hong Kong, tel: 574-2622.
Ikebana International, GPO Box 3029, Hong Kong, tel: 491-1261.
Mountaineering Union, Kowloon GPO Box 70837, Hong Kong, tel: 384-8190.
Orchid Association, GPO Box 9039, Hong Kong, tel: 895-4888.
Press Club, 3rd floor, Capital Bldg, 175 Lockhart Road, Wanchai, Hong Kong, tel: 742-247.

CONSULATES

Antigua & Barbuda: 521A Star House, 3 Salisbury Road, Kowloon, tel: 736-8033.

Argentina: 2510 Jardine House, Connaught Place, Hong Kong, tel: 523-3208.

Australia: 23rd–24th floors, Harbour Centre, 25 Harbour Road, Wanchai, tel: 827-8881.

Austria: Room 2201, Wang Kee Bldg, 34–37 Connaught Road, Central, tel: 522-8086.

Bangladesh: 3807 China Resources Bldg, 26 Harbour Road, tel: 827-4278.

Barbados: 21/f China Building, Central, tel: 526-6911.

Belgium: 9th floor, St John's Bldg, 33 Garden Road, tel: 524-3111.

Belize: 1602 West Tower, Lippo Centre, 89 Queensway, Hong Kong, tel: 521-6063.

Bhutan: Unit B, 1st floor, Kowloon Centre, 29–43 Ashley Road, tel: 376-2112.

Botswana: 4/f Dina House, Ruttonjee Centre, 11 Duddell Street, Central

Brazil: 1504 Dina House, 11 Duddell Street, Hong Kong, tel: 525-7002.

Britain: c/o HK Immigration, Wanchai Tower II, 7 Gloucester Road, Hong Kong, tel: 824-6111.

Burma: See Myanmar.

Canada: One Exchange Square, 11–12/f, Hong Kong, tel: 810-4321.

Chile: 1408 Great Eagle Centre, 23 Harbour Road, Hong Kong, tel: 827-1826.

China (People's Republic of): c/o Ministry of Foreign Affairs, China Resources Bldg, Lower Block, 5/f, 26 Harbour Road, Hong Kong, tel: 585-1700.

Colombia: 6th floor, Unit A, C.M.A. Bldg, 64–66, Connaught Road, Central, tel: 545-8547.

Costa Rica: Flat C-10, Hung On Bldg, 3 Tin Hau Temple Road, tel: 566-5181.

Cote d'Ivoire: 1502 Loong San Bldg, 140 Connaught Road Central, Hong Kong, tel: 522-7460.

Cuba: Flat B, 25th floor, Bellevue Heights, 8 Tai Hang Drive, Hong Kong.

Cyprus: Rm 703, 1 Pacific Place, 88 Queensway, Hong Kong, tel: 820-1100.

Denmark: Suite 2402B Great Eagle Centre, 23 Harbour Road, Wanchai, tel: 827-8101.

Dominican Republic: 706, 59 Queen's Road Central, Hong Kong, tel: 521-2801.

Egypt: Rm 1309, Great Eagle Centre, 23 Harbour Road, Wanchai, tel: 827-0668.

Eire: 23rd floor, Standard Chartered Bank, 4 Des Voeux Road Central, Hong Kong, tel: 821-1212.

El Salvador: 4th floor, Lyton Bldg, 46 Mody Road, Kowloon, tel: 723-2986.

Finland: 1818 Hutchison House, Central, tel: 525-5385.

France: 26th floor, Admiralty Centre, Tower 11, 18 Harcourt Road, tel: 529-4351.

Gabon: P.O. Box 47103, Morrison Hill Post Office, Hong Kong, tel: 572-4062.

Germany: 21st floor, United Centre, 95 Queensway, tel: 529-8855.

Greece: 914 Tower B, Hung Hom Commercial Centre, 37 Ma Tau Wai Road, Kowloon, tel: 774-1682.

Grenada: 4D, 11/f Waterloo Hill, 3 Hok Yu Lane, Kowloon, tel: 762-2972.

Guinea: 4/f, Block E, 702 Castle Peak Road, Hop Hing Industrial Bldg, Kowloon, tel: 744-5211.

Honduras: 1303 Pacific House, 20 Queen's Road Central, Hong Kong, tel: 522-6593.

Iceland: 48th floor, Hopewell Centre, 183 Queen's Road East, tel: 528-3911.

India: 16th floor, Unit D, United Centre, 95 Queensway, tel: 527-5821.

Indonesia: 6–8 Keswick Street, Causeway Bay, tel: 890-4421.

Ireland: See Eire.

Israel: Room 701, Tower Two, Admiralty Centre, Queensway, Hong Kong, tel: 529-6091.

Italy: 805 Hutchison House, Central, tel: 522-0033.

Jamaica: 18th floor, Shanghai Industrial Investment Bldg, 48 Hennessy Road, Hong Kong, tel: 823-8238.

Japan: 25th floor, Bank of America Tower, Central, tel: 522-1184.

Jordan: 1433A Star House, 3 Salisbury Road, Kowloon, tel: 735-6399.

Korea (Republic of): Far East Finance Centre, 5–6/f, 16 Harcourt Road, Hong Kong, tel: 529-4141.

Liberia: 1507, 15th floor, Pacific Place, 88 Queensway, hong Kong, tel: 845-4161.

Luxembourg: Ground Floor, 5 Queen's Road Central, Hong Kong, tel: 877-1018.

Malaysia: 24th floor, Malaysia Bldg, 47–50 Gloucester Road, Wanchai, tel: 527-0921.

Maldives: Rm 211 Kowloon Centre, 29-43 Ashley Road, tel: 367-2114.

Malta: 302 East Ocean Centre, 98 Granville Road, Kowloon, tel: 739-1515.

Mauritius: 4th floor, Wing On Plaza, 62 Mody Road, Kowloon, tel: 731-1615.

Mexico: Room 1809 World-Wide House, 19 Des Voeux Road, Central, tel: 521-4365.

Monaco: 33rd floor, Harbour Centre, 25 Harbour Road, Wanchai, tel: 893-0669.

Morocco: Marine Deck Compartment W1, Ocean Terminal, Kowloon, tel: 736-7286.

Mozambique: 15th floor, World Commercial Centre, 11 Canton Road, Kowloon, tel: 738-4400.

Myanmar: 2421 Sun Hung Kai Centre, 30 Harbour Road, Hong Kong, tel: 827-7929.

Nepal: 14th floor, Liaison Office, Headquarters, Brigade of Gurkhas, H.M.S. Tamar, Central, tel: 588-3253 (10 a.m.–noon, weekdays).

Netherlands: 3/f, China Bldg, 29 Queen's Road Central, Hong Kong, tel: 522-5127.

New Zealand: 3414 Jardine House, Connaught Place, Hong Kong, tel: 525-5044.

Nicaragua: 2/f 51 Nga Tsin Wai Road, Kowloon Tong, tel: 827-8813.

Nigeria: 3309 China Resources Bldg., 26 Harbour Road, Wanchai, tel: 827-8813.

Norway: 1401 AIA Bldg, 1 Stubbs Road, Happy Valley, tel: 873-0888.

Oman: 19th floor, Gee Cheng Hong Centre, 65 Wong Chuk Hang Road, Hong Kong, tel: 873-0888.

Pakistan: 3806 China Resources Bldg, 26 Harbour Road, Hong Kong, tel: 827-1966.

Panama: 1008 Wing On Centre, 111 Connaught Road, Central, tel: 545-2166.

Paraguay: 1207 East Point Centre, 555 Hennessy Road, Hong Kong, tel: 833-6887.

Peru: 10th floor, Wong Chung Ming Commercial House, 16 Wyndham Street, Hong Kong, tel: 868-2622.

Philippines: 21st floor, Regent Centre, 88 Queen's Road Central, Hong Kong, tel: 810-0183.

Poland: Rm 1006 1 Pacific Place, 88 Queensway, tel: 840-0779.

Portugal: 1001–1002, Two Exchange Square, 8 Connaught Place, Central, tel: 523-1338.

Seychelles: Rm 3703 Hong Kong Plaza, 181-191 Connaught Road West, Hong Kong, tel: 549-5337.

Sierra Leone: 1403 Luk Kwok Centre, 72 Gloucester Road, Hong Kong, tel: 834-6961.

Singapore: Unit 901, Admiralty Centre Tower 1, 18 Harcourt Road, Hong Kong, tel: 527-2212.

South Africa: 27th floor, Sunning Plaza, 10 Hysan Avenue, Causeway Bay, tel: 577-3279.

Spain: 8/f Printing House, 18 Ice House Street, Hong Kong, tel: 525-3041.

Sri Lanka: 8/f, Loke Yew Bldg, 50–52 Queen's Road Central, Hong Kong, tel: 523-8810.

St Lucia: 7th floor, Loke Yew Bldg, 50 Queen's Road Central, Hong Kong, tel: 524-5898.

Sweden: 8th floor, The Hong Kong Club Bldg, 3 Chater Road, Central, tel: 521-1212.

Switzerland: 3703 Gloucester Tower, 11 Pedder Street, tel: 522-7147.

Taiwan (Republic of China): c/o Chung Hwa Travel Agency, 4/f Bond Centre, Queensway, Hong Kong, tel: 525-8315.

Thailand: 8/f, Fairmont House, 8 Cotton Tree Drive, Hong Kong, tel: 521-6481.

Togo: 7th floor, Wah Shun Industrial Centre, 4 Cho Yuen Street, Kowloon, tel: 340-0285.

Tonga: 8th floor, Room 84, New Henry House, 10 Ice House Street, Central, tel: 522-1321.

Trinidad & Tobago: 2103 Hollywood Plaza, 610 Nathan Road, Kowloon, tel: 756-8893.

Turkey: 1507 Tower 2, Admiralty Centre, 18 Harcourt Road, Hong Kong, tel: 527-9556.

Tuvalu: M1, 13th floor, Hing Wah Mansion, 1 Babington Path, Hong Kong, tel: 549-4085.

United States of America: 26 Garden Road, Central, tel: 523-9011.

Uruguay: Suite 501, 5/f, Crocodile House, 50 Queen's Road Central, Hong Kong, tel: 544-0066.

Venezuela: D2-J Star House, Kowloon, tel: 730-8099.

Western Samoa: Rm 1301, 1 Pacific Place, 88 Queensway, Hong Kong, tel: 521-5621.

OTHER INSIGHT GUIDES

Other *Insight Guides* which help to make your visit an unforgettable one:

A great, ancient culture comes alive in the pages of *Insight Guide: China*

Isle Formosa – The Beautiful Island – vividly described in *Insight Guide: Taiwan*

Insight Cityguide: Beijing: The Forbidden City beckons....

GETTING THERE

BY SEA

You will not believe the number of ways you can get from Hong Kong to Macau by sea. You could spend a little less than an hour crossing that 40-mile (64-km) stretch of the Pearl River Estuary on a jetfoil or hoverferry, 70 minutes on a jetcat, and, 90–100 minutes on a high-speed ferry.

With all that sea transportation, you would reckon there would always be empty seats. Well, the old timers will tell you how drastically things have improved, but somehow Macau's 6 million visitors per year usually manage to occupy every seat, especially on weekends and public holidays. However, with the advent of computerized ticketing, there are less "full boats" sailing with empty seats. Another innovation which veteran Asia hands just love is the night jetfoil service. This means Hongkongians can whip over after work for a Macanese meal washed down by an inexpensive bottle of Portuguese wine (it is the cheapest vinho in all of Asia, including Australia) and return the same night.

Regardless of when you go, make certain you have your return tickets in your possession before you go. Just about all the Macau ferry sailings use the Macau Ferry Terminal in the Shun Tak Centre, 200 Connaught Road, Central, Hong Kong (the MTR stop is Sheung Wan), with the exception of the hoverferries and a limited number of other services which sail regularly from the China Ferry Pier at China Hong Kong City, 33 Canton Road, Tsimshatsui, Kowloon Pier.

Note: Baggage on the "foils" and "cats" is limited to 20 lbs (9 kg) – but there is no real "check-in" in an airline sense. The main problem is not weight, but space. There just is not much room for large suitcases.

Tax: Add a HK$26 tax to all outward ferry fares and 20 patacas for return fares.

JETFOILS

Jetfoils carry 260 people in two classes and leave either destination for the 55-minute journey at half-hourly intervals from 6 a.m. till 5 p.m. in the winter, 6 p.m. in summer, when the night jet-foils take over till 3 a.m. Upper-deck, first class fares (same airplane seats as lower deck passengers, but free coffee and newspapers, slightly better service, and first crack at exiting upon arrival) are HK$100 on weekdays, daylight sailings; HK$108 on weekends and all public holidays, daylight hours; and HK$132 for the night service, any day. Lower deck economy fares are HK$85 for a weekday, daylight trip; HK$93 on weekends and all public holidays, daylight hours; and HK$112 for all night sailings. Most departures are made from Hong Kong, three from Kowloon. Call 859-3333.

Computer Booking Service: There is a computer booking service for the jetfoils called Ticketmate with 11 outlets in Hong Kong (many of which are in the major Mass Transit Railway stations) and three in Macau where you can buy a passage up to 28 days in advance. Holders of American Express, MasterCard, Visa or Diners Club credit cards can book by phone up to 28 days in advance by dialling 859-6596 in Hong Kong. (The service is not offered in Macau.)

JUMBOCATS/JETCATS

These one-class, jet-propelled catamaran ferries carry up to 215 and 306 people respectively for their 60- and 70-minute trips (daylight hours only). Jetcat fares are HK$70 one-way on weekdays, HK$78 on weekends. For Jumbocats the fares are HK$80 and HK$88 respectively. For telephone bookings and information, call 523-2136. No credit card bookings. Departures from Hong Kong.

Jetcats also sail five times daily (daylight hours only) to the Special Economic Zone of Zhuhai, an oil exploration port, which is only 30 minutes away by road from Macau. One-way fares for the 75-minute trip are HK$105 weekdays, HK$115 weekends and public holidays. Departures are from Kowloon.

HIGH-SPEED FERRIES

These 690-passenger vessels make the 40-mile (64-km) trip in 90–100 minutes, 5 roundtrips daily (an extra during the weekend) between 8 a.m. and 11 p.m. Weekday fares are HK$30 economy, HK$43 tourist and HK$55 first class; HK$45, HK$60 and HK$74 respectively on weekends. The ferries are completely air-conditioned with aircraft seating, luggage racks, snack bars and slot machines. For information call 815-3043. Departures from Hong Kong. Ticketmate computer bookings available.

HOVERFERRIES

Eight 60-minute trips daily during the daylight hours for HK$69 one way on weekdays, HK$84 on weekends and public holidays, HK$96 at night. These 250-passenger vessels leave from the Kowloon Pier. For information call 543-5581.

BY AIR

East Asia Airways operates a number of round trip helicopter trips daily using helipads on the Hong

Kong and Macau Ferry Terminal, Shun Tak Centre, 200 Connaught Road, Hong Kong. (The MTR stop is Sheung Wan.) The fare is HK$986 on weekdays, HK$1086 weekends, one way. The choppers seat eight and the flight takes 20 minutes. Telephone 859-3359 in Hong Kong, or 572983 in Macau.

Travel Essentials

VISAS & PASSPORTS

Visas are NOT required by nationals of Australia, Austria, Belgium, Brazil, Canada, Denmark, France, Germany, Greece, Italy, Japan, Luxembourg, Malaysia, the Netherlands, New Zealand, Norway, Philippines, Thailand, Singapore, South Korea, Spain, Sweden, Switzerland, the United Kingdom and the United States (up to 6 months stay), or Hong Kong residents (British Commonwealth subjects for up to 20 days, other nationalities for up to 3 days.)

Getting a visa is usually painless. It is stamped onto your passport upon arrival for HK$175. A family visa (HK$350) covers an individual or husband travelling with wife and children on the same passport, and is valid for a visit of 20 days or two visits within a 20-day period. (Group visas cost only HK$88 per person in bona fide groups of 10 or more.) Visas obtained from Portuguese consulates (including the one in Hong Kong which is located at 1001–1002, 2 Exchange Square, Connaught Place, Central Hong Kong, tel: 523-1338) cost HK$175 per person.

Nationals of countries who do not have diplomatic relations with Portugal must obtain their visas from Portuguese missions overseas. They cannot obtain them upon arrival in Macau.

If you have entered Hong Kong on a visa, travelling to Macau, or to China (on a day or overnight tour) via Macau, does not affect your Hong Kong visa. If you are on a single-entry visa, however, you will need a re-entry visa (obtainable from the Hong Kong Immigration Department) before leaving.

HEALTH

International inoculation certificates are not normally required, unless cholera has been detected either in Hong Kong or Macau or in the area recently visited by the arrival.

DRINKING WATER

Tap water is usually boiled and provided to hotel rooms by the pitcher – less for safety than to minimize chlorine bouquet. Many residents and visitors nevertheless prefer the local custom of drinking wine.

CUSTOMS

Aside from normal restrictions on drugs, firearms, ammunition and explosives, Macau allows nearly any other items in or out. There are no restrictions on exports and no export duties on Macau purchases.

Hong Kong customs, in addition to restricting drugs, firearms, ammunition and explosives (the last three should be declared upon your original arrival in Hong Kong and left in bond), halves the duty-free tobacco allowance for returnees from Macau to 50 cigarettes, 25 cigars or a quarter pound of tobacco. And the grog allowance is cut to one bottle of wine.

You'll fare better by going into China. There you can have 2–3 bottles of grog and 400 cigarettes. Cameras, watches, radios, tape recorders and the like, and all currencies, have to be declared and are audited on departure. The usual prohibitions against drugs, firearms, ammunitions, explosives and certain printed material apply.

MONEY MATTERS

Macau's pataca is a sort of shadow version of the Hong Kong dollar, the two normally differing in value by less than 5 percent. Hong Kong notes and coins traditionally enjoy a slight premium and (except at the post office and telecoms) circulate freely – with the spender thus taking a slight loss on pataca-denominated transactions. Changing money is the obvious solution, but to avoid double-costly reconversion – pataca are not acceptable in Hong Kong – the best policy is to change enough for basic expenses and cover any excess with HK dollars. (Note: in addition to being roughly equal, both currencies are usually symbolized by "$".) There are no restrictions on the amount or type of currency brought in or out.

AVOS & PATACA

The pataca is divided into 100 avos (¢), with coins and bills as follows: 5, 10 and 50 avos in brass; 1, 5 and 20 patacas in nickel; and 5, 10, 50, 100 and 500 and 1,000 pataca denominations in paper bank notes.

There are no restrictions on moving money in and out of the territory, but the pataca is not used outside of Macau, even in Hong Kong.

MONEY-CHANGERS

Exchange windows at the ferry pier are the simplest place to get reasonable rates for major foreign currencies and traveller's cheques. A dozen-odd banks along Avenida Almeida Ribeiro offer more complete services: 10 a.m.–1 p.m., and 3–4 p.m. business days. There are also the nine casinos and cashiers at most of the major hotels. Major credit cards are accepted in hotels and some of the larger restaurants. Traveller's cheques are accepted everywhere.

GETTING ACQUAINTED

CLIMATE

Forty miles isn't much as a swallow flies, so Macau's weather differs little from its larger colonial neighbour. Climate, though, is a different matter: whatever the skies are doing, Macau's relative lack of grit, noise and towering concrete make the place at least feel pleasant.

Spring and fall, though, are clearly the best times for leisurely visits. The worst times to visit are weekends, when seasonless gambling hordes descend on this Asian Monaco. From May to September, however, there is always the chance of being stranded when a typhoon keeps the ferries in port – but one could suffer a worse fate.

CULTURE & CUSTOMS

Prices in Macau – particularly for food and accommodations – are lower than in Hong Kong. A few restaurants and most hotels add a 10 percent service charge, and all but the smallest villas add a 5 percent government "tourism tax." Tips of 10 percent are standard for residents, but the mostly amiable – and underpaid – waiters are said to be disappointed if visitors don't leave slightly more.

ELECTRICITY

Power in most hotels is 220 volts, but some of the older ones still use 110.

HOLIDAYS

More than 400 years of survival have left Macau plenty of causes to celebrate. With the zeal of true believers on a heathen sea, the Portuguese and their converts to the Roman Catholic faith honour saints' and feast days in high Iberian style, replete with pageants, bright costumes and processions through the streets. And not to be outdone by Christian

foreigners on their home turf, traditional Chinese festivals here turn out throngs armed with crates of local fireworks, traditional Chinese noise-makers that have been banned in Hong Kong since 1967.

But pyrotechnics aside, Macau's moon-determined Chinese festival calendar is nearly identical to that of Hong Kong. Public holidays have little effect on shops or restaurants, but those celebrated in Hong Kong (notably Chinese New Year) invariably jam Macau with gamblers, which makes room reservations here even more difficult. An asterisk (*) indicates that this is a local public holiday.

Among Macau's major holidays are:

January 1: New Year's Day
January–February: Chinese New Year*; Lantern Festival
February–March: Feast of our Lord of Passos (Evening processions from St Augustine's Church to Macau's Cathedral where a night-long vigil is kept. The next day his statue is carried through the streets of Macau – to the Stations of the Cross – and returned to St Augustine's.)
March–April: Feast of the God Tou Tei
April: Ching Ming Festival*; Easter Weekend, including Good Friday and Easter Monday*
April 25: Anniversary of the 1974 Portuguese Revolution*
May 1: Labourers' Day*
May 13: Feast of our Lady of Fatima (procession from Santa Domingo Church to Penha Church, celebrating the 1917 religious miracle that took place at Fatima, Portugal); Feast of the Bathing of Lord Buddha; A-Ma Festival (Tin Hau Festival in Hong Kong); Feast of Tam Kong
June : Dragon Boat Festival*; Feast of Kuan Tai*; Feast of St Anthony of Lisbon
June 10: Camoes and Portugal Communities Day*; Feast of St John the Baptist*
July 13: Feast of Na Cha (July 13)
July–August: Battle of July 13th (islands only); Feast of Lovers; Feast of the Assumption of Our Lady; Festival of Hungry Ghosts
September: Mid-Autumn Festival*; Confucius Day
October: Chung Yeung Festival
October 1: PRC National Day
October 5: Portuguese Republic Day*
November 1: All Saints' Day
November 2: All Souls' Day
December 1: Portuguese Independence Day*
December 8: Feast of the Immaculate Conception*
December 22: Winter Solstice
December 24–25: Christmas*

COMMUNICATIONS

TELEPHONE

Macau offers the standard range of modern international services. Calls and cables can be placed round-the-clock, either through hotel front desks or from the General Post Office on Avenida Almeida Ribeiro just off the main downtown square, or from the Central Post Offices on Taipa and Coloane islands.

In telephone terms, Hong Kong is considered overseas, and 3 minutes cost just over HK$12.40. Local calls – including Taipa and Coloane islands – are 30 avos (three 10-avos coins) from public booths or free on hotel or private lines. Use area code and 070 for Taipa Island and 080 for Coloane Island. Service numbers include:

Directory Information	181
Fire Department	572222
Police	573333
Ambulance	577199

GETTING AROUND

PUBLIC TRANSPORT

Affordable transportation is easily available throughout the island.

PEDICABS

The greatest languor will certainly be encouraged by pedicabs, three-wheeled, two-passenger rickshaws that are pedalled rather than pulled. Still very much in day-to-day use (unlike Hong Kong's rickshaws), their drivers nevertheless – and with some justice – view tourists as walking goldmines. Firm, often largely non-verbal bargaining beforehand is the rule, about Ptc. 15 (for two) for a short ride (say, along the Praia Grande) or HK$50–$60 an hour,

usually enough to keep both sides happy. (Like bicycles, pedicabs cannot cross the bridge and are seldom seen on hills.)

TAXIS

Taxis will of course go anywhere, at rates among the cheapest in the world (Ptc. 6.50 at flagfall, 80 avos each additional 250 metres – or a highly negotiable Ptc. 70 or so per hour). The driver's English abilities (or tourist Portuguese) vary enormously: a few can almost manage guided tours, while others will need to be shown notes in Chinese characters for destinations other than the major hotels. The official surcharges are Ptc. 5 to Taipa and Ptc. 10 to Coloane.

BUSES

The islands – Taipa and Coloane – are a special case. With the demise of ferry runs from the Inner Harbour, the only other access is by public bus. Not all are splendid, open-top doubledeckers, but fairly frequent runs are scheduled from 7 a.m. to midnight. The plaza opposite the Lisboa Hotel is the best place to wait. Fares are: Taipa – Ptc. 2.3; Coloane town – Ptc. 2.8; Hac Sa beach – Ptc. 3.5.

In-town Macau has a number of meandering bus routes, the most useful being perhaps the No. 5, which runs from the Temple of A-Ma out to the Barrier Gate via Avenida Almeida Ribeiro. The No. 3 runs from the Macau Ferry Pier to the city centre. Hours are 7 a.m. to midnight, fares a flat Ptc. 1.80.

PRIVATE TRANSPORT

If you prefer sightseeing at a more leisurely pace, you may want to consider exploring the territory on one of the ways suggested below.

BICYCLES

Off the main streets, a possibly more aesthetic choice is bicycling. Several places around the intersection of Rua do Campo and the Praia Grande, and on Avenida D. Joao IV near the Sintra Hotel rent out very basic models (and occasionally, motorcycles for about Ptc. 50 per hour, depending on the day of the week and time of day. Bikes can also be hired at the Hyatt Regency and Mandarin Oriental Hotels. (Bicycles are not allowed to cross the bridge to Taipa.)

MINI-MOKES

You will no doubt have a ball seeing Macau in these zippy four-seaters, the only rent-a-car service available. Rates range from HK$250–$280 per day, depending on which day. Special hotel/moke rates are available with the Hyatt Regency Hotel or Pousada de San Tiago.

Bookings can be made in Hong Kong at Macau Mokes Ltd., 806 Kai Tak Commercial Bldg, 317 Des

Voeux Road, Central, Hong Kong, tel: 543-4190, fax: 545-5626, telex: 76444 MOKES HX; or in Macau at the Macau Ferry Terminal, tel: 378851, telex: 88251 MX OM.

Avis also has a mini-moke rental service. Reservations can be made world-wide. In Hong Kong call 541-2011 (telex: 76228 KMFTE HX). In Macau, they are located at the Mandarin Oriental Hotel, shopping arcade or carpark, tel: 336789, 567888 ext. 3004. (credit cards accepted).

Note: Only drivers holding International Permits or driving licenses recognized in Portugal are permitted behind the wheel in Macau. Hong Kong driving licenses are not acceptable.

ON FOOT

On foot is in fact undisputedly the best way around. Other matters to consider are summer heat and the several notable hills (Guia, Penha, the Monte Fort and the Camoes Gardens, together roughly bounding the city's old quarter). Fortunately, siestas will preclude the worst of the first, while taxis and buses can handily surmount the others.

WHERE TO STAY

Most visitors on tours to Hong Kong usually enjoy at least a day trip to the Portuguese territory. Some stay overnight. In such cases, the trip is quite pleasant because tour companies prearrange everything. For those interested in making a quick and independent visit to Macau, whether for a day or overnight, arrangements are a bit more difficult. You have to secure two sets of reservations – transportation and hotel – to coincide with your particular needs. A tourist agency should be able to assist you, but of course they charge more, and may want you to include a lot of "options" like organized tours or meals. For a "one-shot approach (transportation and hotel) try a local Hong Kong travel agent or check the *South China Morning Post* classified for tours.

HOTELS

Many of the major hotels in Macau have Hong Kong reservation offices to facilitate matters, but if you choose a smaller hotel or boarding house, you'll have to ring Macau (HK$10.80 for 3 minutes). You should realise that Macau does tend to be filled with ardent Hong Kong gamblers during the weekends and on public holidays. If you have a credit card, you can make telephone reservations. If not, you will have to scamper down to the Macau Ferry Pier on Hong Kong Island or at any Mass Transit Railway station to get your ticket.

But don't let logistical problems discourage you. The visit is worth all the trouble. The Macau Tourist Information Bureau's office in Hong Kong (3704 Shun Tak Centre, 200 Connaught Road Central, Hong Kong Island, tel: 540-8180) and the Macau Government Tourist Office at the Macau Ferry Pier (in Macau) and on Largo do Senado (tel: 315566) can be very helpful.

There is a 10 percent service charge and 5 percent tourism tax on top of the room rates. An asterisk indicates the Hong Kong phone number for booking rooms in that particular hotel. Here is a guide-list of hotels in Macau.

FIRST CLASS

Bela Vista, Rua do Co Comendador Kou Ho Neng 8, Macau, tel: 9635333.
Hyatt Regency, Estrada Alm Marques Espart°2, Taipa, tel: 831234.
Lisboa, Avenida Lisboa, Macau, tel: 577666.
Mandarin Oriental, Avenida da Amizade 965-1110, Macau, tel: 567888.
New Century, Avenida P Tomás Perª, Taipa, tel: 831111.
Pousada Ritz, Rua du Boa Vista 2, Macau, tel: 339955.
Pousada de São Tiago, Avenida de República, Fort Barra, Macau, tel: 378111.
Royal, Estrada da Vitória 2-4, Macau, tel: 552222.
Westin Resort, Estrada de Hac Sa, Coloane, tel: 871111.

MODERATE

Pousada de Coloane, Praia de Cheoc Van, Coloane, tel: 328143, 328144.
Presidente, Avenida da Amizade 69, Macau, tel: 553888.

ECONOMY

Beverly Plaza, Avenida do Dr. Rodrigo Rodrigues, Macau, tel: 782288.
Cantão, Rua do Guimarães 62, off Almeida Ribeiro, Macau, tel: 922416.
Central, Avenida da Almeida Ribeiro 26-28, Macau, tel: 373309.
East Asia, Rua da Madeira 1A, Macau, tel: 922433.
Fortuna, Rua de Cantão Z.A.P.E., Quartiero 15, tel: 786363.
Grande, Avenida da Almeida Ribeiro 146, Macau, tel: 921111.
Guia, Estrada do Engenheiro Trigo 1-5, Macau, tel: 513888.

Hoi Keng, Rua do Guimarães 153, Macau, tel: 572033.
Holiday, Estrada do Repouso 36, Macau, tel: 361696.
Hou Kong, Rua das Lorchas 1, Macau, tel: 937555.
Kingsway, Rua de Luís Gonzaga Gomes, Macau, tel: 700284.
Ko Wah, Rua Felicidade 71, Macau, tel: 375599.
London, Praça Ponte e Horta 4-6, Macau, tel: 937761.
Man Va, Rua Caldeira 32, Macau, tel: 388655.
Masters, Rua das Lorchas 162, Macau, tel: 937572.
Matsuya, Estrada de S. Francisco 5, Macau, tel: 575466.Metropole, Rua da Praia Grande 63, **Macau**, tel: 388166.
Mondial, Rua de António Basto 8, Macau, tel: 566866.
New World Emperor, Rua de Xangai, Macau, tel: 781888.
Península, Rua das Lorchas 14, Macau, tel: 318899.
Sintra, Avenida de D. João IV 58-62, Macau, tel: 385111.
Ung Ieong, Rua das Lorchas 15, (Entrance Bocage 29), Macau, tel: 573814.

FOOD DIGEST

WHAT TO EAT

Liberal use of spices distinguishes Macanese food from normal Portuguese cuisine. The most famous local dish served in Macau is African Chicken. The name, of course, implies that it originated in Mozambique or Angola, where it was called Chicken Biri-Biri (or Piri-Piri, depending on which account you read). Biri-biri is the spicy sauce that enhances food in that part of the world. The chicken itself is spiced, peppered and grilled (properly over charcoal) until dry so that the spices are virtually baked hard by the flames.

Another recipe calls for the marination of the chicken in coconut milk mixed with a strong preparation of spices. Despite its name, some gourmets insist that African Chicken is more closely related to Indian tandoori chicken (presumably served in old Goa). Though the origins of spiced chicken are in doubt, it is a taste treat not to be missed. The same goes for the less popular spiced prawns (Prawns Biri-Biri).

The Portuguese also have adapted Chinese salt and pepper prawns to suit their taste. Yet other treats are prawns, chicken or fish baked in garlic. Some restaurants have also taken succulent crabs found in the area, applied the biri-biri treatment and created a spicy crab dish that's very different from the Chinese version. Quail and pigeon Chinese dishes have also been improvised A La Macanese.

The following is a glossary of basic Macanese food and wine terms which may come in useful when ordering at a local Macanese-Portuguese restaurant:

camaroes	shrimps, prawns
peixe	fish
sopa	soup
carangue jos	crabs
feijoadas	bean stew
cabrito	lamb
coelho	rabbit
galinha	chicken
bacalhau	dried cod, the most common fish served
carne de vaca	beef
vinho	wine
vinho tinto	red wine
vinho branco	white wine
vinho rose	rose wine
vinho verde	young wines (both red and white)
porto	port
coziedu	meat soup
cabidela	duck stew

WHERE TO EAT

Low overheads and cheap family labour have kept prices here well below those for Western food in Hong Kong. For under HK$100 per person you can enjoy a good meal that includes a modest quantity of sturdy Portuguese wine. Portuguese wines, brandies and ports in Macau are the cheapest in Asia. Restaurant reservations are usually required only on weekends and holidays, but even during the slow winter, or at smaller places, calling ahead to book a table is both prudent and polite.

To the occasional rue of the unsuspecting, Macanese dinners (outside of hotels) tend to be eaten early. An arrival at 8.30 p.m. is about the limit, but 7 p.m. or 7.30 p.m. will make local restaurateurs much happier. If you want to dine on Coloane or Taipa, you should remember that after-dark taxis normally ask more than the HK$5 and HK$10 surcharges (to Taipa and Coloane respectively). Furthermore they may be hard to find on the return trip. Buses, however, run until midnight (restaurants will know the schedule), and riding back in an open-topped double-decker on a warm night is certainly no hardship.

MACANESE/PORTUGUESE

1999, Parque de Coloane (Coloane Country Park), Coloane Island, tel: 328295. Named after the year Macau reverts to China, it serves a wide range of

Portuguese dishes, plus those like veal sausages, pig's knuckles and spaghetti. Open noon–3 p.m., 7–10.30 p.m.

A Lorcha, 289 Rua do Almirante Sergio, tel: 313195. A small unpretentious eatery in the Outer Harbour specializing in Portuguese food. Its Chinese dishes are good too as they have a distinct Portuguese flavour. Open noon–3 p.m., 7–10.30 p.m.

A Nau, Cheoc Van Beach, Coloane Island, tel: 328525. A strange combination here – namely Portuguese BBQ on an open terrace overlooking the beach juxtaposed with karaoke. But it works. Try spicy prawns A Nau which are cooked in piri-piri spices. Open 1 p.m.–1 a.m.

Afonso's, Hyatt Regency Hotel, Taipa Island, tel: 831234. One of the top-of-the line Portuguese restaurants. Beautiful seafood. Lovely Portuguese breads. Portuguese buffets on Sundays. Open noon–2.30 p.m., 6.30–11 p.m.

Barra Nova, 287 Rua do Almirante Sergio, tel: 512287. Another small restaurant featuring Portuguese and Macanese cuisine located in the Outer Harbour, located just near the A-Ma Temple. Open noon–3 p.m., 7–11 p.m.

Cafe Leon, 3 Calcada do Gamboa, tel: 316140. the usual variety of Portugese supplemented by selection of spicy African food (from the former Portugese colonies) like African chicken and a selection of piri-piri dishes. Open 11 a.m.–11 p.m.

Fernando's, 9 Praia Hac Sa, Hac Sa Beach, Coloane Island, tel: 328531. Large menu with both Portuguese and Chinese dishes. Seafood, especially clams, and rabbit specialities. Wonderful place to while away an afternoon when you are tired of the beach. Open 11 a.m.–11 a.m.

Flamingo, Hyatt Regency, Taipa Island, tel: 831234. Authentic Portuguese/Macanese food served in the open air in a pavilion over a man-made lake. Marvellous atmosphere. Open noon–3 p.m., 7–11 p.m.

Galo, 47 Rua do Gunha, Taipa Island, tel: 327318. This is the place to go for African Chicken though the other Portugese and Macanese dishes are also on the menu. Open noon–3 p.m., 6–11 p.m.

Henri's, 4 Avenida da Republica, tel: 556251. Try garlic prawns. Open 11 a.m.–11 p.m.

Pinocchio's, 4 Rua do Sol, Taipa Island, tel: 327128. Spicy fish and fowl in a tree-shaded courtyard. Open noon–11.30 p.m.

Portuguese, 16 Rua do Campo, tel: 375445. Bona fide home cooking and no-nonsense red wine. Very cheap. Open 11 a.m.–1 a.m.

Riquexó (means rickshaw), 69 Avenida Sidonia Pais (ask for Park'n Shop), tel: 565655. Everything is literally home-cooked because many of the dishes are prepared at home by Macanese housewives and brought here daily. Open 11 a.m.–3 p.m.

Solmar, 11 Rua da Praia Grande, tel: 574391. Boulevard cafe and bistro, a local favourite. Moderate prices. Open 11 a.m.–11 p.m.

Vasco da Gama, Royal Hotel, tel: 552222. This eatery has lots more European dishes on the menu – and quite imaginative ones at that – than the other Portuguese restaurants. Stewed lamb is a favourite and for aficionados, real Portuguese, a rarity in Macau. Open noon–3 p.m., 6–11 p.m.

INTERNATIONAL

A Galera, Hotel Lisboa, New Wing, tel: 577666 ext 1152. Grill room with live music. Moderately expensive, but half the price of Hong Kong's various hotel grills. Open 12.30–2.30 p.m; 7.30 p.m.–midnight.

A Pousada, Hyatt Regency Hotel, tel: 831234. The hotel calls it a cafe, and the restaurant certainly earns that extra bit of class. Good buffets. Open 7 a.m.–midnight.

Noite e Dia, Hotel Lisboa, 2nd floor, tel: 577666. A high-roller place with dancing and nightly floorshows. Moderately expensive. Open till 1 a.m.

CHINESE

456 (Shanghai Restaurant), Lisboa Hotel, New Wing, tel: 388404. One of the region's best Shanghainese food restaurants, Macau or Hong Kong. Open till 1 a.m.

Dynasty, New World Emperor Hotel, tel: 567888. Another in the New World hotel chain's very up-market, top of the line Cantonese restaurants. Open 7 a.m.–midnight.

Long Kei, 7 Largo do Senado (on the main city square), tel: 573970. By reputation one of the best Chinese restaurants in town. Prices moderate and up. Open 11 a.m.-11 p.m.

ITALIAN

Ristorante Italiano Leong Un, 46 Rua de Cunha, Taipa Island, tel: 2-7061. An Italian bistro with good and filling food. Open 11 a.m.–11 p.m.

JAPANESE

Ginza, Royal Hotel, tel: 552222. As befits a hotel belonging to a Japanese hotel chain (Dai-Ichi), the restaurant's cuisine is authentic. Sashimi and teppanyaki. Open noon–3 p.m., 6–11 p.m.

Furusato, Lisboa Hotel, tel: 388568. Very expensive, but good. Open till 2.30 a.m.

KOREAN

Korean, Hotel Presidente, tel: 569039. The only restaurant in Macau specializes in Korean food. Watch out for the *kimchi*. Open noon–3 p.m., 6 p.m.–midnight.

THAI

Thai, 27E Rua Abreu Nunes, tel: 573288. For the unsuspecting, the cuisine here is some of the hottest in Asia. The *tom yam* is a good test of your endurance. Open noon–6 p.m.

VIETNAMESE

Kam Nau Un, 57 Avenida da Amizade, tel: 309883. A small cheap eatery with a wide of Vietnamese dishes. Open 11 a.m.–2 a.m.

THINGS TO DO

TOUR PACKAGES

Small as it is, Macau is serviced by several commercial sightseeing firms. In addition to multilingual conducted tours, most travel agents will arrange ferry and hotel bookings and complete one or two-day Macau tour packages, some of which may include day trips to China. By using these companies' services, you save the hassle of making such arrangements independently.

TOUR OPERATORS

Licensed Macau tour operators are listed below, but remember that many of the same tours can be arranged from Hong Kong by Hong Kong travel agents.

Able, 5–9 Travessa do Padre Narciso, tel: 89798. Hong Kong office, tel: 545-9993.
Asia, 23-B Rua da Praia Grande, tel: 593844, cable: ASIA-TOURS. Hong Kong office, tel: 548-8806.
China Travel Service (Macau), 63 Rua da Praia Grande, tel: 782331, cable: 9999 MACAU. Hong Kong office, tel: 540-6333.
Estoril, Mezzanine floor, New Wing Hotel Lisboa, Avenida da Amizade, tel: 573614, cable: ESTOURS, telex: 88203 HOTEL OM, fax: 567193. Hong Kong office, tel: 559-1028.
F. Rodrigues, 71 Rua da Praia Grande, tel: 75511. Guangdong (Macau), Ground floor, 37-E Rau da Praia Grande, tel: 588807, telex: 88371 GDMTC OM, fax: 512153. Hong Kong office, tel: 832-9118.
Hi-No-De Caravela, Ground floor, 64–4C Rua de Sacadura Cabral, tel: 338338, fax: 566622. Hong Kong Office, tel: 368-6181.
H. Nolasco, Lda, 20 Avenida Almeida Ribeiro, tel: 76463, cable: POPULAR.
International, Grd. floor, 9 Travessa do Padre Narciso, Loja B, tel: 975183. Hong Kong office, tel: 541-2011.

Lotus, Edificio Fong Meng, Grd. floor, Rua de Sao Lourenco, tel: 81765. Cable: LOTUSTOUR.
Macau Mondial, 74-A, Ground floor, Avenida do Conselheiro Ferreira de Almeida, tel: 566866, fax: 574531.
Macau Star, Room 511, Tai Fung Bank Bldg, 34 Avenida Almeida Ribeiro, tel: 558855, 558866, telex: 88590 STAR OM. Hong Kong office, tel: 366-2262.
Macau Tours, 35 Avenida Dr Mario Soares, tel: 385555, fax: 700050. Hong Kong office, tel: 542-2338.
MBC Tours, 7–9 Rua Santa Clara, Edificio Ribeiro, Loja D, tel: 86462, cable: MACAU BUC, telex: 88251 MBC OM.
Sintra, Hotel Sintra, Avenida Dom Joao IV, tel: 710111, fax: 510527, telex: 88324 SINTA OM. Hong Kong office, tel: 540-8028.
South China, 1st floor, Apt A–B, 15 Avenida Dr Rodrigo Rodrigues, tel: 781811. Hong Kong office, tel: 815-0208.
T.K.W., 4th floor, Apt 408, 27–31 Rua Formosa, tel: 591122. Hong Kong office, tel: 723-7771.
Vacation International, Shopping Arcade/Car Park, Mandarin Oriental, tel: 555686, 567888 ext 3004, fax: 314112.

MACAU-CHINA TRIPS

These modern China days, you can almost go up to Macau's ornate 19th-century Portas do Cerco (border gates) and get a visa. It is easier, though, to go through a travel agency. It takes one day for an individual or a group to process China travel documents at the Chinese frontier post of **Gongbei**. Many visitors travel from Macau because China has created a **Special Tourism Zone** in the **Zhongshan county** area immediately adjacent to this Portugese territory. The area is open for day tours or for longer trips to three resorts that opened in this zone in 1980.

These day trips are made under Chinese supervision with organized tour groups. Travel agents in Macau and Hong Kong arrange everything and, for those really short of time, it is probably the best way to get a quick look at China.

Day tours usually follow two basic itineraries. Both start in **Cuiheng Village**, the birthplace of Dr. Sun Yat-sen, the founding father of modern China who was the first president of the Chinese Republic in 1911 after the Manchus of the Ching dynasty were overthrown. In this village you can visit his residence, a Sun Yat-sen exhibition hall and a memorial school. From there the tours split up and go either to **Shiqi City** or **Zhuhai City**. After lunch in one of those "cities" there are visits to Chinese communes, schools or, possibly, a fishing village. It is possible to do the entire trip in one day which doesn't leave you much time to see Macau en route. The cost starts around HK$400 and includes all transportation to and from Macau.

There are, however, more elaborate tours including, believe it or not, golfing tours (where you do your 18 in China), which have time for visiting Macau. These usually feature an overnight stay in Macau and are available via usual travel agencies.

CHINESE RESORTS

Persons who have more time should visit one of the new resorts just adjacent to the China-Macau border. The **Shi Ching Shan Tourist Centre** and **Zhuhai Resort** are the oldest, only 10 minutes by car from the border gate and offers complete tourist facilities, including air-conditioning, swimming pools, restaurants and local tours. Doubles cost around HK$250–$300.

The **Chung Shan Hot Spring Resort** is a little farther away – 30 minutes by car – and in addition to usual tourist conveniences, it offers therapeutic spa waters from the nearby Iong Mak Hot Springs. These mineral waters are piped directly into the hotel (According to the Chinese, the medicinal qualities of Iong Mak's water are especially good for "joint" or "skin" problems.) At Chung Shan (Zhongshan) you can book double rooms for HK$380 (plus 20 percent for non-members) per weekday nights only. No bookings are accepted for weekends or public holidays as they are reserved for members only. Make reservations at least 24 hours in advance.

Chung Shan's main attraction for foreigners is not so much the medicinal hot springs as the Arnold Palmer-designed, 18-hole, par 72, 19,650-feet (5,991-metre) championship golf course. From padi fields into golf courses? Sounds almost biblical, but there it is. (A second, Jack Nicklaus-designed, 18-hole course will be ready for the first duffers by 1993.) Green fees are HK$350 weekdays per 18 holes, but it is members only at the weekend or on public holidays. Golf clubs can be rented for HK$100 per 18 holes, caddies charge HK$80 each.

Transport to Chung Shan is not difficult once you reach Macau. It costs around HK$20 for a scheduled bus or if you prefer, there are private cars and coaches available. Contact the Chung Shan office in Macau at the Ferry Terminal. The Hong Kong office is in Room 504, Pedder Bldg, Pedder Street, Central, Hong Kong (tel: 521-0377, telex: 75050 WINGS HX). At least 24 hours is needed to obtain visas. Lest you think you misread the previous paragraph about golfing in China, brace yourself for another course in the same area. This one is called the Zhuhai International Golf Club and sports an 18-hole, par 72, 21,054-foot (6,400-metre) course.

Green fees are HK$400 on weekdays for 18 holes, HK$500 on weekends. Golf clubs can be rented for HK$100 for 18 holes, caddies are HK$80. Unlike the Chung Shan resort, there is no hotel on the course which is located some distance outside the town of Zuhai. You can get to Zuhai directly by jetcat from the China Hong Kong City Pier, 33 Canton Road, Tsimshatsui, Kowloon.

The 75-minute jetcat trip costs HK$105 weekdays, HK$115 on weekends. A shuttle bus will fetch you to the course; alternatively, a private car can be arranged for the service. Telephone 526-2136 in Hong Kong for general information, plus golf and jetcat bookings. The course can also be reached by bus from Macau. Do not forget your China visa.

Managed by Japan Golf Promotions Ltd., it also has the adjacent Pearl Land Amusement Park, a 1.35 million-sq. mile (122,000-sq. metre) complex with, among other attractions, a 0.62-mile (1-km) long go-kart track and roller coaster.

Nearby is **Shiqi**. It is designed not only for tourists, but as a rest stop for persons travelling between Canton and Macau. Various tours are available, from a one-day coach or golf tour to the marathon four-day, three-city tours.

At the visa facilities at Gongbei, it is also possible to obtain permission to visit Canton or other parts of China without having to go via Hong Kong. A regular bus service runs to Canton from Macau but the road to Canton is a bit rough.

BEACHES

Macau itself does not have much in the way of beaches, but the islands of Coloane and Taipa do. The best known is Cheoc Van Beach on Coloane Island. Also on Coloane is Hac Sa Beach, a much larger and popular public beach.

NIGHTLIFE

Macau rarely lives up to its historical reputation of sin. Most foreigners would consider it down right dull since the bar/pub scene outside the hotels is virtually non-extistent. And if you are not into casinos, dog- or horse-racing, Chinese- and Japanese-style nightclubs and karaoke bar, and all-night saunas, that leaves only discotheques and TV movies.

BARS

Two of the best hotel bars are the Mandarin Oriental's Bar da Guia and the Hyatt Regency's The Bar though the Greenhouse Cocktail Lounge just off the lobby is pleasant. Sidewalk cafes seem to have all but disappeared in Macau, but there are still a couple of terraces that are pleasant, namely the Pousada de San Tiago and the Pousada de Coloane. (And perhaps the Bela Vista when renovated and re-opened under the management of Mandarin Oriental will have a version of its old terrace, which was the most pleasant in Macau.)

One of the most popular evening activities is the Crazy Paris Show, a sophisticated and risque show, a la Paris's famed Crazy Horse Saloon, which combines a titillating striptease with dance and acrobatics staged in an imaginative tableaux with high-tech lighting. Two shows nightly plus an extra show at 11.30 p.m. on Saturdays in the Lisboa Hotel's Mona Lisa Hall. Ptc. 120. Tickets are available through hotels and travel agencies and at the door. Check times.

NIGHTCLUBS & DISCOS

The Portas do Sol Supper Club in the Lisboa Hotel offers dining, dancing and shows, in the style popular in the era before discotheques. Changing pace, the Paris Nightclub (Avenida Sidonio) is a nightclub with live music and hostesses. Other clubs include the Skylight Disco & Nightclub in the Hotel Presidente, the Guia Disco Nightclub in the Guia Hotel, the Mikado Big I Discotheques at the Lisboa Hotel, and the Karaoki Bar in the Hotel Royal are the top of the list.

There are also sauna and massage parlours in Lisboa, Sintra, Presidente and Royal Hòtels, plus the Estoril (Avenida Sidonio). Most open in the day, some as early as noon, and run to the wee hours. The saunas are famous for their Thai and Filipina masseuses.

Macau's professional girlfriends require the same caveats given to their sisters in Hong Kong. Without a good-sized jackpot in hand, visitors better pass up the opportunities who present themselves around the casinos in favour of the aptly-named Red Lantern tavern, in the Wing Hang Bank Building on Avenida de Almeida Ribeiro.

SHOPPING

WHAT TO BUY

Macau is rarely thought of as a shopping mart, except for its magnificently-priced wines, brandies and ports (which are restricted upon return to Hong Kong). Though it is a duty-free port like Hong Kong, the array of goods available is not nearly so elaborate. Some items, such as cameras or hi-fi systems are more expensive at Macau because of the smaller number sold.

Like Hong Kong, Macau is a clothing manufacturing centre, especially of knitwear, though whatever little that is displayed is apparently not very fashionable.

ANTIQUES & ARTIFACTS

But all is not lost for those who prefer shopping to gambling. Macau is a good place to buy Chinese antiques and artifacts.

The main street, Avenida Almeida Ribeiro, has a few antique shops on both sides of the street as you walk from the Outer Harbour (near the Lisboa and Sintra Hotels, and the hydrofoil/jetfoil piers) towards the Inner Harbour (near the Floating casino).

USEFUL ADDRESSES

TOURIST INFORMATION

In Hong Kong, the Macau Tourist Information Bureau (MTIB) – at 3704 Shun Tak Centre, 200 Connaught Road Central, Hong Kong Island, tel: 540-8180, fax: 559-6513 – is the principal clearing house for questions, recommendations, maps as well as free publications.

In Macau the Macau Government Tourist Office is located at Il Largo do Senado (tel: 315566) or at the Macau Ferry Pier.

Overseas, Macau maintains information offices in Manila, Sydney, Auckland, Tokyo, Bangkok, London, Los Angeles, Honolulu, Chicago, New York, Toronto and Vancouver, or c/o any Portuguese embassy or consulate. Any Portuguese National Tourist office will also be able to answer queries.

The following countries with consulates and commissions in Hong Kong are also accredited by Macau: Austria, Belgium, Brazil, Britain, Canada, Germany, France, Greece, Italy, Japan, Mexico, Norway, Pakistan, Philippines, Sweden, Switzerland, Thailand and the United States.

ART/PHOTO CREDITS

Photography by

Page 80, 120	Dobson, Richard
18/19, 140, 150, 151, 191, 242/243, 250, 257	Dobson, Richard/Globe Press Agency
83, 94, 102/103, 126R	Dugast, Jean-Léo/APA Photo Agency
7, 20, 29L&R, 30L, 32, 33, 56L, 57L&R, 62/63, 71, 72, 91, 97, 104, 108, 111, 123, 129, 134, 141, 142, 164/165, 177R, 183, 202, 204, 206, 226/227, 235, 237, 245, 252, 263, 265, 266	Evrard, Alain/APA Photo Agency
90	Fischbeck, Frank
210/211, 222	Gottschalk, Manfred/APA Photo Agency
50	Government Information Services
137, 203	Heaton, Dallas & John/APA Photo Agency
81, 106/107	Höfer, Hans/APA Photo Agency
26L, 27L&R, 42	Hong Kong Museum of Art Collection
22/23, 24, 213	Hong Kong Museum of Art Collection (Auguste Borget)
Cover, 31, 35, 59, 73, 75, 82, 84, 86, 125, 126L, 133, 139, 157, 193	Jörén, Gerhard/Globe Press Agency
52, 53L&R, 54, 55, 56R, 58, 64, 68, 74, 110, 118L&R, 119, 127, 128, 154R, 169, 209, 238, 244, 249, 256	Kowall, Earl/Globe Press Agency
25, 214	Kugler, Jean/APA Photo Agency
65, 79, 115, 144, 220, 223, 246	Lawrence, Max/APA Photo Agency
40, 44, 48, 92, 131	From the Leo Haks Collection
61, 136, 143, 224, 225L&R	Liau Chung Ren/Globe Press Agency
66, 77, 78, 88L&R, 89L&R	Lloyd, Ian
12/13, 14/15, 85, 100/101, 113, 121, 158/159, 166, 198, 199, 230, 272	McGregor, Keith/Globe Press Agency
28	Martorano, Tony/APA Photo Agency
26R, 41	National Archives & Records Centre
187	Nichols, R.C.A./APA Photo Agency
218	Paramount Pictures
76	Potter, Lincoln
36/37	Public Record Office, London (The 1842 Treaty of Nanking)
122	Reichelt, G.P./APA Photo Agency
1, 117, 232	Strange, Rick/APA Photo Agency
46, 47	*The South China Morning Post*
116, 192, 197	Tovy, Adina/APA Photo Agency
16/17, 30R, 67, 87, 93, 112, 124, 130, 146, 152, 153, 154L, 155, 156, 162/163, 174, 177L, 178, 181, 182, 184, 185, 188, 190, 195, 200, 201, 205, 207, 208, 217, 233, 234, 236, 239, 241, 254, 255, 260, 267, 268, 269, 270, 271	Wassman, Bill
258/259, 264	Yogerst, Joseph
Maps	Berndtson & Berndtson
Illustrations	Geisler, Klaus
Visual Consulting	Barl, V.

INDEX

D

E

F